Requirements for Certification

Requirements for Certification

of Teachers, Counselors, Librarians, Administrators

for Elementary and Secondary Schools

Seventy-sixth Edition, 2011–2012

Edited by
Elizabeth A. Kaye

The University of Chicago Press
Chicago and London

The University of Chicago Press, Chicago 60637
© 2011 by The University of Chicago
All Rights Reserved
Seventy-sixth edition 2011
Published annually since 1935
International Standard Book Number-13: 978-0-226-42864-2
International Standard Book Number-10: 0-226-42864-8
International Standard Series Number: 1047-7071
Library of Congress Catalog Card Number: A43-1905

Contents

Introduction to the Seventy-Sixth Edition
2011–2012

Why do we need a book of requirements for educator certification in our electronic age? This volume provides a concise, accessible summary of relevant information that is simply not consistently available on the websites of individual state certification offices. The goal of our compilation is to provide a "balcony view" of state certification regulations that enables readers to access and compare information either about different positions within a single state or about a single position in one or more states.

Interestingly, states present the material on their certification websites in a variety of formats and levels of accessibility. While some are carefully designed to be user-friendly and intuitively clear to navigate, others are—quite naturally—the electronic version of a procedures manual for staff. With an array of online application forms, automated certification systems, and literally hundreds of pages of state legislative regulations reproduced verbatim, it can be a significant challenge to unearth a clear, consistent overview of the field one is exploring, along with suggestions on where to dive in more deeply when full detail is required. We aim to provide exactly that service.

What we present in *Requirements for Certification* is that much-needed survey of current information on certification requirements for all fifty states and the District of Columbia. Updated annually and presented in a clear, concise outline format, the book provides a fresh overview of certification information for teachers, counselors, librarians, and administrators, as well as those who aspire to join their ranks. For this seventy-sixth edition, forty-eight states have changed their requirements since last year, in degrees ranging from minor to extensive. As this volume moves into its seventy-sixth year of continuous publication, it provides an essential service to both the public and to the professionals who consult it.

Requirements for Certification had its inception in the Board of Vocational Guidance and Placement (now Career and Placement Services) at the University of Chicago. The original study was made by Robert C. Woellner, professor of education and head of the Board, and M. Aurilla Wood, placement counselor. The digest continued under the direction of Elizabeth H. Woellner until her retirement in 1983. Produced only in mimeograph form its first year, the digest was published and made available for sale by the University of Chicago Press in 1935 and has appeared in annual editions since that time.

We continue to express our profound gratitude to the state certification officers for their interest and cooperation under extreme duress. This book simply could not be as current, as accurate, and as helpful as it is without their collaboration. We trust that these efforts, by helping to make the requirements for educator certification as widely available as possible throughout the United States and its possessions and territories, will bear fruit both for the certification professionals and for those who seek access to their knowledge.

Alabama

New legislative Rules governing certification were adopted by the Alabama State Board of Education on December 9, 2010, and are effective February 1, 2011. As of press time for this volume, the Alabama State Department of Education's Teacher Education and Certification website may be accessed at http://tcert.alsde.edu/Portal/Public/Pages/News.aspx The newly enacted certification requirements are prescribed in Rule 290-3-2-.02, Basic Principles, available at http://www.alsde.edu/html/sections/documents.asp?section=66&sort=7&footer-sections The Rule also refers to the current edition of the Subject and Personnel Codes of the Alabama Department of Education; see http://www.alsde.edu/html/sections/documents.asp?section=66&sort=9&footer=sections Finally, for more information on state-approved programs leading to certification, consult the Teacher Education Chapter of the Alabama Administrative Code; contact the Alabama State Department of Education's Teacher Education and Certification website for details at http://tcert.alsde.edu/Portal/Public/Pages/News.aspx

Stages and Titles of Teaching Certificates

I. Professional Educator Certificate (valid July 1–June 30 for 5 years; renewable)
   A. Requirements are prescribed in Rule 290-3-2-.02, Basic Principles, available at http://www.alsde.edu/html/sections/documents.asp?section=66&sort=7&footer-sections
   B. May be issued at the Class B, Class A, or Class AA level
      1. General requirements for all Professional Educator Certificates include holding an earned bachelor's degree from a regionally accredited senior institution or having met requirements spelled out in Rule directly above.
      2. Certificates available in teaching fields listed in the current edition of the Subject and Personnel Codes of the Alabama Department of Education include:
         a. Elementary–secondary (P–12), middle level (4–8), secondary (6–12), and special education (P–12)
      3. Additional certificates available include:
         a. Collaborative special education (K–6, 6–12), early childhood special special education (birth through age 8), early childhood (P–3), elementary (K–6)
      4. Class A level certificates also require that applicants hold an earned master's degree from a regionally accredited senior institution
      5. Class AA level certificates require in addition that applicants complete a planned sixth-year program at a regionally accredited senior institution, which may result in an education specialist degree
   C. Class A or Class AA Professional Educator Certificate for areas of instructional support other than instructional leader

1. Meeting requirements for certification in library-media specialist, school counselor, school psychologist, school psychometrist, and sport manager leads to issuance of the Professional Education Certificate.
   a. Applicants must verify 2 fall years of full-time educational experience in P–12 school system(s), except for those seeking certification through the Council for Accreditation of Counseling and Related Educational Programs (CACREP) approach or the Nationally Certified School Psychologist approach.

II. Professional Leadership Certificate (valid July 1–June 30 for 5 years; renewable)
   A. Requirements are prescribed in Rule 290-3-2-.02, Basic Principles, available at http://www.alsde.edu/html/sections/documents.asp?section=66&sort=7&footer-sections
   B. May be issued at the Class A or Class AA level
      1. Class A level certificates require that applicant hold an earned master's degree from a regionally accredited senior institution.
      2. Class AA level certificates require in addition that applicants complete a planned sixth-year program at a regionally accredited senior institution, which may result in an education specialist degree.
   C. Meeting requirements for certification as career and technical administrator, educational administrator, principal, superintendent, and supervisor leads to the issuance of the Professional Leadership Certificate.
   D. Certificates requiring the Certificate and Experience Reciprocity Option include:
      1. Principal (P–6), principal (7–12), principal (P–12), superintendent (P–12), supervisor (P–12), and career and technical education administrator (6–12)
         a. Applicants for certification in supervision through the certificate and experience reciprocity option must verify 3 full years of full-time supervisory experience in P–12 school system(s).

III. Instructional Leader Certificate
   A. Requirements are prescribed in Rule 290-3-2-.02, Basic Principles, available at http://www.alsde.edu/html/sections/documents.asp?section=66&sort=7&footer-sections
   B. May be issued at the Class A or Class AA level
      1. Class A level certificates require that applicant hold an earned master's degree from a regionally accredited senior institution.
      2. Class AA level certificates require in addition that applicants complete a planned sixth-year program at a regionally accredited senior institution, which may result in an education specialist degree.
   C. Meeting requirements for certification in the area of instructional leader leads to the issuance of the Professional Leadership Certificate.

Requirements for Teaching Certificates

I. The following teaching certificates are available: Early Childhood (P–3), Elementary (K–6), Middle Level (4–8), Secondary (6–12), Elementary–Secondary (P–12), Special Education [P–12 except for early childhood special education (birth to age 8) and collaborative special education (K–6 or 6–12)]

II. State-approved Class B Programs for Teaching Fields
   A. Lead to an initial professional educator certificate on the bachelor's degree level
      1. Available programs include early childhood education, elementary education, and specific teaching fields for middle-level, secondary, career and technical, preschool through grade 12, and special education
      2. Additional information about Class B programs is in the Teacher Education Chapter of the Alabama Administrative Code; contact the Alabama State Department of Education's Teacher Education and Certification website for details at http://tcert.alsde.edu/Portal/Public/Pages/News.aspx
III. State-approved Alternative Class A Programs for Teaching Fields
   A. Lead to an initial professional educator certificate on the master's degree level
   B. Applicants for admission to Alternative Class A programs must meet degree requirements, grade-point average requirements, and prerequisite course-work requirements prior to unconditional admission.
      1. Admission requirements are in the Teacher Education Chapter of the Alabama Administrative Code; contact the Alabama State Department of Education's Teacher Education and Certification website for details at http://tcert.alsde.edu/Portal/Public/Pages/News.aspx
   C. Available teaching fields include:
      1. Early childhood education, elementary education, early childhood special education, and collaborative special education, grades K–6 or 6–12
      2. Middle-level or secondary single teaching fields
      3. Comprehensive middle-level or secondary teaching fields (English language arts, general science, or genera social studies) or career and technical education teaching fields
      4. Preschool through grade 12 programs (visual arts, dance, choral or instrumental music, languages other than English, physical education, theatre, and special education except for early childhood special education and collaborative special education grades K–6 or 6–12)
   D. Additional information about Alternative Class A programs is in the Teacher Education Chapter of the Alabama Administrative Code; contact the Alabama State Department of Education's Teacher Education and Certification website for details at http://tcert.alsde.edu/Portal/Public/Pages/News.aspx
   E. Special Alternative Certificate (SAC)
      1. A superintendent or administrator may recommend issuance of an SAC in order to employ an applicant who is completing requirements for a Class A professional educator certificate in a teaching field through an Alternative Class A state-approved program.
      2. Additional information is in Rule 290-3-2-.08, Rule 290-3:2-.13, and on Supplement SAC; see http://www.alsde.edu/html/sections/documents.asp?section=66&sort=7&footer-sections
IV. State-approved Class A Programs for Teaching Fields
   A. Lead to a Class A Professional Educator Certificate on the master's-degree level
      1. Class A programs for teaching fields are available for:

a. Advanced certification in the same teaching fields for which Class B certification is available
b. Initial certification in English for speakers of other languages, reading specialist, and special education
c. Additional information about Class A programs for teaching fields is in the Teacher Education Chapter of the Alabama Administrative Code and the Rule for the specific teaching field; see http://www.alsde.edu/html/sections/documents.asp?section=66&sort=7&footer=sections

B. Special Alternative Certificate (SAC)
1. A superintendent or administrator may recommend issuance of an SAC in order to employ an applicant who is completing requirements for a Class A Professional Educator Certificate in English for speakers of other languages, readin specialist, or an initial certificate in an area of special education through a Class A state-approved program.
2. Additional information about the SAC for teaching fields is in Rule 290-3-2-.08, Rule 290-3-2-.13, and on Supplement SAC, available at http://www.alsde.edu/html/sections/documents.asp?section=66&sort=7&footer-sections

V. State-approved Class AA Programs for Teaching Fields
A. Leads to a Class AA Professional Educator Certificate on the sixth-year level
1. Some institutions require program completers to earn an education specialist degree.
2. Class AA programs for teaching fields are available for initial certification in special education and advanced certification in the same teaching fields for which Class B and Class A certification is available.
3. Additional information about Class AA programs for teaching fields is in the Teacher Education Chapter of the Alabama Administrative Code; contact the Alabama State Department of Education's Teacher Education and Certification website for details at http://tcert.alsde.edu/Portal/Public/Pages/News.aspx

B. Special Alternative Certificate
1. A superintendent or administrator may recommend issuance of an SAC in order to employ an applicant who is completing requirements for a Class AA Professional Educator Certificate to earn initial certification in an area of special education through a state-approved Class AA program.
2. Additional information is in Rule 290-3-2-.08, Rule 290-3-2-.13, and on Supplement SAC available at http://www.alsde.edu/html/sections/documents.asp?section=66&sort=7&footer-sections

Requirements for Administrative/Supervisory and Support Services Certificates

I. State-approved Class A Programs for Areas of Instructional Support
A. Lead to a Class A Professional Educator Certificate or Professional Leadership Certificate on the master's degree level
1. Class A programs for areas of instructional support are available for instructional leadership (formerly educational administration), library-media, school counseling, school psychometry, and sport management.

        a.   Beginning fall 2007, instructional leadership programs began replacing educational administration programs.

    2.   Additional information about Class A programs for areas of instructional support is in the Teacher Education Chapter of the Alabama Administrative Code

  B. Special Alternative Certificate (SAC)

    1.   A superintendent or administrator may recommend issuance of an SAC in order to employ an applicant who is completing requirements for a Class A Professional Educator Certificate or Professional Leadership Certificate in an area of instructional support through a Class A state-approved program.

    2.   Additional information about the SAC for areas of instructional support is in Rule 290-3-2-.09, Rule 290-3-2-.14, and on Supplement SAC, available at http://www.alsde.edu/html/sections/documents.asp?section=66&sort=7&footer-sections

        a.   The SAC is not available in the area of school psychometry.

II.   State-approved Class AA Programs for Areas of Instructional Support

  A. Leads to a Class AA Professional Educator Certificate or Professional Leadership
Certificate on the sixth-year level.

    1.   Some institutions require program completers to earn the education specialist degree.

    2.   Class AA programs for areas of instructional support are available for:

        a.   Initial certification in school psychology, and

        b.   Advanced certification in instructional leadership or educational administration, library-media, and school counseling.

    3.   Additional information about Class AA programs for areas of instructional support is in the Teacher Education Chapter of the Alabama Administrative Code; see http://www.alsde.edu.html/sections/documents.asp?section=66&sort=9&footer=sections.

Alaska

Levels of Certificates

I. Initial Certificate (valid up to 3 years; nonrenewable). For those seeking first-time Alaska certification or those whose certificates have lapsed more than 12 months
  A. Requirements
    1. Hold bachelor's or higher degree from regionally accredited institution
    2. Complete teacher preparation program,
       or
       Be currently enrolled in teacher preparation program, except for special education applicants, who must complete program prior to application
    3. Passing scores on basic competency examination in reading, writing, and math: Praxis I, California Basic Educational Skills Test (CBEST), WEST-B, or additional exams listed on website
       a. One-year, nonrenewable teaching certificate may be issued for applicants who have not yet met testing requirement but hold current, valid teaching certificate in another state; contact Teacher Certification via email (see Appendix 1) for details and further qualifications for this certificate.
    4. Pass background check
    5. Submit certificate application, completed fingerprint card, and nonrefundable fees
    6. For Type B (administrative) or Type C (special services) certificate, complete 3 semester hours each of approved course work in Alaska Studies and Multicultural/Cross-Cultural Communications
       a. Applicants lacking these courses but meeting all other requirements will be issued a 2-year nonrenewable provisional certificate.
    7. Requirements for Professional or Master certificate must be met during life of Initial certificate.
  B. Initial Certificate Expiration Dates
    1. Tier 1 Initial, Type B and C (Temporary, Provisional and Reemployment)
       a. Effective February 1, 2009, expiration dates of all currently active initial certificates will be changed to June 30 (for certificates issued between January 1 and June 30) or December 31 (for certificates issued between July 1 and December 31).
       b. All new certificates will be set to expire on either June 30 or December 31; see B, 1, a, directly above.
II. Professional Teacher Certificate (valid for 5 years; renewable)
  A. Requirements
    1. Hold Initial Tier I certificate

2. Complete approved teacher preparation program from which either an Institutional or State Recommendation can be obtained

3. Complete 3 semester hours each of approved course work in Alaska Studies and Multicultural/Cross-Cultural Communications

4. Satisfy recency credit by completing 6 semester hours or 9 quarter hours of credit in previous 5 years

5. Pass a content-area examination

6. Submit fingerprint card or acceptable employment verification from an Alaska public school district, application for background check, certificate application, and nonrefundable fees

B. Renewal

1. Satisfy recency credit: see II, A, 4, directly above, except that at least 3 semester hours must be upper-division or graduate credits

2. Verify current employment in Alaska public school district in position requiring certificate

   a. If applicant is not employed in this capacity at time of renewal, fingerprint card is required.

3. Submit renewal application and fees

C. Effective February 1, 2009, as individuals renew, reinstate, or apply for five-year certificates, those certificates will expire on applicant's birthday.

1. Individuals may submit an application packet for renewal 1 year prior to expiration date on certificate being renewed.

III. Master Teacher Certificate (valid 10 years; renewable)

A. Requirements

1. Meet all requirements for Professional certificate; see II, A, 1–6, directly above

2. Hold current Initial or Professional certificate

3. Hold current National Board certification issued by National Board for Professional Teaching Standards (NBPTS),
   or
   Complete 2 performance reviews and achieve required score.

4. Submit certificate application and nonrefundable fees

B. Renewal

1. Hold current or renewed National Board certification

2. Satisfy recency credit: see II, A, 4, directly above, except credit is during previous 10 years

3. See II, B, 2 and 3, directly above

4. Teacher holding Master certificate but not wishing to renew it may move to Professional certificate, provided its renewal requirements are met.

IV. Certification Changes for Current Alaska Certificate Holders

A. Holders of Type A teaching certificate will move directly to Professional level when they renew their current certificate.

B. Holders of Type B Administrative or Type C Special Service certificates will not be affected by these changes.

Administration

I.   Administrative Certificate (Type B; valid 5 years)
    A.   Requirements
        1.   At least 3 years of satisfactory public school teaching experience as certified teacher
            a.   ~~For superintendent endorsement, 5 years of satisfactory employment as~~ teacher or administrator, with at least 3 years of experience as teacher and at least 1 year of experience as administrator with an administrative certificate
        2.   Master's degree from a regionally accredited institution and completion of approved program based on National Council for Accreditation of Teacher Education (NCATE) or equivalent state standards in administrative specialty plus institutional recommendation
        3.   See Levels of Certificates, II, A, 4, above
            a.   Applicants meeting all other requirements except this one may apply for nonrenewable Temporary certificate, valid for 1 year.
        4.   See Levels of Certificates, II, A, 3, above
            a.   Applicants meeting all other requirements except this one may apply for nonrenewable Provisional certificate, valid for 2 years.
            b.   Contact Teacher Education and Certification (see Appendix 1) for complete list of approved courses that meet this requirement
        5.   Submit signed and notarized application, institutional recommendation form, official transcripts, completed fingerprint card, and all processing fees (nonrefundable)
    B.   Renewal. See Levels of Certificates, II, B, and C, above
    C.   Additional Endorsements
        1.   Endorsements will be granted as recommended by the preparing institution.
        2.   To be employed as administrator of special education, the Type B Administrative certificate must be specifically endorsed for special education administration.
            a.   To qualify, applicant must verify at least 3 years of satisfactory employment as certified special education teacher or school psychologist, counselor, or speech pathologist with Type A or Type C certificate or comparable certificate issued by another state, and must have completed approved program as in I, A, 2, directly above, including recommendation specifically for special education administration.
    D.   Exclusions: Type B Administrative certificate does not qualify holder for assignment as a classroom teacher.

Special Services

I.   Special Services Certificate (Type C; valid 5 years)
    A.   Requirements
        1.   Completion of a program through the bachelor's or higher degree from a regionally accredited institution with specialization in a support area that can be utilized by a school district

    2.   Verification from the college that the applicant has completed a program in specific specialization

    3.   See Administration, I, A, 3–5, directly above

B.   Renewal. See Levels of Certificates, II, B, 1 and 2, above

C.   Endorsements

    1.   Type C certificate endorsements are required and include: audiology, occupational therapy, physical therapy, school nursing, school psychology, school psychometry, social work, speech or language pathology, school counselor, and library science–media

       a.   Applicants for School Psychology Endorsement must:

          i.   Also hold a master's or higher degree in school psychology,

          ii.   Secure recommendation by institution whose school psychology program has been approved by NCATE, the National Association of School Psychologists (NASP), or the American Psychological Association,
              and

          iii.   Have completed a 1,200-hour internship with 600 of those hours in school setting. The 600 hours in school setting may be waived if applicant holds certification from the NASP.

       b.   Applicants for endorsement in speech, language, or hearing must:

          i.   Hold either master's or higher degree with major emphasis in speech-language pathology, audiology, or speech-language and hearing science,
              or
              Hold certification of clinical competence from the American Speech-Language-Hearing Association.
              and

          ii.   Secure recommendation for endorsement by institution with program approved by NCATE or the American Speech-Language-Hearing Association.

D.   Exclusions: Type C certificate does not qualify holder for assignment as a classroom teacher.

Additional Certificates

I.   Limited Certificate (Valid 5 years; nontransferable to other school districts)

A.   Requirements for the Vocational Trade Endorsement

    1.   Completion of at least 4 years of full-time work experience in a trade or vocational pursuit, of which not more than 2 years of formal training (trade school or technical institute) are acceptable. Letters of reference from former employers must be submitted.

    2.   Proof of employment in the trade or vocational area by an Alaskan school district having an approved vocational education program

B.   Requirements for the Alaska Native Language or Culture Endorsement

        1.   Submit a résumé demonstrating competency in an Alaskan native language or at least 4 years of experience involving an Alaskan native culture as verified by the school district

   C. Requirements for the Military Science Endorsement

        1.   Meet the criteria of the U.S. Department of Defense to be a Junior Reserve Officer as verified by the school district

        2.   Submit a résumé demonstrating competency in a military sciences specialty

   D. Renewal Requirements

        1.   Three semester hours of professional courses related to applicant's field of employment, or additional training and/or work experience acceptable to the Commissioner, all of which must have been completed within the 5 years immediately preceding the expiration date of the current certificate

        2.   Proof of employment in the trade or vocational area by a school district in Alaska

II.   Temporary Certificate (Type B or C; valid 1 year)

   A. Requirements

        1.   Meet all application requirements except the 6 semester hours of recency and the two Alaska courses

        2.   Proof of satisfactory administrative or special service experience for at least 3 full-time years

        3.   Never possessed an Alaska administrative or special services certificate

   B. Nonrenewable

III. Provisional certificate (Type B or C; valid 2 years)

   A. Requirements

        1.   Meet all application requirements except completion of 3 semester hours in Alaska studies and 3 semester hours in Alaska multicultural education or cross-cultural communication (course work must be approved)

   B. Nonrenewable

IV. Reemployment Certificate, Type B and Type C (valid for 1 year; nonrenewable)

   A. Holders of a certificate that has been expired for more than 12 months may apply for the Reemployment certificate.

   B. During year validity, holder must complete all requirements for regular Type B or Type C certificate (see Administration and Special Services, above) and submit application.

Arizona

Elementary Certificates (K–8)

I. Provisional Elementary Education Certificate (valid 3 years; not renewable, but extendable once for 3 years). Requirements include:
   A. Completed application for certification; appropriate fee; and photocopy of valid Arizona IVP fingerprint card issued on or after January 1, 2008, or photocopy of valid Arizona fingerprint clearance card issued prior to January 1, 2008;
   B. Bachelor's or more advanced degree from an accredited institution, verified by official transcript(s);
   C. One of the following options:
      1. Completion of a teacher preparation program in elementary education from an accredited institution or a Board-approved teacher preparation program,
         or
      2. Forty-five semester hours of education courses from an accredited institution, including at least 8 semester hours of practicum in grades K–8,
         a. Two years of verified full-time teaching experience in grades Prekindergarten–8 may be substituted for the 8 semester hours of practicum.
         b. Courses which teach the knowledge and skills described in the professional teaching standards, such as learning theory, classroom management, methods, and assessment, are acceptable.
            or
      3. A valid elementary education certificate from another state;
   D. Professional Knowledge Elementary Exam—one of the following:
      1. A passing score on the Professional Knowledge Elementary (91) portion of the Arizona Educator Proficiency Assessment (AEPA),
      2. A passing score on a comparable Professional Knowledge Elementary examination from another state or agency,
      3. A valid comparable certificate from the National Board for Professional Teaching Standards,
         or
      4. Three years of full-time teaching elementary education, K–8;
   E. Subject Knowledge Elementary Education Exam—one of the following:
      1. A passing score on the Subject Knowledge Elementary Education (01) portion of the AEPA,
      2. A passing score on a comparable Subject Knowledge Elementary Education examination from another state or agency,
         or
      3. A valid comparable certificate from the National Board for Professional Teaching Standards;

F. Verification of state-approved Structured English Immersion (SEI) training or comparable state-approved SEI training from another state to qualify for the Provisional SET endorsement (valid for 3 years; additional 3 semester hours of state-approved SEI training required to qualify for full SEI endorsement);
    1. If certified before August 31, 2006: verification of 1 semester hour or 15 clock hours of state-approved SEI training
    2. If certified on or after August 31, 2006: verification of 3 semester hours or 45 clock hours of state-approved SEI training
    3. Individuals who hold an Arizona Full Bilingual or Full English as a Second Language (ESL) endorsement are exempt from the SEI endorsement requirement.
    4. The requirement for a Provisional SET endorsement may he waived for a period not to exceed 1 year for individuals who graduate from administrator or teacher preparation programs that are not approved by the Arizona State Board of Education and meet all other applicable certification requirements.
G. Arizona Constitution (a college course or the appropriate examination); *and*
H. U.S . Constitution (a college course or the appropriate examination).
    1. If applicant otherwise qualifies for the certificate but is deficient in Arizona and/or U.S. Constitution, applicant will have 3 years under a valid teaching certificate to fulfill the requirement, except that those teaching an academic course on History, Government, Social Studies, Citizenship, Law, or Civics have 1 year to fulfill the requirement(s).

II. Standard Elementary Education certificate (valid 6 years; renewable). Requirements include:
A. Qualify for and hold the Provisional Elementary Education certificate for 2 years;
B. Two years of verified full-time teaching experience during the valid period of the Provisional certificate may be used to convert the Provisional certificate to a Standard certificate;
C. Three semester hours or 45 clock hours of instruction in research-based systematic phonics from an accredited institution or other provider;
D. Verification of 3 semester hours or 45 clock hours of state-approved SEI training or comparable state-approved SEI training from another state to qualify for the Full SET endorsement;
    1. Individuals who hold a Full Bilingual or Full ESL endorsement are exempt from the SEI endorsement requirement. *and*
E. A photocopy of valid Arizona IVP lingerprint card issued on or after January 1, 2008, or a photocopy of valid Arizona fingerprint clearance card issued prior to January 1, 2008.

Secondary Certificates (7–12)

I. Provisional Secondary Education Certificate (valid 3 years; nonrenewable but extendable once for 3 years). Requirements include:

A. See Elementary Certificates I, A and B, above;
B. One of the following options:
    1. Completion of a teacher preparation program in secondary education from an accredited institution or from a Board-approved teacher preparation program, *or*
    2. Thirty semester hours of education courses, including at least 8 semester practicum in grades 7–12,
        a. Two years of verified full-time teaching experience in grades 7 through Postsecondary may substitute for the 8 semester hours of practicum.
        b. Courses which teach the knowledge and skills described in the professional teaching standards, such as learning theory, classroom management, methods, and assessment, are acceptable. *or*
    3. A valid secondary education certificate from another state;
C. Professional Knowledge Secondary Exam—one of the following:
    1. A passing score on the Professional Knowledge Secondary (92) portion of the AEPA,
    2. A passing score on a comparable Professional Knowledge Secondary examination from another state or agency,
    3. A valid comparable cerlificate from the National Board for Professional Teaching Standards, *or*
    4. Three years of full-time teaching secondary education, 7–12;
D. Subject Knowledge Secondary Education Exam—one of the following:
    1. A passing score on the Subject Knowledge Secondary Education portion of the AEPA
        a. Subject Knowledge assessments offered for the following: art, biology, business, chemistry, economics, English, French, geography, German, health, history, mathematics, music, physics, political science/American government, social studies, and Spanish
        b. If a proficiency assessment is not offered in a subject area, an approved area shall consist of 24 semester hours of subject-related courses from an accredited institution.
        c. An approved area in general science comprises 12 semester hours of life science courses and 12 semester hours of physical science courses.
        d. If a language assessment is not offered through the AEPA, a passing score of Advanced Low on the American Council on the Teaching of Foreign Languages (ACTFL) may demonstrate proficiency of that foreign language in lieu of the 24 semester hours of courses in that subject;
    2. A passing score on a comparable Subject Knowledge Secondary Education examination from another state or agency,
    3. A valid comparable certificate from the National Board for Professional Teaching Standards; *or*

      4.   Master's degree from an accredited institution in the appropriate subject area.
    E.   See Elementary Certificates, I, F, 1–4, above;
    F.   See Elementary Certificates, I, G and H, above.
  II.   Standard Secondary Education Certificate (valid 6 years; renewable). Requirements include:
    A.   See Elementary Certificates, II, A–D, above, except for secondary level

Early Childhood Education Certificate, Birth through Age 8 or through Grade 3

Note: All teachers serving children Birth through Kindergarten must have either an Early Childhood Education certificate or Early Childhood endorsement by July 1, 2012. Also, an individual who holds the Early Childhood Education teaching certificate or the Early Childhood endorsement in combination with an Arizona Cross-Categorical, Emotional Disability, Learning Disability, Mental Retardation, Orthopedic/Other Health Impairment or Severely and Profoundly Disabled Special Education teaching certificate is not required to hold the Early Childhood Special Education certificate.

    I.   Provisional Early Childhood Education Certificate (valid 3 years; nonrenewable but extendable once for 3 years). Requirements include:
    A.   See Elementary Certificates, I, A and B, above
    B.   One of the following 3 options:
        1.   Completion of a teacher preparation program in early childhood education from an accredited institution or a Board-approved teacher preparation program; *or*
        2.   Thirty-seven semester hours of early childhood education courses from an accredited institution, include all of the following areas of study and a minimum of 8 semester hours of practicum;
            a.   Early childhood education courses shall include all of the following areas of study: foundations of early childhood education; child guidance and classroom management; characteristics and quality practices for typical and atypical behaviors of young children; child growth and development, including, health, safety and nutrition; child, family, cultural and community relationships; developmentally appropriate instructional methodologies for teaching language, math, science, social studies and the arts; early language and literacy development; and assessing, monitoring and reporting progress of young children
            b.   Practicum must include a minimum of 4 semester hours in supervised field experience, practicum, internship, or student teaching setting serving children birth through preschool, *or*
One year of full-time verified teaching experience birth through preschool and a minimum of 4 semester hours in a supervised student teaching setting serving children in kindergarten through grade 3, *or*

One year of full-time verified teaching experience kindergarten through grade 3.
   - c. One year of verified full-time teaching experience with children in birth through preschool may substitute for 4 semester hours in supervised field experience, practicum, internship, or student teaching setting serving children birth through preschool.
   - d. One year of verified full-time teaching experience with children in kindergarten through grade 3 in an accredited school may substitute for 4 semester hours in a supervised student teaching setting serving children in kindergarten through grade 3.
      or
   3. A valid early childhood education certificate from another state.
   C. Professional Knowledge Early Childhood Exam—one of the following:
   1. A passing score on the Professional Knowledge Early Childhood (#93) portion of the AEPA,
   2. A passing score on a comparable Professional Knowledge Early Childhood examination from another state or agency,
   3. A valid comparable certificate from the National Board for Professional Teaching Standards,
      or
   4. Three years of full-time teaching early childhood education, birth through grade 3.
   D. Subject Knowledge Early Childhood Education Exam—one of the following:
   1. A passing score on the Subject Knowledge Early Childhood Education (#36) portion of the AEPA,
   2. A passing score on a comparable Subject Knowledge Early Childhood examination from another state or agency,
      or
   3. A valid comparable certificate from the National Board for Professional Teaching Standards
   E. Master's degree in Early Childhood Education from an accredited institution
   F. See Elementary Certificates, I, F, 1–4 above
   G. See Elementary Education, I, G and H, above
II. Standard Early Childhood Education Certificate, Birth through Age 8 or through Grade 3 (valid 6 years; renewable). Requirements include:
   A. Qualify for the Provisional Early Childhood certificate; and acquire 2 years of verified full-time teaching experience during the valid period of the Provisional certificate to convert the Provisional certificate to a Standard certificate;
      or
   B. Hold current National Board Certification in Early Childhood.
   C. See Elementary Certificates, II, D and E, above.
III. Other Special Education Certificates
   A. Consult http://www.azed.gov/certification for complete descriptions of requirements for the following special education certificates: Early Childhood (Birth–5 years);

Cross-Categorical (K–12) Learning Disability (K–12); Hearing Impaired (Birth-Grade 12); Emotional Disability (K–12); Visually Impaired (Birth–Grade 12); Orthopedic Impairments or Other Health Impairments (K–12), Mental Retardation (K–12); Severely and Profoundly Disabled (K–12)

IV. Reciprocal Provisional Teaching Certificates
   A. Consult http://www.azed.gov/certification for complete descriptions of requirements

Endorsements

I. Endorsements are attachments to teaching certificates and indicate areas of specialization. They cover K–12 unless otherwise indicated. See teacher certification website (Appendix 1) for specific requirements for each area. Once issued, endorsements are automatically renewed with the teaching certificate.
   A. Endorsements are issued in following areas: art, bilingual education, computer science, cooperative education, dance, dramatic arts, driver's education, early childhood, elementary foreign language (K–8), English as a second language, gifted education, library-media specialist, mathematics specialist (K–8), middle grade (5–9), music, physical education, reading specialist, and structured English immersion
   B. Changes to the mathematics endorsement will go into effect July 1, 2011; consult http://www.azed.gov/certification for details.

Administrative Certificates

I. Supervisor Certificate, Prekindergarten–12 (valid 6 years; renewable)
   A. Required for all personnel whose primary responsibility is administering instructional programs, supervising certified personnel, or similar administrative duties, except for individuals who hold a valid Arizona Principal or Superintendent Certificate
   B. Requirements for the Supervisor Certificate include:
      1. See Elementary Certificates, I, A, above;
      2. A valid Arizona Early Childhood, Elementary, Secondary, Special Education, Career and Technical Education certificate or other professional certificate issued by the Arizona Department of Education;
      3. Master's or higher degree from an accredited institution;
      4. Three years of verified full-time teaching experience or related education services experience in a Prekindergarten–12 setting;
      5. Completion of a program in educational administration which shall consist of a minimum of 18 graduate semester hours of educational administration courses which teach the knowledge and skills described in the Professional Administrative Standards (R7-2-603);
         a. Courses to include 3 credit hours in school law and 3 credit hours in school finance
      6. A practicum in educational administration or 2 years of verified educational administrative experience in grades Prekindergarten–12;

7. A passing score on the supervisor, principal, or superintendent administrator portion of the AEPA;
8. see Elementary Certificates, F, 1–4, above; *and*
9. See Elementary Certificates, G and H, above.

II. Principal Certificate, Prekindergarten–12 (valid 6 years; renewable)

A. Required for all personnel who hold the title of, or perform the duties of, Principal or Assistant Principal as delineated in Title 15 of the Arizona Revised Statutes, except for individuals who hold a valid Arizona Superintendent Certificate and have completed 3 years of verified full-time teaching experience

B. Requirements include:
1. See Elementary Certificates, I, A, above;
2. Master's or higher degree from an accredited institution;
3. Three years of verified full-time teaching experience in grades Prekindergarten–12;
4. Completion of a program in educational administration for principals, including at least 30 graduate semester hours of educational administration courses teaching the knowledge and skills described in the Professional Administrative Standards (R7-2-603)
    a. Courses to include 3 credit hours in school law and 3 credit hours in school finance
5. A practicum as a principal or 2 years of verified experience as a principal or assistant principal under the supervision of a certified principal in grades Prekindergarten–12
6. A passing score on either the Principal or Superintendent portion of the AEPA;
7. See Elementary Certificates, F, 1–4, above; *and*
8. See Elementary Certificates, G and H, above.

III. Superintendent Certificates, Prekindergarten–12 (valid 6 years; renewable)

A. Individuals who hold the title of Superintendent, Assistant Superintendent, or Associate Superintendent and who perform duties directly relevant to curriculum, instruction, certified employee evaluations, and instructional supervision may obtain a Superintendent Certificate.

B. Requirements include:
1. See Elementary Education Certificates, I, A, above;
2. Master's or higher degree, including at least 60 graduate semester hours from an accredited institution;
3. Completion of a program in educational administration for superintendents, including at least 36 graduate semester hours of educational administrative courses teaching the knowledge and skills described in the Professional Administrative Standards (R7-2-603);
    a. Courses to include 3 credit hours in school law and 3 credit hours in school finance
4. Three years of verified full-time teaching experience or related education services experience in Prekindergarten–12 setting;

5. A practicum as a superintendent or 2 years of verified experience as a superintendent, assistant superintendent, or associate superintendent in grades Prekindergarten–12;
6. A passing score on the superintendent administrator portion of the AEPA;
7. See Elementary Certificates, F, 1–4, above;
   and
8. ~~See Elementary Certificates, G and H, above.~~

Professional Non-Teaching Certificate, (Prekindergarten–12)

I. School Psychologist Certificate, Prekindergarten–12 (valid 6 years; renewable). Requirements include:
   A. Master's or higher advanced degree from an accredited institution;
   B. One of the following 5 options:
      1. Completion of a graduate program in school psychology, consisting of at least 60 graduate semester hours,
         or
      2. Completion of a doctoral program in psychology and completion of a retraining program in school psychology from an accredited institution or Board-approved program with a letter of institutional endorsement from the head of the school psychology program,
         or
      3. Five years experience within the last 10 years working full time in the capacity of a school psychologist in a school setting serving any portion of grades kindergarten through 12, verified by the school district superintendent or human resources department,
         or
      4. A Nationally Certified School Psychologist Credential,
         or
      5. Diploma in school psychology from the American Board of School Psychology;
   C. A supervised internship of at least 1,200 clock hours with a minimum of 600 of those hours in a school setting;
      1. Three years experience as a certified school psychologist within the last 10 years may be substituted for the internship requirement.
   D. See Elementary Certificates, I, A, above.
II. School Psychologist Interim Certificate, Prekindergarten–12 (valid 2 years; nonrenewable). Requirements include:
   A. See Elementary Education certificates, I, A, above
   B. Master's or higher degree in psychology from an accredited institution;
   C. Verification of current enrollment in an accredited school psychology program or a Board-approved school psychology program signed by the dean of a college of education or the administrator of a Board-approved school psychology preparation program;
      and
   D. Verification that the holder of the interim certificate shall be under the direct

supervision of college and certified school personnel, including a school or school district–based certified school psychologist who holds a valid Arizona School Psychologist Certificate.

III. Guidance Counselor Certificate (Prekindergarten–12) (valid 6 years; renewable). Requirements include:

    A. Master's or higher degree from an accredited institution;

    B. Completion of a graduate program in guidance and counseling from an accredited institution, or a valid guidance counselor certificate from another state;

    C. Photocopy of valid Arizona IVP fingerprint card issued on or after January 1, 2008, or photocopy of valid Arizona fingerprint clearance card issued prior to January 1, 2008;
       and

    D. One of the following 3 options:

        1. Completion of a supervised counseling practicum in school counseling,

        2. Two years of verified full-time experience as a school guidance counselor,
          or

        3. Three years of verified full-time teaching experience.

Other Certificates

Certificates are also awarded in adult education, arts education, athletic coaching, career and technical education, foreign language teacher, Junior ROTC, speech-language pathologist, speech-language technician, and teacher intern. For details, please consult http://www.azed.gov/certification

Arkansas

Types of Licenses

I. Initial License: For novice teachers with less than 1 year of teaching experience (valid 1–3 years; nonrenewable)
   A. Prerequisites
      1. Hold a bachelor's or higher degree from an accredited institution
      2. Successfully complete the following tests:
         a. Praxis I: Reading, writing, math
         b. Praxis II: Content test for all parts required, *and*
         c. Praxis II: Principles of Learning and Teaching
      3. Criminal background check by the Arkansas State Police and the FBI
      4. Child Maltreatment Central Registry Check
   B. Induction Program for Novice Teachers
      1. Induction begins upon first-time employment in an Arkansas public school.
      2. Site-based, trained mentor assigned to support novice teacher's practice and professional growth
         a. Pathwise Mentoring Observation system used as a tool for evaluation of classroom performance, grounded in 19 essential teaching criteria
      3. Pass Praxis III : Professional Assessment
II. Standard License (valid 5 years; renewable)
   A. Prerequisites
      1. See Initial License, I, A, 1–4, above
      2. Novice teachers must successfully complete induction program. See Initial License, I, B, 1–3, above.
   B. Renewal Requirements
      1. Beginning with the 2005–06 school year, accrue 60 professional development hours during each year of the 5-year renewal cycle
         a. A 3-hour college credit course may count as 15 hours of professional development, but no more than half of the required 60 hours may be met through college credit hours.
      2. See Initial License, I, A, 3, above, only if never had a background check at first renewal
III. Non-Traditional Licensure
   A. To give talented and highly motivated applicants with college degrees in fields other than education an opportunity to obtain the proper credentials and become teachers in an Arkansas public school. Contact the Office of Professional Quality Enhancement (see Appendix 1) for full details.
      1. Prerequisites: See Initial License, I, A, 1 and 2, a and b, above
      2. Complete application and supporting documents
      3. Successful personal interview

Levels and Areas of Licensure

I.   Levels of Licensure are defined as the grade-age-level parameters of the teaching license. They include the following:
   A.   Early Childhood: Grades Preschool–4
   B.   Preschool/Early Adolescence: Grades Preschool–8
   C.   Preschool/Young Adulthood: Grades Preschool–12
   D.   Middle Childhood/Early Adolescence: Grades 4–8
   E.   Adolescence/Young Adulthood: Grades 7–12
   F.   Postsecondary: Above grade 12
II. Teacher Licensure Competency Areas are defined as the particular content field(s) of the teaching license.
   A.   Areas include adult education; agriculture sciences technology (4–8 and 7–12); art; business technology (4–8 and 7–12); coaching education; drama/speech; early childhood (P–4); early childhood instructional specialist (birth–8); educational examiner; English-language arts/social studies (4–8); English-language arts (7–12); ESL education; family and consumer sciences; foreign language (P–8 and 7–12); gifted and talented education; industrial technology; library media specialist (all levels); life/earth science (7–12); marketing technology (4–8, 7–12, and post-secondary); mathematics/science (4–8); mathematics (7–12); music-instrumental (P–8 and 7–12); music-vocal (P–8 and 7–12); physical/earth science; physical education/health; reading education; speech-language pathologist; school counseling; school psychology specialist; social studies (7–12); special education instructional specialist (4–12); teachers of hearing-impaired students; teachers of visually impaired students.
   B.   Exception areas include special education; added endorsements; educational leadership and supervision; non-instructional student services; and professional and technical
      1.   Applicants cannot test out of exception areas but must complete the program of study and the required Praxis assessment.
III. Adding Areas of Licensure

Note: Questions about adding additional licensure areas may be directed to the Office of Professional Licensure (see Appendix 1). Speak only with a supervisor who works with adding areas of licensure. Be sure to document with whom you spoke and what was said.

   A.   Prerequisites
      1.   Hold a valid Initial or Standard Arkansas teaching license. See Types of Licenses, II, A and B, above.
   B.   To add non-exception teaching areas within the same level of licensure, applicant must pass the State Board–required specialty area assessment(s).
   C.   To add exception areas within the same level of licensure:
      1.   Complete an approved performance-based program of study,
         and
      2.   Pass the State Board–required assessment(s).
   D.   To add non-exception teaching areas outside the current level of licensure:
      1.   See III, C, 1 and 2, directly above

E. To add an area of licensure or endorsement for which there is not a State Board–required specialty area assessment:
  1. Successfully complete an approved performanced-based program of study, *and*
  2. Complete the State Board–required pedagogical assessment.
F. Special Situations
  1. The non-instruction student services areas of school psychology specialist and speech language pathology shall have completed a master's degree and the State Board–required assessment to be licensed.
  2. Teachers or administrators adding early childhood (P–4), all middle school areas, or secondary social studies to their valid standard license shall have completed a 3-credit-hour course in Arkansas history.
  3. Additional areas/levels of licensure or endorsement shall be added to a valid standard license upon receiving documentation that all requirements have been met and upon receiving an application requesting the additional licensure area or endorsement.

Administrative Licensure

I. Levels of Licensure
  A. Building Level Administrator—Principal, assistant principal, or vice principal (P–8 and/or 5–12)
  B. Curriculum/Program Administrator—A school leader responsible for program development and administration, and/or employment evaluation decisions. Each Curriculum/Program Administrator License is limited to one of the following areas:
    1. Special Education (P–12)
    2. Gifted and Talented Education (P–12)
    3. Career and Technical Education (grade levels 4–8, 7–12 and/or Post-Secondary)
    4. Content Area Specialist (P–12)
    5. Curriculum Specialist (P–12)
  C. District Level Administrator—Superintendent, assistant superintendent, or deputy superintendent (P–12)
II. Types of Licensure
  A. Initial License (valid 1–3 years)
    1. Hold a standard teaching license
    2. Have 4 years of classroom teaching experience, with at least 3 of the 4 years at the level of Building Administrator licensure sought
    3. Hold a graduate degree that includes a program of study with an internship and portfolio development, based upon the 5 standards of administrative licensure
      a. For candidates holding a graduate degree in an area other than educational leadership, the Arkansas institution of higher education will review his/her credentials to determine his/her individual needs.

B. Standard License
   1. Participate in a mentoring experience during the period of initial licensure
      a. The mentor provided should have relevant experience sought by the new administrator, at least 3 years of administrator experience, hold a standard teaching license, and have completed the mentorship training.
      b. Districts shall submit their administrator mentoring plans to the Arkansas State Department of Education for approval.
   2. Successfully complete the School Leaders Licensure Assessment (SLLA) with a minimum cut-score of 163
      a. Candidates should practice actual administrative experience during their induction year(s) before attempting the SLLA.
C. District Administrator License
   1. Hold a standard teaching license and a Building-Level Administrator license
   2. Have 4 years of classroom teaching experience and be licensed as a Building-Level Administrator or Curriculum/Program Administrator
   3. Hold an advanced degree or complete an advanced program of study based on individual needs inclusive of an internship and portfolio development based on the Standards for Administrator licensure
   4. Successfully complete the School Superintendent Assessment (SSA) with a score of 156

Reciprocity

I. Eligibility to apply:
   A. Hold a valid or expired teaching license from another state,
      or
   B. Degree must be from an institution that holds regional or national accreditation recognized by the United States Department of Education (USDOE). The education program must also hold national accreditation recognized by the USDOE or be state-approved.
II. A 3-hour Arkansas history course will be required for Arkansas licensure when the licensure area is elementary, any middle school area, or secondary social studies.
III. For full details on exceptions to eligibility requirements as well as information on candidates from other countries, contact the Office of Professional Licensure (see Appendix 1).

California

All multiple and single subject professional teacher preparation programs require candidates to pass an assessment of teaching performance in order to earn a teaching credential. For full details about the Teaching Performance Assessment (TPA), consult the website (see Appendix 1).

Teaching Credentials

I. Multiple Subject Teaching Credential—Commonly used in elementary school service
II. Single Subject Teaching Credential—Commonly used in secondary school service
III. Education Specialist Instruction Credential – Commonly used in special education settings
IV. Five-Year Preliminary Multiple Subject and Single Subject Teaching Credential (nonrenewable)
   A. Requirements for California-Trained Teachers
      1. Bachelor's or higher degree from regionally accredited college or university, except in professional education
      2. Teacher preparation program, including student teaching, completed with grade of C or higher on a 5-point scale at California college or university with a Commission-accredited program
      3. California basic skills requirement*
      4. U.S. Constitution (course or examination)
      5. Subject-matter competence by obtaining passing score on appropriate subject-matter examination or obtaining letter from California college or university with approved subject-matter program (subject-matter letter is not an option for Multiple Subject credential applicants)
      6. Completion of course in developing English language skills, including reading
      7. Completion of course in foundational uses of computers in educational settings
      8. Multiple Subject Teaching Credential only: all California-prepared applicants must pass Reading Instruction Competence Assessment (RICA), unless exempt
   B. Requirements for Teachers Trained in Other States or U.S. Territories
      1. Bachelor's or higher degree from regionally accredited college or university
      2. Possession of comparable teaching credential (does not have to be valid at time of application)
      3. Prior to or within first year of issuance of credential, candidate must satisfy California's basic skills requirement.
         a. Unless the basic skills requirement is satisfied within 1 year of issuance date of credential, credential will not be valid for employment in California's public schools until requirement is met.

4. There are 3 different routes under which an out-of-state-trained teacher may qualify for certification, and each route has specific renewal requirements.
    a. Route 1: Less than 2 years of out-of-state, full-time teaching experience
    b. Route 2:
        i. Two or more years of full-time teaching experience in a public or regionally accredited private school,
          and
        ii. Photocopies of performance evaluations from 2 separate years of the verified out-of-state teaching experience on which the candidate received ratings of "satisfactory" or better.
    c. Route 3: Possess National Board for Professional Teaching Standards (NBPTS) Certificate (results in issuance of clear credential)

C. Requirements for Teachers Trained Outside of the United States
    1. The equivalent of a bachelor's or higher degree from a regionally accredited college or university located in the United States
    2. Completion of a comparable teacher preparation program, including student teaching, that is equivalent to a teacher preparation program from a regionally accredited college or university located in the United States
    3. Possession of, or eligibility for, a comparable teaching credential issued by the country in which the program was completed
    4. Prior to or within first year of issuance of credential, candidate must satisfy California's basic skills requirement
        a. See B, 3, a, above
    5. Individuals trained outside the United States must have their foreign transcripts evaluated by a Commission-approved agency prior to submission of their application packet.

V. Five-Year Clear Multiple Subject and Single Subject Teaching Credential (renewable every 5 years)
A. Requirements for California-Trained Teachers
    1. See IV, A, 1–8, above
    2. Completion of Commission-approved induction program with verification by induction program director
B. Requirements for Teachers Trained in Other States or U.S. Territories
    1. See IV, B, 1–4, above
    2. Complete renewal requirements associated with route under which preliminary teaching credential was issued
        a. Route 1:
            i. Complete Commission-approved induction program with verification by induction program director
            ii. Earn a California English learner authorization
        b. Route 2:
            i. Earn a master's degree (or the equivalent in semester units) from a regionally accredited college or university,
              or

Complete 150 clock hours of professional activities under the California Standards for the Teaching Profession (CSTP).
  ii. Earn a California English learner authorization
 c. Route 3: Individuals who qualify based on National Board (NBPTS) Certification are issued clear credentials.
 C. Requirements for Teachers Trained Outside the United States
  1. See IV, C, 1–5, above
  2. Completion of a course in developing English language skills, including reading (or passage of RICA for holders of Multiple Subject credentials only)
  3. U.S. Constitution course or examination
  4. Subject-matter competence by obtaining a passing score on appropriate subject-matter examination or obtaining letter from California college or university with approved subject-matter program
  5. Commission-approved induction program with verification by induction program director
  6. CPR training for adults, infants, and children
 D. Clear credentials are renewed every 5 years via the Commission's online renewal system.
VI. Authorization for Service for Multiple Subject and Single Subject Teaching Credential
 A. Teacher authorized for multiple-subject instruction may be assigned to teach in any self-contained classroom in preschool and grades K–12 and in classes organized primarily for adults
 B. Teacher authorized for single-subject instruction may be assigned to teach any subject in authorized fields in any grade level: preschool, grades K–12 and in classes organized primarily for adults
  1. Statutory subjects available: agriculture, art, business, English, foundational-level general science, foundational-level mathematics, health science, home economics, industrial and technology education, language other than English, mathematics, music, physical education, science (in one of these areas: biological sciences, chemistry, geosciences, or physics), specialized science (in one of the 4 science areas immediately prior), and social science
VII. Five-Year Clear Specialist Instruction Credential—Covers specialist areas requiring advanced professional preparation or special competencies, including agriculture, bilingual education, early childhood education, gifted education, mathematics, and reading and language arts
 A. Requirements
  1. Hold valid California teaching credential that required bachelor's degree and professional preparation program, including student teaching
  2. Post-baccalaureate professional preparation program in specialist area
  3. Recommendation of California college or university with specific, Commission-accredited specialist program
   a. Applicants trained outside of California who meet requirements in VII, A, 1 and 2, directly above, may still be certified. Student teaching or field work

must have been completed with a grade of C on a 5-point scale and applicant must provide photocopy of out-of-state credential listing a comparable authorization.

    b.   Applicants for Bilingual Education Specialist Credential who trained out of state must apply through and be recommended by California college or university with Commission-accredited program.

  B. Authorization for Service

    1. Credential authorizes holder to teach in area of specialization in preschool, grades K–12, and in classes organized primarily for adults

VIII. Education Specialist Instruction Credential—Available in following specialization areas: mild/moderate disabilities, moderate/severe disabilities, deaf and hard-of-hearing, visual impairments, physical and health impairments, and early childhood special education

  A. Requirements for California-Trained Teachers

    1. Bachelor's or higher degree from regionally accredited college or university

    2. Professional preparation program in education specialist category completed at California college or university with Commission-accredited program

    3. California basic skills requirement*

    4. U.S. Constitution course or examination

    5. Completion of course in developing English-language skills, including reading

    6. Passage of the Reading Instruction Competence Assessment (RICA)

       a. RICA passage is not required for category of early childhood special education.

    7. Verification of subject-matter competence (see IV, A, 5, above)

       a. Verification of subject-matter competence is not required for category of early childhood special education.

    8. Formal recommendation of California college or university with Commission-accredited program

  B. Requirements for Teachers Trained in Other States, U.S. Territories, or outside the United States

    1. See IV, B and C, above

  C. Contact Commission on Teacher Credentialing (see Appendix 1) for full information on Clear or Level II Education Specialist Instruction Credential requirements.

IX. Authorization of Service for Education Specialist Instruction Credential

  A. Authorizes holder to teach in area of specialization and at level listed on credential in following settings: special day classes, special schools, home/hospital settings, correctional facilities, nonpublic schools and agencies, and resource rooms

Services Credentials

I. Five-Year Preliminary Administrative Services Credential (nonrenewable)

  A. Requirements

    1. Possession of valid California credential, which may be in teaching; designated-subjects teaching; pupil personnel services; librarian; health services school nurse; clinical or rehabilitative services; or speech-language pathology

    2. Three years of successful, full-time experience in public or private schools of equivalent status in any of areas listed directly above in A, 1

3. Approved program of specialized and professional preparation in administrative services,
or
Passing score on School Leaders Licensure Assessment (SLLA),
or
Approved administrative internship program from California college or university

4. California basic skills requirement*

5. Recommendation of California college or university with Commission-accredited administrative services program.

6. California-trained applicants must have offer of employment in administrative position from California school district, nonpublic school or agency, or county office of education,
or
May apply for Certificate of Eligibility.

7. Candidates prepared outside of California may satisfy these requirements by:
   a. Verifying completion of bachelor's or higher degree from regionally accredited college or university,
   b. Satisfying California's basic skills requirement (BSR)
      i. The 1-year nonrenewable credential is available to an administrator who prepared out of state if all requirements except BSR are complete.
   c. Completing teacher preparation program and equivalent elementary, secondary, or special education credential based on that program,
   and
   d. Completing administrative preparation program in which candidate was issued, or qualified for, administrative services credential based upon that program,
   or
   Achieving passing score on SLLA.

8. Administrators prepared out of state with pupil personnel, health, speech-language pathology, or clinical or rehabilitative services program will need to obtain prerequisite credential.

II. Five-Year Clear Administrative Services Credential
A. Requirements
   1. Preliminary credential (see I, A, 1–8, above)
   2. Two years of successful full-time experience in position requiring preliminary credential
   3. Complete one of the following:
      a. Obtain the recommendation of a Commission-approved program verifying completion of an individualized program of advanced preparation designed in cooperation with employer and the program sponsor
      b. State Board of Education–approved AB 430 Principal Training Program (completion of Modules 1, 2, and 3 must be submitted with the individual's direct application to the Commission). Information on the Principal Training Program, including approved programs and

proviers, may be accessed through the California Department of Education's website at www.cde.ca.gov

  c. Meet Mastery of Fieldwork Performance Standards through a Commission-approved program (streamlined assessment option to allow candidates to forego the course work component of the program and allow them to demonstrate their knowledge, skills, and abilities through the assessment component of the program)

  d. Commission-approved alternative program based on Commission-adopted guidelines resulting in a formal recommendation from the program sponsor.

  e. Commission-approved performance assessment, when available

 4. Candidates prepared outside of California may earn clear credential without first holding preliminary credential by

  a. Verifying completion of bachelor's or higher degree from regionally accredited college or university,

  b. Satisfying California's basic skills requirement (BSR)

  c. Completing teacher preparation program and earning equivalent elementary, secondary, or special education credential based on that program,

  d. Completing 3 years of elementary, secondary, or special education teaching experience,

  e. Completing administrative preparation program in which candidate was issued, or qualified for, administrative services credential based upon that program,

   or

   Achieving passing score on SLLA,

   and

  f. Completing 3 years of out-of-state public school administrative experience and submitting 2 rigorous performance evaluations.

 5. Administrators prepared out of state with pupil personnel, health, speech-language pathology or clinical or rehabilitative services program will need to obtain prerequisite credential. The 1-year nonrenewable credential is available to administrators who prepared out of state if all requirements except BSR* are complete.

B. Authorization for Service

 1. Administrative Services Credentials authorize holder to provide various duties that may allow holder to serve in a number of positions, including superintendent, associate superintendent, deputy superintendent, principal, assistant principal, dean, supervisor, consultant, coordinator, or in equivalent or intermediate-level administrative positions.

III. Clear Teacher Librarian Services Credential

A. Requirements

 1. Bachelor's degree from regionally accredited college or university

 2. Valid prerequisite California teaching credential that required program of professional preparation, including student teaching

3. Completion of:
   a. Commission-accredited teacher librarian services program and recommendation of California college or university where program was completed,
      or
   b. Out-of-state teacher librarian services program consisting of 30 graduate semester units approved by appropriate state agency in state where program was completed
4. California basic skills requirement (BSR)*
   a. The 1-year nonrenewable credential is available to an individual who prepared out of state if all requirements except BSR are complete

B. Authorization for Service
1. Teacher Librarian Services Credential authorizes holder to assist and instruct pupils in choice and use of library materials; to plan and coordinate school library programs with instructional programs of school district; to select materials for school and district libraries; to conduct planned course of instruction for those pupils who assist in operation of school libraries; to supervise classified personnel assigned to school library duties; and to develop procedures for and management of school and district libraries.

IV. Pupil Personnel Services Credential
A. Authorization for Services
1. Credential available in 4 different areas: school counseling, school social work, school psychology, and child welfare and attendance services

B. Requirements for School Counseling Authorization
1. Post-baccalaureate study consisting of 48 semester units (30 semester units if completed prior to July 1, 2004) specializing in school counseling, including a supervised field experience
2. California's basic skills requirement (BSR)*
   a. The 1-year nonrenewable credential is available to an individual who prepared out of state if all requirements except BSR are complete
3. Recommendation of a California college or university with a Commission-accredited School Counseling program
   a. Individuals who trained out of state must:
      i. Verify possession of, or eligibility for, the equivalent authorization in the state where the program was completed,
         and
   b. Provide written verification from the college or university where the program was completed that:
      i. Program included a minimum of 600 clock hours (450 clock hours if completed prior to July 1, 2004) of supervised field experience with school-aged children in a public school at 2 of 3 school levels (elementary, middle, and high school),
         and
      ii. At least 150 of the required 600 clock hours were devoted to issues of diversity.

C. Requirements for School Social Work Authorization
1. Post-baccalaureate study consisting of 45 semester units specializing in school social work, including a supervised field experience
2. See B, 2, directly above
3. Recommendation of a California college or university with a Commission-accredited School Social Work program
    a. Individuals who trained out of state must:
        i. Verify possession of, or eligibility for, the equivalent authorization in the state where the program was completed, *and*
        ii. Provide written verification from the college or university where the program was completed that program included a minimum of 1000 clock hours (450 clock hours if completed prior to July 1, 2004) of supervised field experience with school-aged children, and at least 450 of the required 1000 clock hours were school-based practice.
D. Requirements for School Psychology Authorization
1. Post-baccalaureate study consisting of 60 semester units specializing in school social work, including a practicum and supervised field experience
2. California's basic skills requirement (BSR)*
    a. The 1-year nonrenewable credential is available to an individual who prepared out of state if all requirements except BSR are complete
3. Recommendation of a California college or university with a Commission-accredited School Psychology program
    a. See B, 3, a, above, except for a Commission-accredited School Psychology program *and*
    b. Provide written verification from the college or university where the program was completed that:
        i. Program included a minimum of 1200 clock hours (540 clock hours if completed prior to July 1, 2004) of supervised field experience with school-aged children, *and*
        ii. Prior to the field experience, applicant completed a minimum of 450 clock hours of practicum, of which 300 clock hours must have been in preschool to grade 12 (up to 150 of the required 300 clock hours may have been offered through on-campus or community agencies).
E. Child Welfare and Attendance Authorization. Contact the Commission (see Appendix 1) for full information

V. For detailed information on credentials in speech-language pathology and clinical or re-habilitative services, consult the website (see Appendix 1).

*   Unless otherwise noted, for initial issuance all applicants must satisfy California's basic skills requirement (BSR). This requirement does not apply to applicants who are having their credentials renewed, reissued, or upgraded. Out-of-state applicants may be issued a 1-year, nonrenewable credential pending satisfaction of the basic skills requirement (BSR) if a California public school employer cannot find a fully credentialed person to fill the position and offers employment to the credential applicant.

Colorado

Effective January 25, 2010, the process for submission of a set of fingerprints requires that the applicant use a fingerprint card provided by a local law enforcement agency; the Colorado Department of Education no longer provides the card. Complete the fingerprint card with the assistance of a qualified law enforcement agency, then submit the completed card, with processing fee, to the Colorado Bureau of Investigation.

Teaching Certificates

I. Interim Authorization (valid 1 year; renewable once)
   A. Issued only to out-of-state applicants who do not have 3 years of full time K–12 work experience
      1. Special services providers do not qualify for this authorization.
   B. Basic Requirements
      1. Bachelor's or higher degree from a regionally accredited institution
      2. Institutional recommendation verifying satisfactory completion of an approved program of preparation that confirms grade level or developmental level(s), subject area(s), or service specialization(s) completed by the applicant
   C. Renewal Requirements
      1. Submission of renewal application and evaluation fee
II. Initial License (valid 3 years; renewable). Note: All applicants begin the licensing process by using the Initial License application, regardless of experience or previous out-of-state license held.
   A. Issued to:
      1. Colorado graduates who have
         a. Passed their required content area exam,
           or
         b. Twenty-four semester hours of credit in specified areas,
           or
      2. Out-of-state applicants who:
         a. Have met Colorado's testing requirement(s),
           or
         b. Have 3 years of out-of-state full-time K–12 work experience.
   B. Requirements
      1. Basic requirements; see I, B, 1–2, directly above
      2. Passing score on Program for Licensing Assessments for Colorado Educators (PLACE) or an approved Praxis II assessment in applicable content knowledge
         a. Out-of-state graduates (except for special services providers) may be exempt from the content area exam if they have 3 years of out-of-state full-time K–12 work experience.

C. Renewal Requirements
    1. Submission of renewal application and evaluation fee
    2. Signature on oath that applicant has not completed induction program

III. Professional License (valid 5 years; renewable)
  A. Issued to:
    1. Applicants who have completed a Colorado-approved induction program, *or*
    2. Out-of-state applicants who have 3 years of out-of-state, full-time, continuous K–12 work experience in their endorsement area.
  B. Requirements
    1. Basic and Initial requirements; see I, B, 1 and 2, and II, B, 1 and 2, directly above
    2. Completion of a Colorado-approved induction program
  C. Renewal Requirements
    1. Submission of renewal application, evaluation fee, and evidence of 6 semester hours or 90 clock hours of professional development activities throughout the 5-year validity of the license
      a. Activities may include credits derived from college or university courses, in-services and workshops, educational travel, involvement in school reform (curriculum development), internships, and other approved ongoing professional development and training experiences.

IV. Master Certificate (valid 7 years; renewable)
  A. Issued to teachers who have successfully completed the National Board for Professional Teaching Standards (NBPTS) voluntary program. Held in conjunction with the Professional License, the Master Certificate will be renewed when the Professional License is renewed.
  B. Must hold current NBPTS certificate to renew

V. Alternative Teacher License (valid 1 or 2 years; nonrenewable)
  A. Issued to applicants accepted to participate in an approved alternative teacher program who hold a bachelor's degree from a fully accredited institution of higher education, show evidence of passing the applicable PLACE or Praxis II assessment in the relevant content area, or meet subject matter requirements.
  B. Upon successful completion of program and recommendation of support team, holder is eligible for Initial Teacher License.

VI. Principal and Administrator Licenses (renewable)
  A. Principal License is valid for all administrative or supervisory positions except chief officer of school district; and Administrator License is valid for all administrative or supervisory positions except building principal and Director of Special Education.
  B. Requirements
    1. Principal
      a. Bachelor's or higher degree from a regionally accredited institution
      b. Institutional recommendation verifying satisfactory completion of the approved graduate program of preparation for the school principalship, including a practicum

        c.   Three or more years as a licensed educator in an elementary or secondary school

        d.   Evidence of passing PLACE assessment in content knowledge

    2.   Professional Principal License requires, in addition to B, 1, a–d, directly above, a master's degree.

    3.   Administrator

        a.   See B, 1, a and b, directly above, except that graduate program is for preparation for school administrators

        b.   See B, 1, d, directly above

    4.   Director of Special Education requires, in addition to B, 3, a and b, directly above, a master's degree in acceptable area and 2 years of K–12 experience working with students with disabilities.

VII.   Special Services License

    A.   Endorsements include audiologist, school counselor, school nurse, orientation and mobility specialist, physical therapist, school psychologist, occupational therapist, speech/language pathologist, and social worker

    B.   Requirements

      1.   See VI, B, 1, a and b, directly above, except that verifications must confirm grade level or developmental level(s) and service specialization(s) completed by the applicant.

      2.   Evidence of passing score on appropriate content area exam

      3.   Requirements are endorsement-specific and can be found on the Department of Education website (see Appendix 1).

Endorsements

I.   Endorsements on licenses and authorizations indicate the grade level(s), subject areas(s), or other areas of specialization that are appropriate to the applicant's preparation, training, and experience. They are typically granted in the major areas of specialization and only in those areas that constitute approved programs.

    A.   Early childhood education (valid for teaching birth to ages 8)

    B.   Elementary education (valid for teaching multiple subjects in self-contained classroom)

    C.   Secondary endorsement areas (valid for grades 7–12 or middle school)

      1.   Agriculture and renewable natural resources, art,* business education, drama, English language arts, family and consumer studies, foreign language(s),* health,* instructional technology teacher,* linguistically diverse, linguistically diverse bilingual specialist,* marketing, mathematics, music,* physical education,* school librarian,* science, social studies, speech, teacher librarian,* technology education (industrial arts), and trade and industry education

      2.   Special education endorsements

        a.   Early childhood special education, early childhood special education specialist, gifted and talented specialist, special education generalist, special education specialist, special education specialist: deaf and hard of hearing, special education specialist: blind/visually impaired

3. Graduate endorsements
   a. Instructional technology specialist, director of special education (administrative), reading specialist, reading teacher, teacher librarian
4. Special services provider endorsement areas (Birth–21)
   a. Audiologist, occupational therapist, orientation and mobility (peripatology), physical therapist, school nurse, school psychologist, school social worker, school counselor, and school speech/language pathologist
5. Administrative Endorsements
   a. Principal, superintendent, director of special education

*   Endorsements in these areas are issued for K–12.

Connecticut

Several recent changes to Connecticut educator statutes may have an important impact on the ability of some educators to advance from the provisional to the professional educator level of certification. Please note that:

— On or after July 1, 2012, experience teaching in a nonpublic school will no longer be accepted to advance certificates to the professional educator level, but may be accepted to renew a provisional educator certificate.

— On or after July 1, 2016, 30 hours of graduate course work will be required to advance teaching certificates to the professional level. Undergraduate course work will no longer be accepted.

For more information, go to www.ct.gov/sde/cert and click on "Maintaining Connecticut Educator Certification."

General Requirements

I. In addition to the specific requirements noted below, individuals seeking certification in Connecticut must fulfill the following teacher assessment requirements:
   A. Demonstrate essential skills in mathematics, reading, and writing by passing the Praxis I Academic Skills Assessments or by receiving a waiver
   B. Demonstrate subject matter competence by receiving a satisfactory evaluation on the Praxis II Academic Skills Assessments test for certification in specific endorsement areas (including elementary and middle grades education, secondary and special subjects) or the language proficiency assessments
   C. Demonstrate professional knowledge through the Beginning Educator Support and Training Program (BEST), consisting of assignment to mentor teachers or teams and performance assessments (completed prior to second level of certification)
II. Connecticut requires each candidate for certification to present the recommendation of the preparing institution for the certification sought in the absence of 2 years of verified successful experience in the type of position to be covered (experience in an approved private or out-of-state public school is acceptable).

Integrated Early Childhood Special Education (Birth–K or Nursery–Grade 3)

I. Initial Educator Certificate for Birth–K and N–3
   A. Bachelor's degree from an approved institution
   B. General education, including study in 5 out of 6 of the following areas, as well as a survey course in U.S. history, semester hours 39
      1. English
      2. Science

3. Mathematics
4. Social studies
5. Fine arts
6. Foreign language

C. Human growth and development, including typical and atypical development, psychology of learning, and family studies (may be part of a subject area major or general academic courses), semester hours... 15

D. Completion of a major awarded by an approved institution in any 1 subject area (a major or courses in professional education may not be counted),
or
Completion of an interdisciplinary major consisting of 39 semester hours with a concentration of at least 18 semester hours in human growth and development, including typical and atypical development, psychology of learning, and family studies, with the remainder distributed among no more than 3 additional subjects related to human growth and development (a major or course work in professional education may not be counted)

E. Professional education in early childhood education in each of the following areas, semester hours.. 36
   1. Foundations of education
   2. Curriculum and methods of teaching
      a. Required courses differ for Birth–K and N–3 endorsements; contact the Bureau of Educator Preparation and Certification (Bureau) for details (see Appendix 1).
   3. Supervised student teaching at the level of the endorsement, semester hours.. 6–12
      a. Contact the Bureau for additional details (see Appendix 1).

II. Provisional Educator Certificate
   A. Evidence of meeting the general conditions and requirements for an initial certificate
   B. Completion of beginning educator support and assessment program as may be available from the Department of Education and 10 school months of successful service under the interim or initial certificates or durational shortage area permit,
   or
   Thirty school months of successful teaching in the same area for which the provisional educator certificate is being sought, in a school approved by the appropriate governing body in another state, within 10 years prior to application

III. Professional Educator Certificate
   A. Thirty school months of successful teaching under the provisional educator certificate
   B. Course work beyond bachelor's degree, semester hours 30
   To include:
      1. A planned program at an approved institution of higher education, related directly to the subject areas or grade levels of the endorsement or in an area or areas related to the teacher's ability to provide instruction effectively or to meet locally determined goals or objectives,
      or

2. An individual program that is mutually determined or approved by the teacher and the employing agent of the Department of Education and is designed to increase the ability of the teacher to improve student learning

Elementary Education (K–6)

I. Initial Educator Certificate
   A. See Integrated Early Childhood Special Education, I, A, above
      1. General education, including study in 5 out of 6 of the following areas, as well as a survey course in U.S. history, semester hours 39
         English, science, mathematics, social studies,
         and either
         Fine arts,
         or
         Foreign language
      2. Must include 6 semester hours in child and/or human growth and development
   B. Completion of a major awarded by an approved institution in any 1 subject area (a major or courses in professional education may not be counted),
      or
      Completion of an interdisciplinary major consisting of 39 semester hours, with a concentration of at least 18 semester hours in any 1 subject area and the remainder distributed among no more than 3 subjects related to the concentration (a major or courses in professional education may not be counted)
   C. Professional education in each of the following areas, semester hours................. 30
      1. Foundations of education
      2. Educational psychology
      3. Curriculum and methods of teaching
         a. Must include 6 semester hours in language arts
      4. Supervised observation, participation, and full-time, responsible student teaching, semester hours... 6–12
      5. Course of study in special education of at least 36 clock hours (contact the Bureau for additional details; see Appendix 1).
II. Provisional Educator Certificate
   A. See Integrated Early Childhood Special Education, II, A and B, above
III. Professional Educator Certificate
   A. See Integrated Early Childhood Special Education, III, A and B, above

Middle Grades (4–8)

Note: The middle grades subject-specific certificate or a secondary academic certificate authorizes the teaching of specific subjects in a middle school setting. Middle grades certificates shall be endorsed for the subject in accordance with the recommendation of the preparing institution.

I. Initial Educator Certificate
    A. See Integrated Early Childhood Special Education, I, A and B, above
    B. Completion of any 1 of the following
        1. A subject area major in any of the following areas: English, mathematics, biology, physics, chemistry, earth science, general science, social science, history, political science, economics, geography, anthropology, sociology, *or*
        2. An interdisciplinary major in humanities, history/social science, or integrated science, *or*
        3. Twenty-four semester hours of study in 1 of the subjects (except general science) listed directly above in B, 1, *and either*
            a. Fifteen semester hours in a second subject of those listed directly above in B, 1 (except general science), which will result in endorsements in 2 subject areas, *or*
            b. Fifteen semester hours in an all-level endorsement that will not qualify for an additional teaching endorsement
    C. See Elementary Education, I, C, 1, 2, 4 and 5, above
        1. Curriculum and methods of teaching (6 credits minimum) to include
            a. Reading and writing across middle grades curriculum, *and*
            b. Methods for teaching at the middle grades level
    D. For middle grades endorsement in English, history or social science, mathematics, humanities, and integrated science, special courses are required. Contact the Bureau for additional information (see Appendix 1).
II. Provisional Educator Certificate
    A. See Integrated Early Childhood Special Education, II, A and B, above
III. Professional Educator Certificate
    A. See Integrated Early Childhood Special Education, III, A and B, above

Secondary Academic (7–12)

I. Initial Educator Certificate
    A. Bachelor's degree from an approved institution
    B. General education, including a survey course in U.S. history and including study in 5 of the 6 following areas, semester hours 39
        1. English
        2. Natural sciences
        3. Mathematics
        4. Social studies
        5. Arts
        6. Foreign languages

C. Completion of a subject area major awarded by an approved institution in the subject for which endorsement is sought (professional education majors may not be used to fulfill this requirement),

or

Completion of at least 30 semester hours in the subject for which certification is sought and a minimum of 9 semester hours in a subject or subjects directly related to the subject for which certification is sought (professional education majors or courses may not be used to fulfill this requirement or to fulfill the requirements for the specific endorsements listed below)

1. General science endorsement—Major may be met by completion of at least 39 semester hours in science, including study in biology, chemistry, physics, and earth science.
2. History and social studies endorsement—Requirements may be met by completion of a major in 1 of the following areas:
    a. History (including 18 semester hours in social studies)
    b. Political science, economics, geography, or anthropology/sociology (including at least 18 semester hours in history)
    c. An interdisciplinary major of at least 39 semester hours in subjects covered by the endorsement, with at least 18 semester hours in history, including U.S. history, Western civilization, or European history, and with at least 1 course each in political science, economics, geography, anthropology, sociology, and psychology
3. Business endorsement—Major awarded by an approved institution in business or in any 1 of the subjects covered by the endorsement or an interdisciplinary major consisting of 39 semester hours of credit in subjects covered by the endorsement
4. Foreign language endorsement—24 semester hours in the foreign language in which endorsement is sought

D. Completion of a planned program of study and experience in professional education, including study in the following areas, semester hours 18
1. Foundations of education
2. Educational psychology
3. Curriculum and methods of teaching
4. Supervised observation, participation, and full-time responsible student teaching, semester hours 6–12
5. Course of study in special education of at least 36 clock hours covering specific areas

II. Provisional Certificate
  A. See Integrated Early Childhood Special Education, II, A and B, above
III. Professional Certificate
  A. See Integrated Early Childhood Special Education, III, A and B, above

Special Subjects

Special subject endorsements, taught at the elementary and secondary levels, are agriculture, art, health, home economics, technology education, music, and physical education.

I.   Initial Educator Certificate
   A.   Bachelor's degree from an approved institution
   B.   General education, semester hours 39
      1.   See Secondary Academic, I, B, above
   C.   Completion of a subject area major awarded by an approved institution in the subject for which endorsement is sought (professional education majors, except those in physical education and technology education, may not be used to fulfill this requirement), *or*

Completion of at least 30 semester hours in the special subject or field for which certification is sought and a minimum of 9 semester hours in a subject or subjects directly related to the subject for which certification is sought (professional education majors or courses, except those in physical education and technology education, may not be used to fulfill this requirement)
   D.   Professional education, semester hours 18
      1.   See Secondary Academic, I, D, above
II. Provisional Certificate
   A.   See Integrated Early Childhood Special Education, II, A and B, above
III. Professional Certificate
   A.   See Integrated Early Childhood Special Education, III, A and B, above

School-Library Media (PreK–12)

I.   Initial Educator Certificate
   A.   Bachelor's degree from an approved institution
   B.   Holds or is eligible for a Connecticut teaching certificate
   C.   Ten months of successful teaching experience
   D.   Completion of at least 24 semester hours of credit in an approved graduate program of certification for school-library media specialists in specified areas, including a course of study in special education of at least 36 clock hours

Note: Connecticut has several alternative routes to initial certification in school-library media.

II. Provisional Certificate
   A.   See Integrated Early Childhood Special Education, II, A and B, above
III. Professional Educator Certificate
   A.   Thirty school months of successful teaching under the Provisional Certificate
   B.   Master's degree or a sixth-year program in school-library media at an approved institution, *or*

Master's degree in another field from an approved institution, plus 30 semester hours of graduate credit in school-library media from an approved institution

School Counselor

I.   Initial Educator Certificate
   A.   Holds a Professional Educator Certificate,

or

    Holds or is eligible for an Initial Educator Certificate with 3 years of successful teaching experience, or completion of a 1-year, full-time supervised school internship as school counselor

  B. Master's degree

  C. Study in an approved institution, to include 30 semester hours in a planned program in school counseling

  D. Recommendation by preparing institution based on knowledge, skills, and understanding in the following areas: principles and philosophy of developmental guidance and counseling; psychological and sociological theory as related to children, youth, and family; career development theory and practice; individual and group counseling procedures; organizational patterns and relationship of pupil services to total school and community programs; pupil appraisal and evaluation techniques; and school-based consultation theory and practice

  E. Evidence of progression of supervised experience in counseling and guidance through laboratory and practicum

  F. Course of study in special education of at least 36 clock hours

 II. Provisional Educator Certificate

  A. See Integrated Early Childhood Special Education II, A and B, above, except that successful service must be in a school counseling capacity

III. Professional Educator Certificate

  A. Thirty school months of successful service under the provisional educator certificate, interim educator certificate, or provisional teaching certificate

  B. Completion of at least 45 semester hours of graduate credit at an approved institution in counseling and related courses

Intermediate Administration or Supervision

 I. Initial Educator Certificate for Intermediate Administration or Supervision (deputy or assistant superintendent, principal or assistant principal, etc.)

  A. Eighteen semester hours of graduate credit in addition to the master's program

  B. Fifty school months of successful teaching or administrative service in public schools or approved nonpublic schools, or as a professional or managerial staff member in a state education agency

  C. Recommendation of an approved institution where the applicant has completed a planned program of preparation for administrative and supervisory personnel

  D. See Superintendent of Schools, I, E, 1–5, below, except in a program for intermediate administrators

  E. See Superintendent of Schools, I, F, below.

 II. Provisional Educator Certificate for Intermediate Administration or Supervision

  A. Same as Integrated Early Childhood Special Education, II, A and B, above, except that successful service must be in an administrative capacity

III. Professional Educator Certificate for Intermediate Administration or Supervision
    A. Thirty school months of successful service under the provisional educator certificate, interim educator certificate, or provisional teaching certificate
    B. Completion of at least 30 semester hours of graduate credit at an approved institution, in addition to the master's degree

Superintendent of Schools

I. Initial Educator Certificate (superintendent of schools or executive director of a regional educational service center)
    A. Master's degree from an approved institution, as well as 30 semester hours of graduate credit beyond the master's degree
    B. Completion of 80 school months of successful teaching or service, at least 50 of which shall have been in public schools or approved nonpublic schools, or as a professional or managerial staff member in a state education agency. This total may include the 30 school months of required administrative experience (see I, C, directly below).
    C. Thirty school months of full-time administrative or supervisory experience in public schools or approved nonpublic schools, or as a managerial staff member in a state education agency in position(s) that would have required certification had the service been in Connecticut public schools. On specific recommendation of the preparing institution, consideration may be given to applicants who have completed a substantial period of internship in general school administration as part of a supervised, planned program of preparation for the superintendency.
    D. Recommendation of an approved institution where the applicant has completed an approved program specifically in preparation for the position of superintendent of schools. The program shall be no less than 30 graduate semester hours, at least 15 of which have been completed at that institution and the remainder approved by it.
    E. Graduate study in each of the following areas:
        1. Psychological and pedagogical foundations of learning
        2. Curriculum development and program monitoring
        3. School administration
        4. Personnel evaluation and supervision
        5. Contemporary educational problems and solutions from a policy-making perspective
    F. Course of study in special education of at least 36 clock hours
II. Provisional Educator Certificate
    A. See Integrated Early Childhood Special Education, II, A and B, above
III. Professional Educator Certificate
    A. Present evidence of having served successfully under the provisional educator, interim provisional educator, or provisional teaching certificates for a period of at least 30 school months

Other Certificates

I. Teaching Certificates
    A. Comprehensive Special Education (K–12)
    B. Teaching English to Speakers of Other Languages
    C. Bilingual Education
    D. Remedial Reading and Remedial Language Arts (1–12)
    E. Occupational subjects in vocational-technical schools
    F. Applied curriculum and technology subjects
    G. Adult Education
    H. School nurse–teacher
    I. School dental hygienist–teacher
II. Special Service Certificates
    A. Speech and language pathology,
    B. School psychology,
    C. School social work.
III. Administrative Certificates
    A. Reading and language arts consultant,
    B. Department chairperson,
    C. School business administrator.

Please contact the Bureau (see Appendix 1) for the requirements for these certificates.

Delaware

Delaware has a Licensure and Certificate system for teacher, administrator, and specialist certification. The license gives an educator the right to work, and the certificate defines what the educator may do. Consult Delaware Educator Data System (DEEDS) at the Delaware Department of Education for full details (see Appendix 1).

Licensure

I. Initial License (valid 3 years; nonrenewable but extendable upon proof of exigent circumstances or up to 3-year leave of absence)
   A. In-State Requirements
      1. Bachelor's degree from regionally accredited college or university
      2. Complete approved student teaching program,
         or
         Complete 91 days "in lieu of student teaching" in 1 assignment in a Delaware public/charter school within the last year before application for license, with supporting evidence of satisfactory performance from evaluations,
         or
         Enrollment in the Alternative Routes to Teacher Licensure and Certification Program,
         and
         Meet or exceed cut-off scores on Praxis I: Reading 175 (322), Writing 173 (319), Math 174 (319).
   B. Out-of-State or Lapsed Requirements
      1. Department of Education may issue an initial license/certificate to applicant licensed as an educator in another jurisdiction if applicant has less than 3 years teaching experience, or to an applicant who previously held a valid Delaware Standard. Professional Status certificate who has been out the profession for more than 3 years
   C. In addition to an Initial License, applicants must also apply for a standard certificate in the appropriate area; see standard certificate below.
   D. Preparations for Continuing License Application
      Before expiration of Initial License, applicant must:
      1. Complete professional development and mentoring activities
      2. Receive 2 out of 3 satisfactory evaluations
      3. Disclose any criminal conviction history
II. Continuing License (valid 5 years; renewable and extendable upon proof of exigent circumstances or up to 3-year leave of absence)
   A. General Requirements
      1. Successfully complete requirements for Initial License (see I, A–C, directly above),
         and

Receive no more than 1 unsatisfactory annual evaluation, as defined by the Delaware Performance Appraisal System, during period of Initial License.
2. Hold educator license in another jurisdiction with evidence of completing 3 or more years of successful teaching experience
B. Requirements for Licensed Educators Returning to Work
1. Continuing license issued upon employment for current holders of standard or professional status license
2. Holders of expired licenses out of the profession for less than 3 years may apply with evidence of Delaware certification and will receive an Initial License.
3. Holders of expired licenses out of the profession for more than 3 years must also, within first year of employment, successfully complete district-sponsored mentoring program.
C. An educator holding a current or expired Professional Status or Standard Certificate who is assigned to work outside the area covered by that credential will be issued a Continuing License, with an Emergency Certificate for the new area, for a period of 3 years to enable the educator to fulfill the new area's Standard Certificate requirements.
D. Continuing License Renewal (valid 5 years; renewable)
1. Fulfill 90-clock-hour requirement for professional development
a. At least 45 hours every 5 years must be in activities related to educator's work with students or staff
b. Professional development hours must take place during term of continuing license
c. See Department of Education (Appendix 1) for detailed options
d. Disclose any criminal conviction history
III. Advanced Licensure (valid 10 years; renewable)
A. Requirements
1. Application by holder of National Board of Professional Teaching Standards certification or equivalent program approved by Professional Standards Board
B. Renewal
1. Renewable for additional 10-year term provided that educator maintains proficiency under program for which license was first issued
2. If holder does not renew the Advanced License, a Continuing License will be issued upon expiration of the Advanced License.

Alternative Routes to Teacher Licensure and Certification Program

I. Candidates seeking participation in the Alternative Routes to Teacher Licensure and Certification Program shall be issued an Initial License of no more than 3 years' duration.
II. Requirements:
A. Hold a bachelor's degree from a regionally accredited college or university, with a major appropriate to the instructional field they desire to teach
B. Pass an examination of general knowledge, such as Praxis I, or provide an acceptable alternative

C. Pass an examination of content knowledge, such as Praxis II, in the instructional field they desire to teach, if applicable and available

D. Obtain acceptable health and criminal background check clearances

E. Obtain and accept an offer of employment in a position that requires licensure and certification

III. Components of the Alternative Routes Program

A. Summer institute of approximately 120 instructional (clock) hours completed by candidates prior to the beginning of teaching assignments

B. One-year, full-time practicum experience that includes a period of intensive on-the-job mentoring and supervision beginning the first day of classroom teaching and continuing for 30 weeks

C. Seminars on teaching that provide Alternative Routes to Teacher Licensure and Certification teachers with approximately 200 instructional (clock) hours or equivalent professional development during the first year of their teaching assignment and during an intensive seminar the following summer

Standard Certificate

I. Issued to an educator who holds a valid Delaware Initial, Continuing, or Advanced License; or a Limited Standard, Standard, or Professional Status Certificate issued prior to August 31, 2003, who has met the following requirements

II. Preliminary Requirement

A. Certification from the National Board for Professional Teaching Standards in area of certification;
   or

B. Meeting the requirements of the relevant Department or Standards Board regulation for obtaining a Standard Certificate in area of certification;
   or

C. Graduation from a National Council for Accreditation of Teacher Education (NCATE) approved educator preparation program, or from a Delaware-approved educator preparation program using National Association of State Directors of Teacher Education and Certification (NASDTEC) or NCATE standards, with a major or its equivalent in area of certification;
   or

D. Satisfactory completion of the Alternative Routes to Teacher Licensure and Certification Program, the Special Institute for Licensure and Certification, or other approved alternative educator preparation programs;
   or

E. Bachelor's degree from a regionally accredited college or university in any content area including 15 credit hours or their equivalent in professional development related to their area of certification, of which at least 6 credit hours must focus on pedagogy, selected by the applicant with the approval of the employing school district or charter school;
   and

III. Additional Requirements
    A. Meet or exceed Praxis II scores in the area of certification, if applicable and available
       or
    B. Hold a valid and current license/certificate in certification area from another state.

Early Childhood Teacher Standard Certificate (Birth–Grade 2)

I. Issued to an applicant who holds a valid Delaware Initial, Continuing, or Advanced License; or a Limited Standard, Standard, or Professional Status Certificate issued prior to August 31, 2003
II. Requirements
    A. See Standard Certificate, I and II, above
    B. If an examination of content knowledge such as Praxis II is not applicable and available in Early Childhood Education, and if the educator is applying for his/her second Standard Certificate, then the applicant must satisfactorily complete 15 credits or its equivalent in professional development related to Early Childhood Education, selected by the applicant with the approval of the employing school district or charter school, which is submitted to the Department of Education.

Elementary Teacher Standard Certificate (Grades K–6)

I. Issued to an educator who holds a valid Delaware Initial, Continuing, or Advanced License; or a Limited Standard, Standard, or Professional Status Certificate issued by the Department prior to August 31, 2003
II. Requirements
    A. See Early Childhood Teacher Standard Certificate, II, A and B, above

Administration

I. School Principal/Assistant Principal
    A. Educational Requirements
        1. Master's degree in educational leadership from NCATE- or state-approved program from a regionally accredited college or university,
          or
        2. Master's degree in education from NCATE- or state-approved program from a regionally accredited college or university and a current and valid principal or assistant principal certificate from another state,
          or
        3. Master's degree in any field from regionally accredited college or university and successful completion of Delaware-approved Alternative Routes to Teacher Licensure and Certification Program for School Leaders (until available, see I, A, 4, immediately below),
          or

        4. Master's degree in any field from regionally accredited college and successful completion of graduate-level course work including:

            a. School administration (at level to be initially assigned); supervision / evaluation of staff; curriculum development; school business management; school law/legal issues in education; human relations; and—if not taken at undergraduate level—child, adolescent, or human development

  B. Experience Requirement

      1. Minimum of 3 years of teaching experience at level to be initially assigned, except for middle level, where teaching experience may be at PK–12 level, or as a Principal or Assistant Principal of a school for exceptional students

        a. Teaching experience means meeting students on a regularly scheduled basis, planning and delivering instruction, developing or preparing instructional materials, and evaluating student performance in any PK–12 setting.

            i. Experience must be in categories of children served (example: autistic)

            ii. Principal of Exceptional Children must have teaching experience with exceptional children.

II. School Leader I: Director, Supervisor, Administrative Assistant, Coordinator, and Manager in Instructional Areas

  A. General Requirement

      1. See School Principal/Assistant Principal, I, A, 1–3 directly above, except that applicant hold a current and valid equivalent central office administrative certificate from another state,
        or

      2. Master's degree in any field from regionally accredited college and minimum of 24 semester hours of graduate-level course work, completed either as part of master's degree or in addition to it, in Administration, including:

        a. Curriculum development; supervision/evaluation of staff; human relations; school law/legal issues; and 12 credits in area to be supervised. Additional semester hours may include courses in curriculum, instruction and/or methods.

  B. Experience Requirement

      1. Minimum of 3 years of teaching experience at the PK–12 level

      2. For Directors, Supervisors, Administrative Assistants, Coordinators, and Managers of programs for exceptional students, teaching experience must be with exceptional children.

III. School Leader II: Superintendent/Assistant Superintendent

  A. Educational Requirements

      1. Doctoral degree in educational leadership from a regionally accredited college or university using an NCATE- or state-approved educator preparation program,
        or

      2. Master's or doctoral degree in education from regionally accredited college and a current superintendent or assistant superintendent certificate from another state,
        or

3. Master's or doctoral degree in any field from regionally accredited college and successful completion of Delaware-approved Alternative Routes to Teacher Licensure and Certification Program for School Leaders/Superintendents (until available, see III, A, 4, immediately below),
    or

4. Master's or doctoral degree in any field from regionally accredited college and successful completion of graduate-level course work in the following areas, either as part of the master's or doctoral degree program or in addition to it:
    a. Personnel administration; supervision/evaluation of staff; curriculum development and instruction; school business management; school law/legal issues in education; human relations; organization management; and—if not taken at undergraduate level—child or adolescent development

B. Experience Requirement
1. Minimum of 5 years teaching experience at the PK–12 level
    a. Teaching experience means meeting students on a regularly scheduled basis, planning and delivering instruction, developing or preparing instructional materials, and evaluating student performance in any PK–12 setting,
    or
2. Minimum of 5 years of full-time PK–12 leadership experience,
    or
3. Any combination of these types of experiences that totals a minimum of 5 years.
4. Experience may be acquired at either the building or district level.

Guidance Counselor

I. Elementary School Counselor
A. Requirements
1. Holds a valid Delaware Initial, Continuing, or Advanced License or a Limited Standard, Standard, or Professional Status Certicate issued prior to August 31, 2003; and meets the following requirements:
2. Graduated from an NCATE-specialty-organization-recognized educator preparation program or from a state-approved educator preparation program offered by a regionally accredited college or university, with a master's degree in Elementary School Counseling,
    or
3. Holds a master's degree from a regionally accredited college in any field; with a minimum of 27 semester hours of graduate course work in the areas of principles and practices of the counseling program, individual counseling skills, group counseling skills, human development, developmental group guidance, individual and group testing for counselors, supervised practicum in elementary counseling, counseling theory, and consultation;

and one of the following:
a.   Minimum of 3 years of professional experience in an elementary school setting

or
b.   Three years of equivalent experience as approved by the Department of Education

or
c.   Supervised school counseling internship of 1 full year in an elementary school setting as part of a graduate degree program in elementary school counseling or arranged by the Department of Education; may be completed over a 2-year period on a half-time basis.

II.   Secondary School Counselor
A.   Requirements—the same as for Elementary School Counselor, but at the secondary school level

School Psychologist

I.   Licensure Requirements
A.   Bachelor's degree in any content area from a regionally accredited college or university
B.   Graduate-level program of study, approved by the National Association of School Psychologists (NASP) or the American Psychological Association (APA), offered by a regionally accredited college or university titled "School Psychology," consisting of a minimum of 60 graduate-level credit hours, of which at least 54 credits are exclusive of an internship,
and
Supervised internship of no less than 1,200 hours, completed at or near the end of the program, and completed either full time or half time over a period of no more than 2 consecutive years, at least 600 hours of which must be in a school setting,
or
C.   Completion of an organized graduate-level program of study offered by a regionally accredited college or university titled "School Psychology," consisting of a minimum of 60 graduate level credit hours, of which at least 54 credits are exclusive of an internship,
and
Evidence of substantial graduate-level preparation.
D.   Valid certificate from the National School Psychology Certification Board,
or
Valid certificate in school psychology from another state department of education in the U.S.,
or
Valid license as a psychologist issued by the Delaware Board of Examiners of Psychologists.

School Social Worker

I. Requirements
    A. Standard Certificate as a School Social Worker will be given to an applicant who has the following:
        1. Valid Delaware Initial, Continuing, or Advanced License,
            or
            Standard or Professional Status Certificate issued by the Department prior to August 31, 2003;
        2. Master's Degree School Social Worker (MSW) from a regionally accredited college or university;
        3. Two years of successful full-time work experience as a social worker;
        4. One year of supervised experience in a school setting,
            or
            One-year internship of 1,000 hours approved by the Department of Education and supervised by an appropriate school designee.

Library/Media Specialist

I. Licensure Requirements
    A. The Department shall issue a Standard Certificate to an applicant meeting the requirements below who holds
        1. A valid Delaware Initial, Continuing, or Advanced License,
            or
        2. A Standard or Professional Status Certificate issued prior to August 31, 2003.
II. Education Requirements
    A. Bachelor's degree in any content area from a regionally accredited college/university, with completion of a master's degree from a regionally accredited college/university in an American Library Association (ALA)–approved program in School Library/Media,
        or
    B. Master's degree from a regionally accredited college/university in any other content area, including a general Media Library Specialist (MLS) degree, and completion of a program in School Library/Media approved by the Department pursuant to 14 DE Administrative Code 399 which meets ALA standards

District of Columbia

Teaching Licenses/Credentials

I. Regular I License (valid 2 years; nonrenewable; upgrades to Regular II) Requirements
   A. Bachelor's degree;
   B. Verification of current enrollment in state-approved teacher preparation program;
   C. Verification of current employment as teacher in Washington, D.C. (DC), local education agency (LEA);
   D. Passing scores for all portions of Praxis I examination;
      and
   E. Passing score for Praxis II Content Knowledge exam in content area of teaching assignment; for details, visit the Educator Licensure and Accreditation website at www.osse.dc.gov

II. Regular II License (valid 4 years; renewable) Requirements
   A. Bachelor's degree;
   B. Verification of successful completion of state-approved teacher preparation program with Praxis testing;
   C. Holds valid level II license from a US state/territory with 3 years of valid full-time teaching experience within past 7 years in licensure subject area,
      or
      Full completion of all content and teacher education course work required under DC Municipal Regulations as determined by Office of State Superintendent of Education (OSSE) transcript review;
   D. Passing scores for all portions of the Praxis I;
      and
   E. Passing scores for all applicable Praxis II Content Knowledge and Pedagogy exams in area of license being requested (where applicable); for details, visit the Educator Licensure and Accreditation website at www.osse.dc.gov

III. Transitional License (valid 1 year; nonrenewable) Requirements
   A. Bachelor's degree;
   B. May only be requested by a DC LEA;
   C. Candidate has never been previously employed as a DC public school teacher;
      and
   D. Candidate has major in content area of teaching assignment (liberal arts for elementary education teaching assignments),
      or
      Candidate has verification of completion of state-approved teacher education program or holds a valid level II license from another state and only needs to complete DC's testing requirements.

IV. Past Licenses. As of 2009, the following changes apply:
   A. Three-year Provisional license is now a two-year Regular I license.

B. Five-year Standard license is now a four-year renewable Regular II license.

C. Five-year Professional license is now a four-year renewable Regular II license.

D. Limited Term Substitute licenses will no longer be issued or renewed.

    1. All applicants must have bachelor's degree to be eligible for substitute licensure.

E. Licensure changes for current license holders will be effective upon application for licensure renewal or upgrade.

V. Adding Additional Teaching Endorsements

A. Individuals that currently hold Standard, Professional or Regular II teaching licenses may obtain Regular II endorsement licenses in additional teaching areas by successfully completing required Praxis II Pedagogy exam (where applicable); *and*

B. Successfully completing Praxis II Content Exam,

or

Demonstrating evidence of completion of content course work required in DC municipal regulations from accredited college/university,

or

Having a major or major equivalent (30 semester hours); visit the Educator Licensure and Accreditation website at www.osse.dc.gov for full details.

VI. Service Provider Licenses

A. School Psychologist

    1. Conferred master's degree in school or educational psychology from accredited institution, including at least 42 semester hours of graduate-level course work with content in the following:

        a. Fifteen semester hours to include: introduction to school psychology; child adolescent psychology or developmental psychology; psychology of abnormal behavior/psychopathy of childhood and adolescence (mental hygiene); statistics, tests, and measurements, evaluation, or research methods; and seminar in school psychology;

        b. Six semester hours from among the following: neurology or neuropsychology and brain behavior; biological basis of behavior; theories of learning; or theories of personality;

        c. Nine semester hours from the following: history and systems of psychology; psychology of the exceptional child; sociocultural education; survey of problems and issues in special education; or public school law, urban issues, legal and ethical issues;

        d. Six semester hours to include the following: individual assessment of cognitive abilities; and behavioral assessment (behavioral checklist, classroom observation techniques); *and*

        e. Six semester hours from the following: evaluation and diagnosis of exceptional children; diagnosis and remedial techniques in arithmetic; the learning disabled child/learning disabilities; or personality assessment; *and*

    2. At least 500 clock hours of satisfactory field experience in PreK–12 school setting under supervision of certified school psychologist.

B. School Counselor
1. Conferred master's degree in school counseling from accredited institution that includes at least 300 clock hours of graduate-level university-supervised field experience in counseling in PreK–12 grade school setting.
    a. One hundred of these required hours (20 hours per year) may be granted prior to classroom teaching experiences.
    b. Hours of field experience shall be performed in pre-practicum, practicum, or internship and shall include demonstration of skills/competencies in the following:
        i. Individual, group, play therapy; family therapy; consultation; career development, measurement, and evaluation; placement and follow-up; computer literacy; and multicultural education.
    c. Field experience requirement may be met by completion of degree in school counseling from program approved by Council for Accreditation of Counseling and Related Educational Programs (CACREP) or National Board of Certified Counselors (NBCC) certificate.
        i. Degree program shall include graduate-level course work with content in the following: philosophy and principles underlying guidance and other pupil personnel services; the theory and practice of counseling, including work with exceptional and culturally diverse students; educational and psychological measurement; career development theory including career planning and decision-making techniques and the use of occupational and educational information; understanding the individual (i.e., the nature and range of human characteristics); group counseling and group guidance processes; research and evaluation; elementary, middle, and secondary school counseling;
2. Minimum of 2 successful academic years of full-time teaching or other professional, school-based experience, or experience in nonschool setting
C. School Librarian/Media Specialist
1. Conferred master's degree from accredited institution;
    and
2. Twenty-one semester hours in library or information science content that includes the following: cataloging and classification; computerized applications of library automation and information access; instructional media design and production; organization of school library media programs and collections; reference sources and services; evaluation, selection and utilization of instructional media for children and young people; and integration of library resources in the curriculum;
    and
3. Directed field experience in school library media center with experienced media specialist;
    or

Two years of successful recognized teaching experience;
or
One year of library experience.

    D.   The OSSE issues additional service provider licenses; visit the Educator Licensure and Accreditation website at www.osse.dc.gov for full details on the following:

        1.   Audiologist

        2.   Attendance Officer

        3.   Psychometrist

        4.   Pupil Personnel Worker

        5.   School Social Worker

        6.   Speech Language Pathologist

VII.   Teacher and Service Provider Licensure Renewal Requirements

    A.   Note for all Standard and Professional license holders regarding renewal:

        1.   Per teacher licensure regulations effective January 9, 2009, standard and professional license holders will receive a 4-year Regular II license upon renewal.

        2.   Applicants may submit renewal credits completed within 5 years prior to date of licensure application submission.

        3.   Upon issuance of a Regular II license, acceptable span for renewal credits will be 4 years prior to the date of licensure application submission.

    B.   To renew a Standard, Professional, or Regular II District of Columbia license, applicants must submit evidence of:

        1.   Six semester hours or 90 contact hours (or a combination of the two) of professional development activities completed within the 4 years prior to date of licensure application submission.

            a.   Minimum of 3 semester hours/45 clock hours of professional development activities must be directly related to field (subject content) of license being renewed;

            b.   Remaining required 3 semester hours/45 clock hours may include any professional development activity relevant to Pre-K–12 education and/or serving Pre-K–12 students.

            c.   Examples of acceptable renewal activities include: course work at accredited college or university; workshops, seminars, or conferences sponsored by a local education agency/school district and/or other education/professional organization

            d.   For information on translating college/university credit hours, Continuing Education Units (CEUs), and Professional Learning Units (PLUs) into contact hours, visit the Educator Licensure and Accreditation website at www.osse.dc.gov

        2.   Individuals with more than 1 license must meet subject matter requirements for each licensure area separately (3 credits or 45 contact hours per license). The same general education credits/hours may be used to renew more than one license.

VIII.   School Administrator Licensure

    A.   Administrative Services Credential Requirements

        1.   Option 1

      a.   Bachelor's degree from accredited college or university;

      b.   Completion of state-approved program in K–12 School Leadership/Administration;

      c.   Successful completion of 2 years of full time PreK–12 school-based teaching or pupil services experience,

          or

          Two years of other full-time PreK–12 school-based instructional leadership work experience;

          and

      d.   Official verification of passing score for School Leaders Licensure Assessment (SLLA) as required by DC.

  2. Option 2

      a.   Master's degree or higher from accredited college or university;

      b.   Successful completion of 2 years of full-time PreK–12 school-based teaching or pupil services experience,

          or

          Two years of other full-time PreK–12 school-based instructional leadership work experience;

          and

      c.   Official verification of passing score for the SLLA as required by DC.

B. License Types

  1. Regular Administrator (valid 4 years, renewable)

      a.   For applicants who successfully meet all requirements outlined in Option 1 or 2, directly above.

  2. Transitional Administrator (valid 1 year; nonrenewable)

      a.   For applicant who holds current out-of-state license that authorizes him/her to operate as full or lead principal in a K–12 grade school but who have not completed the SLLA as required by DC

  3. Please note that DC issues a combined principal/assistant principal license.

      a.   License holders from other states who only hold assistant principal's license will not qualify for DC license under the Interstate Licensure Agreement, but may qualify for licensure by meeting requirements as stated directly above in A, 1 and 2.

C. School Administrator License Renewal Requirements

  1. Completion of 200 clock hours of approved professional development activities and services completed within previous 5 years from date renewal application is filed.

      a.   Professional development hours may be accrued by completion of activities from 1 or more of following options: college credit, professional workshops presented by approved nationally recognized entities, and professional development activities approved by employing local educational agencies.

Florida

The Bureau of Educator Certification at the Florida Department of Education determines individualized testing requirements for certification. After your application for certification is on file, the Bureau will issue you an Official Statement of Status of Eligibility. This statement will indicate your individualized testing requirements; these may include the Florida Teacher Certification Exams (FTCE) or, for candidates seeking certification in educational leadership, the Florida Educational Leadership Exam (FELE). Contact the Bureau (see Appendix 1) for complete information.

Professional Certificate
(Valid for 5 Years)

I. General Requirements
    A certificate may be issued to an applicant who meets the following:
    A. Files a completed application, including official degree transcripts and a complete fingerprint report that has been cleared by the Florida Department of Law Enforcement and the FBI
    B. Holds a bachelor's or higher degree from an acceptable institution of higher learning
    C. Has an acceptable major in a single subject in which Florida offers certification or meets specialization requirements in the subject
    D. Meets professional preparation requirements (see III, below)
    E. Has obtained a 2.5 grade-point average on a 4.0 scale in each subject shown on the certificate
    F. Has received a passing score on the Florida General Knowledge Test or on the College Level Academic Skills Test (CLAST) earned prior to July 1, 2002.
    G. Has received a passing score on the Professional Education Subtest of the Florida Teacher Certification Examination
    H. Has received a passing score on the Florida state-approved subject area examination for each subject or field shown on the certificate
    I. Successfully demonstrates professional education competencies identified by Florida statutes
II. Renewal
    A. Completion of 6 semester hours of appropriate college credit; or 120 approved Florida staff-development points specific to the subject(s) shown on the certificate; or training/course work related to the educational goals and performance standards outlined in Florida statutes during each 5-year validity period
III. Professional Preparation Requirements for Academic, Administrative, and Speciality Class Coverages (PreK–12)
    A. Completes an undergraduate teacher education program at an institution approved by the Florida State Board of Education or another state, or the National Council for the Accreditation of Teacher Education,
        or

Possesses a valid full-time standard teaching certificate issued by another state,
or

B. Professional preparation
    1. Completes 15 semester hours in the following professional development areas:
        a. Classroom management, including safe learning environments,
        b. Human development and learning,
        c. Educational assessment, to include the content measured by state achievement tests and the interpretation and utilization of data to improve student achievement,
        d. Effective instructional strategies, including the needs of diverse learners,
        e. For the middle (grades 5–9) and subject coverages for secondary (grades 6–12) and K–12 level: art, music, dance, computer science, health, foreign languages, humanities, curriculum and special methods of teaching the subject,
            and
        f. For the middle (grades 5–9) and secondary (grades 6–12) level subject coverages, foundations of research-based practices in teaching reading (competency 2 of the State Board–approved reading endorsement competencies).
    2. Practical experience in teaching, satisfied by 1 of the following methods:
        a. One year of full-time teaching experience in an approved elementary or secondary school,
            or
            Six semester hours earned in a college student teaching or supervised internship completed in an elementary or secondary school.
    3. Additional requirements in teaching reading and professional education for grades K–6 and for exceptional education students are included in the separate certification subject specialization State Board Rules.
    4. All the professional education requirements for preschool and prekindergarten–grade 3 subject coverages in lieu of the requirements in B, 1, directly above, are included in the separate certification subject specialization State Board Rules.
    5. The requirements of professional preparation in B, 1, directly above, are not applicable and shall not be required for school social worker or speech-language impaired certification.

C. Professional preparation for agriculture (grades 6–12)
    1. Complete 15 semester hours with credit in the following professional agricultural education areas:
        a. Curriculum development and educational assessment in agriculture,
        b. Instructional strategies in teaching agriculture,
        c. Program planning in agricultural education,
        d. An agriscience teaching induction course that includes basic principles and philosophy of agricultural education, and strategies for classroom management.

2. The practical teaching experience requirement may be satisfied as in professional preparation in B, 2 (see above).

D. For other options, see http://www.fldoe.org/edcert/mast_prof.ASP

Elementary School

I. General Requirements
    A. General and professional preparation. See Professional Certificate, above.

II. Specific Requirements
    A. Bachelor's or higher degree with a major in elementary education that includes teaching reading at the elementary or primary level,
        or
        See www.fldoe.org/edcert/rules/6a-4-0151.asp

Middle Grades (5–9)

I. General Requirements
    A. General and professional preparation. See Professional Certificate, above.

II. Specific Requirements
    A. Middle Grades English: a bachelor's or higher degree major in middle grades English or a bachelor's or higher degree in another subject or field and 18 semester hours above the freshman level in English, including specific courses in grammar, composition, and 9 semester hours of literature and speech
    B. Middle Grades Mathematics: a bachelor's or higher degree major in middle grades mathematics or a bachelor's degree in another subject or field and 18 semester hours in mathematics, including specific courses in calculus, geometry, probability, or statistics
    C. Middle Grades General Science: a bachelor's or higher degree major in middle grades general science or a bachelor's or higher degree in another subject or field and 18 semester hours in science, including specific courses in biology, earth-space science, and chemistry or physics
    D. Middle Grades Social Science: a bachelor's or higher degree major in middle grades social science or a bachelor's or higher degree in another subject or field and 18 semester hours in social science, including specific courses in history, economics, United States government, geography, and United States history (6 hours)
    E. Middle Grades Integrated Curriculum
        1. A bachelor's or higher degree with a degree major in middle grades education that includes a minimum of 12 semester hours in each of the following areas: English, mathematics, science, and social science,
            or
        2. A bachelor's or higher degree with a degree major in a subject other than middle grades education and 54 semester hours in English, mathematics, science, and social science
            a. Eighteen semester hours to be completed in 1 of the 4 subject areas. The 18 semester hours shall be the same required for middle school

certification in that area (see II, A–D, directly above). At least 12 semester hours to be completed in each of the remaining subject areas.

Secondary School (6–12)

I. General Requirements
   A. General and professional preparation. See Professional Certificate, above.
II. Special requirements for subject fields: agriculture, biology, business education, chemistry, earth-space science, English, home economics, education, marketing, mathematics, physics, social science (general), and technology
   A. Florida offers alternative plans for certification in the subject fields.
      1. For all subject fields, applicants may qualify by having a bachelor's or higher degree with a major or 30 semester hours of specified courses in the field for which certification is being sought.
      2. For English and social science, applicants may also qualify by having a bachelor's or higher degree with at least 30 semester hours in the field or in related fields for which certification is being sought. (Contact Florida's Bureau of Educator Certification—see Appendix 1—for details on specific course distributions.)
      3. For mathematics and the sciences, applicants may also qualify by two additional certification routes. In all cases, the applicant must have a bachelor's or higher degree with at least 30 semester hours of specified courses in the field or related fields for which certification is being sought. (Contact Florida's Bureau of Educator Certification—see Appendix 1—for details on specific course distributions.)

Administration

I. General Requirements
   A. General and professional preparation. See Professional Certificate, above.
II. Educational Leadership, Level One Certificate
   A. Holds a master's or higher degree from an accredited institution
   B. Documentation of successful completion of the Florida Educational Leadership Core Curriculum, through one of the following plans:
      1. Successful completion of a Florida Department of Education–approved preservice program in educational leadership offered by an accredited institution,
         or
      2. A graduate degree major in educational administration, administration and supervision, or educational leadership awarded by a Florida Department of Education–approved institution,
         or
      3. Successful completion of an Educational Leadership training program approved by the Florida Department of Education and offered by a Florida public school district,
         or

4. A graduate degree with a major in a subject other than educational administration, administration and supervision, or educational leadership, *and*
   Successful completion of a Department of Education–approved modified Florida program in educational leadership offered by an accredited institution, *or*

5. A graduate degree with a major in a subject other than educational administration, administration and supervision, or educational leadership awarded by an accredited institution, and 30 semester hours of graduate credit in each of the Florida-specified principal leadership standard areas and an internship or a course with associated field experience in educational leadership.

III. School Principal, Level Two Certificate
   A. Holds a valid professional certificate covering educational leadership, school administration, or school administration/supervision
   B. Documents successful performance of the duties of school principalship
   C. Demonstrates successful performance of the competencies of the school principalship, which shall be documented by the Florida district school superintendent

Educational Media Specialist (PreK–12)

I. General Requirements
   A. General and professional preparation. See Professional Certificate, above.
II. Specialization Requirements
   A. Bachelor's or higher degree with a major in educational media,
      or
   B. Bachelor's or higher degree in another subject with courses in educational media, including the following areas, semester hours 30
      1. Management of library media programs
      2. Collection development
      3. Library media resources
      4. Reference sources and services
      5. Organization of collections
      6. Design and production of educational media

Guidance Counselor (Grades PreK–12)

I. General Requirements
   A. General and professional preparation. See Professional Certificate, above.
II. Specialization Requirements
   A. Master's or higher degree with a graduate major in guidance and counseling or in counselor education that includes 3 semester hours in a supervised counseling practicum in an elementary or secondary school,
      or

B. Master's or higher degree with 30 semester hours of graduate credit in guidance and counseling, including (semester hours)

1. Principles and administration of guidance 3
2. Student appraisal 3
3. Education and career development 3
4. Learning theory and human development 3
5. Counseling theories and techniques 3
6. Group counseling 3
7. Consultation skills 3
8. Legal and ethical issues 3
9. Counseling techniques for special populations 3
10. Supervised practicum in an elementary or secondary school 3

Note: Noncitizens, exchange teachers, and resident aliens and refugees may be issued a certificate on the same basis as citizens of the United States, provided they meet exact and specific qualifications established by the Florida State Board of Education. Proof of eligibility to work in the United States is required for noncitizens.

Georgia

Certification Classification

I. Categories
   A. Renewable (valid 5 years, during which educator must satisfy standard renewal requirements)
      1. Clear Renewable: indicates all professional and Georgia-specific requirements for certification in the field have been met
      2. Performance-Based (PB): issued prior to 1990 under the Teacher Performance Assessment Instrument (TPAI) and remains in effect for certificates originally issued under the system
      3. Performance-Based (P): issued only for Educational Leadership performance-based programs
         a. Individual must be employed in leadership position and have the certificate requested by employing school system.
         b. During validity period of certificate, individual must complete specific requirements of performance-based leadership program.
   B. Non-Renewable (valid from 1 to 3 years, except for Performance-Based Leadership Certificate): issued at request of a Georgia employing school system when 1 or more conditions must be met
      1. Non-Renewable Professional Certificate (valid 3 years, nonrenewable, nonextendable)
         a. Recognizes initial preparation for certification in the field including, but not limited to, former Georgia educators or out-of-state certificate holders who do not meet or exempt Special Georgia Requirements; professional certificate holders assigned to another field who do not meet all certificate requirements for new field; and certificate holders who must obtain higher degree level.
         b. During validity period, individual must complete specific requirements outlined in Georgia Professional Standards Commission (PSC) correspondence that accompanies the certificate.
      2. Non-Renewable Non-Professional Certificate (valid 3 years, nonrenewable, nonextendable)
         a. Issued to applicants who have satisfied minimum content standards but must complete pedagogy and/or Special Georgia Requirements and/or who must obtain a higher degree level.
         b. During validity period, individual must complete specific requirements outlined in PSC correspondence that accompanies the certificate.
      3. Advanced Degree Alternative Certificate (ADAC) (issued in 1-year increments for a total of 3 years; nonextendable)
         a. Issued to individuals accepted into ADAC Program.

        b.   During each 1-year validity period, applicant must satisfy specified requirements outlined in the rule and in PSC correspondence that accompanies the certificate.

    4.   Core Academic Certificate (valid 3 years; nonrenewable and nonextendable)

        a.   Issued to individuals accepted into Core Academic Preparation Program path for middle grades (4–8) or secondary grades (6–12) only

        b.   Issued for core academic subjects as defined in section 4.01 of the Georgia Implementation Guidelines for Title II-A which is found on the PSC website at: http://www.gapsc.com/EducatorPreparation/NoChild LeftBehind/Admin/Files/ImpPolicy.pdf

    5.   Clinical Practice Certificate (valid 3 years; nonrenewable and nonextendable). Issued to:

        a.   Individuals who have held Georgia permit at bachelor's degree or higher level, with exception of JROTC, for a minimum of 3 years,
or
Individuals who have completed an education program and are eligible for college or university student teaching but elected to accept a degree without student teaching.

    6.   Intern Certificate (valid 3 years; nonrenewable and nonextendable)

        a.   Issued to individuals accepted into Teacher Academy for Preparation and Pedagogy (TAPP).

    7.   International Exchange Certificate (valid 3 years; nonrenewable and nonextendable)

        a.   Issued to educators certified in other nations who wish to teach in Georgia schools

    8.   Life Certificate: although discontinued in 1974, valid for current holders

    9.   One-Year Supervised Practicum Certificate (valid 3 years; nonrenewable and nonextendable)

        a.   Issued to individuals accepted into One-Year Supervised Practicum Program path

II.   Certificate Type: consult PSC website at http://www.gapsc.com for specific eligibility requirements

    A.   Teaching: issued in fields that prepare individual to teach subject matter offered as part of school curriculum

    B.   Service: issued in fields that prepare individual to provide support services to students, school personnel, and school operations

    C.   Leadership: issued in fields that prepare individual to administer or supervise a school system, school, or school program

    D.   Paraprofessional: issued to eligible individuals hired as paraprofessionals; no assigned level

    E.   Noninstructional Aide: issued to eligible individuals hired to perform routine noninstructional tasks; no assigned level

    F.   Technical Specialist: issued to eligible individuals in Technology/Career Education areas of Trade & Industry Education and Healthcare Science & Technology Education

1. May be issued to those holding high school diplomas/GED or associate degrees, as well as those with bachelor's degrees or higher

G. Permits: issued at request of employing school system to individuals with specific experience in teaching fields of performing arts (music, dance, drama), foreign language (for native speakers), and educational leadership positions of superintendent.

H. Support Personnel Licenses: issued at request of employing school system to individuals who serve in position of leadership over support functions in local school system

1. Such positions include, but are not limited to, finance, transportation, public relations, personnel, staff development, facilities, planning, evaluation, research, assessment, and technology coordination

I. Adjunct Licenses (valid 1 year; renewable): issued at request of employing school system to:

Individuals with specific knowledge, skills, and experience in engineering, medical, dental, pharmaceutical, veterinarian, legal, accounting, or arts profession, or any other professional position approved by PSC,

or

Who have instructional experience in branch of U.S. military (except for JROTC),

or

Who are in a PSC-accepted accredited college or university.

1. Holders are eligible to provide instruction for one-half day in core academic subjects in grades 6–12 only, as defined in Section 4.01 of Georgia Implementation Guidelines for Title II-A.

III. Certificate Fields

A. P–5: Pre-Kindergarten through grade 5

B. 4–8: Middle Grades

C. 6–12: High School

D. P–12: special education, art, music, health, physical education, etc.

E. P–12: service and leadership

IV. Certificate Levels: Determined by highest degree awarded on official transcript from PSC-accepted accredited institution to educator, this single level is assigned to all certificate fields held by that educator.

A. Level One (Selected Technology/Career Education fields only): completion of high school diploma or GED equivalent

B. Level Two (Selected Technology/Career Education fields only): completion of associate's degree or 1 of following options:

1. 54 semester hours of acceptable college credit,

2. Two-year program consisting of minimum of 2,000 clock hours through regionally accredited postsecondary vocational/technical school in field in which certification is requested,

or

3. Minimum of 27 semester hours of acceptable college or university credit and minimum of 1,000 clock hours through accredited vocational/technical school in field in which certification is requested.

    C.   Level Four: completion of bachelor's degree or PSC's determined degree equivalent
    D.   Level Five: completion of master's degree or PSC's determined degree equivalent
    E.   Level Six: completion of education specialist's degree or PSC's determined degree
         equivalent;
         or
         Completion of a minimum of 36 semester hours of course work required for
         level seven doctoral degree, and successful completion of oral and/or written
         comprehensive examinations or the institution's determined equivalent.
    F.   Level Seven: completion of Ph.D. or Ed.D. degree or PSC's determined degree
         equivalent
  V. Endorsements
    A.   Each endorsement requires a prerequisite certificate and may be added by
         completing course work within an approved college or staff development
         endorsement program.
         1.   Most endorsement fields require 10 to 20 quarter hours of credit for completion.
         2.   Fields carry same expiration date as their prerequisite certificate, and both are
              renewed at same time.
    B.   Teaching Endorsements. Contact PSC at http://www.gapsc.com for its official rule
         for any endorsement or to see a list of Georgia institutions offering preparation in a
         specific endorsement
         1.   Birth through five; career exploration (PECE); computer science; coordinator of
              cooperative education (CVAE); culinary arts; diversified cooperative training
              (DCT); early childhood mathematics; early childhood science; English to
              speakers of other languages (ESOL); gifted in-field; intervention specialist; K–5
              mathematics: K–5 science; middle grades; online teaching; reading; related
              vocational instruction (RVI); safety and driver education; special education deaf
              education; special education physical and health disabilities; special education
              preschool (ages 3–5); special education transition specialist; special education
              visual impairment
    C.   Service Endorsements
         1.   Teacher support specialist; student support team (SST) coordinator
    D.   Leadership Endorsements
         1.   Teacher Leader
 VI. Standard Renewal Requirements
    A.   Clear Renewable and Performance-Based certificates are eligible for renewal.
         Requirements include:
         1.   6 semester hours of college course work; or 10 Professional Learning Units
              (PLUs); or 10 Continuing Education Units (CEUs), or 10 credits based on U.S.
              Department of Education Teacher-To-Teacher Workshops; or, completion of
              1 full year of acceptable school experience while working in another state on a
              valid certificate issued by that state;
              and
              criminal record check by employing school system.
    B.   Certificate holders employed by Georgia public school must have an individual
         professional development plan aligned with their system's Comprehensive School

Improvement Plan (CSIP). To be acceptable for certificate renewal, credit must be included in the individual plan and be directly associated with at least 1 of the following:
1. Field(s) of certification held;
2. School/district improvement plan;
3. Annual personnel evaluation;
   or
4. State/federal requirements.
C. Renewal Cycle
1. Georgia certificates usually have beginning date of July 1 and ending date of June 30.
2. Valid certificates may be renewed from October 1 in year preceding ending validity date to September 30 of calendar year in which validity date expires.
   a. Grace period between July 1 and September 30 allows completion of acceptable course work during summer period, so validity continues with no break in dates.

Routes to Certification

I. Traditional Routes to Clear, Renewable Certificate
A. College/university with state-approved educator preparation program
1. Complete bachelor's or higher degree from institution of higher education along with all program requirements for certificate field
2. Obtain recommendation from educator preparation program
3. Complete appropriate content assessment before certification
B. Holders of bachelor's degree may enroll in state-approved program for certificate only (post-baccalaureate program)
1. Complete all program requirements
2. See I, A, 2 and 3, directly above
C. Interstate Mobility (Reciprocity)
1. Hold out-of-state professional certificate,
   or
   Have completed and hold recommendation from approved out-of-state educator preparation program.
2. The PSC will determine specific Georgia requirements to be completed based on individual experience and credentials.
II. Alternative Route Certification
A. The Georgia Teacher Academy for Preparation and Pedagogy (GaTAPP) oversees multiple program paths to Georgia Clear Renewable Certification. Preliminary requirements include:
1. Hold a bachelor's degree or higher from an accredited institute
2. Have not completed teacher education degree programs
B All program paths involve:
1. Structured supervision and coaching by team of qualified mentors and coaches called the Candidate Support Team (CST)

    a. CST is composed of a school-based administrator, a school-based mentor/coach, a program provider supervisor, and a content specialist.

    b. CST assesses the level of knowledge and skills with which a transition teacher enters the program and recommends the appropriate path for the teacher candidate to take in order to meet 24 teaching competencies.

    c. Through continuous monitoring and assessment of the transition teacher's classroom performance, CST provides recommendations for advancement or retention in the program.

    d. Throughout transition, or induction phase, transition teachers provide evidence of the knowledge, skills, and dispositions required in the 24 teaching competencies and for successful completion of the program.

    e. Upon meeting all the required teacher competencies, including the Special Georgia Requirements and a minimum of one year of mentoring/coaching, transition teachers are recommended by the CST for Georgia Clear Renewable Certification.

C. For full details, consult http://www.gapsc.com/EducatorPreparation/GaTapp/home.asp

Special Georgia Requirements

I. Content Knowledge

  A. Appropriate content knowledge assessments are required of all persons seeking initial certification, except for those specifically exempted below. Contact the PSC at http:www.gapsc.com for full and current details.

  B. Exemptions from content knowledge assessments

    1. Hold or have held a professional certificate in another state, having passed appropriate statewide or national content knowledge assessment(s) required in that state for that certificate field,

      or

    Satisfy out-of-state certificate criteria and have 3 full years of acceptable, successful education experience under that certificate in a field comparable to Georgia certificate field within 5 years of application date,

      or

    Hold valid National Board for Professional Teaching Standards (NBPTS) certification in the specific field, except for the Middle Grades Generalist field,

      or

    If the PSC has not adopted a content assessment for certificate field being sought.

    2. Graduates of Georgia state-approved programs who have satisfied all program requirements except the content knowledge assessment(s), including a valid recommendation, may be issued a 1-year Waiver certificate at request of employing school system.

    3. See Testing Requirements below for specific details.

II. Standards of Conduct
   A. Applicant must comply with the profession's ethical standards.
   B. FBI background check (fingerprint) required for professional employment in Georgia public schools.
   C. Every 5 years, a Georgia criminal history check required for certificate renewal.
   D. Applicants for certification must also respond to background check questions on application form.
III. Recency of Study
   A. Certification applicants must verify study or experience within 5 years preceding date of application in one of the following ways:
      1. Complete 6 semester hours or 10 PLU credits or 10 CEU credits within 5 years, *or*
      2. Complete 1 year of out-of-state teaching experience on a certificate within 5 years, *or*
      3. Hold either a valid NBPTS certificate or a valid Georgia Master Teacher certificate, *or*
      4. Complete 1 year of full-time college teaching experience within 5 years, *or*
      5. In fields of audiology, school psychology, school social work, and speech and language pathology, provide a valid State of Georgia license issued by the Examining Boards Division of the Office of the Secretary of State.
IV. Special Education
   A. Any person certified in a teaching field, the leadership field of Educational Leadership, the service fields of Media Specialist and School Counseling, or holders of permits or Technical Specialist certificates shall complete course work approved by the PSC (3 semester hours of college credit or 5 PLUs) in the identification and education of children who have special educational needs, *or*
   B. Hold NBPTS-valid certification in this area.
V.   Veteran out-of-state educators moving into Georgia may be eligible to exempt all Special Georgia Requirements except Standards of Conduct. Contact PSC at http:www.gapsc.com for full requirements for exemption.

Testing Requirements

I.   Georgia Assessments for the Certification of Educators (GACE) is the educator licensure assessment in Georgia. Full information about the GACE program and certification requirements is available at www.gace.nesinc.com.
   A. GACE assessments include Basic Skills, Paraprofessional, Professional Pedagogy, and content assessments.
      1. There is no GACE broad field social studies test for high school (6–12); instead separate tests are available for history, economics, geography, and political science that an educator seeking authorization to teach multiple social science

subjects at that level will need to pass. However, GACE includes a middle grades social studies test to support Middle Grades Social Studies (4–8) certification.

2. For certification candidates in the field of Speech and Language Pathology, the Praxis II test 0330 will remain the required test.

B. The PSC will not accept Praxis II scores for Educational Leadership assessments that reflect a score report date of March 15, 2008, or later unless the applicant completed any approved Georgia Educational Leadership program on or before September 30, 2009.

Leadership Certificate Requirements

Requirements for the Performance-Based Leadership Certificate are listed below. For implementation details, including clarification and guidelines for the transition between the previous and current leadership certification systems, consult the PSC at http://www.gapsc.com and reference Rule 505-2-300.

I. Clear Renewable Certificate Requirements
A. Performance-Based Leadership (PL) Certificate (available after September 30, 2009)
1. Complete a PSC-approved Georgia performance-based leadership program at the specialist (level 6) or doctoral (level 7) degree,
   or
2. Hold a level 6 or level 7 degree in another field and complete the performance-based certification requirements
   and
   Be recommended by a PSC-approved program provider.
B. Leadership (L) Certificate
1. Hold a clear-renewable L certificate issued prior to September 30, 2009
   or
   Apply through the out-of-state reciprocity process if never held a Georgia certificate,
   or
   Under specified conditions, convert a permit in leadership to the clear renewable leadership certificate

Hawaii

As of February 2011, public hearings are being held on the adoption of certain administrative rules for Hawaii's teacher licensing. Please check with the Hawaii Teacher Standards Board (HTSB) website at www.htsb.org for updates. Also, since Praxis testing requirements have recently changed, check with HTSB for current information on the correct tests.

Licenses

I. Provisional License (valid 3 years, nonrenewable)
   A. Minimum requirements: applicant must:
      1. Complete State-Approved Teacher Education Program (SATEP);
      2. Pass Hawaii subject area examinations in field of applicant's SATEP,
         or
         Pass subject area examinations for licensure in the state where applicant completed SATEP,
         or
         Complete a major in field of applicant's SATEP if there is no subject area examination for applicant's licensure area;
      3. Meet professional fitness requirements listed on Hawaii's application, section 2;
         and
      4. Pay license fees.
   B. Effective date of license will be date when all requirements are met and all required documentation is submitted.
      1. Periodically check HTSB website for any revisions to licensing requirements and watch for announcements about launch of online licensing system.
II. Standard License (valid 5 years, renewable)
   A. Minimum requirements: applicant must:
      1. Complete SATEP, except for applicants who are:
         a. National Board for Professional Teaching Standards (NBPTS)–certified teachers holding a current, valid out-of-state teaching license,
            or
         b. Teachers with a current, valid out-of-state teaching license with the Meritorious New Teacher Candidate (MNTC) designation;
      2. Pass basic skills, pedagogy, and content knowledge tests, except for those who meet the following conditions:
         a. Hold NBPTS certificate,
         b. Hold teaching license with MNTC designation,
            or
         c. Teachers holding current, valid out-of-state license may be able to use out-of-state licensure tests in lieu of Hawaii Praxis tests;

3. Meet professional fitness requirements listed on Hawaii's application, section 2; *and*
4. Pay license fees.
B. See I, B, 1, directly above

III. Advanced License (valid 5 years, renewable)
A. Minimum requirements: applicant must:
1. Possess current, valid Standard License from Hawaii or its equivalent from another state;
2. Possess current, valid NBPTS certification, *or*
    Possess master's, specialist, or doctoral degree from regionally accredited institution in area relevant to teaching field for which license is sought or field that improves the practice of teaching;
    a. Applicant may not use degree with which Standard License was obtained to also obtain Advanced License.
3. Five years of satisfactory full-time teaching experience completed within 8 years of application in state which issued Standard License.
4. Meet Professional fitness requirements listed on Hawaii's application, section 2; *and*
5. Pay license fees.
B. See I, B, 1, directly above

IV. Add Field to Existing License
A. Minimum requirements. Applicant must:
1. Complete an SATEP in new license field; *or*
2. Complete 18 hours of course work from SATEP in new field, *and*
    Complete 2 years of satisfactory contracted K–12 teaching experience in new field within last 5 years of added field application date;
    a. Total teaching experience must be equivalent to at least 1 year of full-time teaching in new field. *or*
3. Submit passing Praxis subject area examinations in new field, *and*
    Complete 2 years of satisfactory contracted K–12 teaching experience in new field within last 5 years of added field application date.
    a. Total teaching experience must be equivalent to at least 1 year of full-time teaching in new field.

V. License Renewal Requirements
A. Go to www.htsb.org for current instructions

VI. Permits
A. Career and Technical Education (CTE) Permit minimum requirements:
1. Hawaii Department of Education must submit recommendation to receive CTE Special Permit directly to HTSB on behalf of applicant, who must:

        a.   Possess valid trade/industry license or certification, if one exists in trade/industry in field in which instruction will be offered;

        b.   Have 3 years of satisfactory full-time experience in field in which instruction will be offered;

        c.   Meet professional fitness requirements listed on Hawaii's application, section 2;

            and

        d.   Pay permit fees.

    2.   Effective date of permit will be date when all requirements are met and all required documentation is submitted.

        a.   Periodically check HTSB website for any revisions to permit requirements and watch for announcements about launch of online application system.

B.   Ni'ihau Permit minimum requirements provide that applicant must:

    1.   Be recommended by Hawaii Department of Education for showing strong progress towards meeting the licensing requirements and thus, qualifying for the Ni'ihau Special Permit;

        a.   Meet professional fitness requirements listed on Hawaii's application, section 2;

            and

        b.   Pay permit fees.

    2.   Effective date of permit will be date when all requirements are met and all required documentation is submitted.

    3.   This permit will expire on last day of school year in which it is issued, so applicant must reapply for permit each year.

        a.   Periodically check HTSB website for any revisions to permit requirements and watch for announcements about launch of online application system.

VII.   Praxis Test Information

    A.   All teachers applying for Hawaii Provisional or Standard License take the PPST Reading, Writing, and Mathematics Tests.

        1.   Tests and qualifying scores are:

            a.   PPST Reading (test code 10710 or 5710) score 172+

            b.   PPST Writing (test code 20720 or 5720) score 171+

            c.   PPST Mathematics (test code 10730 or 5730) score of 173+

        2.   Hawaii utilizes a composite score; refer to http://htsb.org/html/details/licensing/prasixcompositescore.html for explanation.

    B.   Exemptions and Exceptions

        1.   NBPTS-certified and MNTC-licensed teachers holding current, valid licenses from another state are exempt from all Praxis examinations.

        2.   Teachers with valid out-of-state licenses should refer to Standard License applicant instructions regarding required tests.

        3.   Teacher candidates should periodically check the HTSB website (www.htsb.org) for updates to testing requirements.

Teacher Performance Standards

Teachers, counselors, and librarians must meet specific performance criteria for each standard. Contact HTSB (see Appendix 1) for details.

I. Standard 1: Focuses on the Learner
   A. Candidate consistently engages students in appropriate experiences that support their development as independent learners.
II. Standard 2: Creates and maintains a safe and positive learning environment
   A. Candidate consistently creates a safe and positive learning environment that encourages social interaction, civic responsibility, active engagement in learning, and self-motivation.
III. Standard 3: Adapts to Learner Diversity
   A. Candidate consistently provides opportunities that are inclusive and adapted to diverse learners.
IV. Standard 4: Fosters effective communication in the learning environment
   A. Candidate consistently enriches communication in the learning environment.
V. Standard 5: Demonstrates knowledge of content
   A. Candidate consistently demonstrates competency in content area(s) to develop student knowledge and performance as specified in the Hawaii Content and Performance Standards.
VI. Standard 6: Designs and provides meaningful learning experiences
   A. Candidate consistently plans and implements meaningful learning experiences for students.
VII. Standard 7: Uses active student learning strategies
   A. Candidate consistently uses a variety of active learning strategies to develop students' thinking, problem-solving, and learning skills.
VIII. Standard 8: Uses assessment strategies
   A. Candidate consistently applies appropriate assessment strategies to evaluate and ensure the continuous intellectual, social, physical, and emotional development of the learner.
IX. Standard 9: Demonstrates professionalism
   A. Candidate continually evaluates the effects of his or her choices and actions and actively seeks opportunities to grow professionally.
X. Standard 10: Fosters parent and school community relationships
   A. Candidate establishes and maintains strong working relationships with parents and members of the school community to support student learning.
XI. School Librarians add performance standard 11: Designs and provides quality library media programs and services
   A. The effective school librarian establishes and administers quality library media center programs and services that support and enhance student learning. Consult HTSB (see Appendix 1) for full performance criteria.
XII. School Counselor performance standards are adaptations of the teacher standards adapted to counseling responsibilities. Consult HTSB (see Appendix 1) for complete standards statements and performance criteria.

XIII.   HTSB has developed a Code of Ethics intended to advance the teaching profession, to guide the professional behavior of P–12 educators, and to form the basis for disciplinary action taken by the Board. Consult HTSB (see Appendix 1) for the full text of its 3 principles: commitment to students, to the profession, and to the community.

Idaho

General Requirements for All Teachers and Administrators

I. Testing Requirements
   A. Applicants for certificates/endorsements in Standard Elementary, Standard Secondary, Early Childhood/Early Childhood Special Education Blended, and/or Standard Exceptional Child must meet or exceed qualifying score(s) for appropriate Praxis II test(s).
      1. Applicants for certificates in Administration or Pupil Personnel Services are exempted from this requirement.
II. Out-of-State Applications
   A. Applicants from regionally accredited institutions meeting bachelor's degree–based requirements for certification or equivalent in other states may be certified by the Idaho Department of Education when they substantially meet the requirements for Idaho certification. Contact the Bureau of Certification/Professional Standards (see Appendix 1).
III. Contact the Certification/Professional Standards Commission (see Appendix 1) for full details on State Board of Education–approved alternate routes to Idaho certification that became effective July 1, 2006.
   A. Alternative Authorization—Teacher to New Certification
   B. Alternative Authorization—Content Specialist
   C. American Board for Certification of Teacher Excellence (ABCTE; see abcte.org)
IV. Professional-Technical Education
   A. Idaho State Division of Professional-Technical Education is authorized to determine whether applicants meet requirements for instructing or administering professional-technical programs at the secondary and postsecondary levels.
V. Renewal of Certification
   A. All credentials may be renewed upon completion of at least 6 semester credits of college courses within the 5-year period of validity.
VI. Criminal History and Background Check
   A. All adults working in Idaho public schools (certificated and noncertificated), or applying for certification, are currently required to have results of a criminal history check on file with the State Department of Education. Proposed temporary rules for these are receiving public comment. Check with the Idaho Certification/Professional Standards Commission (see Appendix 1) for details and current information.

Early Childhood/Early Childhood Special Education (Birth–Grade 3)

I. Early Childhood/Early Childhood Special Education Blended Certificate (valid 5 years, renewable). Minimum requirements:
   A. Bachelor's degree from accredited college or university
      1. Complete general education requirements

2. Professional education requirements:
   a. Minimum of 30 semester credit hours, or 45 quarter credit hours, in philosophical, psychological, and methodological foundations; in instructional technology; and in professional subject matter of early childhood and early childhood–special education.
   b. Professional subject matter of early childhood and early childhood–special education shall include course work specific to young child from birth through grade 3 in areas of: child development and learning; curriculum development and implementation; family and community relationships; assessment and evaluation; professionalism; and application of technologies.
   c. Required 30 semester credit hours, or 45 quarter credit hours, shall include not less than 6 semester credit hours, or 9 quarter credit hours, of early childhood student teaching; and 3 semester credit hours, or 4 quarter credit hours, of developmental reading.
3. Institutional recommendation from accredited college or university, and passage of Idaho Comprehensive Literacy Exam.
4. Each candidate shall meet or exceed state qualifying score on the following approved early childhood assessments:
   a. Education of Young Children, Praxis II #0021 (qualifying score—169)
   b. Special Education: Pre-School/Early Childhood, Praxis II #0690 (qualifying score—550)

Elementary School (Grades K–8)

I. Standard Elementary Certificate (valid 5 years; renewable)
   A. Bachelor's degree from accredited college or university
   B. Professional requirements to include the following areas, total semester hours 24
      1. Philosophical, psychological, and methodological foundations of education
      2. Elementary student teaching, semester hours 6
         or
         Two years of successful teaching in an elementary school
      3. Developmental reading, semester hours 6
   C. Passing score on the Idaho Comprehensive Literacy Assessment (Idaho graduates only).
   D. Completion of Idaho Comprehensive Literacy Course or passage of Idaho Comprehensive Literacy Assessment (all applicants)

Secondary School (Grades 6–12)

I. Standard Secondary Certificate (valid 5 years; renewable)
   A. Bachelor's degree
   B. Professional requirements, semester hours 20
      1. Philosophical, psychological, and methodological foundations of education
      2. Secondary student teaching, semester hours 6
         or
         Two years of successful teaching in a secondary school

      3.   Reading in the content area, semester hours 3

  C. Preparation in at least 2 fields of secondary teaching

      1.   Major subject, semester hours 30

           and Minor subject, semester hours 20

           or

      2.   Preparation in a single area, in lieu of a major and minor, ... 45
semester hours

The Exceptional Child

I.   Standard Exceptional Child Certificate (valid 5 years; renewable)

  A. Generalist (Educationally Handicapped) Endorsement

      1.   Completion of a program in Special Education approved by Idaho State Board of Education, *or* by the state educational agency where the program was completed

      2.   Special education courses, semester hours 30

          a.   To include developmental processes; evaluation; individualization of instruction for exceptional child; instructional experience; individual and group classroom management; knowledge of and coordination with other school personnel; knowledge of state and community ancillary services; work with parents

      3.   Pass appropriate Praxis II assessments

      4.   Completion of Idaho Comprehensive Literacy Course or passage of Idaho Comprehensive Literacy Assessment

  B. Specialized Endorsement

      1.   Hearing and visually impaired

      2.   Requirements

          a.   Baccalaureate degree

          b.   Completion of approved program in area of endorsement, as recommended by the training institution

      3.   Pass appropriate Praxis II assessments

  C. Consulting Teacher Endorsement (valid 5 years; renewable)

      1.   Valid Standard Exceptional Child Certificate

      2.   Valid Standard Elementary or Secondary teaching certificate

      3.   Completion of fifth-year or master's degree program

      4.   Three years of teaching experience, with at least 2 years in a special education classroom setting

      5.   Demonstration of competencies

  D. Supervisor/Coordinator Endorsement

      1.   Master's degree

      2.   Standard Exceptional Child Certificate, or Pupil Personnel Services Certificate endorsed for School Psychologist, Communication Disorders Specialist, or School Social Worker

      3.   Three years of experience in special education

      4.   Demonstration of competencies

Administration

I. Administrative Certificates
    A. School Principal Endorsement (K–12) (valid 5 years; renewable)
        1. Master's degree from an accredited institution
        2. Four years of full-time experience (under certification) working with K–12 students while under contract in a school setting
        3. Completion of an administrative internship or 1 year of experience as an administrator
        4. Completion of a state-approved program of at least 30 semester hours of graduate study in school administration for the preparation of school principals at an accredited institution
            a. To include competencies in supervision of instruction; curriculum development; school finance; administration; school law; student behavior management; and education of special populations
        5. Institutional recommendation
    B. Superintendent Endorsement (valid 5 years; renewable)
        1. Educational specialist or doctorate degree or a comparable post-master's sixth-year program at an accredited institution
        2. See School Principal Endorsement I, A, 2 and 3, directly above.
        3. Completion of a state-approved program of at least 30 semester hours of post-master's graduate study in school administration for the preparation of school superintendents at an accredited institution
            a. In addition to the competencies required for the principal (see I, A, 4, a, above), this program will include competencies in advanced money management, budget, and accounting principles; district-wide support services; employment practices and negotiations; school board and community relations; and special services and federal programs.
        4. Institutional recommendation
    C. Director of Special Education Endorsement (K–12)
        1. See School Principal Endorsement I, A, 1 and 2, above.
        2. Institutional verification of competencies in organization and administration of special services; school finance and school law as related to special education; supervision of instruction; practicum experience in special education administration; counseling parents of exceptional children; foundations of special education; curriculum and methods in special education; and diagnosis and remediation in special education
        3. Competency checklist forms from the applicant's institution may be requested by the Certification Division.

Pupil Personnel Services

I. Standard Counselor Endorsement (K–12) (valid 5 years; renewable)
    A. Requirements
        1. Master's degree plus verification of completion of approved program of graduate study in school guidance and counseling from an institution approved

by the Idaho State Board of Education or the state educational agency of the state in which the program was completed

    a.   The program must include successful completion of 700 hours of supervised field experience, 75 percent of which must be in a K–12 school setting to include substantial amounts of experience in elementary, middle/junior high, and high school

  2. Institutional recommendation

II. School Psychologist Endorsement (valid 5 years; renewable)

  A. Requirements

    1. Graduate semester hours 60

       a. Master's degree program of 30 semester hours in education or psychology, plus 30 hour School Psychology Specialist degree program, *or*

       b. Sixty semester hours in master's degree program in School Psychology, *or*

       c. Sixty semester hours in School Psychology Specialist program that does not require a master's degree; laboratory experience; and a minimum 1200 clock-hour internship.

    2. Institutional recommendation

III. Speech-Language Pathologist Endorsement (valid 5 years; renewable)

  A. Requirements

    1. Completion of state-approved program in speech-language pathology

    2. Master's degree in speech-language pathology

    3. Institutional recommendation

IV. Audiology Endorsement (valid 5 years; renewable)

  A. Same as for Speech-Language Pathologist Endorsement, but substitute "audiology" for "speech-language pathology."

V. School Social Worker Endorsement (valid 5 years; renewable)

  A. Requirements

    1. Master's degree in social work from an approved program, *or*

    2. Master's degree in guidance and counseling, sociology, or psychology, plus graduate work in social work education, semester hours 30

    3. Valid social work license issued by the Idaho Bureau of Occupational Licenses

    4. Institutional recommendation

VI. School Nurse Endorsement (valid 5 years; renewable)

  A. Requirements

    1. Valid registered nursing license issued by the Idaho State Board of Nursing

    2. Bachelor's degree in nursing, education, or a health-related field. *or*

Nine semester credits in at least 3 of the following areas: health program management; child and adolescent health issues; counseling/psychology/social work; and methods of education instruction.

Illinois

Additional new rules became effective in September of 2010—including redesign of the Basic Skills test—and more, will become effective on February 1, 2012. In addition to information below, contact the Illinois State Board of Education (ISBE) website at http://www.isbe.net/certification/default.htm and the Illinois Certification Testing System (ICTS) website at http://www.icts.nesinc.com for full details.

Professional Teaching Certificates

I. Professional Teaching Certificate Types
    A. Early Childhood: Valid for teaching children birth through grade 3 (Birth–Grade 3)
    B. Elementary: Valid for teaching children in self-contained classrooms from kindergarten through grade 9 (K–9)
        1. One must meet additional requirements to teach at the middle grades level
    C. Secondary: Valid for teaching children from grade 6 through grade 12 (6–12)
        1. One must meet additional requirements to teach at the middle grades level
    D. Special: Valid for teaching children in the subject specified from kindergarten through grade 12 (K–12)
    E. Special/Special Education: Valid for teaching children with disabilities from PreK through age 21 (PreK–21)
II. Professional Teaching Certificate Levels
    A. Initial Level (valid 4 years; expires on June 30 of 4th year of experience)
        1. Issued to new teachers and valid until 4 years of teaching have been obtained
        2. Holders must complete one of professional development options for obtaining Standard Certificate during time they hold Initial Certificate.
        3. Initial certificate holders must qualify for Standard level once they have completed 4 years of teaching on Initial Certificate.
    B. Standard Level (valid 5 years; renewable at end of each registration period)
        1. Standard certificate holders must complete continuing professional development requirements by end of each registration period to renew certificate.
        2. Once teachers obtain a Standard certificate, any subsequent teaching certificates issued to them will also be Standard level.
        3. Teachers from other states with 4 years of teaching experience on valid, comparable certificate are eligible to apply for Standard certificate.
    C. Master Level (valid for 10-year periods; renewable)
        1. Master Certificate is issued to persons who have met the standards of the National Board for Professional Teaching Standards WPTS).
        2. Renewal requirement is same as for 5-year Standard certificate
        3. No application fee or testing requirement for Master-level certificate
III. Requirements for Applicants Prepared in an Illinois Institution

A. Traditional program graduates must follow application procedures on ISBE website at http://www.isbe.net/certification/default.htm

B. Alternative program graduates complete certification in 2-step process; details at http://www.isbe.net/certification/default.htm

IV. Requirements for Applicants Trained or Certified in Another State

A. All course work must be from regionally accredited institution and appear on official college or university transcript.

B. Applicants from other states who have completed approved programs in their states, or who hold out-of-state certificates comparable to certificates they want in Illinois, may be eligible to obtain Illinois certificates when they:

1. Are of good character;

2. Are U.S. citizens, or are legally present and eligible for employment;

3. Have a bachelor's degree;

4. Have completed pre–student teaching field experience;

5. Have completed student teaching;

   a. Student teaching must be demonstrated on an official transcript from a regionally accredited 4-year institution of higher education (IHE).

   b. Those without student teaching credit may obtain a waiver of student teaching when they present proof of 1 year of teaching experience on a valid certificate.

6. Have completed course work addressing the psychology of, the identification of, and the methods of instruction for the exceptional child, including without limitation the learning disabled child;

7. Have a major specified on the transcript appropriate to the certificate sought (early childhood education, elementary education, art, music, etc.) or have 32 semester hours in content appropriate to the certificate sought;

8. Have passed the Illinois Basic Skills test, appropriate content area test(s), and the assessment of professional teaching test required for the grade level of the certificate;

   a. Applicants who hold a valid out-of-state certificate that is comparable to the certificate sought in Illinois will be considered to have passed a test of basic skills and will be exempt from the Illinois Basic Skills test unless they have taken and failed it in the past.
   and

9. Apply for a provisional certificate.

   a. Provisional certificate (valid 2 full fiscal years, with 1st fiscal year ending on June 30 following issue date). Applicants who hold valid, comparable certificates from another state may be issued a provisional certificate for Elementary, Early Childhood, Secondary, Special, School Service Personnel, and Administrative certificates when an evaluation indicates the applicant has some deficiency that must be removed before the regular certificate may be issued.

   b. Individuals with testing deficiencies who pass the tests and remove all other deficiencies by June 30 following the date of issue can exchange their provisional certificates for regular certificates without additional application or fee.

    c.   If all deficiencies are not removed by the end of the first fiscal year, a new application and fee will be required for the regular certificate to be issued when all deficiencies have been removed.

    d.   Applicants will be subject to current rules, including testing requirements, when the new application is submitted.

  10. See ISBE website at http://www.isbe.net/certification/default.htm for:

    a.   Checklist of requirements for out-of-state applicants

    b.   Certification for individuals educated in countries outside of the United States

    c.   Subsequent Illinois teaching certification by transcript evaluation

V.   **Endorsement of Teaching Certificates**

  A. Elementary and secondary certificates must be endorsed at the time of issuance in all subjects for which the holder meets applicable requirements.

    I.   These endorsements indicate the subjects that the teacher is qualified to teach and may be issued at various grade levels.

    2.   Teachers are not required to be endorsed in every subject for which they are qualified, and they may continue to be placed in assignments where they met previous requirements for the subject, provided the requirements were in effect at the time the teacher met the requirements and held the required certificate.

    3.   Special certificates must be endorsed for the grade level of the certificate upon issuance in the area of specialization, but may also have endorsements added at other grade levels.

  B. Subsequent Endorsements

    1.   Universities may award subsequent endorsements in a manner similar to when they recommend issuance of an initial teaching, school service personnel, or administrative certificate.

    2.   Applicants may also apply for subsequent endorsements from the ISBE website at http://www.isbe.net/certification/default.htm

  C. Endorsement Requirements at the Secondary Level (9–12)

    1.   Endorsements are designed to meet the No Child Left Behind (NCLB) requirements for all core academic subjects; however, secondary endorsement requirements do not meet the NCLB requirements for highly qualified teachers unless a test or major area of concentration was completed. The applicant must meet one of the following requirements:

        a.   Have a major in the content area, either indicated on the transcript or demonstrated by having a total of 32 semester hours in the content area, *or*

        b.   Pass a content-area test in the endorsement area and have at least 24 semester hours of course credit in the content area.

    2.   The following content areas are exceptions to the above general rules: bilingual education; driver education and safety; English as a Second Language (ESL); foreign languages; library information specialist; reading specialist; reading teacher; sciences; self-contained general education; social sciences; technology specialist; and supervisory endorsement on special (K–12 or Pre-K – age 21) certificates

  D. Endorsements at the Middle Grades Level (Grades 5–8 for elements certificates and 6–8 for secondary certificates)

     1.   Endorsements at the middle grades level require a minimum of I8 semester hours of course work in the endorsement areas as well as the following pedagogy courses:

        a.   Three semester hours of course work that includes middle-grade philosophy, curriculum, and methods including content-area reading instruction; and

        b.   Three semester hours of educational psychology course work that focuses on the developmental characteristics of early adolescence.

     2.   These endorsement requirements alone will not make a teacher highly qualified in the core academic areas for NCLB purposes.

     3.   Elementary, secondary, and special certificates may be endorsed for teaching at the middle school level.

     4.   Specific requirements apply for certain middle grades endorsements, including: bilingual, ESL, foreign languages, mathematics, library information specialist, reading specialist, reading teacher, self-contained general education, and technology specialist. Consult ISBE website at http://www.isbe.net/certification/default.htm for details.

   E. Primary-Level Endorsements

     1.   Some subjects require 18 hours or more to teach at the primary level.

     2.   Teachers may request primary-level endorsements in the following subjects: English as a second language; bilingual education; reading teacher; library information specialist; and technology specialist.

     3.   Except for the middle grades pedagogy courses, the requirements in the content area are identical with those for the middle grades for each subject.

   F. For a comprehensive list of endorsements available at each level, see http://isbe.net/certification/default.htm

School Service Personnel Certificates

   I. School Service Personnel Certificates (valid 5 years; renewable upon registration)

     A. Certificates awarded include School Counselor, School Nurse, School Psychologist, School Social Worker, or Speech/Language Pathologist (non-teaching)

     B. General requirements are to be of good character; be in good health; and to be a U.S. citizen or to document being legally present and eligible for employment.

     C. Persons who hold only school service personnel certificates may not be employed as teachers.

     D. Provisional Certificates (valid 2 full fiscal years with 1st year ending on June 30 following issue date)

        1.   Available to applicants from other states who hold out-of-state certificates with comparable endorsements to allow time to complete testing requirements and remove other deficiencies found during the evaluation.

        2.   Individuals who hold valid, comparable certificates from other states will be exempt from taking the Basic Skills test, unless previously failed, but must take the content test.

     E. Supervisory Endorsement on the School Service Personnel Certificate

        1.   The holder of the School Service Personnel Certificate may have the added endorsement for supervision upon presentation of evidence of each of the following:

       a.   Hold a master's or higher degree,

       b.   Have completed 8 semester hours of graduate professional education including at least 1 course related primarily and explicitly to the supervision of personnel and 1 course primarily and explicitly related to the administration and organization of schools,
           and

       c.   Have at least 2 years of appropriate school service personnel experience.

  F.   For full and detailed information, including specific application procedures, see http://www.isbe.net/certification/default.htm

II. Certification of School Counselors

  A.   Applicants for the school service personnel certificate endorsed for school counseling shall:

      1.   Hold a master's or higher degree awarded by a regionally accredited IHE in school counseling, another counseling or related field (e.g., social work or psychology), or an educational field,

      2.   Have completed an Illinois program approved for the preparation of school counselors or a comparable approved program in another state or country, and/or hold a comparable certificate issued by another state or country,
          and

      3.   Have completed a supervised counseling practicum of at least 100 clock hours that provided interaction with individuals and groups of school age and included at least 40 hours of direct service work.

      4.   Each applicant shall have completed a structured and supervised internship that is part of an approved program.

          a.   The internship shall be of a length that is determined by the approved program to be adequate to enable candidates to meet the standards but shall entail at least 600 hours and last no less than 1 semester, during which candidates shall engage in the performance of various aspects of the counseling role and shall be gradually introduced to the full range of responsibilities associated with that role.

          b.   However, the internship for an individual with at least 2 years of teaching experience may, at the discretion of the institution offering the approved program, consist of no fewer than 400 hours.

          c.   In each case at least 240 hours of the internship shall involve direct service work with school-age individuals and groups.

          d.   The internship shall occur in a school setting except that, at the discretion of the institution, a maximum of one-third of the hours required may be credited for experiences in other related settings such as hospitals or day care settings that, in the judgment of the institution, expose the candidates to the needs of school-aged children and prepare the candidates to function as school counselors.

          e.   Each applicant shall either hold or be qualified to hold a teaching certificate; or have completed, as part of an approved program, course work addressing each of the following:

              i.   The structure, organization and operation of the educational system, with emphasis on PreK–12 schools,

  ii. The growth and development of children and youth, and their implications for counseling in schools,

  iii. The diversity of Illinois students and the laws and programs that have been designed to meet their unique needs, *and*

  iv. Effective management of the classroom and the learning process.

 f. Certain specific exceptions of internship requirements may be made for applicants who hold another state's certification in school counseling; see http://www.isbe.net/certification/default.htm for details.

 g. Candidates shall be required to pass the School Counselor (#181) test as well as the test of basic skills, except for applicants who hold a valid school counselor certificate from another state, since they are assumed to have passed a test of basic skills and are exempt from the Illinois test. See http://www.icts.nesinc.com for additional information regarding testing.

 h. Applicants who hold a master's degree in any field other than school counseling, or who hold a bachelor's degree only, shall be required to complete the equivalent of all requirements of an approved school counseling preparation program.

  i. The Illinois institution offering the program shall review the individual's educational and experiential background and identify any of the standards or other applicable requirements that the individual's preparation has not addressed.

  ii. Upon successful completion of the course work and experiences offered by the institution that address the identified standards, the applicant shall be eligible to be recommended for certification by entitlement.

B. For detailed requirements for interim certification of school counselor interns, as well as all other school service personnel certificates, see ISBE website at http://www.isbe.net/certification/default.htm

Administrative Certificates

I. Administrative Certificates (valid 5 years; renewable)

 A. Administrative Certificates are required for persons serving in administrative roles.

  1. Applicants for these certificates must complete the appropriate content-area test as well as the Basic Skills test.

II. Provisional Administrative Certificates (valid 2 full fiscal years; not renewable)

 A. For applicants from another state or country who hold a valid, comparable certificate from their state or country and do not meet all of Illinois's requirements.

 B. The educator must pass all required tests and meet all other certification requirements.

 C. Applicants who hold a valid, comparable certificate from another state will receive a waiver of the Basic Skills test unless they have previously attempted and failed the test.

III. General Administrative Endorsement is required for principals, assistant principals, assistant or associate superintendents, and staff filling other similar or related positions.

    A. Candidates shall hold a master's degree awarded by a regionally accredited institution of higher education that encompasses the course work in educational administration and supervision.

    B. Candidates shall have completed an Illinois program approved for the preparation of administrator, or a comparable approved program in another state or country, or hold a comparable certificate issued by another state or country.

    C. Candidates shall have 2 years of full-time teaching or school service personnel experience in public schools, schools under the supervision of the Department of Corrections, schools under the administration of the Department of Human Services, or nonpublic schools recognized by the State Board of Education or meeting comparable out-of-state recognition standards.

    D. Beginning with applications submitted on or after February 1, 2012, candidates must also meet each of the following requirements:

        1. Teaching experience shall have been accrued while the individual held a valid early childhood, elementary, secondary, special K–12, or special preschool–age 21 certificate.

        2. School service personnel experience shall have been accrued while the individual held a valid school service personnel certificate.

IV. Alternative Route to Administrative Certification for National Board Certified Teachers

    A. A teacher who meets all of the following criteria may be eligible to apply to an Illinois institution of higher education that has an approved Alternative Route to Administrative Certification for National Board Certified Teachers program, which will allow the holder to work as a school principal in Illinois. Contact an Illinois institution for details about becoming a candidate.

        1. Hold certification from the National Board for Professional Teaching Standards (NBPTS)

        2. Hold a Teacher Leader Endorsement

        3. Hold master's degree in Teacher Leadership

    B. Candidates for administrative certification must complete 15 semester hours of course work in which the candidate must show evidence of meeting competencies for each of the following:

        1. Organizational management and development

        2. Finance

        3. Supervision and evaluation

        4. Policy and legal issues

        5. Leadership

    C. Eligible candidates must pass the Illinois Certification Testing System content-area test #186—Principal and the Basic Skills test. Consult http://www.icts.nesinc.com for testing information.

V. Chief School Business Official Endorsement

    A. Required for chief school business officials

        1. Candidates shall hold a master's degree awarded by a regionally accredited IHE

2. Candidates, whose master's degrees were earned in business administration, finance, or accounting, shall be required to pass the basic skills and content area tests. Consult http://www.icts.nesinc.com for testing information.
3. All other candidates shall meet each of the following sets of requirements:
    a. Have completed an Illinois program approved for the preparation of school business officials or a comparable approved program in another state or country and/or hold a comparable certificate issued by another state or country; and
    b. Have 2 years of administrative experience in school business management.
4. Each candidate shall be required to pass the applicable content-area test, as well as the test of basic skills; however, individuals who hold valid, comparable certificates from other states will receive a waiver of the Basic Skills test unless previously attempted and failed.

VI. Superintendent Endorsement
A. Required of school district superintendents. Note that the superintendent's endorsement shall not be issued as an individual's first endorsement on the administrative certificate unless issued on the basis of a comparable out-of-state credential. Consult the ISBE website at http://www.isbe.net/certification/default.htm for full details.
1. Candidates for the superintendent's endorsement shall hold a master's degree awarded by a regionally accredited IHE.
2. Candidates shall have completed an Illinois program approved for the preparation of superintendents or a comparable approved program in another state or country or hold a comparable certificate issued by another state or country.
3. Candidates shall have at least 2 years of full-time administrative or supervisory experience in schools, on a general supervisory, general administrative, director of special education, or all-grade supervisory endorsement on an administrative certificate, or a comparable out-of-state credential.
4. Candidates shall be required to pass the applicable content-area test, as well as the test of basic skills. Individuals who hold valid, comparable certificate from other states will receive a waiver of the Basic Skills test unless previously attempted and failed. Consult http://www.icts.nesinc.com for testing information.
5. The educator must have completed 30 semester hours of graduate credit beyond the master's degree in a program for superintendents with 16 semester hours in professional education.

VII. Director of Special Education
Consult the ISBE website at http://www.isbe.net/certification/default.htm for full details.

Test Required for Illinois Certificates

I. General Testing Information
A. All applicants for early childhood, elementary, secondary, special K–12/PreK–age 21 teaching certificates and all applicants for school service personnel and administrative certificates are required to pass a test of basic skills and content knowledge applicable to the endorsement on the certificate sought.

1. The Basic Skills test assesses reading comprehension, grammar and writing, and mathematics.
   a. Individuals who pass the Basic Skills test and receive Illinois certificates based in part on passage of that test are not required to take the Basic Skills test for any subsequent Illinois certificates.
   b. Unless the Illinois test was previously failed, a test waiver option for the Basic Skills test may apply to applicants with valid, comparable out-of-state certificates; contact ISBE (Appendix 1) for a final determination regarding waivers.
2. The content-area tests are aligned with the Illinois Learning Standards for the content area of each endorsement attached to a certificate.
   a. The content-area tests are also required for the issuance of some subsequent endorsements.
   b. A listing of all content-area tests is available at http://www.icts.nesinc.com
B. Applicants for early childhood, elementary, secondary, special K–12/PreK–age 21 teaching certificates are also required to pass an Assessment of Professional Teaching (APT) test appropriate to the grade level of the certificate sought.
   1. The APT assesses candidates on professional and pedagogical knqwledge and skills and is available in 4 levels: birth to grade 3, grades K–9, grades 6–12, and grades K–12.
C. Applicants for most special education Certificates are required to take the Special Education General Curriculum test.
   1. The Special Education General Curriculum (# 163) test is required for the following special education teaching certificates: Learning Behavior Specialist I, Teachers of Students with Deafness/Hard of Hearing, Teachers of Students with Blindness/Visual Impairments, and Speech and Language Pathologist: Teaching.
D. The language proficiency tests, which target specific languages other than English, are for individuals seeking transitional bilingual certificates, endorsements, or approvals.
   1. A test of language proficiency is required unless the applicant received a degree from an institution where the target language was the medium of instruction.
   2. A test in English Language Proficiency is required unless the applicant received a degree from an institution where English was the medium of instruction.
   3. A listing of all language proficiency tests is available at http://www.icts.nesinc.com
E. Applicants completing approved Illinois entitlement programs are required to pass the Illinois certification tests; and IHEs cannot waive certification tests.
F. Tests Required for Endorsements
   1. Individuals who hold Illinois certificates may apply for subsequent endorsements on their existing certificates, and many applicants seeking subsequent secondary level endorsements have an option of fulfilling the endorsement requirements by completing 24 semester hours of course work and passing the content-area test.
   2. Some designations, however, will require a test regardless of the number of content-area credits the applicants have.
G. Full information regarding test dates, study guides, test selection, and registration is available at http://www.icts.nesinc.com

Indiana

Stages and Titles of Teaching Certificates

I. Reciprocal Permit. Issued on the basis of:
A. Completion of an out-of-state teacher preparation program and valid (unexpired) out-of-state license comparable to either the Indiana Initial Practitioner or Proficient Practitioner license when there are licensing deficiencies such as the Pre-Professional Skills Test (PPST) and appropriate Praxis II exam(s)

II. Initial Practitioner (valid 2 years).
A. Issued on the basis of:
1. Completion of bachelor's or higher degree,
2. Teacher preparation program,
3. Institution of higher education (IHE) recommendation, *and*
4. Passing scores on the PPST and appropriate Praxis II exam(s).
B. Successfully complete the two-year Indiana Mentoring and Assessment Program (IMAP): required for all beginning teachers with less than 2 year of full-time, creditable experience.

III. Proficient Practitioner (valid 5 years; renewable)
A. Issued on the basis of successful completion of IMAP or 2 years of full-time, out-of-state, creditable teaching experience under a valid out-of-state license
B. Renewable every 5 years with completion of a Professional Growth Plan and 90 professional growth experience points

1V. Accomplished Practitioner (valid 10 years initially; then renewable every 5 years)
A. Issued on the basis of the appropriate graduate degree and appropriate years of full-time, creditable teaching experience
B. After the first 10 years, renewable every 5 years with completion of a Professional Growth Plan (PGP) and 90 professional growth experience points.

Requirements for Teaching Certificates

Consult http://www.doe.in.gov/dps/licensing/apbysubject2002/welcome.html for a complete listing of the content/developmental areas available for teaching.

I. Reciprocal Permit (valid 1 year)
A. Available only to candidates who have completed an out-of-state education program at a 4-year, regionally accredited IHE
B. Requirements include:
1. Bachelor's or higher degree;
2. Teacher preparation program, including field experience, practicum, and/or student teaching; *and*

      3. Valid (unexpired) out-of-state license equivalent to the Indiana Initial or Proficient Practitioner license with an equivalent content (subject area) and school setting (grade level).

II. Initial Practitioner License (valid 2 years)
  A. Requirements include:
    1. Recommendation of the Indiana IHE approved to offer the program
    2. Out-of-state graduates may be eligible if all Indiana licensure requirements are met and the applicant has less than 2 years of full-time, creditable teaching experience.
    3. Successful completion of IMAP.

III. Proficient Practitioner License (valid 5 years)
  A. Requirements include:
    1. Successful completion of IMAP or recommendation of the Indiana IHE approved to offer the program
      a. Conditional upon applicant completion of a beginning teacher internship under a valid Indiana license issued under a prior bulletin or rules or having 2 years of full-time, creditable teaching experience under a valid Indiana license issued under a prior bulletin or rules
    2. Out-of-state graduates may be eligible if all Indiana licensure requirements are met and the applicant has at least 2 years of full-time, creditable out-of-state teaching experience under a valid out-of-state license.

IV. Accomplished Practitioner License (valid 10 years initially; then renewable every 5 years)
  A. Requirements include:
    1. Recommendation of the Indiana IHE approved to offer the appropriate graduate degree and verification of 2 years of full-time, creditable teaching experience under a valid license.
    2. Out-of-state graduates may be eligible if all Indiana licensure requirements are met and the applicant holds the appropriate graduate degree and has 2 years of full-time, creditable teaching experience under a valid out-of-state license.
    3. An individual who obtains national board certification (NBCT) is immediately eligible for the accomplished practitioner license.

V. Renewal Requirements
  A. Licenses issued under bulletins/rules prior to Rules 2002 may be renewed with:
    1. Six semester hours of course work,
    2. Ninety preapproved Continuing Renewal Units (CRUs) if the teacher has a master's degree,
    or
    3. Completion of a Professional Growth Plan Renewal Report along with documentation and verification of 90 professional growth experience points.
  B. Licenses issued under Rules 2002 must be renewed with:
    1. A Professional Growth Plan Renewal Report,
      a. Materials for the PGP can be found at: http://www.doe.in.gov/dps/renewal/growth/welcome.html
      and
    2. Documentation and verification of 90 professional growth experience points.

Requirements for Administrative/Supervisory Certificates

I. The following areas are available for administration and supervision licensure:
    A. Building Level Administrator (Principal)
    B. Superintendent
    C. Director of Exceptional Needs
    D. Director of Curriculum and Instruction
    E. Director of Career and Technical Education
II. All administrative licenses are K–12
III. Types of Certificates
    A. Reciprocal Permit (valid 1 year)
        1. Available only to candidates who have completed an approved out-of-state program at an IHE regionally accredited to offer the appropriate graduate degree.
        2. Requirements include:
            a. Master's or higher degree,
            b. Education leadership program,
            c. Two years of full-time, creditable teaching experience, *and*
            d. Valid (unexpired) out-of-state license equivalent to the Indiana Initial or Proficient Practitioner license.
    B. Initial Practitioner License (valid 2 years)
        1. Requirements include:
            a. Recommendation of the Indiana IHE approved to offer the program
            b. Out-of-state graduates may be eligible if all Indiana licensure requirements are met, including passing score on Praxis School Leaders Licensure Assessment (SLLA) exam, and the applicant has less than 2 years of full-time, creditable administration and supervision experience.
            c. Successful completion of IMAP.
    C. Proficent Practitioner License (valid 5 years)
        1. Requirements include:
            a. Successful completion of IMAP or recommendation of the Indiana IHE approved to offer the program if the candidate holds another Indiana administrative license issued under a prior bulletin or rules
            b. Out-of-state graduates may be eligible if all Indiana licensure requirements are met (including passing score on Praxis SLLA exam) and the applicant has at least 2 years of full-time, creditable out-of-state administration and supervision experience under a valid out-of-state license.
    D. Accomplished Practitioner License (valid 10 years initially; then renewable every 5 years)
        1. Requirements include:
            a. For Building Level Administrator: Education Specialist degree or higher and 7 years of full-time, creditable administration and supervision experience under the appropriate license
            b. For District Level Administrator: Doctorate in Education Administration

and 7 years of full-time, creditable administration and supervision experience under the appropriate license

E.   Renewal Requirements

    1.   Licenses issued under bulletins/rules prior to Rules 2002 may be renewed with:

        a.   Six semester hours of course work,

        b.   Ninety preapproved CRUs,

           or

        c.   Completion of a Professional Growth Plan Renewal Report along with documentation and verification of 90 professional growth experience points.

    2.   Licenses issued under Rules 2002 must he renewed with:

        1.   A Professional Growth Plan Renewal Report,

           a.   Materials for the PGP can be found at: http://www.doe.in.gov/dps/renewal/growth/welcome.html

               and

        2.   Documentation and verification of 90 professional growth experience points.

Requirements for School Services Certificates

I.   The following content/developmental areas are available for school services:

A.   School Counselor

B.   School Nurse

C.   School Social Worker

D.   School Psychologist

II.   Types of Certificates

A.   Reciprocal Permit (valid 1 year)

    1.   Available only to candidates who have completed an out-of-state education program at a four-year, regionally accredited IHE

    2.   Requirements include:

        a.   Bachelor's or higher degree for school nurse and appropriate license from the Indiana Professional Licensing Agency (see IPLA at www.pla.in.gov);

        b.   Master's or higher degree for school social work and accompanying license from the Indiana Professional Licensing Agency (see IPLA at www.pla.in.gov);

        c.   Master's or higher degree for school counseling and school psychology and equivalent out-of-state license.

B.   Initial Practitioner License (valid 2 years)

    1.   Requirements include:

        a.   Recommendation of the Indiana IHE approved to offer the program

        b.   Out-of-state graduates may he eligible if all Indiana licensure requirements are met and the applicant has less than 2 years full-time, creditable experience in the school services area.

        c.   Successful completion of IMAP.

C. Proficient Practitioner License (valid 5 years)
   1. Requirements include:
      a. Successful completion of IMAP
      b. Out-of-state graduates may be eligible if all Indiana licensure requirements are met and the applicant has at least 2 years of full-time, creditable out-of-state school services experience under a valid out-of-state license.

D. Accomplished Practitioner License (valid 10 years initially; then renewable every 5 years)
   1. Requirements include:
      a. Recommendation of the Indiana IHE approved to offer the appropriate graduate degree and verification of creditable experience under a valid license
      b. Out-of-state graduates may be eligible if all Indiana licensure requirements are met and the applicant holds the appropriate graduate degree and appropriate number of years of creditable experience in the school services area under a valid out-of-state license.

E. Renewal Requirements
   1. Licenses issued under bulletins/rules prior to Rules 2002 may be renewed with:
      a. Six semester hours of course work,
      b. Ninety preapproved CRUs if the teacher has a master's degree,
         or
      c. Completion of a Professional Growth Plan Renewal Report along with documentation and verification of 90 professional growth experience points.
   2. Licenses issued under Rules 2002 must be renewed with:
      1. A Professional Growth Plan Renewal Report.
         a. Materials for the PGP can be found at: http://www.doe.in.gov/dps/renewal/growth/welcome.html
            and
      2. Documentation and verification of 90 professional growth experience points.

F. License Renewal Requirements
   For information regarding the renewal of licenses, go to http://www.doe.in.gov/dps/faq/renewal.html

Iowa

Types of Licenses

I. Initial License (valid 2 years; renewable under prescribed conditions)
   A. Baccalaureate degree from an approved institution
   B. Completion of an approved teacher education program
   C. Completion of an approved human relations component
   D. Completion of requirements for one of the teaching endorsements
   E. Meets the recency requirement listed under the Class A License (V, A, 3, directly below)

II. Standard License (valid 5 years; renewable under prescribed conditions)
   A. See I, A–E, above
   B. Two years of successful, verifiable teaching experience (based on a local evaluation process)

III. Master Educator License (valid 5 years; renewable)
   A. Holder of or eligible for a standard license
   B. Five years of verifiable teaching experience
   C. Master's degree in an area of one of the teaching endorsements
   D. Meets the recency requirement listed under the Class A License (V, A, 3, directly below)

IV. Professional Administrator's License (valid 5 years; renewable)
   A. Holder of or eligible for a standard license
   B. Three years of teaching experience
   C. Completion of requirements for 1 of the administrative endorsements

V. Class A License (valid 1 year; not renewable)
   A. Issued to applicant under the following conditions:
      1. Has completed a practitioner preparation program (e.g., a teacher or administrator program), but has not completed all required components in the professional education core
      2. Has not completed an approved human relations component
      3. Recency: meets requirements for a valid license but has less than 160 days of teaching during last 5-year period

VI. Exchange License (valid 1 year; not renewable)
   A. Baccalaureate degree from a regionally accredited institution
   B. Completion of a state-approved teacher preparation program
   C. Hold a valid teaching license in the state in which the teacher preparation program was completed
   D. No disciplinary action pending
   E. Has not completed all Iowa requirements for a teaching endorsement
   F. Must meet any and all licensure deficiencies during the 2-year period of the license

VII. Professional Service License (valid 2 years; renewable). For service as school audiologist, school psychologist, school social worker, speech-language pathologist, supervisor of special education (support), director of special education of an area education agency, or school counselor

A. Master's degree in a recognized professional educational service area from a regionally accredited institution

B. Has completed a state-approved program which meets the requirements for an endorsement in a professional educational service area

C. Has completed the requirements for one of the professional educational service area endorsements

D. Meets the recency requirement; see V, A, 3, directly above

Teaching Endorsements

I. Subject Area (K–6 and 7–12)
   A. See Types of Licenses, I, A–C, above
   B. Professional education core. Completed course work or evidence of competency in
      1. Student learning
      2. Diverse learners
      3. Instructional planning
      4. Instructional strategies
      5. Learning environment/classroom management
      6. Communication
      7. Assessment
      8. Foundations, reflection, and professional development
      9. Collaboration, ethics, and relationships
      10. Computer technology related to instruction
      11. Completion of pre–student teaching field-based experiences
      12. Methods of teaching with an emphasis on the subject and grade-level endorsement desired
      13. Student teaching in the subject area and grade-level endorsement desired
   C. Curriculum content
      1. Teaching major that must include the requirements for at least one subject endorsement, semester hours 30

II. Elementary (1–6)
   A. See Types of Licenses, I, A–C, above
   B. Subject Area—see I, B, directly above
   C. Curriculum content
      1. Methods and materials of teaching a variety of elementary subjects
      2. Pre–student teaching experience in at least 2 different grades
      3. Specialization in a single discipline or a formal interdisciplinary program of at least 12 semester hours

III. Prekindergarten/kindergarten
   A. See Types of Licenses, I, A–C, above
   B. Subject Area—see I, B, directly above
   C. Curriculum to include courses related to young children

IV. English as a second language (K–12)
    A. See Types of Licenses, I, A–C, above
    B. Subject Area—see I, B, directly above
    C. Completion of 18 semester hours of course work in English for Speakers of Other Languages (ESOL)
V. Elementary counselor (K–8)
    A. Master's degree
    B. Completion of 27 semester hours focusing on guidance and counseling on the elementary level, including
        1. Practicum in elementary school counseling
VI. Secondary counselor (5–12)
    A. Requirements are identical to those for elementary counselor, except that course work and practicum focus on the secondary level.
VII. Reading specialist (K–12)
    A. Master's degree
    B. Holder of or eligible for the Standard License and a teaching endorsement
    C. One year of experience, which included the teaching of reading as a significant part
    D. Completion of 27 semester hours focusing on reading, including
        1. Practicum on reading
VIII. Elementary school teacher librarian (K–8)
    A. See Types of Licenses, I, A–C, above
    B. Completion of 24 semester hours in school media course work, including
        1. Practicum in an elementary school media center
IX. Secondary school teacher librarian (5–12)
    A. Requirements are identical to those for elementary school teacher librarian, except that course work and practicum focus on the secondary level.
X. School teacher librarian (K–12)
    A. See Types of Licenses, I, A–C, above
    B. Master's degree
    C. Completion of 30 semester hours in school media course work, including
        1. Practicum at both the elementary and secondary levels

Administrative Endorsements

I. Principal (PreK–12)
    A. Master's degree
    B. Completion of at least 27 semester hours of course work in elementary and secondary administration, supervision, and curriculum
    C. Three years of teaching experience on the PreK–12 level
II. Superintendent (PreK–12)
    A. Master's degree, plus at least 30 semester hours of planned graduate study in administration beyond the master's degree. Overall, at least 45 semester hours of course work must be in school administration and related subjects.
    B. Three years' experience as a building principal or other PreK–12 district-wide education agency administrative experience

Note: Graduates from institutions in other states who are seeking initial Iowa licensure and an administrative endorsement must also meet the requirements for the Standard License.

Special Education Endorsements

I.   Program requirements for special education teaching endorsements
  A.   See Types of Licenses I, A–C, above
  B.   Twenty-four semester hours in special education, as well as other specific requirements, are necessary for teaching endorsements in the areas of mental and learning disabilities, hearing and visual impairment, the physically handicapped, and early childhood–special education.

II. Special education support personnel
  A.   Requirements for endorsements in this category vary greatly. Often a master's degree is necessary, and several endorsement areas have alternative routes for authorization. Requirements for school psychologist, school audiologist, speech and language clinician, school social worker, and other support personnel are available from the Board of Educational Examiners (see Appendix 1).

Reciprocity

Iowa participates in the Central Region Educator Certificate/License Exchange Agreement with the following states: Illinois, Indiana, Kansas, Michigan, Minnesota, Missouri, Nebraska, North Dakota, Ohio, Oklahoma, South Dakota, and Wisconsin

Kansas

License Types and Requirements

I. Initial Teaching License (valid 2 years; renewable)
   A. In-state applicants
      1. Bachelor's degree from a regionally accredited college or university
      2. Completion of a state-approved teacher preparation program
      3. Recency: have at least 8 credit hours or 1 year of accredited teaching experience completed within the last 6 years
      4. Passing scores on the content assessment in each of the endorsement areas on license
      5. Passing scores on the pedagogy assessment: Principles of Learning and Teaching (PLT)
   B. Out-of-state applicants
      1. See I, A, 1–3, directly above;
         and
      2. Passing scores on content and pedagogy tests: tests completed to achieve the out-of-state license may be acceptable;
         or
      3. May be issued a 2-year exchange license, if applicable;
         or
      4. May be issued a 1-year nonrenewable license;
         or
      5. May be issued a substitute license;
         or
      6. Meet experience requirements to come in at the professional license level.
II. Professional Teaching License (valid 5 years; renewable)
   A. In-state applicants
      1. Hold a currently valid Initial teaching license
      2. During its validity period, successfully complete the prescribed performance assessment
   B. Out-of-state applicants
      1. Bachelor's degree
      2. Completion of a state-approved preparation program in subject or field in which licensure is sought
      3. Recency: at least 1 year of accredited teaching experience or 8 semester hours of college credit within the 6 year period immediately prior to application
      4. Out-of-state professional license,
         and
      5. Three years of recent accredited experience under a standard teaching license
         or

Passing scores on assessments in content and pedagogy, with an already completed performance assessment.

III.   Accomplished Teaching License (valid 10 years; renewable)

A.   Available only to teachers who have achieved National Board certification from the National Board for Professional Teaching Standards (NBPTS) through completion of their advanced-level performance assessment process.

1.   Kansas licensed teachers must also hold a currently valid Kansas professional level teaching license as well as achieving National Board certification.

2.   National Board–certified teachers coming from out-of-state may apply for this license as their initial Kansas license, as long as they also hold a currently valid professional-level teaching license in another state.

a.   Accomplished license will be valid for the validity length of National Board certification.

IV.   One-Year Nonrenewable Teaching License (valid only for current school year)

A.   Meet all requirements for an Initial license (see I, A, 1–5, directly above) except for all or part of the prelicensure tests

B.   Tests in which individual is deficient must be completed during the school year in order to upgrade to the Initial license.

V.   Two-Year Exchange (Teaching or School Specialist) License (valid 2 years)

A.   Exchange Teaching

1.   Complete a state-approved teacher education program through college in home state

2.   Hold a standard valid license in that state

3.   Rectify all deficiencies in initial Kansas requirements during 2-year period

B.   Exchange School Specialist (school counselor, library media, reading specialist)

1.   Complete a state-approved school specialist program in home state

2.   Hold a standard valid school specialist license in that state

3.   Rectify all deficiencies in initial Kansas requirements during 2-year period

a.   Deficiencies may include completion of the content licensure examination; a 3.25 cumulative GPA in graduate course work; and/or recency credit.

4.   Hold a Kansas professional-level teaching license

5.   Neither leadership licenses nor alternative routes to licensure are eligible for exchange licensure.

VI.   Substitute Licenses

A.   Standard Substitute License (valid 5 years; renewable)

1.   Hold a bachelor's degree

2.   Complete a teacher preparation program

3.   Submit 1 fingerprint card for an FBI and Kansas Bureau of Investigation (KBI) background clearance report

B.   Emergency Substitute License (valid for current school year)

1.   Complete a minimum of 60 semester credit hours from regionally accredited college or university

2.   Submit 1 fingerprint card for an FBI and KBI background clearance report

VII.   Provisional License (valid 2 years; renewable)

A.   Provisional Teaching Endorsement License

1. Fifty percent of the program for the new teaching area is complete.
2. A Kansas district must verify assignment of teacher in the provisional subject area at the appropriate level.
3. To qualify for a second provisional, complete half the remaining course work deficiencies (have 75 percent of approved program completed).
4. For Provisional Teaching Endorsement License in Special Education, see VII, A, 1, directly above.
   a. A valid license for general education is required.
   b. Course work in areas of methodology, characteristics, and a practicum is already completed.
   c. Kansas district must verify assignment of teacher in provisional special education area at the appropriate level.
B. Provisional School Specialist License for school counselor, library media, or reading specialist
   1. Hold a valid 5-year professional teaching license
   2. Fifty percent of the school specialist program is completed
   3. Kansas district must verify assignment of applicant as a school specialist.
C. Provisional license is not available for school leadership licenses.
VIII. Restricted Teaching License Alternative Pathway (valid 3 years while employed in school system)
A. Meet all eligibility requirements:
   1. Hold a bachelor's degree or higher from a regionally accredited university
   2. Degree must be in a regular education content area in which applicant desires to teach or equivalent content course work must be completed.
   3. Complete college course work with a cumulative GPA of 2.50
B. Request that the university hosting the alternative route program evaluate transcript to ensure that content requirements for subject matter teaching area are adequate
   1. Develop a plan of study with the alternative certification program staff; program length may vary depending on situation.
C. Locate and apply for a teaching position, verifying that a restricted license is appropriate for it
D. Apply for restricted license, coordinating application among individual, employing school district, and higher education institution providing the course work.
E. Once license is issued, applicant will teach full time while completing required professional education course work towards full licensure.
F. Submit a progress report every year verifying appropriate progress towards a full license; otherwise, restricted license will be cancelled
   1. During first year of teaching, pass content assessment
G. Apply for a full Kansas license with institutional recommendation once applicant successfully completes all course work and testing requirements on plan of study
H. Complete the PLT assessment
IX. School Specialist License
A. Initial School Specialist License
   1. Graduate degree from a regionally accredited college
   2. Complete graduate-level state-approved program

3. 3.25 cumulative GPA in graduate course work
4. Recency: have at least 8 credit hours or 1 year of accredited experience completed within the last 6 years
5. Currently valid Kansas professional teaching license (if applying for library media, reading specialist)
6. Successfully complete a school specialist content assessment
    a. School counselor content test: complete Praxis II test number 0420 — School Guidance and Counseling—with score of 600 or above
    b. Library media specialist content test: complete Praxis II test number 0311—Library Media Specialist—with score of 630 or above
    c. Reading specialist content test: complete Praxis II test number 0300—Reading Specialist—with score of 560 or above
B. Professional School Specialist License
    1. In-state applicants
        a. Hold a currently valid Initial School Specialist License; see IX, A, 1–6, directly above
        b. Complete the performance assessment while employed as a school specialist
    2. Out-of-state applicants
        a. See IX, A, 1–5, directly above,
        and
        b. Successfully complete a school specialist content and performance assessment,
        or
        Three years of recent accredited experience in a school specialist position with a valid professional level license.
X. School Leadership Licenses: includes Program Leadership (supervisor/coordinator); Building Leadership (principal); District Leadership (superintendent)
    A. Initial School Leadership License (valid 2 years)
        1. Graduate degree from a regionally accredited college
        2. Complete graduate-level state-approved program in school leadership
        3. 3.25 cumulative GPA in graduate course work
        4. Recency: at least 8 credit hours or 1 year of accredited experience completed within the last 6 years
        5. Minimum of 3 years of accredited experience under a valid professional license/certificate
        6. School leadership licensure assessment
    B. Professional School Leadership license (valid 5 years)
        1. Hold a currently valid Initial School Leadership License
        2. Complete performance assessment while employed as an administrator
    C. Out-of-state applicants
        1. See X, A, 1–6, directly above
        and
        2. Successfully complete a school leadership content and performance assessment
        or

Three years of recent accredited experience in a school leadership position with a valid professional school leadership license

XI.   New Licenses: Contact the Kansas State Department of Education (see Appendix 1) for full details
   A.   Transitional License (valid 1 year)
      1.   Provides immediate access to practice for:
         a.   Out-of-state applicant without recent credit or experience
         b.   Kansas educator with expired full license who is retired or out of practice
   B.   Interim Alternative License (valid 1 year; renewable for another year)
      1.   Guarantees license for immediate access to practice to out-of-state applicant whose preparation was through an alternative pathway
   C.   Restricted School Specialist License (for school counselor or library media)
      1.   Requires graduate degree and 3 years of professional experience in the counseling or library field
      2.   Must complete professional education during 3-year restricted license period while employed in school system

Endorsements by Levels

I.   Early Childhood: Birth–Grade 3 or Birth–K
   A.   Requires combined general education and special education curriculum: Early Childhood Unified
   B.   Must be done with a general education license: Deaf or Hard-of-Hearing; Visually Impaired; School Psychologist
II.   Early Childhood–Late Childhood: K–6
   A.   Elementary
   B.   Provisional is available for: Adaptive; Functional; Gifted; English for Speakers of Other Languages (ESOL)
III.   Late Childhood–Early Adolescence: Grades 5–8
   A.   Provisional is available for: History Comprehensive; Science; English Language Arts; Mathematics
IV.   Early Adolescence–Late Adolescence/Adulthood: Grades 6–12
   A.   Provisional is available for: English Language Arts; Mathematics; Agriculture; Biology; Business; Chemistry; Earth and Space Science; Family & Consumer Science; History and Government; Journalism; Physics; Psychology; Speech/Theatre; Technology Education; Communication Technology; Power, Energy, Transportation Technology; Production Technology; Adaptive; ESOL; Functional; Gifted
V.   Early Childhood–Late Adolescence/Adulthood: PreK–12
   A.   School Psychologist; Building Leadership; District Leadership; Program Leadership
   B.   Provisional is available for: Deaf or Hard-of-Hearing; Visually Impaired; Adaptive, Functional; Gifted; ESOL; Library Media Specialist; Music; Instrumental Music; Vocal Music; Physical Education; Reading Specialist; School Counselor

Kentucky

General Requirements

I. Recency of preparation
   A. Completed program of preparation within 5 years preceding date of receipt of certification application form,
      or
      Completed 6 semester hours of additional graduate credit within preceding 5 years.
      1. Applicants who have completed a 5th-year program and have 2 years of successful teaching experience within the last 10 years are exempt from the 6-hour requirement.
   B. Initial 1-year certification for special circumstances
      1. Those not meeting recency requirements in I, A, directly above, who have not previously held a regular Kentucky teaching certificate, but who otherwise qualify for certification shall be issued a 1-year initial certificate that
         a. Ends June 30 of next calendar year
         b. Is conditional on 6 semester hours of graduate credit applicable toward the usual renewal requirements being completed by September 1 of year of expiration

II. Duration of teaching certificates
   A. Issued for 5 years, with provisions for subsequent 5-year renewals, provided that by September 1 of the year of expiration, the applicant has completed
      1. Three years of successful teaching experience,
         or
         At least 6 semester hours of graduate credit or the equivalent.
   B. One-year certificates shall be issued for
      1. Beginning teacher internship
         a. Upon successful completion of such internship as judged by majority vote of beginning teacher committee, 1-year certificate will be extended for remainder of the 5-year period.
      2. Initial certification for applicants not meeting recency requirements in I, A, directly above.

III. Renewal of teaching certificates
   A. Requirements for subsequent 5-year renewals
      1. Completion by September 1 of the year of expiration of
         a. Three years of successful teaching experience,
            or
            Six semester hours of graduate credit or the equivalent.
      2. Those who have not yet completed the planned 5th-year program shall
         a. Complete at least 15 semester hours of graduate credit applicable to the program for the first renewal,

and

    b.   Complete the remainder of the program for the second renewal.

  3.   Credits for certificate renewal shall be earned after the issuance of the certificate.

    a.   Any credits earned in excess of minimum requirements shall accumulate and apply toward subsequent renewals.

  4.   Applicants holding a lapsed regular Kentucky teaching certificate shall not be required to take the written tests or to participate in the beginning teacher internship program.

IV.   Out-of-State Applicants

    A.   Those who have completed 2 or more years of acceptable teaching experience outside of the Commonwealth of Kentucky and who otherwise qualify for certification shall not be required to take the written tests or to participate in the beginning teacher internship program.

V.   Requirements for 1-year certificate for beginning teacher internship

    A.   Completion of an approved program of preparation that corresponds to the certificate desired

    B.   Passing scores on the Praxis II Subject Assessment appropriate for each content area in which certification is requested, in addition to the appropriate Principles of Learning and Teaching (PLT) test

      1.   All new teachers are required to take the PLT test in addition to the specialty(ies) test appropriate for the certification they are seeking. Contact the Education Professional Standards Board (see Appendix 1) for detailed information.

    C.   Evidence of full-time employment in a Kentucky school as attested by the prospective employer

VI.   Upon successful completion of the approved program of preparation and upon completion of the designated tests with acceptable scores, the Education Professional Standards Board shall issue a statement of eligibility for employment that shall serve as evidence of eligibility for the 1-year certificate once a teaching position is secured. The statement of eligibility shall be valid for a 5-year period.

Approved Programs

The Commonwealth of Kentucky follows the "approved program" approach to certification. An individual should follow the program in effect at the college or university with the guidance of the college advisor and meet the General Requirements (see above). Applicants interested in certification should contact the Division of Certification (see Appendix 1) for the latest information.

    I.   Interdisciplinary Early Childhood Education (Birth to Primary)

   II.   Elementary School (Primary through Grade 5)

  III.   Middle School (Grades 5 through 9)

    A.   Preparation in one major or equivalent,

       or

    B.   Preparation in two teaching fields selected from the following: English and communications, mathematics, science, and social studies

1. Candidates who choose to prepare simultaneously for teaching in the middle school and for teaching exceptional children are required to complete only one middle school teaching field.

IV.   Secondary School (Grades 8 through 12)

    A. Preparation includes one or more of the following specializations: English, mathematics, social studies, biological science, physics, chemistry, or earth science.

V.   Middle/Secondary School (Grades 5 through 12)

    A. Preparation includes one or more of the following specializations: agriculture, business and marketing, family and consumer science, industrial education, technology education.

VI.   Elementary/Middle/Secondary School (Primary through Grade 12)

    A. Preparation includes one or more of the following specializations: art, foreign language (Arabic, Chinese, French, German, Japanese, Latin, Russian, or Spanish), health, physical education, integrated music, vocal music, instrumental music, school media librarian.

VII.   Exceptional Children (Primary through Grade 12, and for collaborating with teachers to design and deliver programs for pre-primary children)

    A. Preparation includes one or more of the following specializations: learning and behavior disorders; moderate and severe disabilities; hearing impaired or hearing impaired/sign proficiency; visually impaired; communication disorders (master's level); speech language pathology assistant (bachelor's level).

VIII.   Endorsements to Certificates (Primary through Grade 12)

    A. Computer science (8–12), English as a second language (P–12), gifted education (P–12), driver education (8–12), reading and writing (P–12), instructional computer technology (P–12), learning and behavior disorders (8–12), school nutrition (P–12), and school safety (P–12)

    B. Restricted Base Certificates: psychology (8–12), sociology (8–12), journalism (8–12), speech/media communications (8–12), theater (P–12), dance (P–12), computer information systems (P–12), English as a second language (P–12), school nurse (P–12), school social worker (P–12), junior reserve officer training corps (8–12)

IX.   Professional Certificate for Instructional Leadership

    A. Certification is offered for the following positions: Supervisor of Instruction, Level 1; Supervisor of Instruction, Level 2; Principal, All Grades, Level 1; Principal, All Grades, Level 2; Director of Special Education; Director of Pupil Personnel; School Psychologist; Guidance Counselor; and School Superintendent.

Principal, All Grades

I.   Requirements for Principal, All Grades, Level 1

    A. As prerequisites for the Level 1 program of preparation for the initial Professional Certificate for Instructional Leadership, the candidate shall

        1. Have been admitted to the preparation program on the basis of criteria, developed by the teacher-education institution,

        2. Have completed 3 years of full-time teaching experience,

        3. Have completed the master's degree,

4. Qualify for a Kentucky teaching certificate.
5. Successfully complete the new School Leaders Licensure Assessment (SLLA) and the Kentucky-developed Educational Administration test.
    a. Applicants with out-of-state principal certification and 2 years of verified full-time principal experience are exempt from the SLLA.
6. All applicants without 2 years of verified full-time principal experience must successfully complete a 1-year Kentucky principal internship program.
B. The initial Professional Certificate for Instructional Leadership shall be issued for a period of 1 year upon successful completion of Level 1 preparation and the tests prescribed and upon obtaining employment for an internship position as principal or assistant principal. Upon proof of employment as a principal/assistant principal, the certificate shall be extended for 4 years.
C. The certificate shall be renewed subsequently for 5-year periods. The first renewal shall require the completion of the curriculum identified as the Level 2 program in the curriculum standards. Each 5-year renewal thereafter shall require the completion of 2 years of experience as a principal, or 3 semester hours of additional graduate credit related to the position of school principal, or 42 hours of approved training selected from programs approved for the Kentucky Effective Leadership Training Program.
D. If a lapse in certification occurs because of lack of completion of the Level 2 preparation, the certificate may be reissued for a 5-year period upon successful completion of the Level 2 preparation. If a certificate lapses with Level 2 preparation, but because of lack of the renewal requirements, the certificate may be reissued after the completion of an additional 6 semester hours of graduate study appropriate to the program.
E. Persons applying for the Professional Certificate for Instructional Leadership who satisfy the curriculum requirements and all other prerequisites and who have completed at least 2 years of successful full-time experience, including at least 140 days per year, as a school principal, within a 10-year period prior to making application will be exempt from the internship requirements for school principals but shall be required to pass the written examinations.
II. Standards for School Principal
A. Individuals must meet the standards for principals taken from the Standards for School Leaders developed by the Interstate School Leaders Licensure Consortium (ISLLC). Please contact the Kentucky Division of Certification (see Appendix 1) for additional information.

Guidance Counselor

I. Provisional Certificate Requirements, Primary–Grade 12 (valid 5 years)
A. Complete an approved master's level program in guidance counseling
B. Renewable with proof of completion of at least 9 semester hours of graduate credit in areas of counseling or guidance counseling
II. Standard Certificate Requirements, Primary–Grade 12 (valid 5 years)
A. Option 1

1. Successfully complete an approved master's level program in guidance counseling
2. Successfully complete additional 3–6 credit hours from an approved graduate-level counseling or guidance counseling program
3. One year of full-time employment as a provisionally certified guidance counselor in an accredited public or private school
4. Hold a valid Kentucky Professional teaching certificate, *and*
5. Complete at least 1 year of full-time classroom teaching experience

B. Option 2
   1. See II, A, 1 and 2, directly above
   2. Complete at least 2 years of successful employment as a provisional full-time certified guidance counselor

C. Renewable upon completion of Effective Instructional Leadership Act (EILA) hours as specified by the Kentucky Department of Education by September 1 of the year of expiration

Library Media Specialist

I. This standards- and performance-based credential is awarded for work with all grade levels after the following requirements have been met:
   A. Transcript reflecting appropriate grades and courses,
   B. Recommendation of the college or university,
   C. Praxis II: Library Media Specialist test with satisfactory score, *and*
   D. Internship.
II. For applicants with 2 years of experience as a Library Media Specialist, C and D, directly above, may be waived. Contact the Education Professional Standards Board (see Appendix 1) for more detailed information.

School Psychologist

I. Provisional Certificate for School Psychologist
   A. Requirements
      1. Recommendation of the applicant's preparing institution
      2. Successful completion of the institution's approved program of preparation
      3. Passing score on the required assessment
   B. Issued for a duration period of 1 year; may be renewed for an additional year if the individual is serving in the position of the school psychologist on at least a half-time basis.
   C. Individual serves under the supervision of the preparing institution. During this first year of service, the employer of the Provisional Certificate shall permit the individual to engage in the preparing institution's internship component.
   D. Internship may be served full-time during 1 school year or half-time during 2 consecutive years.

II. Standard Certificate for School Psychologist
   A. Option 1
      1. Completion of an approved program of preparation that corresponds to the certificate at a teacher-education institution that adheres to the National Association of School Psychologists Standards for Training Programs
      2. Completion of the appropriate assessment and a passing score as established in state regulations
   B. Option 2
      1. Possession of a valid certificate as a nationally certified school psychologist issued by the National School Psychology Certification System
   C. The Standard Certificate for School Psychologist shall be issued for a period of 5 years and may be renewed for subsequent 5-year periods with completion of one of the following:
      1. At least 3 years of experience as a school psychologist within each certification period and 72 hours of continuing professional development activities, *or*
      2. Six semester hours of graduate training related to school psychology.

Teacher for Gifted Education

I. Standards for Certificate Endorsement
   A. Classroom teaching certificate
   B. One year of teaching experience
   C. The completion of an approved graduate-level curriculum
      1. At least 9 semester hours of credit giving emphasis to the following content:
         a. Nature and needs of gifted education
         b. Assessment and/or counseling of the gifted
         c. Curriculum development for the gifted
         d. Strategies and materials for teaching the gifted
         e. Creative studies
      2. At least 3 semester hours of credit in a supervised practicum for gifted education; however, with 2 years of experience as a teacher for gifted, the practicum requirement may be waived.

Louisiana

Standard Certificates

I. Type C/Level 1 (valid for 3 years)
   A. Baccalaureate degree, including an approved teacher-education program, student teaching, and 1-year internship,
      or
      3 years of teaching experience in the program area
   B. Credits distributed among general education, content focus area, knowledge of the learner, and methodology in teaching
   C. Appropriate NTE/Praxis scores for initial certification
II. Type B (valid for life for continuous service)/Level 2 (valid for 5 years)
   A. Baccalaureate or higher degree, including completion of an approved teacher-education program
   B. See I, B, directly above
   C. Three years of successful teaching experience in certified field
   D. Successful completion of the State Evaluation Program
III. Type A (valid for life for continuous service)/Level 3 (valid for 5 years)
   A. Baccalaureate degree, including completion of an approved teacher-education program
   B. See I, B, directly above
   C. Master's or higher degree from an approved institution
   D. Five years of successful teaching experience in certified field
   E. Successful completion of the State Evaluation Program

Basic Certification

I. Grades PK–3
   A. General education course work hours: English (12), mathematics (9), sciences (9), social studies (6), and arts (3)
   B. Focus areas course work hours: nursery school and kindergarten (12); reading/language arts (12); and mathematics (9)
II. Grades 1–5
   A. General education course work hours: English (12), mathematics (12), sciences (15), social studies (12), and arts (3)
   B. Focus areas course work hours: reading/language arts (12); and mathematics (9)
III. Grades 4–8
   A. Focus on greater depth in content in generic or 2 in-depth teaching areas
   B. General education course work hours: English (12), mathematics (12), sciences (15), social studies (12), and arts (3)

    C.   Focus areas course work hours
        1.   In-depth teaching areas #1 and #2 each require:
            a.   Seven or more hours in English/social studies/mathematics *or* science, *and*
            b.   Nineteen total hours in general education and focus area courses.

IV. Grades 6–12
    A.   Focus on greater depth in content in primary and secondary teaching area
    B.   General education course work hours: English (6), mathematics (6), sciences (9), social studies (6), and arts (3)
    C.   Primary teaching area requires 22 or more hours if in science,
        or
        Twenty-five or more hours if in English, social studies, or mathematics,
        or
        Thirty-one or more hours if in other areas.
        1.   General education (if applicable) and focus area hours should equal 31 total hours.
    D.   Secondary teaching area requires 13 or more hours if in English, social studies, or mathematics,
        or
        Ten or more hours if in science,
        or
        Nineteen or more hours if in other areas.
        1.   General education (if applicable) and focus area hours should equal 19 total hours.

New Certification Areas and Courses

I. Common Elements of Basic Certification for All Grade Levels
    A.   General education course work
        1.   Same general course work areas and hours (e.g., 54 hours) for Grades 1–5 and 4–8
    B.   Knowledge of the learner and learning environment: 15 hours
        1.   Same general course work areas and hours (e.g., 15 hours) for all PK–12 teachers
    C.   Teaching Methodology
    D.   Student Teaching
        1.   Same requirements and hours (e.g., 9 hours) for all PK–12 teachers
    E.   Total hours: 124

II. Grades PK–3
    A.   Methodology and Teaching
        1.   Teaching Methodology: 6 hours
        2.   Student Teaching: same requirements and hours (e.g., 9 hours) for all PK–12 teachers
            a.   Students must spend a minimum of 270 clock hours in student teaching with at least 180 of such hours spent in actual teaching, a substantial portion of which shall be on an all-day basis.

B. See I, B, 1, directly above
C. Flexible hours for the university's use: 22 hours
   1. It is recommended that preservice teachers be provided a minimum of 180 hours of direct teaching experience in field-based settings prior to student teaching.
D. See I, E, directly above

III. Grades 1–5

A. See II, A–D, directly above, except that flexible hours for university's use are 19

IV. Grades 4–8

A. Methodology and Teaching
   1. Teaching Methodology: 9 hours
   2. Student Teaching: See II, A, 2, a, directly above
   3. Reading: 6 hours
B. See I, B, 1, directly above
C. Flexible hours for the university's use
   1. Two in-depth teaching areas: 17–20 hours
D. See I, E, directly above

V. Grades 6–12

A. Methodology and Teaching
   1. Teaching Methodology: 6 hours
   2. Student Teaching: See II, A, 2, a, directly above
   3. Reading: 3 hours
B. See I, B, 1, directly above
C. Flexible hours for the university's use: 17–26
D. See I, E, directly above

General/Special Education, Mild-Moderate Certification

I. Elementary Grades 1–5

A. Complete approved blended general/special education mild-moderate program for elementary grade levels 1–5, with program focus on areas of reading/language arts and mathematics. Total required semester hours in program 126
   1. General education, semester hours 54
   To include English (12), mathematics (12), sciences (15), social studies (12), and arts (3)
   2. Focus area, special education semester hours 21
   Must meet Council for Exceptional Children (CEC) performance-based standards for accreditation and licensure
   3. Knowledge of the learner and learning environment, with emphasis on the elementary school student, semester hours 15
   Course work to address needs of regular and exceptional child, including child/adolescent development or psychology, educational psychology, the learner with special needs, classroom organization and management, and multicultural education

4. Methodology and teaching, semester hours.. 33
   Teaching methodology and strategies, including science and social
   science (6), math content/methodology (6), student teaching, 50% of which
   must include working with and actual teaching of students with disabilities (9)
5. Flexible hours for university's use, semester hours 3
6. In addition to the student teaching experience, actual teaching experiences
   (in addition to observations) in classroom settings during sophomore, junior,
   and senior years within schools with varied socioeconomic and cultural
   characteristics are required.
   a. A minimum of 180 hours of direct teaching experience in field-based
      settings prior to student teaching is required.

II. Middle Grades 4–8
   A. Complete approved blended general/special education mild-moderate program
      for middle grades 4–8, with program focus on special education and one
      middle school content area. Total required semester hours in program 123
      1. See I, A, 1, directly above
      2. Focus area, special education and 1 middle school content area,
         semester hours.. 42
         Combined general education and focus area (19); middle school content
         area—English, mathematics, science, or social studies (21); special
         education content, which must meet CEC performance-based standards
         for accreditation and licensure (21).
      3. See I, A, 3, directly above, except with emphasis on the middle school
         student
      4. Methodology and teaching, semester hours.. 21
         Reading and literacy content/methodology (6), teaching methodology
         and strategies (6), student teaching, 50% of which must include working
         with and actual teaching of students with disabilities (9)
      5. Flexible hours for university's use, semester hours 3–16
      6. In addition to the student teaching experience, actual teaching experiences
         (in addition to observations) in classroom settings during sophomore,
         junior, and senior years within schools with varied socioeconomic and
         cultural characteristics are required.
         a. A minimum of 180 hours of direct teaching experience in field-based
            settings prior to student teaching is required.

III. Secondary Grades 6–12
   A. Complete approved blended general/special education mild-moderate
      program for secondary grade levels 6–12, with program focus on special
      education and one high school content area. Total required semester hours
      in program 123
      1. General education, semester hours 30
         To include English (6), mathematics (6), sciences (9), social studies (6),
         and arts (3)
      2. Focus area, special education and 1 high school content focus area,
         semester hours.. 51

Combined general education and focus area (31); secondary school content area (30); special education content, which must meet CEC performance-based standards for accreditation and licensure (21).

3. See I, A, 3, directly above, except with emphasis on the secondary school student
4. Methodology and teaching, semester hours 21
   Reading and literacy content/methodology (6), teaching methodology and strategies (6), student teaching, 50% of which must include working with and actual teaching of students with disabilities (9)
5. Flexible hours for university's use, semester hours 16–29
6. In addition to the student teaching experience, actual teaching experiences (in addition to observations) in classroom settings during sophomore, junior, and senior years within schools with varied socioeconomic and cultural characteristics are required.
   a. A minimum of 180 hours of direct teaching experience in field-based settings prior to student teaching is required.

Administrators, Supervisors, and Special Service Personnel

I. Educational Leadership Certificate—Level 1. For school and district leadership positions such as principal, assistant principal, parish or city supervisor of instruction, supervisor of child welfare and attendance, or comparable positions
   A. Eligibility Requirements
      1. Hold or be eligible to hold valid Louisiana Type A or Level 3 teaching certificate; see Standard Certificates, III, A–E, above
      2. Have completed competency-based graduate degree preparation program in area of educational leadership from regionally accredited institution of higher education
      3. Earn passing score on School Leaders Licensure Assessment (SLLA), in accordance with state requirements
      4. Those meeting requirements in I, A, 1 and 2, directly above, are eligible for a Level 1 Educational Leader Certificate. Upon employment as school district educational leaders, new employees must enroll in 2-year Educational Leader Induction Program—to be completed in no more than 3 years—under direction of Louisiana Department of Education.

II. Educational Leadership Certificate—Level 1 (Alternate Path). For same positions as in I, directly above.
   A. Eligibility Requirements
      1. See I, A, 1, directly above
      2. Have completed a graduate degree program from a regionally accredited institution of higher education
      3. Have met competency-based requirements by completing individualized program of educational leadership—based on screening of each candidate's competencies when entering program—from a regionally accredited institution of higher education

4. Earn passing score on SLLA in accordance with state requirements
5. See I, A, 4, directly above, except candidates must meet requirements listed in II, A, 1–4, directly above

III. Educational Leadership Certificate—Level 2: Professional (valid for 5 years; renewable)
A. Eligibility Requirements for Initial Certification
1. Hold a valid Level 1 Educational Leader Certificate
2. Complete 2-year induction program—in no more than 3 years—under guidance of mentor trained in accordance with standards set by Louisiana Department of Education. Induction period begins upon individual's first full-time administrative appointment (whether permanent or acting) as assistant principal, principal, parish or city supervisor of instruction, supervisor of child welfare and attendance, or comparable school district leader position.
3. Earn passing score on Interstate School Leaders Licensure Consortium (ISLLC) School Leader Portfolio Assessment, in accordance with state requirements
B. Renewal Requirements
1. Complete minimum of 150 continuing learning units of professional development over 5 years. These must be consistent with leader's Individual Professional Growth Plan (IPGP) and must include updating educational leader portfolio.

IV. Education Leader Certificate—Level 3: Superintendent (valid 5 years; certification period activated with candidate's first full-time appointment as Superintendent)
A. Eligibility Requirements
1. Hold valid Louisiana Level 2 Educational Leader Certificate
2. Have completed 5 years of successful administrative or management experience in education at level of principal or above
3. Earn passing score on the School Superintendent Assessment (SSA), in keeping with state requirements
B. Renewal Requirements
1. See III, B, 1, directly above

V. Teacher Leader Endorsement (Optional). Teachers who hold valid Type B or Level 2 or higher Louisiana teaching certificate may add this endorsement to their certificate. Contact Louisiana Department of Education (see Appendix 1) for eligibility requirements and renewal guidelines.

Counselor K–12

I. Counselor in the School Setting
A. Hold a valid Louisiana teaching certificate
B. Hold a master's degree
1. In school counseling from a regionally accredited institution,
or
2. With the equivalent hours and courses required for a master's degree in school counseling

C. Complete a total of 24 semester hours of graduate course work distributed so that at least 1 course is in each of these basic areas:
   1. Principles and administration of school counseling programs
   2. Career and lifestyle development
   3. Individual appraisal
   4. Counseling theory and practice
   5. Group processes
   6. Human growth and development
   7. Social and cultural foundations in counseling
   8. Supervised practicum in a school setting

II. Professional Counselor in the School Setting
   A. Issued to an applicant who has met the requirements for counselor in the school setting (I, A–C, directly above), and holds current licensure as a Licensed Professional Counselor (LPC) in Louisiana

III. Please contact the Louisiana Department of Education (see Appendix 1) for information on certification as Ancillary Counselor K–12 without a teaching certificate.

School Librarian

I. Requirements
   A. Elementary or secondary school teaching certificate
   B. Library science courses, semester hours 18
       To include elementary and/or secondary school library materials (9); organization, administration, and interpretation of elementary and/or secondary school library services (6); and elementary and/or secondary school library practice (3)

Regulations for Out-of-State Application for Classroom Teacher

I. Requirements for Level 1 Certificate
   A. Bachelor's degree from a regionally accredited institution, completion of an approved teacher-education program, including student teaching, and a regular certificate from the state where the applicant completed the program,
       or
       Bachelor's degree from a regionally accredited institution, a regular certificate from another state, and student teaching or 3 years of teaching in certified field
   B. If applicant has not taught within 5 years immediately preceding date of application or if this will be a first employment in Louisiana, he or she must complete 6 hours of resident credit, or extension credit, in areas relative to his or her field.
   C. Appropriate NTE/Praxis scores
   D. These certificates are governed by laws and regulations applying to certification in Louisiana.
   E. An applicant who lacks the appropriate NTE/Praxis scores but meets all other requirements may be issued a 3-year nonrenewable certificate.

Maine

Fingerprinting through a Maine-approved site/process is required prior to issuing any certificate, whether new or renewing, regardless of whether the applicant is employed. The same process is required for all contracted personnel, such as speech clinicians, psychologists, and occupational therapists, as well as substitute teachers and all support staff.

Teacher and Educational Specialist Certificates

I. Targeted Need Certificate (valid 1 year; renewable twice)
   A. Bachelor's degree from accredited college
   B. Teaching in a subject area designated as a shortage area
   C. Six semester hours in the content area
   D. Affidavit of employment from local school district
II. Conditional Certificate (valid 1 year; renewable twice)
   A. Bachelor's degree from a regionally accredited college
   B. Completion of all content area (24 semester hours) course requirements
   C. Affidavit of employment from local school district
III. Provisional Certificate (valid 2 years; renewable in special circumstances)
   A. Bachelor's degree from regionally accredited institution with a 2-year concentration in liberal arts
   B. Completion of an approved teacher-education program (professional and subject matter), including student teaching
   C. Qualifying scores on the Pre-Professional Skills Test Praxis I
   D. Qualifying scores on Praxis II
IV. Professional Certificate (valid for 5 years; renewable)
   A. Meet requirements of a provisional certificate
   B. Two years of teaching experience
   C. Recommendation for professional certificate from support system following successful completion of a Teacher Action Plan, including 6 classroom observations
V. Master Certificate (valid for 5 years; optional; renewable)
   A. Recommendation for a master certificate from the support system following completion of a Teacher or Educational Specialist Action Plan based on the standards for National Board certification as developed by the National Board of Professional Teaching Standards

Endorsements

I. Elementary Teacher (K–8)
   A. Bachelor's degree from an accredited institution in an approved program for the education of elementary teachers which includes at least 6 semester hours in each

of the 4 liberal arts areas (math, English, science, social sciences), together with the formal recommendation of the preparing institution, Praxis I and Praxis II,

or

Bachelor's degree from an accredited institution with at least 6 semester hours in each of the 4 areas noted above, professional course work, student teaching, Praxis I, Praxis II, and PLT (Principles of Learning and Teaching);

and

Affidavit of employment from local school district.

    B.   Professional education courses, to include:

        1.   Teaching exceptional children in the regular classroom

        2.   Effective instruction through content area methods

            a.   At least 12 semester hours to include all of the following: mathematics, reading, science, and social studies

            b.   At least 3 semester hours from one of the following: language arts, process writing, children's literature, and whole language

        3.   One academic semester or 15 weeks of full-time student teaching experience or a combination of part-time and full-time student teaching equivalent to 15 weeks

    C.   Renewal for a professional certificate

        1.   Completion of 6 hours of approved study, preferably academic study in the endorsement area

        2.   Recommendation of the support system

II.   Middle Level (5–8): endorsements for English/language arts, mathematics, science, social studies, or a world language

    A.   Possession of a valid provisional or professional Maine teaching certificate (K–8, K–3, 7–12, or K–12),

    B.   7–12 endorsement area of authorization, semester hours 24

        1.   Science endorsement must include at least 9 semester hours each in life science and physical science

    C.   Other K–12 or foreign-language endorsement areas, semester hours 24

    D.   Praxis II middle level content exam

III.   Secondary Level (7–12): endorsements for English/language arts, mathematics, life science, physical science, and social studies

    A.   Bachelor's degree from an accredited institution in an approved program for teachers in the relevant subject area that includes a major in that subject area, together with the formal recommendation of the preparing institution,

or

Bachelor's degree from an accredited institution with a concentration in the liberal arts, plus

        1.   At least 24 semester hours of credit in the relevant subject area for English/language arts, mathematics, social studies, and life science or physical science

    B.   Professional education courses

        1.   Teaching exceptional children in the regular classroom

        2.   Content area methods

        3.   One academic semester or 15 weeks of full-time student teaching experience

C. Praxis I, Praxis II, and PLT
D. Renewal for a professional certificate
    1. See Endorsements, I, C, 1.

Administration Certificates

I. Superintendent Certificate (valid for 5 years; renewable with specific requirements)
    A. Bachelor's degree and master's degree (at a minimum) from an accredited institution. It is recommended, but not required, that the master's degree be in educational administration.
    B. Evidence of 3 years of satisfactory teaching experience or 3 years of equivalent teaching experience in an instructional setting
    C. Evidence of 3 years of previous administrative experience in schools or equivalent experience as an administrator in an institutional setting
    D. Evidence of a basic level of knowledge appropriate to the certificate demonstrated by course work in 13 specified categories
        1. Past experience—such as performance upon examinations or completion of specialized programs approved for this purpose—may be accepted, upon documentation, in lieu of one or more of these course requirements.
    E. A candidate may demonstrate a basic knowledge of I, D, directly above, through course work, equivalent training experiences, or by meeting a minimum score of 165 on the School Superintendent Assessment. For details, contact the Maine Department of Education (see Appendix 1).
    F. Knowledge of Maine education laws
    G. Completion of an approved internship or practicum in a school setting
        1. Graduate-level, state-approved administrator internship or practicum program of at least 15 weeks,
            or
            One full year of employment as an assistant supervisor or a superintendent,
            or
            Mentorship program lasting 1 academic year in which the mentor is a school superintendent
II. Assistant Superintendent Certificate (valid for 5 years)
    A. See Administration Certificates, I, A–F, directly above, except that only 1 year of previous administrative experience (or an approved 1-year administrative internship) is required.
III. Principal Certificate (valid for 5 years)
    A. See Administration Certificates, I, A, B, and D, directly above
IV. Assistant Principal Certificate (valid for 5 years)
    A. Bachelor's degree from an accredited institution
    B. Evidence of 3 years of satisfactory public school teaching experience or 3 years of equivalent teaching experience
    C. Evidence of a basic level of knowledge appropriate to the certificate demonstrated by course work in 3 specified areas

V.   Other Administrative Certificates (valid for 5 years) Teaching principal, curriculum coordinator/instructional supervisor, director of special education, director of secondary vocational education, assistant director of secondary vocational education, adult and community education director, and assistant adult and community education director. For details, contact the Maine Department of Education (see Appendix 1).

School Guidance Counselor (K–12)

I.   Requirements
- A.   Master's or doctorate degree from an accredited institution and an approved program to prepare school guidance counselors, together with the formal recommendation of the preparing institution
- B.   Minimum of 33 semester units in specified areas
- C.   Completion of an approved graduate-level, K–12 internship of 1 academic year that relates to the duties of a school guidance counselor in a school setting
- D.   Two full years of work experience
- E.   Praxis II
- F.   Renewal
    1.   Completion of 6 hours of approved study, preferably academic study in the certificate area, and recommendation by local support system

Library-Media Specialist (K–12)

I.   Academic Requirements
- A.   Holder of a Maine provisional or professional-level certificate with a subject area endorsement
- B.   Completion of an approved graduate program for the preparation of school library-media specialists,
    and
    Specified area courses in library science, semester hours 24
- C.   Praxis II

II.   Valid 2 years

III.   Renewal
- A.   See School Guidance Counselor, I, F, 1, above.

Maryland

Types of Certificates

Note: Individuals seeking employment with local school systems in positions requiring a certificate issued by the Maryland State Department of Education are required to undergo a criminal background investigation. Contact the Certification Branch of the State Department of Education (see Appendix 1) for details.

I. Professional Eligibility Certificate and Standard Professional Certificate I
  A. Definitions
    1. The Professional Eligibility Certificate (valid for 5 years; renewable) is the initial certificate issued to an applicant who meets all certification requirements but is not currently employed as a professional in a Maryland local school system.
    2. The Standard Professional Certificate I (valid for 5 years; renewable once) is issued to an applicant who meets all certification requirements and is employed by a Maryland local school system or an accredited nonpublic school.
      a. Complete 6 semester hours of acceptable credit to obtain the 5-year renewal, *or*
      b. Before the expiration of the Standard Professional Certificate I, the holder, employed as a professional with 3 years of satisfactory, professional, school-related experience, shall meet the requirements for the Standard Professional Certificate II or the Advanced Professional Certificate.
  B. Requirements
    1. All applicants must hold a bachelor's or higher degree from an institution of higher education,
      a. An applicant for certification in a vocational education area that does not require a bachelor's degree is exempt from this requirement as well as from I, B, 7, a–c, directly below
      and either
    2. Complete a Maryland-approved program for teacher certification (consult list on website—see Appendix 1—under "Teacher Preparation"), *or*
    3. Complete an approved out-of-state teacher education program offered by an institution of higher education (IHE) leading to teacher certification,
      a. IHE must be in the state in which the institution is located, for which a comparable Maryland certificate is issued *or*
    4. Complete a graduate program offered by an IHE leading to specialist, administrator, or supervisor certification, if the requisite experience is submitted,
      a. See I, B, 3, a, directly above *or*

5. Present a valid professional state certificate,
   a. Also, present verification of at least 27 months of satisfactory school-related experience on the basis of which application is being made for a like or comparable Maryland certificate during the past 7 years
   b. If applicable to the certification being sought, meet the degree requirement under the Code of Maryland Regulations (COMAR) for specialists, administrators, and supervisors,
   or
6. Present a valid professional certification from a country other than the United States
   a. See I, B, 5, a and b, directly above,
   or
7. Present verification of satisfactory completion of the requirements of a specific area under COMAR for teachers, specialists, or administrators and supervisors, with their required grade,
   or
8. A local school system may request a Maryland Resident Teacher Certificate for an applicant who does not meet the requirements for a professional certificate, if specific requirements are satisfied. Contact Department of Education (see Appendix 1) for details.
9. All candidates applying for initial teacher certificate are required to present qualifying scores on the Praxis I Academic Skills Assessments, ACT, SAT, or GRE as well as the appropriate content and pedagogy assessments where required (Praxis II or ACTFL).
   a. While out-of-state candidates who do not hold a professional certificate from their respective state must meet Maryland's qualifying scores, some out-of-state candidates may be eligible for a test exemption. Contact Department of Education (see Appendix 1).

II. Standard Professional Certificate II (valid 5 years; not renewable)
   A. Complete the Standard Professional Certificate I
   B. Verify 3 years of satisfactory professional experience
   C. Complete 6 semester hours of acceptable credit
   D. Submit a professional development plan for the Advanced Professional Certificate
   E. Before the expiration of the Standard Professional Certificate II, the holder shall meet the requirements for the Advanced Professional Certificate.

III. Advanced Professional Certificate (valid 5 years; renewable)
   A. Verify 3 years of full-time professional school-related experience
   B. Complete 6 semester hours of acceptable credits
   C. Hold master's or higher degree in a certification area directly related to public school education, including 6 semester hours related to the professional's discipline,
   or
   D. Complete 36 semester hours of post-baccalaureate course work, including 21 hours of graduate credit and a minimum of 6 credits related to the professional's discipline

1. Only courses that carry grades of C or higher are eligible to fulfill this requirement.

    or

E. Obtain National Board certification and earn a minimum of 12 semester hours of approved graduate course work related to the professional's discipline

F. An applicant for the Advanced Professional Certificate in a vocational education area that does not require a bachelor's degree for initial certification shall also complete

    1. A planned program of 36 semester hours taken at an accredited institution (of which no more than 6 may be Department-approved continuing education units for trade-related courses)

IV. Conditional Certificate (valid 2 years; may be reissued once only)

   A. Issued at request of local superintendent of schools only if local school system is unable to fill a position with a qualified person holding a professional certificate

   B. Applicant must

    1. Hold a bachelor's or higher degree from an IHE but fail to meet requirements for the Standard Professional Certificate

      a. If hired in a vocational education area that does not require a bachelor's degree, applicant may be issued the Conditional Teacher Nondegree Certificate.

    2. Present a professional development plan

V. Resident Teacher Certificate (valid 2 years; nonrenewable)

   A. Requirements

    1. Bachelor's degree from an institution of higher learning

    2. Qualifying score on a Department-approved test in basic skills or a comparable state-approved test in basic skills

    3. Qualifying score on a Department-approved content area test or a comparable state-approved content test

    4. Official documentation from local superintendent of schools of completion of standards-based pre-employment training, including:

      a. Minimum of 90 hours of study [which may be a combination of semester and clock hours, based on Maryland Essential Dimensions of Teaching or the Interstate New Teacher Assessment and Support Consortium standards] and include:

        i. Elementary reading processes and acquisition,

          or

        ii. Secondary teaching reading in the content areas part I.

      b. Enrollment in a Department-approved alternative preparation program

      c. Internship that was part of a Department-approved alternative preparation program

   B. Instead of V, A, above, applicant may present official verification from local superintendent of schools of a Department-approved valid alternative certificate.

   C. Local superintendent of schools shall file a written request with State Superintendent of Schools for Resident Teacher Certificate to be issued after applicant has met requirements of V, A, directly above.

D. Applicant holding Resident Teacher Certificate shall be eligible for Standard Professional Certificate upon receipt by Department of the following:
1. Completion of approved alternative program as verified by program provider,
2. Qualifying score on applicable Department-approved pedagogy test, *and*
3. Satisfactory teaching performance during period of residency as verified by local superintendent of schools.

Early Childhood Education (PreK–Grade 3)

I. Complete approved teacher preparation program that leads to certification in Early Childhood Education, PreK through grade 3, *or*

II. Complete the following requirements:
A. General Education
1. Bachelor's or higher degree from IHE with a major in interdisciplinary studies or a major in an academic field taught in early childhood education, including course work (semester hours) in mathematics (12), science (12), social studies (9), and English (9), *or*
2. Bachelor's or higher degree from an IHE and no less than 48 semester hours of content course work, including mathematics (12), science (12), social studies (9), and English (9).
B. Professional Education
1. Twenty-seven semester hours of course work, including 12 semester hours of specific course work in reading instruction and a course in each of the following at appropriate age or grade level of certificate:
a. Child development
b. Human learning
c. Teaching methodology
d. Inclusion of special needs student populations
e. Assessment of students
f. Processes and acquisition of reading skills
g. Best practices in reading instruction that include cueing systems of graphophonics, semantics, and syntactics
h. Use of reading assessment data to improve instruction
i. Materials for teaching reading to gain literary experience, to perform a task, and to read for information
C. Teaching Experience
1. Supervised experience in a public or accredited nonpublic school setting at the prekindergarten or kindergarten or primary age/grade level, *or*
2. One year of satisfactory full-time teaching experience in a public or accredited nonpublic school setting at the prekindergarten or kindergarten and primary age/grade level

3.   Course work listed in II, B, 1, f–i, directly above, may also be taken through Maryland local school system–sponsored CPDs approved by the Department of Education.

D.   At least 50 percent of the course work in II, A and B, directly above, must be taken at same institution or consortium of institutions, and each course submitted to fulfill credit requirement must be completed with a grade of C or better.

Elementary Education (Grade 1–6) and Middle School

I.   Complete approved teacher preparation program that leads to certification in Elementary Education, grades 1–6,
or

II.   Complete the following requirements:
A.   Identical to Early Childhood Education, II, A–D, above, except professional education courses and teaching experience should be at elementary and middle school level

Secondary Education (Grade 7–12)

I.   Secondary Academic Certification Areas
Note: Areas marked with asterisk (*) apply only to those not completing a state-approved teacher preparation program and have specific requirements. Contact the Department of Education (see Appendix 1).
A.   Agriculture (agribusiness) and renewable natural resources;* biology; business education; chemistry; computer science; data processing;* earth/space science; English; environmental science; family and consumer sciences;* family and consumer sciences/career technology education;* foreign language (classical); foreign language (modern); geography; health occupations education;* history; marketing education–teacher-coordinator;* mathematics; physical science; physics; social studies;* speech communication; technology education;* theater; trades and industry;* work-based learning coordinator*
B.   Specialty areas (PreK–12): art; English for speakers of other languages; environmental education; health; music; physical education

II.   Requirements
A.   General Education
1.   Bachelor's or higher degree from an IHE with a major in a certification area,
or
2.   Complete 36 semester hours of content course work in one of the certification areas
a.   No less than 50 percent of content course work shall be taken at same institution
b.   No less than 12 semester hours of content course work shall be upper-division course work
B.   Professional Education
1.   Twenty-one semester hours of course work, including a course of at least 3 semester hours in each of the following at the appropriate age or grade

level of the certificate: child or adolescent development; human learning; teaching methodology; inclusion of special needs student populations; and assessment of students,
and

2. Six semester hours covering specific course work in reading instruction, which may also be taken through Maryland local school system–sponsored CPDs that are Department-approved. Contact the Department of Education (see Appendix 1) for details.

3. No less than 50 percent of the required professional education course work in B, 1 and 2, directly above, shall be taken at the same institution.

C. Teaching Experience

1. Supervised experience in a public or accredited nonpublic school setting at appropriate age or grade level and in subject area for which applicant is seeking certification,
or

2. One year of satisfactory full-time teaching experience in a public or accredited nonpublic school setting at appropriate age or grade level and in certification subject area.

D. See Early Childhood Education, II, A and D, above

Administration

I. Administrator I (supervisor of instruction, or assistant principal) requirements:

A. Master's degree from an IHE

B. Twenty-seven months of satisfactory performance either teaching, or on a professional certificate, or as a certified specialist,
and

C. Complete one of the following:

1. Department-approved program that includes outcomes in Maryland instructional leadership framework and leads to certification as supervisor of instruction, assistant principal, or principal,
or

2. Approved program in accordance with interstate agreement that leads to certification as supervisor of instruction, assistant principal, or principal,
or

3. Eighteen semester hours of graduate course work at an IHE to include balance of content in these categories:

   a. Curriculum, instruction, and assessment
   b. Development, observation, and evaluation of staff
   c. Legal issues and ethical decision making
   d. School leadership, management and administration,
   and
   e. Practicum, internship, or collaboratively designed and supervised experience by local school system and IHE to include Department-approved

       instructional leadership outcomes with verification of experience submitted by applicant

II.   Administrator II (school principal)
- A. Complete requirements for Administrator I certification
- B. Qualifying score on Department-approved principal certification assessment
- C. Principal from another state may obtain Administrator II certificate if applicant held valid professional certificate in that state and verifies at least 27 months of satisfactory performance as principal during past 7 years.
- D. Standard Professional or Advanced Professional certificates shall be considered valid for service as principal of an elementary school of not more than 6 teachers if the principal teaches at least 50 percent of the school day.

III. Superintendents
- A. Eligibile for a professional certificate in early childhood education, elementary education, or secondary education
- B. Master's degree from an accredited institution
- C. Three years of satisfactory teaching experience and 2 years of administrative and/or supervisory experience
- D. Successful completion of a 2-year program with graduate courses in administration and supervision in an approved institution. A minimum of 60 semester hours of graduate work done for III, B, directly above, can be used to complete this program.

Massachusetts

Professional Standards for Teachers

Specific standards are used by teacher-preparation providers in preparing their candidates and by the Department of Elementary and Secondary Education (ESE) in reviewing programs seeking state approval or as the basis of the performance assessments of candidates. Contact the ESE (http://www.doe.mass.edu/Educators) for full listing of standards.

I. Candidates demonstrate that they meet Professional Standards by passing a performance assessment
    A. In practicum phase of preparation for Initial license
    B. As part of Performance Assessment Program option for earning Professional license
    C. As one option for relicensure during each 5-year cycle after Professional license is obtained

PreK–12 Teacher Licenses

I. Preliminary license (valid 5 years for teachers, exclusive of specialist teachers): For applicants who have not completed Approved Educator Preparation Program. Requirements:
    A. Bachelor's degree
    B. Passing score on the communication and literacy skills test
    C. Passing score on the subject matter knowledge test(s) appropriate to the license sought, based on the subject matter knowledge requirements, where available
    D. Competency Review for candidates seeking licensure in fields for which there are no subject matter knowledge tests available and for the following licenses: teacher of students with moderate disabilities; teacher of students with severe disabilities; teacher of the deaf and hard of hearing, and teacher of the visually impaired
    E. Evidence of sound moral character
    F. Additional requirements for the early childhood, elementary, and teacher of students with moderate disabilities and teacher of the visually impaired licenses:
        1. Seminars or courses that address the teaching of reading, English language arts, and mathematics
        2. Seminars or courses on ways to prepare and maintain students with disabilities for general classrooms; for example, use of strategies for learning and of behavioral management principles
        3. Passing score on Foundations of Reading test
    G. Additional requirements for the teacher of students with severe disabilities and teacher of the deaf and hard of hearing licenses
        1. See I, F, 1 and 2, directly above
        2. Passing score on either Department-approved test of teaching of reading to deaf and hard-of-hearing students, when available, or Foundations of Reading test

II. Temporary License (valid for 1 year). For experienced teachers from another state. Requirements:

  A. Three years of teaching experience under valid out-of-state license

  B. Possession of a valid educator license/certificate from another state/jurisdiction that is comparable to at least an Initial license in Massachusetts; see III, A–E, directly below

  C. Meet the terms of Massachusetts' interstate agreements; for details, consult http://www.doe.mass.edu/edprep/nasdtec.html

III. Initial license (valid for 5 years; renewable for an additional 5 years). Requirements:

  A. Bachelor's degree from an accredited college or university

  B. Passing score on the communication and literacy skills test

  C. Passing score on the subject matter knowledge test(s) appropriate to the license sought, based on the subject matter knowledge requirements

  1. Where no test has been established, completion of an approved program will satisfy this requirement.

  D. Completion of an approved program for Initial license sought

  E. Evidence of sound moral character

IV. Professional license (valid for 5 years; renewable for additional 5-year terms). Requirements:

  A. Possession of an Initial license in same field as Professional license sought

  B. Completion of a 1-year induction program with a mentor

  C. At least 3 full years of employment under Initial license

  D. At least 50 hours of mentored experience beyond induction year; may be fulfilled as part of IV, E, directly below

  E. Completion of ONE of the following:

  1. Approved district-based program for Professional license sought,
    or

  2. Master's or higher graduate-level program in accredited college or university that is or includes ONE of the following:

    a. Approved program for Professional license sought

    b. Master's degree program or other advanced graduate program in academic discipline appropriate to license sought in graduate or professional school other than education,
      or

  3. For those who have completed any master's or higher degree or other advanced graduate program not described directly above, ONE of the following:

    a. Approved, non-degree, 12-credit program of which no fewer than 9 credits are in academic discipline appropriate to instructional field of Professional license sought

    b. Twelve credits of graduate-level courses in academic discipline appropriate to instructional field of Professional license sought (which may include credits earned prior to license application),
      or

  4. Programs leading to eligibility for master teacher status, such as those sponsored by the National Board for Professional Teaching Standards and others accepted by the Commissioner,
    or

      5.   Department-sponsored Performance Assessment Program, when available.

V. Additional Licenses

    A. New Field

        1.   Teachers holding an Initial or a Professional license in one field may earn a license of same type and same level in new field by achieving a passing score on appropriate subject matter knowledge test of Massachusetts Tests for Educator Licensure (MTEL),

                or

                Passing a competency review for those licenses for which there is no subject matter knowledge tests

        2.   Additional requirement for earning a license as an early childhood or elementary teacher: completion of a practicum or practicum equivalent of 150 hours in role of license sought in appropriate classroom

        3.   Additional requirements for earning a license as teacher of students with moderate disabilities, teacher of students with severe disabilities, teacher of the deaf and hard of hearing, or teacher of the visually impaired are completion of both:

            a.   Competency review

            b.   Practicum, practicum equivalent, or internship of 150 hours in role of license sought in appropriate classroom

    B. New Level

        1.   Teachers holding an Initial or a Professional license at one grade level may obtain license at new grade level of same type and in same field by:

            a.   Achieving a passing score on appropriate subject matter knowledge test(s) at new level,

                or

            b.   By passing a competency review for those licenses with no such tests.

        2.   Teachers must complete one of the following:

            a.   Department-approved seminar, institute, or course addressing curriculum and developmental characteristics of appropriate age group,

                or

            b.   Practicum, practicum equivalent, or internship of 150 hours in role of license sought in appropriate classroom.

        3.   Guidance counselors holding an Initial or a Professional license at one grade level may obtain a license of same type and in same field at a new grade level by completing ONE of the following:

            a.   Department-approved seminar, institute, or course addressing curriculum and developmental characteristics of age group appropriate to license sought,

                or

            b.   Practicum, practicum equivalent, or internship of 150 hours in role of license sought in appropriate classroom.

    C. New Field and New Level

        Holders of an Initial or a Professional license in one field may earn a license of same type in new field and new grade level by meeting requirements listed in IV, A and B, directly above.

VI. Recertification
   A. Individuals with a Professional license must engage in recertification process
      1. All educators prepare an Individual Professional Development Plan for each 5-year renewal cycle. This plan must:
         a. Be consistent with educational needs of school and/or district
         b. Enhance ability of educator to improve student learning
      2. Educators must obtain initial approval and final endorsement of their plans from their supervisor.
      3. Professional licenses may be renewed by successful completion of the appropriate number of professional development points (PDPs) within a 5-year cycle as detailed by ESE (see Appendix 1).
VII. Additional Educator Licenses
   A. Vocational Technical Education
      1. Licenses for teachers, administrators and cooperative education coordinators are generally required for employment in state-approved vocational technical education programs.
   B. Adult Basic Education
      1. The ABE License is a voluntary license. By statute, ESE does not require this license; however, employers have the option of using this license as part of their hiring criteria.

Licenses Issued

The following licenses will be issued and will be valid for employment at the grade levels indicated. Practicum requirements are specified for all positions, and subject matter knowledge requirements are specified for each teacher and specialist teacher license. Contact ESE (see Appendix 1) for details.

   I. Teacher Licenses and Levels: Biology (5–8; 8–12); Business (5–12); Chemistry (5–8; 8–12); Dance (All); Early Childhood: Teacher of Students With and Without Disabilities (PreK–2); Earth Science (5–8; 8–12); Elementary (1–6); English (5–8; 8–12); English as a Second Language: ESL (PreK–6; 5–12); Foreign Language (PreK–6; 5–12); General Science (5–8); Health/Family and Consumer Sciences (All); History (1–6, 5–8; 8–12); Instructional Technology (All); Latin and Classical Humanities (5–12); Library (All); Mathematics (1–6, 5–8; 8–12); Middle School: Humanities (5–8); Middle School: Mathematics/Science (5–8); Music: Vocal/Instrumental/General (All); Physical Education (PreK–8; 5–12); Physics (5–8; 8–12); Political Science/Political Philosophy (5–8; 8–12); Speech (All); Teacher of Students with Moderate Disabilities (PreK–8; 5–12); Teacher of Students with Severe Disabilities (All); Teacher of the Deaf and Hard of Hearing (All); Teacher of the Visually Impaired (All); Technology/Engineering (5–12); Theatre (All); Visual Art (PreK–8; 5–12)
  II. Specialist Teacher Licenses and Levels: Academically Advanced (PreK–8); Speech, Language, and Hearing Disorders (All); Reading (All)
 III. Administrator Licenses and Levels

    A.   Superintendent/Assistant Superintendent (All); School Principal/Assistant School Principal (PreK–6; 5–8; 9–12): see detailed requirements below

    B.   Supervisor/Director (All); Special Education Administrator (All); School Business Administrator (All): contact ESE (see Appendix 1) for detailed requirements.

IV.   Professional Support Personnel Licenses and Levels: School Guidance Counselor (PreK–8; 5–12); School Nurse (All); School Psychologist (All); School Social Worker/School Adjustment Counselor (All): contact ESE (see Appendix 1) for detailed requirements.

Superintendent/Assistant Superintendent (All)

I.   Preliminary license requirements:

    A.   Completion of at least 3 full years of employment in executive management/ leadership role or in supervisory, teaching, or administrative role in public/charter school, private school, higher education, or other educational setting accepted by Department of Education

        1.   Passing score on the Communication and Literacy Skills test

II.   Initial license requirements:

    A.   Possession of at least an Initial license in another educational role, or Preliminary/ Assistant Superintendent license, and completion of 3 years of employment in a district-wide, school-based, or other educational setting

    B.   Demonstration of successful application of the Professional Standards for Administrators through completion of a Performance Assessment for Initial license and one of the following:

        1.   Completion of an approved post-baccalaureate program of studies, including a supervised practicum/practicum-equivalent (300 hours) in the superintendent/ assistant superintendent role

        2.   Administrative apprenticeship/internship (300 hours) in superintendent/ assistant superintendent role with a trained mentor, using Department guidelines

        3.   Panel Review

    C.   Passing score on the communication and literacy skills test

III.   Professional license requirements:

    A.   Possession of an Initial license at the appropriate level

    B.   Completion of a 1-year induction program with a trained mentor

    C.   At least 3 full years of employment under the Initial superintendent/assistant superintendent license

IV.   Additional Licenses for Experienced School Administrators.
Contact ESE (see Appendix 1) for details.

School Principal/Assistant Principal (PreK–6; 5–8; 9–12)

I.   Initial license requirements:

    A.   Prerequisite experience: Completion of at least 3 full years of employment in executive management/leadership role or in supervisory, teaching, or administrative role in a public or private school, higher education, or other educational setting accepted by ESE.

B. Demonstration of successful application of Professional Standards for Administrators through completion of Performance Assessment for Initial license and ONE of the following:
  1. Approved post-baccalaureate program of studies including supervised practicum/practicum equivalent (300 hours) in principal/assistant principal role and at level of license sought,
      or
  2. Administrative apprenticeship/internship (300 hours) in principal/assistant principal role and at level of license sought with a trained mentor, using Department guidelines
      or
  3. Panel Review. Eligibility for a Panel Review is limited to candidates who have completed either a post-baccalaureate program in management/administration at accredited college or university, *or* 3 full years of employment in executive management/leadership, supervisory, or administrative role.
C. Passing score on the communication and literacy skills test
II. Professional license requirements:
A. Possession of Initial license as principal/assistant principal
B. Completion of 1-year induction program with a trained mentor
C. At least 3 full years of employment under Initial school principal/assistant principal license

Note: Administrative licenses are also available at all levels for Supervisor/Director, Special Education Administrator, and School Business Administrator. Contact ESE (see Appendix 1) for details.

School Guidance Counselor (PreK–8, 5–12)

Note: Candidates seeking professional support personnel licenses who have substantial experience and formal education relevant to the license sought but who do not meet all of the specific requirements listed may demonstrate that they meet the requirements, with the exception of a passing score on the Communication and Literacy Skills test, through a Panel Review administered by the Department in accordance with their guidelines.

  I. Initial license requirements
A. Master's degree with major in counseling
B. Subject matter knowledge
  1. Contact ESE (see Appendix 1) to review their 14 detailed standards
C. Practicum of 450 hours in an educational setting
D. Passing score on communication and literacy skills test
II. Professional license
A. Possession of an Initial license
B. Employment for 3 years as a school guidance counselor
C. Completion of ONE of the following:
  1. Sixty credits of graduate course work that may include credits earned in master's degree program for Initial license in a discipline appropriate to license sought,

including (but not limited to) school counseling, mental health counseling, school psychology, or clinical psychology,
or

2. Achievement and maintenance of certification or licensure from either National Board of Certified Counselors (NBCC) or National Board for School Counseling.

Note: Licensure is also available for all levels of School Nurse; School Psychologist; and School Social Worker/School Adjustment Counselor—contact ESE (see Appendix 1) for details.

Michigan

Certificates and Credentialing

I. Provisional Certificate
   A. Minimum requirements for initial teaching license
      1. Successful completion of approved elementary or secondary teacher preparation program, including student teaching;
      2. Recommendation of state-approved institution of higher education (IHE) or demonstration of completion of approved teacher preparation program at out-of-state IHE;
      3. Valid cardiopulmonary resuscitation (CPR) training certificate from approved provider; includes child and adult CPR with first aid training; *and*
      4. Passing all components of the Michigan Test for Teacher Certification (MTTC), including Basic Skills test (reading, writing, and math) and appropriate subject area examinations prior to recommendation for certification.
         a. Out-of-state applicants should register for MTTC only on written advice of Michigan Department of Education (MDE).
         b. Temporary Teacher Employment Authorization (valid up to 6 years when specific conditions are met) may be issued to out-of-state candidate for purpose of employment before required teacher tests are passed if candidate holds valid certificate in another state, meets all requirements for Michigan certificate except passing teacher test, and has submitted completed application, including all fee payments. Contact MDE (see Appendix 1) for full details.
   B. Renewal of Provisional Certificate (each renewal valid for up to 3 years)
      1. First renewal requires completion of 9 semester hours in planned course of study.
      2. Second renewal requires completion of 18 semester hours in planned course of study.
      3. Additional 3-year renewal requires sponsorship of local school district or private school and approval of MDE.
   C. Two-year Provisional Extension
      1. Specific requirements apply to this extension, which is nonrenewable by statute. Contact MDE (see Appendix 1) for details.
   D. New Teacher Induction/Teacher Mentoring Guidelines
      1. Contact MDE (see Appendix 1) for recommendations on implementing revised school code requiring all new classroom teachers in first 3 years of classroom teaching experience to be mentored by 1 or more master teachers and be provided 15 days of intensive professional development.
II. Professional Education Certificate (valid 5 years)

A. Minimum requirements for advanced teaching license
1. Completion of 18 semester hours in planned course of study after issuance of approved initial teaching certificate (or approved master's degree earned at any time);
2. Three years of successful teaching experience;
3. Meet reading requirement: 6 semester hours of teaching of reading or reading methods for elementary, and 3 semester hours for secondary;
   and
4. Completion of additional reading course with appropriate field experiences in diagnosis, remediation of reading disabilities, and differentiated instruction.
B. Renewal of Professional Education Certificate
1. Meet continuing education requirements every 5 years by;
   a. Completing 6 semester hours at approved teacher preparation institution or State Board–approved institution (see MDE for details);
      or
   b. Completing 18 State Board–Continuing Education Units (SB-CEUs) or a combination of the two (3 SB-CEUs are equivalent to 1 semester hour of credit).
      i. Semester hour credits or SB-CEUs must have been completed within 5-year period preceding date of application and after date of issuance of previous certificate.

III. School Administrator Certificate
A. Requires completion of master's or higher degree from approved program in educational leadership or administration; contact MDE (see Appendix 1) for full history and details of this program, including random continuing education audits.
B. Renewal of School Administrator Certificate
1. Meet same continuing education requirements as renewal policy for Professional Education teaching certificate; see II, B, 1, a and b, directly above.

IV. Professional School Support Personnel Credentials
A. School Guidance Counselor Endorsement
1. Available as additional endorsement (elementary grades K–8 or K–9, secondary grades 6–12, or as K–12 endorsement on either elementary or secondary certificate) to those who hold valid teaching certificate.
2. Requires completion of approved school counselor preparation program offered by teacher preparation institution and by passing Guidance Counselor subject area exam of MTTC.
B. Preliminary Employment Authorization for School Guidance Counselor (valid 3 years; nonrenewable)
1. Available to candidate of Michigan teacher preparation institution who has completed 30 semester hours of course work in approved school guidance counseling program and has passed Guidance Counselor subject area exam of MTTC.
2. During 3-year validity period, holder must complete remainder of any outstanding courses/practicum to be recommended for school counselor endorsement on Michigan teaching certificate or School Counselor License.

C. School Counselor License (valid 5 years; renewable)
   1. Eligible in-state candidates must fulfill 1 or more of following criteria:
      a. Hold master's or higher degree awarded after completion of approved School Counselor Education program that includes at least all skills and content areas or their equivalent required by Michigan law;
         or
         Work with in-state university to complete approved school counselor program after completion of counseling or other advanced degree program;
         or
         Successfully complete MTTC Guidance Counselor examination;
         and
      b. Receive recommendation by approved School Counselor Education program.
   2. Requirements for out-of-state candidates
      a. At least 5 years of successful experience serving in school counseling role within immediately preceding 7-year period;
      b. Passed MTTC Guidance Counselor examination;
         and
      c. Hold either bachelor of science or bachelor of arts degree, and can provide copy of credential or approval document required by state to serve in school counseling role in which counseling experience is documented.
   3. License Renewal
      a. Complete 6 semester credit hours or 18 State Board–Continuing Education Units (SB-CEUs) or a combination of the two (3 SB-CEUs are equivalent to 1 semester credit hour).
   4. Temporary School Counselor Authorization (valid 1 year; nonrenewable)
      a. Issued to out-of-state candidates who meet either the educational or experience requirement but have yet to take and pass required examination; apply directly to MDE (see Appendix 1).
   5. For full information on authorizations, endorsements, school counselor hiring/noncompliance issues, tenure of school counselors, and approved administrative rules that govern school counselors, contact MDE (see Appendix 1).
D. School Psychologist Credentials
   1. Initial School Psychologist Certificate (valid 3 years; renewable once)
      a. Issued upon completion of approved school psychologist program offered at approved teacher preparation institution.
      b. During validity period, holder is expected to gain experience as practicing professional and to complete all academic training program requirements.
      c. To renew once, complete 6 semester hours of credit pertinent to school psychology at approved preparation institution.
   2. Advanced School Psychologist Certificate (valid 5 years; renewable)
      a. Issued upon completion of supervised work experience requirement and additional academic study.

         b.   Out-of-state candidate who holds national certification with at least 1 year of professional experience after completing all internships can apply directly to MDE (see Appendix 1) for School Psychologist certificate.

         c.   To renew, complete 6 semester hours of credit from approved institution, or 18 State Board–Continuing Education Units (SB-CEUs), or a combination of both. Contact MDE (see Appendix 1) for full details.

V.   Validity Levels

   A. Elementary

      1.   Elementary certificate issued after September 1, 1988, is valid for teaching all subjects grades K–5, all subjects grades K–8 in a self-contained classroom, and subject area endorsements, as listed on the certificate, in grades 6–8.

   B. Secondary

      1.   Secondary certificate issued after September 1, 1988 is valid for teaching subject area endorsements, as listed on the certificate, in grades 6–12.

VI. No Child Left Behind (NCLB) Requirements for Highly Qualified Teachers

   A. Elementary and Secondary Education Act/NCLB Act of 2001 requires that all teachers of core academic subjects be Highly Qualified at time of employment.

      1.   Core academic subjects include English, reading, language arts, mathematics, science, foreign languages, civics and government, economics, the arts, history, and geography

   B. New teachers trained at approved Michigan teacher preparation institution and assigned in compliance with validity of their certificates will meet definition of Highly Qualified because they are required to take and pass the MTTC subject area examinations, except for special education teachers.

   C. Additional information regarding highly qualified requirements can be found at www.michigan.gov/mde-hq.

Minnesota

First-Time Licensure Requirements

I. Teachers and School Administrators
   A. Completion of a state-approved teacher education and/or administrative preparation program through a regionally accredited institution
      1. Certifying officer of the college/university through which the state-approved program was completed must recommend the applicant for Minnesota licensure.
   B. Testing Requirements
      1. Beginning in September 2010, the Minnesota Teacher Licensure Examinations (MTLE) will be the sole means of assessing the basic skills, pedagogical, and content-area knowledge of candidates for Minnesota licensure.
      2. All candidates for an initial license will be required to pass the MTLE basic skills tests as well as pedagogy and content area tests; for full details, consult http://education.state.mn.us/mde/Teacher_Support/Educator_Licensing/index.html
   C. Minnesota Human Relations Program
      1. Human Relations Requirement is a state mandate directing licensure applicants to show evidence of the following:
         a. Understanding the contributions and lifestyles of the various racial, cultural, and economic groups in our society
         b. Recognizing and dealing with dehumanizing biases, discrimination, and prejudices
         c. Creating learning environments that contribute to the self-esteem of all persons and to positive interpersonal relations
         d. Respecting human diversity and personal rights
         e. The study of American Indian language, history, government, and culture
      2. Applicants may fulfill this requirement through one of the following options:
         a. Graduate from a Minnesota teacher preparation program—verified by licensure recommendation;
         b. Graduate from a teacher preparation program in states with which Minnesota has reciprocity of Human Relations, including Iowa, Ohio, Nebraska, South Dakota, or Wisconsin—verified by licensure recommendation;
         c. Evidence of program completion through Peace Corps, AmeriCorps, Vista, or Teacher Corps;
            or
         d. Complete one of Minnesota's approved Human Relations Programs—designed for applicants prepared outside of Minnesota and offered throughout the state—verified by a transcript or completion certificate.
      3. Applicants prepared outside of Minnesota may be granted a 1-year temporary license to teach while completing a human relations program.

4. Applicants who have not completed one of the options above but believe that they can demonstrate meeting all 5 Human Relations components/objectives may submit evidence by completing the Human Relations Verification Chart and attaching verifying documents.

5. For detailed information and list of approved Human Relations programs, consult http://education.state.mn.us/mde/Teacher_Support/Educator_Licensing/index.html

D. Fingerprinting Requirements

1. All applicants for an initial educator license in Minnesota are required by state law to obtain a criminal background check including a fingerprint check. Contact the Educator Licensing office (651/582-8691 or via e-mail at mde .educator-licensing@state.min.us) with your name and mailing address to request a fingerprint card, a list of local agencies providing these services and their fees, and detailed instructions on how to complete the card.

II. Teachers and School Administrators (outside Minnesota)

A. Minnesota does not have licensure reciprocity with any other state.

B. Applicants prepared out of state may be granted a Minnesota professional license when the following criteria are met:

1. The teacher preparation institution is accredited by the regional association for the accreditation of colleges and secondary schools;

2. The program leading to licensure has been recognized by the other state as qualifying the applicant completing the program for current licensure within that state;

3. The program leading to licensure completed by the applicant is essentially equivalent in content to approved Minnesota programs and the grade-level range of preparation is the same as, greater than, or not more than 1 year less than the grade-level range of the Minnesota licensure field for which application is made;

4. The preparing institution verifies applicant completion of the approved licensure program and recommends the applicant for a license in the licensure field and at the licensure level;

5. Program completion is verified by an official transcript issued by the recommending institution;

6. The applicant has completed instruction in methods of teaching in the licensure field and at the licensure level of the program; *and*

7. The applicant has completed student teaching or essentially equivalent experience.

C. Applicants who complete online preparation programs meeting these 7 criteria will be eligible to apply for a temporary limited teaching license which provides time for the applicant to complete Minnesota-specific licensure requirements in II, D and E, directly below. Such online programs must be:

1. Regionally accredited (see http://www.ncahighlerlearningcommission.org/) and approved by the state in which the program is offered;

2. In a licensure field for which Minnesota has licenses and rules;

3. Essentially equivalent in content and scope to approved programs offered by Minnesota institutions;

4. Able to qualify the graduate for kill licensure in the state in which the program was offered;

5. Providing supervised clinical experiences, including 10 weeks of full-time student teaching in the subject and grade level of licensure requested;

6. Including instruction in methods of teaching in the licensure field and at the licensure level;
   and

7. Providing evidence that the applicant has a bachelor's degree with a major, or the equivalent, in the field of intended licensure.

D. In addition to the above stipulations, applicants for teacher and administrative licenses must satisfy Minnesota requirements for:

1. MTLE testing; see I, B, directly above;

2. Minnesota Human Relations Program; see I, C, directly above;
   and

3. Fingerprinting requirements; see I, D, directly above

E. For teachers educated out of state or online whose initial Minnesota teaching license has a renewal condition requiring completion of one or more reading courses, consult http://www.education.state.mn.us/MDE/Teacher_Support/Educator_ Licensing/Licensing_Info/License_Renew/index.html for a current list of reading programs which will meet the specific requirement for licensure.

III. Related Services Personnel

A. Includes School Counselors, School Nurses, School Psychologists, School Social Workers, and Speech/Language Pathologists

B. Licensure in these fields does not require compliance with the Minnesota Human Relations or MILE testing requirements.

C. In addition, applications for School Counselor (if the program completed is accredited by the Council for the Accreditation of Counseling and Related Educational Programs [CACREP]), School Nurse, School Psychologist, School Social Worker, and Speech/Language Pathologists do not require a recommending signature.

D. An applicant seeking School Counselor licensure through a non–CACREP accredited program must be recommended for licensure by the certifying officer of the college/university through which the program was completed. For full details, contact Educator Licensing at the Minnesota Department of Education (see Appendix 1). Consult http://education.state.mn.us/mde/Teacher_Support/Educator_ Licensing/index.html

E. See Fingerprinting Requirements, I, D, 1, directly above.

Licensure Requirements and Levels

I. For the most accurate information on the approximately 32 programs approved for licensing in Minnesota, view the Teacher Preparation Institutions with contact information document at http://education.state.mn.us>Educator Licensing>First-Time Licensure.

II.   For a detailed listing of the 77 teacher licensure fields, 4 administrative licenses, and 5 related licenses, contact Educator Licensing at http://education.state.mn.us/mde/Teacher_Support/Educator_Licensing/index.html

Administration

I.   Licensure for superintendent, principal, or special education director. Requirements for all three positions include:

A.   Three years of successful classroom teaching experience while holding a classroom teaching license valid for the position or positions in which the experience was gained;
and

B.   Completion of a specialist or doctoral program, or a program consisting of 60 semester credits beyond the bachelor's degree that includes a terminating graduate degree and topics preparatory for educational administration and specified Minnesota competencies.

1.   Each program must be approved by the Board of School Administrators and be offered at a regionally accredited Minnesota graduate school.

C.   Additional position-specific requirements include:

1.   An applicant for licensure as a superintendent or principal must have field experience of at least 320 hours or 40 eight-hour days to be completed within 12 continuous months in elementary, middle or junior high, and high schools as an administrative aide to a licensed and practicing school principal or superintendent, depending on the licensure sought.

a.   The field experience must include at least 40 hours or one week at each level not represented by the applicant's primary teaching experience.

i.   A person licensed as an elementary school principal must complete a field experience of at least 200 hours in secondary administration to qualify for licensure as a K–12 principal.

ii.   A person licensed as a secondary school principal must complete a field experience of at least 200 hours in elementary administration to qualify for licensure as a K–12 principal.

2.   An applicant for licensure as a director of special education must have a practicum or field experience that includes a minimum of 320 hours in an administrative position under the immediate supervision of a licensed and practicing director of special education.

a.   The field experience will include at least 40 hours or one week at a special education administrative unit other than the primary experience of the applicant.

II.   Provisional license (valid 2 years, nonrenewable)

A.   Currently licensed elementary and secondary school principals seeking entry into a position as a K–12 principal may apply for a provisional license.

1.   Applicant must provide evidence of enrollment in an approved administrative licensure program for licensure as a K–12 principal.

III. Administrative Licensure Without Teaching Experience for Superintendents, Principals, and Directors of Special Education. Requirements include:
   A. Meet the degree requirement specified in I, B, directly above;
   B. Satisfactorily complete a field experience in school administration as an intern in the license area sought:
      1. In a school district setting appropriate for the license sought,
      2. Under the supervision of educators from an approved college or university school administration program and a licensed practicing school administrator working in the area of the intern's field experience,
         and
      3. The field experience must consist of at least 320 hours, of which at least 40 must be in each school level: elementary, middle grades, and high school, and is in addition to the teaching internship requirement below;
   C. Demonstrate required basic teaching knowledge and skills by:
      1. Presenting a portfolio or other appropriate presentation as determined by the approved school administration program demonstrating appropriate teaching knowledge and skills;
         or
      2. Meet the examination requirement of part 8710.0510, subpart 1, items A and B, and subpart 3, items A and B;
         and
   D. Fulfill teaching internship requirement insuring that applicant shall have experience and knowledge in curriculum, school organization, philosophy of education, early childhood, elementary, junior high, middle school, and senior high schools through an internship that:
      1. Includes 1 school year with a minimum hour equivalency of 1,050 hours of classroom experiences, including 8 weeks of supervised teaching;
      2. Is under the supervision of a licensed practicing school administrator;
      3. Includes supervision provided by educators from an approved school administration program;
         and
      4. Is based on a written agreement between the intern, the approved school administration preparation institution, and the school district in which the internship is completed.
IV. Licensure for Directors of Community Education For specific requirements, consult http://educaton.state.mn.us/mde/Teacher_Support/Educator_Licensing/index.html

School Counselor (K–12)

I. Requirements for Entrance License
   A. Hold a master's degree from a college or university that is regionally accredited by the association for the accreditation of colleges and secondary schools.
   B. Complete an approved teaching preparation program leading to the licensure of school counselors or provide evidence of having completed a preparation program in

school counseling accredited by the Council for the Accreditation of Counseling and Related Educational Programs.

C. Complete a preparation program that must demonstrate specific knowledge and skills. For details, contact the Minnesota State Department of Education (see Appendix 1).

II. Renewal of Continuing License

A. See detailed rules governing continuing licensure at http://education.state.mn.us/mde/Teacher_Support/Educator_Licensing/index.html

Mississippi

Standard Educator Licenses

I. Five-year Educator License, Traditional Teacher Education Route
   A. Class A Five-Year Educator License (valid for 5 years; renewable)
      1. Bachelor's degree in teacher education from a state-approved or a National Council for Accreditation of Teacher Education (NCATE)–approved program from a regionally/nationally accredited institution of higher learning
      2. Passing scores on Praxis II (Principles of Learning and Teaching Test)
      3. Passing scores on Praxis II (Specialty Area Test) in degree program
   B. Class AA Five-Year Educator License (valid for 5 years; renewable)
      1. See I, A, 1–3, directly above
      2. Master's degree in the endorsement area in which license is requested *or* Master of Education degree
   C. Class AAA Five-Year Educator License (valid for 5 years; renewable)
      1. See I, A, 1–3, directly above
      2. Specialist degree in the endorsement area in which license is requested
         or
         Specialist of Education degree
   D. Class AAAA Five-Year Educator License (valid for 5 years; renewable)
      1. See I, A, 1–3, directly above
      2. Doctoral degree in the endorsement area in which license is requested
         or
         Doctor of Education degree
II. Five-Year Educator License, Alternate Route
   A. Class A Five-Year Educator License
      1. Route One
         a. Bachelor's degree (noneducation) from a regionally/nationally accredited institution of higher learning
         b. Passing scores on Praxis I (Pre-Professional Skills Test—PPST)
         c. Passing scores on Praxis II Specialty Area Test
         d. Successful completion of a 1- or 2-year state-approved alternate route program
         e. Application for a 5-year educator license,
            or
      2. Route Two
         a. Hold a bachelor's degree with a minor or concentration in secondary education (7–12)
         b. Passing scores on Praxis I (Pre-Professional Skills Test—PPST)
         c. Passing scores on Praxis II Specialty Area Test

        d.   Documentation of completion of student teaching from a state- or NCATE-approved program.

   B. Class A, Class AAA, and/or Class AAAA Five-Year Educator License

      1. Meet the requirements for a Class A license

      2. Master's, specialist, or doctoral degree in the endorsement area in which license is requested,

        or

        Master's of Education degree, Specialist of Education degree, or Doctor of Education degree.

III. Reciprocity

   A. Class A Five-Year Educator License (valid for 5 years; renewable)

      1. Valid out-of-state Five-Year Class A (bachelor's-degree-level) License in a Mississippi endorsement area

   B. Class AA Five-Year Educator License (valid for 5 years; renewable)

      1. Valid out-of-state Five-Year Class AA (master's-degree-level) License in a Mississippi endorsement area

   C. Class AAA Five-Year Educator License (valid for 5 years; renewable)

      1. Valid out-of-state Five-Year Class AAA (specialist-degree-level) License in a Mississippi endorsement area

   D. Class AAAA Five-Year Educator License (valid for 5 years; renewable)

      1. Valid out-of-state Five-Year Class AAAA (doctorate-degree-level) License in a Mississippi endorsement area

IV. Five-Year Educator License—Guidance and Counseling

   A. Class AA Option One (valid 5 years; renewable)

      1. Hold a Five-Year teaching certificate

      2. Complete a master's degree program in guidance and counseling,

        or

        Hold a master's degree in another area and complete an approved program for guidance and counseling.

      3. Passing score on Praxis II (Specialty Area for Guidance Counselor)

   B. Class AA Option Two (valid 5 years; renewable)

      1. Complete an approved master's degree program for guidance and counseling that includes a full year internship

      2. Passing score on Praxis I (Pre-Professional Skills Test—PPST) or on Praxis I (Computer-Based Test—CBT)

      3. Passing score on Praxis II (Specialty Area Test for Guidance Counseling)

   C. Class AA Option Three (valid 5 years, renewable)

      1. Hold National Certified School Counselor (NCSC) credential issued by National Board of Certified Counselors (NBCC)

   D. Class AAA (valid 5 years; renewable)

      1. Meet requirements for Class AA License (see III, B, 1, directly above)

      2. Specialist degree in guidance and counseling

   E. Class AAAA (valid 5 years; renewable)

      1. Meet requirements for Class AA License (see III, B, 1, directly above)

      2. Doctoral degree in guidance and counseling

V. Five-Year Educator Licenses for Audiologist, Child Development Speech Pathologist, School Psychologist, and in Emotional Disability, Dyslexia, Psychometry, Library/Media, and Performing Arts

    A. Contact Mississippi State Department of Education (see Appendix 1 for contact information) to obtain details on these licenses.

Alternate Routes to Licensure

I. Three-Year Alternate Route Educator License—Master of Arts in Teaching (MAT) Program (valid 3 years; nonrenewable): issued to applicant with a bachelor's degree who has not completed a state or nationally accredited teacher education program and who is enrolled in an approved Master of Arts in Teaching program

    A. Bachelor's degree from a regionally/nationally accredited institution of higher learning

    B. Passing score on *one* of the following:

        1. Praxis I (Pre-Professional Skills Test–PPST)

        2. Praxis II (Specialty Area Test)

    C. Complete 6 hours preteaching course requirements from an approved Master of Arts in Teaching program

    D. Institutional recommendation

    E. Complete 1-year teaching internship

II. Mississippi Alternate Path to Quality Teachers

    A. One-Year Alternate Route License: contingent upon completion of II, A, 1–4, immediately below, and proof of employment by a local school district

        1. Bachelor's degree (non-education) from a nationally/regionally accredited institution of higher learning; minimum grade-point average (GPA) required

            a. GPA of 2.0 overall for those who graduated from college 7 or more years ago

            b. GPA of 2.5 overall or 2.75 in major for those who graduated from college less than 7 years ago

        2. Passing scores on Praxis I

        3. Passing score on Praxis II (Specialty Area Test) in area of endorsement

        4. During first year of employment, teacher must complete the following

            a. Nine New Teacher Practicum weekend sessions held in fall and spring that focus on classroom management; peer coaching; school law; data analysis and using test results to improve instruction; and other topics as needed

            b. New Teacher Training Modules: interactive video training

            c. Local district evaluation

            d. Intensive induction program and mentoring provided by local school district

III. Teach Mississippi Institute (TMI) (For grades 7–12)

    A. One-Year Alternative Teaching Route License

        1. Bachelor's degree or higher from a nationally/regionally accredited institution of higher learning

        2. Passing scores on Praxis I (PPST)

3. Passing score on Praxis II (Specialty Area Test) in area of endorsement
    a. Areas open to endorsement with a Teach Mississippi Institute Alternate Route License include: biology; business education; chemistry; English; French; German; home economics; marketing; mathematics; physics; social studies; Spanish; special education (7–12 only); speech communications
4. Complete Teach Mississippi Institute: an 8-week online program

or

an 8-week, 9-semester hour summer program that shall include, but is not limited to, the following: instruction in education; effective teaching strategies; classroom management; state curriculum requirements; planning and instruction; instructional methods and pedagogy; using test results to improve instruction

5. Once employed as a teacher, successfully complete at least a 1-year beginning teacher mentoring and induction program administered by the employing school district.

B. Five-Year License—Nontraditional Route (valid for 5 years; renewable)
    1. Complete III, A, 1–5, directly above.
    2. Submit to Office of Educator Licensure (see Appendix 1) application, certificate of completion of internship, and letter from school

IV. American Board Certificate for Teacher Excellence (ABCTE) Alternate Route for Teachers
    A. Subject Areas of Licensure: biology, chemistry, English, math, physics (7–12)
    B. Program Entrance Requirements
        1. Bachelor's degree from a regionally/nationally accredited institution of higher learning
        2. Fees plus background check
        3. Two assessments in a subject area and pedagogy test
        4. Assignment of advisor and prescribed individual study profile
        5. Enrollment in ABCTE program
    C. Requirements for Five-Year Alternate Route License
        1. One-year teaching internship with certified mentoring
            a. Mentor must be National Board– or Mississippi Department of Education–trained mentor, or have completed ABCTE mentoring program
        2. Completion of training in one of the following
            a. Mississippi Alternate Path to Quality Teachers (MAPQT) 3-week summer training
            b. Mississippi Department of Education 8-week online training
            c. MAT 6 hours of initial graduate university courses (may be applied to master's degree)

VI. Licenses
    A. Contact the Mississippi Department of Education (see Appendix 1) to obtain details on these licenses.
        1. Three-Year Class A Vocational Educator License for Non-Degree Applicants (valid 3 years; nonrenewable)
        2. Three-Year Class A Vocational Educator Licenses and Vocational Licenses for Applicants without a Teacher Education Degree

3. Five-Year Vocational Licenses for Non–Education Degree Applicants (Class A, AA, AAA, and AAAA)

Administrator Licenses

I. Nonpracticing Administrator License (Class AA, AAA, or AAAA; 5 years renewable): issued to an educator not currently employed in an administrative position
   A. Hold 5-year standard educator license
   B. Verfication of 3 years of education experience
   C. Completion of an approved master's, specialist, or doctoral degree in educational administration/leadership from a state-approved or regionally/nationally accredited institution of higher learning
   D. Successful completion of School Leaders Licensure Assessment (SLLA), Educational Testing Service
   E. Institutional recommendation documenting completion of an approved planned program in educational leadership/supervision through a state-approved or regionally/nationally accredited institution of higher learning
   F. Validity is based upon validity of period of standard license currently held.
II. Entry Level Administrator License (Class AA, AAA, or AAAA; valid 5 years; nonrenewable): issued to an educator employed as a beginning administrator
   A. See I, B and C, directly above.
   B. Valid for 5 years, in which time applicant is expected to complete School Executive Management Institute (SEMI) entry-level requirements, which consist of five 2-day training modules
III. Career Level Administrator License (Class AA, AAA, or AAAA; 5 years renewable)
   A. See II, B, directly above
IV. Alternate Route Administrator License (Class AA, AAA, or AAAA)
   A. One-year Alternate Route Administrator License (Class AA; valid 1 year; convertible to IV, B, directly below)
      1. Requirements
         a. Completion of master's of education (MED) or higher education degree
         b. Passing score on Praxis I (Pre-Professional Skills Test PPST) and Praxis II (Principles of Learning and Teaching Test)
         c. Three years teaching experience for MED
         d. Successful completion of alternate route training
         e. Priority will be given to Superintendent/Board recommendation for admittance into an alternate route program.
      2. Conversion to Five-Year Entry Level Alternate Route Administrator License
         a. Complete Alternate Route program
         b. See I, B, directly above.
   B. Five-year Entry Level Alternate Route Administrator License (Class AA; valid 5 years; nonrenewable)
      1. Requirements
         a. See IV, A, 1, a–d, directly above.
         b. See I, B, directly above.

2. Conversion to Career Level Standard License within 5 years—see III, A, directly above.
    a. Completion of SEMI entry-level OSL requirements
    b. Completion of 16 hours of educational leadership course work; courses must be in school law, school finance, school administration, curriculum and instruction

Missouri

Contact Educator Certification at the Missouri Department of Elementary and Secondary Education (http://www.dese.mo.gov/divteachqual/teachcert.index.html) for the most current regulations.

Educator Certification, Classification, and Renewals

I. General Qualifications for Certification
Identical for all teaching certificates, except for some areas of Vocational Education
   A. Baccalaureate degree from college/university with teacher education program approved by Missouri Department of Elementary and Secondary Education (DESE) or with teacher education program approved by state education agency in states other than Missouri
      1. No formal reciprocity for certification with other states; however, graduates from approved teacher-education programs within other states may obtain Missouri certificate based on meeting certain requirements.
   B. Recommendation for certification from designated official for teacher education in college/university where program was completed; not required with possession of a valid out-of-state certificate
   C. Grade-point average of 2.5 on a 4.0 scale, both overall and in content area.
   D. Successful completion of required Praxis test(s)
      1. Consult DESE website (see Appendix 1) for list of the Missouri Specialty Area Tests and qualifying scores
      2. Educators who completed teacher-education program and were certificated before September 1, 1990, are exempt from this requirement
   E. Meet educational, professional, and subject area requirements as specified
   F. Applicants are required to complete a Missouri background check, including fingerprinting; for details, consult http://www/dese.mo.gov/divteachqual/teachcert/index.html
II. Classifications
   A. Initial Professional Certificate (valid 4 years)
      1. Assigned to new graduates of teacher-education programs and to individuals with less than 4 years of DESE-approved teaching experience who meet the minimum requirements and qualifications
      2. See I, A–E, directly above.
      3. To advance to next level, during valid dates of classification, the teacher must meet all of following requirements:
         a. Participate in district-provided and -approved mentoring program for 2 years
         b. Successfully complete 30 contact hours of professional development that may include college credits

      c.   Participate in Beginning Teacher Assistance Program

      d.   Successfully participate in a yearly performance-based teacher evaluation

      e.   Complete 4 years of approved teaching experience

B.   Career Continuous Professional Certificate, or CCPC (valid continuously if following requirements are met):

    1.   Successfully complete each year 15 contact hours of professional development that may include college credits,
       and

    2.   Have a local professional development plan.

    3.   If in possession of 2 of the 3 following items, applicant is exempt from reporting yearly professional development

      a.   Ten years of teaching experience,
         or

      b.   Master's degree,
         or

      c.   Certification from National Board for Professional Teaching Standards (NBPTS) or National Association of School Psychologists.

C.   Administrative Classification

    1.   Elementary Principal K–8 and Secondary Principal

      a.   Initial Administrator Certificate (valid for 4 years)

        i.   Permanent or professional Missouri teaching certificate
           or
           Baccalaureate degree and recommendation from state-approved teacher-preparation program; and qualifying score on designated assessment for initial certification

        ii.   Minimum of 2 years of approved teaching experience

        iii.   Complete designated building-level administrator's assessment

        iv.   Course in psychology and education of the exceptional child

        v.   Master's degree in educational leadership from approved college/university

        vi.   Recommendation for certification from approved college/university program with at least 24 semester hours of approved graduate education courses

      b.   Transition Administrator Certificate—Principal (valid for 6 years)

        i.   4 years of state-approved administrator experience

        ii.   2 years of designated district-provided mentoring.

        iii.   Development, implementation, and completion of approved professional development plan

        iv.   Annual performance-based evaluation that meets or exceeds Missouri Performance Based Principal's Evaluation

        v.   Completion of 8 semester hours towards advanced degree in educational leadership or 120 contact hours in professional development activities

  c. Career Continuous Administrator Certificate—Principal
      i. Educational specialist degree or higher in educational leadership, reading/literacy or curriculum/instruction.
      ii. Performance-based principal evaluation
      iii. 30 contact hours of professional development annually
2. Middle School Principal 5–9
    a. Initial Administrator Certificate (valid for 4 years)
        i. Valid Missouri professional elementary or secondary, initial, transition, or career principal's certificate
        ii. Recommendation for certification as a middle school principal from approved college/university program to train principals
        iii. Specified undergraduate or graduate credit
        iv. Planned program of at least 6 semester hours in education courses focusing on: middle school philosophy, organization, and curriculum; and intellectual, physiological, emotional and social development of the transescent child (10–14 year old)
    b. Transition Administrator Certificate—Principal (valid for 6 years)
        i. See II, E, 1, b, i–v, directly above
    c. Career Continuous Administrator Certificate—Principal
        i. See II, E, 1, c, i–iii, directly above
3. Superintendent
    a. Initial Administrator certificate (valid for 4 years)
        i. Must complete Ed.S. or Ed.D. in educational administration and be recommended by the degree-granting University; must complete designated district level administrator's assessment.
        ii. Minimum of 1 year of experience as a building- or district-level administrator at public or accredited nonpublic school
        iii. See II, E, 1, a, i–vi, directly above
    b. Career Continuous Professional Certificate—Administrator
        i. See II, E, 1, c, i–iii, directly above
4. Special Education Administrator K–12
    a. Initial Administrator Certificate—Special Education Director (valid for 4 years)
        i. Professional teaching certificate for an area of special education or student services
            or
            Baccalaureate degree and recommendation from state-approved teacher-preparation program in an area of special education; and qualifying score on designated assessment
        ii. Minimum of 2 years of approved special education or student services teaching experience
        iii. See II, E, 1, a, i–vi, directly above
    b. Transition Administrator Certificate—Special Education Director (valid for 6 years)
        i. See II, E, 1, b, i–v, directly above

        c.   Career Continuous Administrator Certificate—Special Education Director
           i.   See II, E, 1, c, i–iii, directly above

    5. Career Education Director
        a.   Initial Administrator Certificate—Career Education Director (valid for 4 years)
           i.   Permanent or professional or career education Missouri teaching certificate

                 or

                 Baccalaureate degree and recommendation from state-approved teacher-preparation program; and qualifying score on designated assessment
           ii. See II, E, 1, a, ii–vi, directly above
        b.   Transition Administrator Certificate—Career Education Director (valid for 6 years)
           i.   See II, E, 1, b, i–v, directly above
        c.   Career Continuous Administrator Certificate—Career Education Director
           i.   See II, E, 1, c, i–iii, directly above

D. Student Services Classification
    1. Counselor K–8 (valid for 4 years)
        a.   Recommendation for certification from college/university approved to train elementary school counselors
        b.   Master's degree with major emphasis in guidance and counseling from approved college/university based upon completion of approved program of at least 24 semester hours of approved graduate courses in guidance and counseling, with at least 12 semester hours focused upon guidance in elementary schools,

           or

           Master's or higher degree in education, school counseling, counseling, counseling psychology, or a closely related mental health discipline; and additional graduate course work specific to school counseling, as designated by the state-approved recommending certification offical, including supervised internship or field experience of at least 300 hours in appropriate school setting
        c.   Bachelor's degree in education from state-approved teacher preparation program

           or

           Completion of specified curriculum in teaching methods and practices, classroom management, and psychology of the exceptional child, as specified by the recommending certification officer of a state-approved program
        d.   Qualifying score on designated assessment, not to include the principles of learning and teaching
    2. Counselor 7–12 (valid for 4 years)
        a.   See II, F, 1, a–d, directly above

    3. Career Continuous Student Services (valid for 99 years)
        a. Four years of state-approved school counseling experience
        b. Participation in 2 years district-provided mentoring during the first 2 years of student services experience
        c. Development, implementation, and completion of a professional development plan of at least 40 contact hours of professional development or 3 semester hours of graduate credit towards an advanced degree
        d. Successful participation in an annual performance-based evaluation
    4. For related certificates listed here, contact Educator Certification at Missouri's Department of Elementary and Secondary Education (http://www.dese.mo.gov/divteachqual/teachcert/index.html)
        a. Psychological Examiner K–12
        b. School Psychologist K–12
        c. Speech-Language Pathologist
        d. Career Education Adult Supervisor
        e. Career Education Counselor Certificate
        f. Career Services Coordinator Certificate

E. Classifications involving district application. For detailed information on these, contact Missouri Department of Elementary and Secondary Education (http://www.dese.mo.gov/divteachqual/teachcert/index.html)
    1. Substitute Classification (valid 1 year)
    2. Temporary Authorization Classification (valid 1 year; renewable yearly)

F. Career (Vocational) Classification Applicants may seek licenses below; for full details, contact Missouri Department of Elementary and Secondary Education (http://www.dese.mo.gov/divteachqual/teachcert/index.html)
    1. Secondary Career Education License
    2. Postsecondary/Adult Career Education License
    3. Career Continuous Career Education (CCCE) License

G. Doctoral Route to Classification
    1. Individual who has earned a doctoral degree (Ph.D., Ed.D., M.D., etc.) from accredited institution of higher education may apply for Missouri certification based on major area of postgraduate study.
    2. Certificate issued by doctoral route to certification will be limited to major area of postgraduate study for which there is a Missouri teaching certificate.
    3. Applicant can be granted only an initial professional classification certificate of license to teach; there is no provision to receive a career classification
    4. Applicants must submit the following:
        a. Completed application for Missouri Teacher's Certificate for Holders of Doctorate Degree
        b. Official transcript showing a doctoral degree conferred in major area of postgraduate study, including official transcripts from all other institutions attended
        c. Praxis II Assessment score report showing successful completion of appropriate required exit exam (Praxis II: The Principles of Learning and Teaching, grades 7–12)

H. Alternative Routes
1. Available at some colleges/universities for college graduates who have not completed a teacher-education program. This certification is offered through an approved Missouri college/university and includes specific qualifications for acceptance. It also requires employment with a district prior to being accepted into the college's alternative program.

Areas and Types of Certification

I. Certification Levels
A. Early Childhood (Birth–Grade 3)
B. Elementary Education (1–6)
C. Middle School (5–9)
1. Language Arts
2. Mathematics
3. Science
4. Social Studies
5. Other Middle School Endorsements
D. Secondary Education (9–12) (except as noted)
E. Special Education
F. Student Services
G. Administration
H. Career Education (vocational)
I. Other

II. Subject Areas
Agriculture; Art (K–12, 9–12); Blind & Partially Sighted (B–12);[#] Building-Level Administrator;[*] Business Education; Deaf and Hearing Impaired (B–12);[#] District-Level Administrator (Superintendent, K–12);[*] Early Childhood Education (B–Grade 3); Early Childhood Special Education (B–Grade 3); English; English for Speakers of Other Languages (ESOL) (K–12); Family and Consumer Science (B–12); Foreign Languages [French (K–12); German (K–12); Spanish (K–12)]; Gifted Education (K–12); Health (K–12, K–9, 9–12); Industrial Technology; Library Media Specialist (K–12); Marketing Education; Mathematics; Music (Instrumental, Vocal) (K–12); Physical Education (K–9, K–12, 9–12); Principal (K–8, 5–9, 9–12);[*] School Counselor (K–8, 7–12);[*] School Psychologist K–12;[*] Science (Biology; Chemistry; Earth Science; General Science; Physics); Severely Developmentally Disabled (B–12);[#] Social Science; Special Education Administrator; Mild/Moderate Cross-Categorical K–12; Special Reading (Remedial) (K–12); Speech and Language Pathologist (B–12);[*] Speech/Theater; Unified Science[+] (Biology; Chemistry; Earth Science; Physics); Vocational School Director

[*] Not available by completion of the designated assessment only; also requires completion of a program of study and a recommendation from a state-approved institution.
[+] Not available by completion of designated assessment only; also requires completion of program of study in unified science core with area of specialization from a state-approved institution
[#] Not available by completion of the designated assessment only; also requires completion of a program of study with the area of specialization from a state-approved institution.

Montana

Educator Licensure

I. Minimal educator licensure requirements
   A. Bachelor's degree from regionally accredited college or university,
   B. Six semester credits in department of education course work from accredited education preparation program either in Montana or elsewhere,
   and
   C. Verification of student teaching or 1 year of teaching experience in elementary and/or secondary school or school district either in Montana or elsewhere,
   or
   Eligibility for a Class 5 alternative license to complete this requirement.

Teacher Licenses

I. Class 2 Standard Teacher's License (valid 5 years)
   A. Applicant must submit verification of all of the following:
      1. Meeting or exceeding minimal educator licensure requirements; see Educator Licensure, I, A–C, above,
      2. Completion of accredited professional educator preparation program,
      and
      3. Qualification for 1 or more endorsements as outlined in Class 1 and 2 Endorsements; see III, directly below.
   B. Class 2 standard teacher's license shall be renewable with 1 of the following combinations of college credit and renewal units:
      1. Three semester credits and 15 renewal units,
      2. Four semester credits,
      3. Four quarter credits and 20 renewal units,
      4. Five quarter credits and 10 renewal units,
      or
      5. Six quarter credits.
   C. A lapsed Class 2 standard teacher's license may be reinstated by showing verification of 60 renewal units, 40 of which must be earned by college credit during the 5-year period preceding the validation date of the new license.
II. Class I Professional Teacher's License (valid 5 years)
   A. Applicant must submit verification of all of the following:
      1. Eligibility for the Class 2 standard teacher's license; see I, A, 1–3, directly above,
      2. Master's degree in professional education or endorsable teaching area(s) from accredited college or university,
      and
      3. Three years of successful teaching experience employed in accredited school

organization consistent with Montana's K–12 pattern during school fiscal year as licensed member of instructional staff.

    a.   Experience gained prior to basic eligibility for initial licensure is not considered.

B.   Class 1 standard teacher's license shall be renewable with 60 renewal units.

C.   A lapsed Class 1 professional teacher's license may be reinstated by showing verification of 60 renewal units earned during 5-year period preceding validation date of new license.

III.   Class 1 and 2 Endorsements

    A.   Areas approved for endorsement on Class 1 and 2 licenses include the following: agriculture, art K–12, biology, business education, chemistry, computer science K–12, drama, earth science, economics, elementary education, English, English as a second language K–12, family and consumer sciences, geography, health, history, history–political science, industrial arts, journalism, library K–12, marketing, mathematics, music K–12, physical education K–12, school counseling K–12, science (broadfield), social studies (broadfield), sociology, special education P–12, speech-communication, speech-drama, technology education, trade and industry, traffic education K–12, and world languages

    B.   License holder may qualify for a statement of specialized competency by completing at least 20 semester college credit hours or equivalency in approved areas of permissive specialized competency, including: early childhood education, gifted and talented education, and technology in education.

    C.   To obtain elementary endorsement, applicant must provide verification of completion of accredited elementary teacher education program, including student teaching, or university-supervised teaching experience.

    D.   To obtain secondary endorsement, applicant must provide verification of at least:

        1.   Sixteen semester credits in professional educator preparation program, including student teaching or appropriate college waiver, and 30 semester credits in approved major and 20 semester credits in approved minor,
           or

        2.   Forty semester credits in an extended major.

    E.   Both elementary and secondary preparation, including student teaching or university-supervised teaching experience, are required for endorsement in any approved K–12 endorsement area.

        1.   The K–12 endorsement areas outlined in III, A, directly above, may also be endorsed at elementary or secondary level depending on verified level of preparation.

    F.   Class 1 or 2 license may be endorsed in special education P–12 with program preparation at elementary or secondary levels, or balanced K–12 program of comparable preparation.

    G.   Balanced K–12 license level option is available through Montana Board of Public Education–approved special education programs for those individuals with:

        1.   Minimum of completed bachelor's degree,
           and

        2.   Verified completion of out-of-state approved special education program that includes student teaching or university supervised teaching experience.

H. Completion of accredited professional educator preparation program in any disability area shall result in a special education endorsement.

I. Applicants with graduate degrees in endorsable field of specialization may use experience instructing in relevant higher education courses as credit in that endorsement area for licensure.

Administrative Licenses

I. Class 3 Administrative License (valid 5 years)

   A. Appropriate administrative areas acceptable for license endorsement are the following: elementary principal, secondary principal, K–12 principal, K–12 superintendent, and supervisor

   B. To obtain Class 3 administrative license, applicant must hold at least the appropriate master's degree and qualify for 1 of the endorsements set forth directly below; see Administrative Licenses, II–VII.

   C. Lapsed Class 3 administrative license may be reinstated by showing verification of 60 renewal units earned during 5-year period preceding validation date of new license.

II. Class 3 Administrative License—Superintendent Endorsement

   A. Applicant must provide verification of all of the following:

      1. Minimum of 3 years of successful teaching experience as appropriately licensed and assigned Class 1 or 2 teacher or Class 6 school counselor, *and*

      2. Minimum of 18 semester graduate credits in school administrator preparation program, of which 12 must be beyond the master's degree, in each of the following content areas: organizational leadership; instructional leadership; facilities planning and policy; personnel and labor relations; community and board relations; policy development; and 3 semester credits of college course work each in Montana school law and in Montana school finance.

   B. In addition to the requirements in A, 1 and 2, directly above, every applicant must provide verification of either:

      1. Education specialist degree or doctoral degree in education leadership from professional educator preparation program accredited by either the National Council for the Accreditation of Teacher Education (NCATE) or by a Montana Board of Public Education (BPE)–approved organization, *and*

         Minimum of 1 year of administrative experience as appropriately licensed principal or 1 year of supervised Montana BPE-approved administrative internship as a superintendent; *or*

      2. Master's degree in educational leadership from accredited professional educator preparation program or master's degree in education from accredited program, *and*

         Licensure and endorsement as a K–12 principal,

and

Minimum of 1 year of employment in accredited school during school fiscal year as licensed member of supervisory or administrative staff in school organization consistent with Montana's K–12 pattern,
or

3. Minimum of 1 year of supervised Board of Public Education–approved administrative internship as superintendent.

C. Class 3 administrative license endorsed as superintendent shall be renewed as follows:

1. For applicants meeting all licensure requirements at time of initial application, verification of 60 renewal units earned during valid term of license,
or

2. For applicants not meeting the requirement of 3 semester credits of college course work each in Montana school law and in Montana school finance, verification of those 6 semester credits earned during valid term of initial Class 3 license.

III. Class 3 Administrative License—Elementary Principal Endorsement

A. Applicant must provide verification of:

1. Minimum of 3 years of successful experience as appropriately licensed and assigned Class 1 or 2 teacher or Class 6 school counselor at elementary level,
and

Master's degree in educational leadership from professional educator preparation program accredited by either NCATE or by a Montana BPE-approved organization,
or

2. Master's degree from any accredited professional educator preparation program and minimum of 24 graduate semester credits from school administrator preparation program in following content areas: school leadership; instructional leadership to include supervision and elementary curriculum; successful completion of 3 semester credits of college course work in Montana school law; and school and community relations.

IV. Class 3 Administrative License—Secondary Principal Endorsement

A. Applicant must provide verification of:

1. Minimum of 3 years of successful experience as appropriately licensed and assigned Class 1 or 2 teacher or Class 6 school counselor at the secondary level,
and

Master's degree in educational leadership from professional educator preparation program accredited by either NCATE or by a Montana BPE-approved organization,
or

2. Master's degree from any accredited professional educator preparation program and minimum of 24 graduate semester credits from school administrator preparation program in following content areas: school leadership; instructional leadership to include supervision and secondary curriculum; successful

completion of 3 semester credits of college course work in Montana school law; and school and community relations.

    B. Class 3 administrative license endorsed as a secondary principal shall be renewed upon verification of 60 renewal units earned during valid term of the license.

  V. Class 3 Administrative License—K–12 Principal Endorsement

    A. Applicant must provide verification of:

1. Master's degree in educational leadership from professional educator preparation program accredited by either NCATE or by a Montana BPE-approved organization,
2. Full eligibility for elementary or secondary principal endorsement or current endorsement as Montana elementary or secondary principal,
3. Minimum of 3 years of successful experience as appropriately licensed and assigned Class 1 or 2 teacher or Class 6 school counselor at any level within K–12,
   and
4. If eligible at secondary level, at least 6 graduate semester credits in educational leadership and curriculum at elementary level; or, if eligible at elementary level, at least 6 graduate credits in educational leadership and curriculum at secondary level.

    B. Class 3 administrative license endorsed as K–12 principal shall be renewed upon verification of 60 renewal units earned during valid term of the license.

  VI. Class 3 Administrative License—Supervisor Endorsement

    A. Issued in specific fields such as math, music, and school counseling, or in general areas such as elementary education, secondary education and curriculum development.

    B. Applicants must submit verification of:

1. Successful completion, at accredited college or university, of master's degree in area requested for endorsement,
2. Meeting eligibility requirements for Class 1 or Class 2 teaching license endorsed in field of specialization,
3. Three years of successful experience as an appropriately licensed and assigned teacher,
4. At least 14 graduate semester credits in education or equivalent to include: general school administration; administration in specific area to be endorsed; supervision of instruction; basic school finance; and school law,
   and
5. Supervised practicum/internship (minimum of 4 semester credits or appropriate waiver), with recommendation of appropriate official(s) required.

    C. Class 3 administrative license endorsed as supervisor shall be renewed upon verification of 60 renewal units earned during valid term of license.

  VII. Class 3 Administrative License—Special Education Supervisor Endorsement

    A. Issued in specific field of special education to applicants who submit verification of:

1. Successful completion, at accredited college or university, of master's degree in special education or master's degree in special education–related service field, e.g., school psychologist, speech-language pathologist, audiologist, physical therapist, occupational therapist, registered nurse, clinical social worker, or clinical professional counselor,

2. Full licensure in field of specialization,
3. Three years of successful experience in accredited school setting as appropriately licensed and assigned teacher, or 5 years of successful experience in accredited school setting as fully licensed and assigned related services provider,
4. At least 14 graduate semester credits in education or equivalent to include: general school administration; administraion in specific area to be endorsed; supervision of instruction; basic school finance; and school law, *and*
5. Supervised practicum/internship (minimum of 4 semester credits or appropriate waiver), with recommendation of appropriate official(s) required.

B. Class 3 administrative license endorsed as special education supervisor shall be renewed upon verification of 60 renewal units earned during valid term of license.

Additional Licenses

I. Class 4 Career and Technical Education License (valid 5 years)
   A. Three types of Class 4 licenses:
      1. Class 4A license issued to individuals holding valid Montana secondary level teaching license, but without appropriate career and technical education endorsement,
      2. Class 4B license issued to individuals with at least bachelor's degree, but who do not hold valid Montana secondary-level teaching license with appropriate career and technical education endorsement,
      3. Class 4C license issued to individuals who hold at least high school diploma or GED and meet minimum requirements for endorsement.
   B. Class 4 license renewal requires 60 renewal units.
      1. Class 4A licenses (with bachelor's degree) shall be renewable by earning 60 renewal units, 40 of which must be earned through college credit. Endorsement related to technical studies may be accepted with prior approval. The first renewal must show evidence of renewal units earned in the following content areas: principles and/or philosophy of career and technical education; or safety and teacher liability.
      2. Class 4A licenses (with master's degree) shall be renewable by earning 60 renewal units. The first renewal must show evidence of renewal units earned in the following content areas: principles and/or philosophy of career and technical education; or safety and teacher liability.
      3. Class 4B or 4C licenses shall be renewable by earning 60 renewal units, 40 of which must be earned through college credit. Appropriate course work to renew a Class 4B or 4C license includes the following: principles and/or philosophy of career and technical education; curriculum and instruction in career and technical education; learning styles/teaching styles, including serving students with special needs; safety and teacher liability; classroom management; teaching methods; career guidance in career and technical education; or endorsement related technical studies, with prior approval.

C. Lapsed Class 4 license may be reinstated by showing verification of following:

1. For Class 4A licenses:

    a. If licensee does not have master's degree, 60 renewal units, 40 of which must be earned by college credit or prior approved endorsement-related technical studies, earned during 5-year period preceding validation date of new license;

    or

    b. If licensee has master's degree, 60 renewal units earned during 5-year period preceding validation date of new license.

    c. For Class 4B and 4C licenses, licensee must verify completion of 4 semester credits of course work in following areas: principles and/or philosophy of career and technical education; curriculum and instruction in career and technical education; learning styles/teaching styles, including serving students with special needs; safety and teacher liability; classroom management; teaching methods; career guidance in career and technical education; or endorsement-related technical studies, with prior approval.

II. Class 4 Endorsements

A. Recognized occupations eligible for Class 4 license shall be evaluated on annual basis by Superintendent of Public Instruction. Appropriate career and technical education areas acceptable for endorsement on Class 4 license include, but are not limited to, the following: automotive technology, welding, auto body, industrial mechanics, small engines, heavy equipment operations, electronics, horticulture, agriculture mechanics, building trades, building maintenance, culinary arts, metals, drafting, computer information systems, graphic arts, aviation, health occupations, machining, diesel mechanics, videography, and theater arts.

    1. Endorsements not on list of recognized occupations may be retained as long as holder continues to renew license.

B. To obtain an endorsement on a Class 4 license, applicant must provide the following:

    1. Verification of minimum of 10,000 hours of documented work experience, which may include apprenticeship training, documenting knowledge and skills required in specific trade in which they are to teach. Acceptable documentation is determined by the superintendent and may include, but is not limited to:

        a. Work experience completed and verified by previous employers, to include detailed description of duties performed during employment,

        b. For self-employed individuals, examples of projects completed, letters of verification from clients or customers, profit and loss statements demonstrating viability of business or self-employment,

        c. Verification of teaching experience in area requested for endorsement, accompanied by verification of substantial work experience in area requested for endorsement,

        d. Certificates of completion of appropriate technical programs or related college degrees and course work, and industry certification (e.g., ASE, AWS).

2. For health occupations or computer information systems, an alternative to above requirement of 10,000 hours work experience may be substituted as approved by Superintendent of Public Instruction as follows:
    a. For health occupations:
        i. Hold Class 1 or 2 license with endorsement in health or any of science areas;
        ii. Verification of participation in or completion of approved internship program in medical setting,
            and
        iii. Successful completion of course work in human biology and anatomy and physiology,
            or
        iv. Hold current professional license or certificate in related health occupation field.
3. For computer information systems, individual may provide verification of completion of approved technical program in recognized training institution and hold professional license or recognized industry standard certificate.

C. Class 4A, 4B, or 4C career and technical education license may be approved to teach traffic education if the license meets specific requirements; contact Montana Office of Public Instruction (OPI)—see Appendix 1—for full details.

III. Class 6 Specialist License (valid 5 years)
    A. Class 6 specialist licenses may be issued with following endorsements:
        1. School psychologist,
            or
        2. School counselor.
    B. Class 6 specialist license renewal requires college credit or renewal units as follows:
        1. Four graduate semester credits,
        2. Six graduate quarter credits,
            or
        3. Sixty renewal units.
    C. Lapsed Class 6 specialist license may be reinstated by showing verification of 4 graduate semester credits or equivalent renewal units earned during 5-year period preceding validation date of new license.

IV. Class 6 Specialist License—School Psychologist
    A. To obtain Class 6 specialist license with school psychologist endorsement, applicant must provide verification of:
        1. Current credentials as nationally certified school psychologist (NCSP) from the National Association of School Psychologists (NASP),
            or
        2. Master's degree in school psychology or education specialist degree in related field from accredited institution
            and

Recommendation from Montana Association of School Psychologists Competency Review Board after completion of oral examination.

V. Class 6 Specialist License—School Counselor
 A. To obtain Class 6 specialist license with a school counselor endorsement, applicant must provide verification of:
  1. Master's degree in school counseling (K–12),
   or
  2. Master's degree with equivalent graduate-level school counseling content, *and*
   Supervised internship of at least 600 hours in school or school-related setting.
 B. Class 6 specialist license endorsed in school counseling may be approved to teach traffic education if the licensee is approved by Superintendent of Public Instruction and meets specific requirements; contact OPI (see Appendix 1) for full details.

VI. Class 7 American Indian Language and Culture Specialist (valid 5 years)
 A. Superintendent of Public Instruction shall issue Class 7 license based upon verification by the American Indian tribe for which the language and culture licensure is desired that the individual has met tribal standards for competency and fluency as a requisite for teaching that language and culture.
  1. Candidates for Class 7 licensure must meet all nonacademic requirements for licensure in Montana.
 B. The board will accept and place on file the criteria developed by each tribe for qualifying an individual as competent to be a specialist in its language and culture.
 C. A Class 7 American Indian language and culture specialist licensee may be approved to teach traffic education if the licensee is approved by the Superintendent of Public Instruction and meets specific requirements; contact OPI (see Appendix 1) for full details.
 D. Sixty units of renewal activities authorized and verified by the tribe will be required for renewal of a Class 7 license.
 E. A school district may assign an individual licensed under this rule only to specialist services within the field of American Indian language and culture under such supervision as the district may deem appropriate. No teaching license or endorsement is required for duties within this prescribed field.

VII. Class B Dual Credit-Only Postsecondary Faculty License (valid 5 years)
 A. A faculty member of a postsecondary institution is required to hold a Class 8 dual credit license, unless already licensed Class 1, 2, or 4 and properly endorsed, whenever a faculty member is teaching a course for which one or more students will earn both high school and college credit. Contact OPI (see Appendix 1) for full details.

Nebraska

Note: Recent changes include the addition of a Dual Credit certificate for college staff providing instruction to high school students and of a career education certificate for those hired by districts to provide a specific class to students. Also, the Nebraska Certification Office will begin to send certificates as e-mail attachments after January 1, 2011, to reduce printing and postage fees.

Teaching Certificates

I. Initial Certificate (valid 5 years; renewable with provisions)
    A. Requires completion of:
        1. Bachelor's degree
            and
        2. An approved teacher education program with an endorsement recommendation from an approved institution.
            a. Six semester hours must be completed within the past 5 years.
    B. Renewable with 6 semester hours or 1 year of documented experience teaching in an approved school.
II. Standard Certificate (valid 5 years; renewable with provisions)
    A. Requirements include holding a valid Initial Certificate and at least 2 consecutive years of teaching experience.
    B. Renewable with 6 semester hours or 1 year of teaching experience within the past 5 years.
III. Professional Certificate (valid 10 years; renewable with provisions)
    A. Issued with completion of master's degree in curriculum and instruction, educational technology, or in the applicant's content field.
    B. Renewable with 6 approved semester hours or 1 year of teaching experience within the past 5 years.

Requirements for Teaching Certificates

I. Professional, Standard and Initial Certificates. Requirements for all include:
    A. Completion of a bachelor's degree;
        1. Originals of all college transcripts required
    B. Recommendation by college for teacher training program completed;
    C. Completion of at least 6 hours of college course work in the past 5 years;
    D. Complete Praxis Series I PPST—Basic, Skills test, a human relations course addressing the 6 competencies found in statute, and a general special education course;
        1. The basic skills test (PPST) requirement is waived for persons who have 3 years of teaching experience in another state while holding a valid certificate with no deficiencies.

and

E. Fingerprinting for any person who has not held a previous Nebraska certificate or lived in Nebraska for 5 consecutive years prior to the date of application.

   1. Applicant must have no felony convictions.

II. Standard and Professional Certificates Additional Requirements:

A. Both require 2 years of teaching experience during the previous 5 years.

B. Professional certificate also requires a master's degree in curriculum and instruction, educational technology, or in the person's content area.

III. Certificates with deficiencies. Consult the website for more detailed information at www.education.ne.gov/TCERT

A. Provisional Teaching Certificates

   1. Provisional Teaching Certificate (valid 1 year; renewable with provisions)

      a. Issued to persons reentering the profession who do not have recent teaching experience but otherwise meet all requirements

      b. Renewable with completion of 6 hours of course work

   2. Provisional Commitment certificate

      a. Issued at the request of a school district to employ a person who has completed 50 percent of their pre–student teaching requirements and 75 percent of their content courses to take a difficult-to-fill position

B. Substitute Teaching Certificates

   1. State Substitute Certificate (valid 5 years)

      a. Issued to applicants with a bachelor's degree who have completed an education program

      b. Allows holder unlimited days per year to substitute provided no one position is longer than 90 days

   2. Local Substitute Certificate (valid 3 years)

      a. Issued to applicants with at least 60 college hours including 1 education class

      b. Allows holder to substitute only in 1 district for no more than 40 days per year

C. Temporary Teaching Certificate (valid 2 years)

   1. Issued to those persons who have not completed the human relations training but have met all other requirements for a regular certificate

D. Conditional Teaching Certificate (valid for up to 1 year)

   1. Allows teaching while fingerprints are being processed or at the direction of the Commissioner when existing deficiencies prevent the issuance of a regular certificate in a timely manner

E. Transitional Teaching Certificate (valid 1 year in 1 district only)

F. Career Education Certificate (valid 5 years)

   1. Issued to a person with a particular area of expertise who is offering a program to students in 1 school district

G. Dual Credit Certificate (valid 5 years)

   1. Issued to college employees who are teaching high school classes for both college and high school credit

Administrative Certificates

I. Professional Administrative Certificate (valid 10 years). Requirements include:
 A. Two years of teaching experience;
 B. Completion of a specialist or doctorate degree in educational administration;
 C. Six semester hours of graduate work in educational administration within 5 years of the date of application,
  or
  Have been serving as a school administrator for 2 or more years within the past 5;
  and
 D. Successful completion of Praxis Series 1 PreProfessional Skills Test, human relations and special education (SPED) training.

II. Standard Administrative Certificate (valid 5 years). Requirements include:
 A. Two years of teaching experience;
 B. Completion of a master's degree in educational administration;
 C. Six semester hours of graduate work in educational administration within 5 years of the date of application,
  or
  Have been serving as a school administrator for 2 or more years within the past 5;
  and
 D. Human relations, PPST, and SPED training completed.

III. Provisional Administrative Certificate (valid 1 year; renewable with provisions)
 A. Candidate must have at least 75 percent of a superintendents program completed or 50 percent of a principal's program completed.
  1. Candidate must complete at least 15 hours in the first 3 years.
 B. Renewable by completing 6 hours of course work as identified by a plan drafted by a Nebraska college.

IV. Temporary Administrative Certificate (valid 2 years)
 A. Issued to applicant to complete human relations training

Support Services Certificates

I. School Psychologist, School Nurse, Educational Audiologist, Speech Technician and Coaching
 A. Standard Special Services Certificate (valid 5 years). Requirements include:
  1. Human relations training;
  2. Additional subject-specific required training or course work;
  3. Completion of an approved program in candidate's specialty;
   and
  4. Six hours of college credit within the past 5 years or one year of valid experience.
 B. Provisional Special Services Certificate (valid 1 year). Requirements include:
  1. Human relations training;

    2.   Completed 75 percent of the course requirements;
        and

    3.   Submit a signed statement of intent to fulfill the remaining requirements.

C. Temporary Special Services Certificate (valid 2 years). Requirements include:

    1.   Signed affidavit indicating lack of completion of the human relations training; and

    2.   Have met all other requirements for a Special Services Certificate

Nevada

Teaching Certificates and Requirements

I. Renewable License (valid for 5 years)
   A. Bachelor's degree from a regionally accredited college/university and completion of a program that meets approved program standards.
   B. Renewal is based on 6 semester hours of college/university credit, or 6 Nevada approved in-service credits, or a combination of both to equal a total of 6 renewal credits.
II. Non-Renewable Three-year License
   A. Same requirements as the Renewable License except with provisions for testing and course work.
   B. All provisions must be met prior to the expiration date. Once all provisions are satisfied prior to expiration date, license may be changed to Standard or Professional.
III. Professional License
   A. Meet requirements for the renewable license, submit master's degree from a regionally accredited college/university, and verify 3 years of successful teaching experience at the K–12 grade level.
   B. Renewal is based on 6 semester hours of college/university credit, or 6 Nevada approved in-service credits, or a combination of both to equal a total of 6 renewal credits.
IV. Specialist License (valid for 8 years)
   A. Meet requirements for the Renewable License, complete an educational specialist degree program from a regionally accredited college/university, and verify 3 years of successful teaching experience at the appropriate K–12 grade level. Renewal requirement is submission of professional development credit.

Basic Qualifications for Licensure

I. An applicant must be a citizen or a lawful permanent resident of the United States.
II. Degree(s) and credits for courses must have been earned from a regionally accredited college or university.
III. Foreign transcripts must be accompanied by a course-by-course and degree equivalency evaluation done by an approved evaluator service (list available on website; see Appendix 1) before applicant applies for licensure.
IV. A license is issued based on the evaluation of the applicant's official transcript(s).
V. Within 3 years from date the license is issued, all applicants will be required to submit verification of completion of course work, or pass the Education Commission–approved examination(s) in Nevada School Law, Nevada Constitution, and the U.S. Constitution, as well as competency testing examinations with the passing score established by the Department of Education.

Elementary School
(Kindergarten–8th Grade)

I.   Elementary License Requirements
    A.   Bachelor's degree from accredited college or university and completion of a State Board of Education–approved program of preparation for teaching in elementary grades
    B.   Completion of the following:
        1.   Elementary professional education, semester hours 32
            a.   Supervised student teaching.. 8
            b.   Teaching methods of teaching basic elementary subjects, including, but not limited to, mathematics, science, and social studies 9
            c.   Teaching of literacy or language arts... 9
            d.   Professional education course work.. 6
        These may include: classroom management; English as a second language; technology; evaluation of pupils; child development; special education; or social and cultural issues
II. Professional Elementary License Requirements
    A.   Meet all requirements for Elementary License
    B.   Hold a master's degree in education
    C.   Have 3 years of verifiable elementary teaching experience in state-approved schools
III. Elementary License Endorsement
    A.   Credit within the area of endorsement, semester hours.. 12
        1.   Recognized endorsement areas are art; computers and technology; English; health; mathematics; literacy; science; social studies; physical education; bilingual education; and music.
            a.   Endorsement for English requires 3 semester hours of credit in each of the following: advanced composition, descriptive grammar, and speech.
            b.   Endorsement to teach pupils enrolled in bilingual education program requires applicant to pass appropriate examination (see website in Appendix 1 for details).
    B.   Endorsement on an elementary license is not required by the Department of Education to teach kindergarten through 8th grade, although a school district may require such.

Middle School
(7th–9th Grades)

I.   Requirements to teach in designated middle school or junior high school
    A.   Hold bachelor's or higher degree from accredited college or university, *and*
        1.   Complete Board-approved preparation program for teaching at this level *or*
        Complete professional education course work, semester hours 24

Hours to include:

    a.   Supervised student teaching in designated middle or junior high school, semester hours 8

    b.   A course in methods and materials for teaching major or minor field of specialization at middle school, junior high school, or secondary grade level, or a middle or junior high school level integrated methods course

    c.   Course of study regarding education or curricular adaptation for pupils with disabilities and/or a course or study regarding educational foundation or methods in teaching English language learners, semester hours 3

    d.   Course work in at least 2 of following areas: Middle school foundations, history, theory or philosophy; middle school curriculum, pedagogy, or assessment; adolescent growth and development; nature and needs of the adolescent including social, emotional, and cultural concerns; classroom management strategies; school/family/community collaboration; or supervision and evaluation of programs and pupils in a middle school, semester hours in each of 2 areas................................. 6
       and

    e.   Course work in any of the following subjects: English as a second language/bilingualism or biculturalism; educational technology; tests and measurement; educational psychology; education of the exceptional child; multicultural education; or educational research, semester hours 6
       and

  2.   Credits in a major field of endorsement or area of concentration, semester hours.. 24

  B.   Subsequent minor fields of endorsement may be added to the license upon verification of 14 semester hours of credit.

II.   Endorsement areas: Art; English/language arts; foreign language (see Department of Education in Appendix 1 for specifics); mathematics; music; science; and social science

  A.   Mathematics endorsement requires completion of 3 semester credits, to include a course in college algebra or concepts of calculus, including an introduction to limits, derivatives and integrals, precalculus, or differential calculus.

  B.   Major or minor fields of endorsement or area of concentration shall be deemed to be met if applicant holds bachelor's degree or a higher degree with a major, minor, or area of concentration identified on official transcript of record conferred by regionally accredited college or university.

Secondary School

I.   Authorization

  A.   A license endorsed in a recognized teaching field is required for teaching in departmentalized seventh and eighth grades, junior high schools, senior high schools, and designated and approved middle schools. Endorsements are dependent upon the applicant's field of specialization or concentration, usually designated as majors or minors or areas of concentration.

II. Initial Secondary License Requirements
   A. Bachelor's degree and completion of an approved program of preparation for secondary school teaching,
      or
   B. Bachelor's degree and completion of the following:
     1. A teaching field major from a regionally accredited institution
     2. Secondary professional education, semester hours 22
       a. Supervised teaching and/or teaching internship..................................... 8
       b. A course in methods and materials of teaching in field of specialization.
       c. Check with Department of Education (see Appendix 1) for specific requirements in occupational education

III. Professional Secondary License Requirements
   A. Meet all requirements for Initial Secondary License
   B. Hold a master's degree
   C. Have 3 years of verified teaching experience in state-approved secondary schools

IV. Teaching Endorsements
   A. Academic endorsements: art, biological science, business, English as a second language, English, general science, mathematics (major/minor), music (major/minor in instrumental or instrumental and choral; major only in choral and vocal), physical education, physical education and health, physical science, recreational physical education, social studies, and speech and drama
   B. Occupational endorsements: agricultural education, automotive technology, business education, child care, commercial housekeeping, communications and media, construction technology, drafting and design, electronic technology, food services, health occupations, home economics, hospitality and recreation, housing and home furnishing, human services, industrial arts, manufacturing technology, marketing education, stage and theater technology, technology education
   C. Comprehensive fields of concentration
     1. Majors, semester hours 36
       a. Music major, semester hours... 36
     2. Minors, semester hours 24
   D. Single-subject majors and minors
     1. Majors, semester hours 30
     2. Minors, semester hours 16
     3. For complete list of academic and occupational single-subject majors or minors, see Department of Education Teacher Licensing website (see Appendix 1).

Special Education

Available endorsements include: adaptive physical education, audiology, autism, traumatic brain injury, early childhood developmentally delayed, serious emotional disturbances, generalist, gifted and talented, health impairments, hearing impaired, specific learning disabilities, mental retardation, orthopedic impairments, speech and language impairments, and visual impairments. Contact the Teacher Licensing Office (see Appendix 1) for more detailed information in this area.

Administration

I. Authorization
    A. A Professional Administrator of a School endorsement is required for the following: superintendent, associate superintendent, assistant superintendent, principal, vice principal, supervisor, administrative assistant, and program supervisor or coordinator
    B. A Professional Administrator of a Program endorsement is required for an individual who supervises or coordinates a program of nursing, school psychology, speech therapy, physical therapy, occupational therapy, or any other program area unless that person holds a Professional Administrator of a School endorsement.
    C. A Supervisor of Curriculum and Instruction endorsement is also issued.

II. Professional Administrator of a School Endorsement: meet requirements A or B below
    A. Complete the following:
        1. Master's degree
        2. Valid teaching license for elementary, secondary, or K–12 special
        3. Three years of verified teaching experience at the K–12 level in state-approved schools
        4. Thirty-six semester hours of graduate courses in school administration, to include: administration and organization of schools; supervision of instruction; development of personnel; school finance; school law; curriculum; educational research; internship or field experience in school administration; and other courses considered to be part of an administrative program for educators;
            or
    B. Hold a qualifying valid teaching license with the appropriate teaching experience (see II, A, directly above) and have a master's degree or higher in educational administration from an accredited institution

III. Professional Administrator of a Program Endorsement
    A. Hold a master's degree
    B. Hold a valid license in program for which endorsement is requested
    C. Have and submit to Department evidence of 3 years of experience as licensed employee in kindergarten or grades 1–12
    D. Have completed at least 27 semester hours in administration courses (which may not be taken as independent study), to include:
        1. Administration and organization of a school or the role of a program administrator in the applicant's endorsement area,
        2. General principles of supervision of personnel or supervision of personnel for a program in the applicant's endorsement area,
        3. Finances of a school or finances of a program in the applicant's endorsement area,
        4. The laws that apply to schools,
        5. The evaluation and development of personnel for a school or for a program in the applicant's endorsement area,
            and

6. Any other courses that are required for a degree in the administration of a program in the applicant's endorsement area.

School Counselor

I. Endorsement as a School Counselor
    A. Hold a master's degree or higher in school counseling from a regionally accredited college and/or university,
        or
    B. Hold a master's degree or higher from a regionally accredited college and/or university and a specialty credential as a national certified school counselor issued by the National Board for Certified Counselors,
        or
    C. Hold a master's degree or higher with a major in counseling from a regionally accredited college or university and fulfill requirements in I, E, 1 and 2, directly below,
        or
    D. Hold a master's degree or higher from a regionally accredited college or university and have at least 2 years of teaching experience, or at least 2 years of school counseling experience, and fulfill requirements in I, E, 1 and 2, directly below
    E. Complete the following:
        1. At least 280 hours of a practicum, internship, or field experience in school counseling at any grade level in grades K–12,
            and
        2. At least 36 semester hours of graduate credits in school guidance and counseling in the following areas of study
            a. The process of individual counseling
            b. The process of group counseling
            c. Testing and educational assessments
            d. Legal and ethical issues in counseling
            e. Career counseling
            f. Organization and administration of school counseling programs
            g. Multicultural counseling
            h. Child and family counseling,
                and
            i. Complete 2 of the following:
                i.   The use of technology in education
                ii. Exceptional children
                iii. Human growth and development
                iv. Substance abuse counseling

Library Media Specialist

I. Endorsement as School Library Media Specialist, K–12
    A. Hold a valid elementary, secondary, or special teaching license, excluding a business and industry endorsement or a special qualification,

and

B. Complete a program for school library media specialists that has been approved by the board or a regional accrediting association,
or

C. Hold a master's degree in library science, with specialization in school librarianship, from a school accredited by the American Library Association,
or

D. Complete 21 semester hours of course work in the following subjects
   1. Organization and administration of a school library
   2. Cataloging and classification of materials for a library
   3. Reference, bibliography, and information skills
   4. Use and selection of educational media for a library
   5. Children's and young adults' literature
   6. Computers in the library
   7. A supervised practicum in an elementary or secondary school library

II. Endorsement as Professional School Library Media Specialist
   A. Hold a master's degree in any field,
   B. See I, A–C, directly above,
   C. Complete an additional 9 semester hours in curriculum and instruction, educational technology, or information technology,
   and
   D. Have 3 years of experience in state-approved schools or accredited private schools as a librarian or school library media specialist.

New Hampshire

Alternatives for Certification

I. General Requirements for Certification Alternatives 1–5, below
   A. This basic academic skills requirement applies to all five certification alternatives.
      1. Passing score on Praxis I Pre-Professional Skills Test or Computer-Based Test,
         or
         passing score on Praxis I composite score option,
         or
         equivalent test
      2. Exemptions: Ed 513.01 (b) (July 2003)
         a. Master's degree or higher,
            or
         b. Seven or more years of educational experience under a credential issued by another state
   B. This subject area assessment applies to all five certification alternatives.
      1. Passing score on Praxis II subject-specific tests for initial certification in English, French, German, Spanish, social studies, general science, biology, chemistry, earth/space science, middle school mathematics, secondary mathematics, physical science, physics, elementary education, early childhood, middle school, social studies and middle school English
      2. See I, A, 2, a and b, above
   C. Criminal record check, which is conducted at the district level upon employment
II. Alternative 1—Approved Programs in New Hampshire
   A. New Hampshire State Department of Education–approved programs of professional preparation in education
   B. Certification for teachers, education specialists, and administrators
      1. Successful completion of the approved program
      2. Written recommendation by designated official of the institution
      3. Application to New Hampshire State Department of Education, Bureau of Credentialing
      4. Praxis I and Praxis II, if applicable
III. Alternative 2 has 2 distinct sets of requirements, known as Alternatives 2A and 2B.
   A. Alternative 2A concerns applicants from other states party to the National Association of State Directors of Teacher Education and Certification (NASDTEC) Interstate Contract and shall consist of the following:
      1. Individuals shall qualify for a beginning or experienced educator credential by:
         a. Completing a program in another state party to the NASDTEC Interstate Contract that would qualify the applicant for certification as an educator in the other state. This includes, but is not limited to, an alternative

certification program consistent with the terms of the NASDTEC Interstate Contract with New Hampshire,
or

    b. Holding an equivalent, valid credential from such a state and having 3 years of educational experience in the last 7 years under a credential from a participating state

  2. Applicants seeking to obtain certification under Alternative 2A shall apply to the Bureau of Credentialing pursuant to Ed 508.

B. Alternative 2B concerns applicants from states not signatory to the NASDTEC Interstate Contract.

  1. Individuals from a state not party to the NASDTEC Interstate Contract shall qualify for a beginning or experienced educator credential by:

    a. Completing a program in such a state that would qualify the applicant for certification as an educator in that state, including but not limited to an alternative certification program approved by the department of education in such a state,
or

    b. Holding an equivalent, valid credential from such a state and having at least 3 years of experience as an educator in the last 7 years under a credential issued by that state.

IV. Alternative 3—Demonstrated Competencies and Equivalent Experiences—has 3 distinct sets of requirements, known as Alternatives 3A, 3B, and 3C.

A. Alternative 3A for Educators

  1. An applicant who has acquired competencies, skills, and knowledge through means other than Alternatives 1 or 2 may request a credential by submitting to the Bureau:

    a. A completed official application form,

    b. Official college or university transcripts verifying that the applicant holds a bachelor's degree,
and

    c. A letter from an employer verifying completion of at least 3 months of full-time experience in the area of the endorsement sought

  2. The Bureau shall evaluate the materials listed above to determine whether or not the individual qualifies under this method.

    a. If not, the Bureau shall notify the individual within 15 days of its decision, providing reasons for the determination and recommending another appropriate application method, if applicable

    b. If so, the applicant shall attend on oral interview with a duly appointed review board, which shall make a written recommendation to the administrator whether or not to certify the applicant.

    c. If denied credentialing, the applicant may appeal the administrator's decision.

B. Alternative 3B for National or Regional Certification

  1. An applicant eligible for a credential because of national or regional examination results may submit an official application for certification along

with his or her examination scores to the Bureau with appropriate filing fees and accompanying documentation of:

    a.   A national-level or regional certification validated by passing a national or regional examination designed to assess the individual's skills in the area of certification sought,

        or

    b.   Proof of completion of a specialized program such as, but not limited to, a bachelor's degree in social work, culminating in a bachelor's degree from an accredited college or university.

  C. Alternative 3C for Administrators

    1. Applicants for superintendent, principal, or special education administrator shall submit an official application for certification to enable the Bureau to determine by transcript analysis whether the applicant meets the appropriate program requirements:

        a.   For superintendent applicants, Ed 614.05

        b.   For principal applicants, Ed 614.04

        c.   For special education administrator applicants, Ed 506.07(d)

V. Alternative 4 — Critical Shortage Areas, Career & Technical Education, and Business Administrator

  A. Alternative 4 is a qualifying method for certification that requires:

    1. Bachelor's degree from an approved institution,

    2. Completion of a professional development plan in a critical shortage teaching area, career & technical education and/or business administration. New Hampshire Department of Education, Bureau of Credentialing website has a complete list of Critical Shortage areas (see Appendix 1),

    3. Successful teaching under a mentor teacher,

        and

    4. Recommendation for certification from the local Superintendent of Schools.

  B. An applicant may be employed as an educator after obtaining a statement of eligibility from the Bureau of Credentialing (see Appendix 1) and while completing an approved individualized professional development plan.

  C. Applicant who holds a Statement of Eligibility may be hired by a Superintendent or agency head to pursue Alternative IV. This document is not a teaching certificate. The Superintendent will submit an "In Process of Certification" form while the plan is being developed and the basic academic skills requirement is being met. Exemptions to the basic academic skills requirement include:

    1. Master's degree or higher,

    2. Seven or more years of educational experience under a credential issued by another state,

        or

    3. New Hampshire certification in another content area.

VI. Alternative 5 — Site-Based Certification Plan

  A. Available in elementary and secondary teaching areas, excluding vocational and special education

B.   Qualifications
1.   A bachelor's degree from an approved institution
2.   The applicant shall meet one of the following criteria:
a.   For secondary education, at least 30 credit hours in the subject to be taught and an overall grade-point average of at least 2.5, or equivalent
b.   For elementary education, successful completion of courses in mathematics, English, social studies, and science with an overall grade-point average of at least 2.5, or equivalent
3.   An individual who fails to meet the grade-point average requirement shall still qualify for site-based certification plan provided that:
a.   All other requirements are met,
b.   Collegiate graduation occurred more than 5 years prior to application for the site-based plan,
and
c.   Occupational experience totaling 5 years directly related to the area to be taught is documented by letter from previous employers; employment contracts; or letters of commendation and recommendations from parties knowledgeable about the applicant's backround and experience.
C.   Candidates must complete a specifically designed site-based educational plan, normally during the first 1 to 2 years of service.

Levels of Professional Certification

I.   Beginning Educator Certificate (valid 3 years)
A.   Successful completion of an approved program of professional preparation in education
B.   Recommendation by designated official of preparatory institution
C.   Upon recommendation of Superintendent of Schools, a beginning educator may be eligible for Experienced Educator Certificate at the close of the 3-year period.
II.   Experienced Educator Certificate (valid 3 years)
A.   Has met all requirements for previous levels of certification
III.   Educator Recertification
A.   Every educator applying for credential renewal must acquire all of the following:
1.   A minimum of 75 hours of approved professional development activity every 3 years
2.   A minimum of 45 hours of the total hours required shall be devoted to approved professional development activities meeting district needs, school goals, and/or school improvement plans.
3.   A minimum of 30 hours of the total hours required shall be devoted to approved professional development activity in each subject area and/or field of specialization for which recertification is sought.
4.   For each endorsement, an additional 30 hours shall be devoted to approved professional development activity in each subject area and/or field of specialization.

New Jersey

Applicants are strongly advised to consult the New Jersey Licensing Code, available at http://www.state.nj.us/education/educators/license/, for specific eligibility requirements for obtaining certificates.

Certification Overview

I. New Jersey certificates are issued under 4 categories; for detailed listings of the many certificates and specific requirements for them, go to http://www.state.nj.us/education/educators/license/
    A. Teacher certificates for classroom teachers
    B. Educational Services Personnel certificates for such positions as school social worker, school psychologist, learning disabilities teacher-consultant, substance awareness coordinator, etc.
    C. School Leaders certificates for school administrator, principal, supervisor, and school business administrator
    D. Career and Technical Education certificates for positions such as automotive technology, carpentry, cosmetology/hair styling, plumbing, etc.
    E. In addition, the following certificates may be issued when the appropriate requirements have been satisfied:
        1. Emergency Certificate: a substandard 1-year license issued only in limited fields of educational services
        2. County Substitute Credential: a temporary certificate issued by the county office which allows the holder to temporarily perform the duties of a fully licensed and regularly employed teacher when none is available

II. Endorsement and Highly Qualified Status
    A. An endorsement is an area of certification with distinct grade-level and subject matter authorizations in which a certificate holder is authorized to serve.
    B. Although an endorsement authorizes the holder to teach in the area of their endorsement, the individual must also meet the highly qualified requirements required by the federal government. For further information on meeting the highly qualified requirements, go to http://www.nj.gov/education/profdev/nclb/

III. Certification Process for Novice Educators
    A. Certificate of Eligibility (CE): for applicants who did not complete a teacher preparation program. Requirements:
        1. Hold bachelor's or advanced degree from regionally accredited college or university
        2. Students graduating on or after September 1, 2004, must achieve cumulative minimum GPA of 2.75 (when 4.00 GPA equals an A grade) in baccalaureate, higher degree, or state-approved post-baccalaureate certification program with at least 13 semester-hour credits

       a.   For students graduating before September 1, 2004, same requirements apply except minimum GPA is 2.50

3.   For subject area endorsements, complete at least 30 credits in coherent course sequence appropriate to instructional area (at least 12 of such semester-hour credits must be at advanced level, including junior-, senior-, or graduate-level study)

    a.   For elementary school endorsement, complete liberal arts, science, dual content, or interdisciplinary academic major, or minimum of 60 semester hour credits in liberal arts and/or science

4.   All course work must appear on transcript of regionally accredited 4-year college or university

5.   Pass appropriate state test of subject matter knowledge; and

6.   Pass examination in physiology, hygiene, and substance abuse issues

7.   Elementary school (K–5) CE, Instructional Area CE, or Preschool through Grade Three CE

    a.   Effective October 31, 2009, candidates for the Elementary school (K–5) CE or Instructional Area CE must demonstrate knowledge of basic pedagogical skills appropriate to the area of endorsement through transcripts showing successful completion of a minimum of 24 hours of study offered through a state-approved provider or through approved course work at a New Jersey state-approved college.

       i.   Exceptions: Holders of a CEAS, provisional, or standard certificate in another instructional area are exempt from this requirement.

    b.   Effective September 1, 2009, candidates for the Preschool through Grade Three CE must also follow procedures described directly above in 7, a, i.

B. Certificate of Eligibility with Advanced Standing (CEAS): for applicants who did complete a teacher preparation program. Requirement:

1.   The candidate shall meet the requirements in I, A, 1–7, directly above and complete one of the following programs of teacher preparation:

    a.   A New Jersey college program, graduate or undergraduate, approved by the Department for the preparation of teachers;

    b.   A college preparation program included in the interstate certification reciprocity system of the National Association of State Directors of Teacher Education and Certification (NASDTEC);

    c.   An out-of-state teacher education program approved by the National Council for the Accreditation of Teacher Education (NCATE), Teacher Education Accreditation Council (TEAC), or any other national professional education accreditation body recognized by the Council on Higher Education Accreditation approved by the Commissioner;

    d.   A teacher education program approved for certification by the Department in one of the states party to the NASDTEC Interstate Contract, provided the program was completed on or after January 1, 1964, and the state in which the program is located would issue the candidate a comparable endorsement;

       or

   e.   An out-of-state college teacher education program approved by the state department of education in which the program is located.
2.   The teacher preparation programs listed in I, B, 1, a–e, directly above must culminate in college supervised student teaching.
3.   A candidate who graduates on or after September 1, 2004, will meet the requirements in I, B, 1, a–e directly above if they fall within the parameters in 3, a and b, directly below. For details, consult http://www.state.nj.us/education/educators/license/gpa.htm
   a.   A GPA that is below 2.75, but at least 2.50 and whose score in the appropriate state test of subject matter knowledge exceeds the passing score by 10 percent or more;
        or
   b.   A GPA that is 3.50 or higher, but whose score in the appropriate State test of subject matter knowledge falls below the passing score by no more than five percent.
C.   Standard Certificate: for applicants who have at least 1 year of full-time teaching experience under a valid out-of-state license and have completed a full-time teacher preparation program that included student teaching. Requirements:
   1. Possess a provisional certificate;
        and
   2.   Successfully complete a state-approved district training program while employed provisionally in a position requiring the appropriate instructional certificate.
   3.   Further eligibilities and their restrictions are available at http://www.state.nj.us/education/educators/license/
   4.   A candidate who holds National Board professional Teacher Standards (NBPTS) certification and the corresponding out-of-state license or out-of-state certificate shall be eligible for the standard certificate in the NBPTS certificate field without additional requirements.
   5.   Completion of an out-of-state non-traditional or alternate route teacher preparation program that is determined by the Department to be comparable to the state's school-based training and evaluation program provided to all New Jersey novice teachers;
        and
        A valid standard certificate from the state in which the above was completed.
IV.   Provisional Teacher Program
A.   School-based training and evaluation program provided to all novice teachers during first year of New Jersey teaching
B.   Building principal recommends standard certification at completion of program requirements
C.   Both alternatively and traditionally prepared teacher candidates participate and receive support by veteran teachers in their school. Contact Department of Education (see Appendix 1) for full details.
D.   Alternate route candidates complete 200 hours of formal instruction in professional education aligned with New Jersey Professional Standards for Teachers.

V. Reciprocity
    A. Out-of-state applicants qualifying under any form of reciprocity [i.e., ICC (International Code Council), NCATE (National Council for Teacher Education), TEAC (Teacher Education Accreditation Council), or locally approved, out-of-state college teacher education program] will have met content area and professional education requirements.
    B. Such candidates must also meet required GPA, pass required state test of subject matter knowledge, and state test of physiology, hygiene, and substance abuse issues.

Educational Services Certification

New Jersey issues 21 educational service endorsements, including school psychologist, school nurse, school social worker, and speech-language specialist. For a full listing of available endorsements, authorizations, and related requirements, see the New, Jersey Department of Education website: http://www.nj.gov/njded/code/current/title6a/chap9.pdf, beginning on page 79.

Administrator Certification

I. Standard Certificate for Principal, School Administrator, or School Business Administrator
    A. Candidate must:
        1. Complete advanced degree in one of recognized fields of leadership or management, or in curriculum and instruction, including study area requirements
            a. School business administrator certificate requires either a master's degree or a certified public accountant license.
        2. Pass written examination
            a. School Leaders Licensure Assessment for principal; and School Superintendent Assessment for school administrator
        3. Apply for Certificate of Eligibility (CE)
    B. When candidate obtains position requiring principal, school administrator, or school business administrator certification, school district must
        1. Register candidate into Administrator Training Program (2 years in length)
        2. Send Statement of Assurance of Position and Standard Residency Agreement to initiate residency period
    C. When mentor is assigned to candidate, a training program is developed by district, mentor, and candidate, subject to Department of Education approval. A provisional certificate (valid 2 years) is then issued to candidate.
    D. Upon satisfactory completion of residency (candidate is evaluated 3 times) and recommendation of mentor, State Board of Examiners may issue standard certificate.
II. Standard Certificate for Supervisor
    A. Three years of full-time teaching or educational services experience
    B. Valid New Jersey instructional or educational services certificate or out-of-state equivalent

C. Master's degree from regionally accredited college or university
D. Twelve graduate credits in supervision and curriculum development, to include the following:
    1. A course in general staff supervision for grades PK–12
    2. A course in general curriculum development for grades PK–12
    3. An elective course in curriculum development
    4. An elective course in either curriculum development or staff supervision
III. For more detailed information on available administrative endorsements, authorizations, and related requirements, see the New Jersey Department of Education website: http://www.nj.gov/njded/code/current/title6a/chap9.pdf, beginning on page 67
IV. For administrative certification application information, see Certification Application Process, I–III, above

New Mexico

Licensure Levels

I. Initial Licensure—Level 1 (classroom instruction)
   A. Valid for 5 years; renewable if license not used during its term, or extended if only partially use
   B. Thirty to thirty-six semester hours in elementary education (see Elementary Education, below, for details)
   C. Professional education courses that incorporate the Professional Licensure Bureau's prescribed pedagogical competencies
   D. Teaching field in at least one content area that incorporates the Professional Licensure Bureau's teaching field competencies
   E. Pass, with a minimum score of 240, the New Mexico Teacher Assessments (NMTA), including the New Mexico Assessment of Teacher Basic Skills, New Mexico Assessment of Teacher Competency (Elementary, Secondary, or Early Childhood) and New Mexico Content Area test in the applicable subject area

II. Continuing Licensure—Level 2 (classroom instruction)
   A. Valid for 9 years; renewable
   B. Fulfillment of Level 1 requirements; see I, B–E, directly above
   C. Minimum of 3 years of teaching experience at Level 1
   D. Submission and passage of a Professional Development Dossier; see details at http://www.teachnm.org
   E. Every public school teacher must successfully meet requirements of the state's high objective uniform standard of evaluation through an annual performance evaluation based on annual professional development plan
   F. Verification by local superintendent or private school official that applicant has met Professional Licensure Bureau's prescribed teaching competencies

III. Continuing Licensure—Level 3-A (instructional leadership)
   A. Valid for 9 years; renewable
   B. Fulfillment of Level 2 requirements; see II, B–F, directly above
   C. Master's degree or National Board for Professional Teaching Standards (NBTPS) certification
   D. Minimum of 3 years of teaching experience at Level 2
   E. Verification by local superintendent or private school official that applicant has met the Professional Licensure Bureau's prescribed Level 3-A competencies

IV. Initial Licensure—Level 3-B (educational administration/management)
   A. Valid for 9 years; renewable
   B. Fulfillment of Level 3-A requirements; see III, B–E, directly above
   C. Master's degree
   D. Completion of an administrative internship or apprenticeship

E.   Eighteen semester hours of graduate credit in educational administration that incorporates the Professional Licensure Bureau's prescribed Level 3-B competencies

Note: Detailed competencies for each level of certification are available from the New Mexico Professional Licensure Bureau website (http://www.ped.state.nm.us/Licensure; then click Licensure Pathways/Requirements).

Out-of-State Application for Licensure

I.   Those seeking New Mexico teacher or administrator licensure must show:
A.   Bachelor's and/or master's degree from a regionally accredited college or university
B.   Completion of an educator preparation program accepted by the New Mexico Professional Licensure Bureau
C.   Valid standard certificate or license issued by another state, or valid certificate issued by the National Board for the Professional Teaching Standards for the appropriate grade level and type
D.   Proof of passing test scores from another state in core content areas and verification of teaching experience
1.   If this information is not specifically required, submit notarized statement verifying it.
E.   If seeking licensure at levels 2 or 3, provide official verification signed by a school district official of out-of-state teaching experience.
II.   Administrative Licensure
1.   Bachelor's and master's degrees from a regionally accredited college or university
2.   Valid teaching license accepted by the New Mexico Professional Licensure Bureau
3.   Valid administrator license from another state
4.   If candidate entered an administrator preparation program after April 2003, 6 years of teaching experience

Elementary Education (K–8)

I.   Requirements for Level 1 Licensure (valid 5 years)
A.   Bachelor's degree from regionally accredited institution
B.   General education, total semester hours 30–36
1.   English, semester hours 12
2.   History (including American history and Western civilization), semester hours 12
3.   Mathematics, semester hours 6
4.   Government, economics, or sociology, semester hours 6
5.   Science (including biology, chemistry, physics, geology, zoology, or botany), semester hours 12
6.   Fine arts, semester hours 6

C. Professional education, semester hours 30–36
   1. Completion of the Professional Licensure Bureau's approved functional areas and related competencies in professional education
   2. Completion of a student teaching component
   3. Placement on a continuous Professional Development Plan (PDP) with structured support or mentoring by the school district
   4. Six hours in teaching of reading if program started after August 2001
D. Teaching field, semester hours 24–36
  (such as mathematics, science(s), language arts, reading, social studies, or other content-related areas)
   1. Completion of Professional Licensure Bureau's approved functional areas and related competencies in the teaching field
E. Testing requirement: see Licensure Levels, I, E, above

Middle-Level Education (5–9)

I. Requirements for Level 1 Licensure (valid 5 years)
  A. See Elementary Education, I, A, B, C, and E, above
  B. Same as Elementary Education, I, D, except that 6 semester hours of the 24 required must be in upper-division courses
  C. Middle-level education course work, semester hours 12
   To include representation in any combination of the New Mexico Middle-Level Competencies,
   or
   Five years of teaching experience in middle-level grades
   or
   A valid certificate issued by the National Board for Professional Teaching Standards for the appropriate grade level and type
  D. Testing requirement: see Licensure Levels, I, E, above

Secondary Education (7–12)

I. Requirements for Level 1 Licensure (valid 5 years)
  A. See Elementary Education, I, A, B, and E, above
  B. Professional education, semester hours 24–30
   1. See Elementary Education, I, C, 1 and 2
   2. Three hours in teaching of reading if program started after August 2001
  C. Teaching field, semester hours 24–36
   1. Twelve semester hours must be in upper-division courses as defined by the institution.
   2. See Elementary Education, I, D, 1
  D. Testing requirement: see Licensure Levels, I, E, above

Educational Administration (K–12)

I.   Requirements for Level 3-B Licensure (valid 9 years; renewable)
A.   Valid New Mexico teaching license, Level 3-A
B.   Bachelor's and master's degrees from regionally accredited institution. For students first entering a college or university in Fall 1986 and thereafter, an apprenticeship is required.
1.   The apprenticeship may be completed at an institution with an approved program in educational administration and must consist of at least 180 clock hours, to include time at both the beginning and the end of the school year,
or
The apprenticeship may be completed under the supervision of a local school superintendent or a private school official at the school and consist of at least 180 clock hours during 1 complete calendar year, to include time at both the beginning and the end of the school year.
C.   Eighteen semester hours of graduate credit in an approved educational administration program that incorporates the Professional Licensure Bureau's approved functional areas and related competencies in educational administration and must be from a regionally accredited institution
D.   Pass the Licensure assessment in administration.

School Counseling (Pre K–12)

I.   Requirements for Level 1 Licensure (valid 3 years)
A.   National certified school counselor credential issued by the National Board for Certified Counselors,
or
B.   Licensed professional mental health counselor credential or licensed professional clinical mental health counselor credential issued by the New Mexico Counseling & Therapy Board, and a minimum of 6 semester hours of graduate credit in school counseling,
or
C.   Bachelor's and master's degrees from regionally accredited institutions
1.   Master's degree in school counseling from a New Mexico institution that must incorporate the Professional Licensure Bureau's prescribed competencies in the area of school counseling,
or
2.   Master's degree from an out-of-state institution in a school counseling program approved by the Professional Licensure Bureau,
or
3.   If master's degree is in a discipline other than school counseling, 36–42 semester hours of graduate credit from a New Mexico institution that incorporates the Professional Licensure Bureau's prescribed competencies in school counseling and includes a practicum in a school setting,
or

4. If master's degree is in a discipline other than school counseling, 36–42 semester hours of graduate credit from an out-of-state institution in school counseling that is approved by the Professional Licensure Bureau and includes a practicum in a school setting

D. Pass the Licensure assessment in school counseling.

Additional Licenses/Endorsements

For details, please visit the New Mexico Professional Licensure Bureau website: http://www.ped.state.nm.us/licensure

I. Additional Licenses Offered
Athletic Coach (7–12), Certified Occupational Therapist Assistant (preK–12), Early Childhood (Birth–Grade 3), Educational Assistant (preK–12), Educational Diagnostician (preK–12), Grades preK–12 Teaching, Interpreter for the Deaf (preK–12), Mobility Trainer for the Blind (preK–12), Native American Language and Culture (preK–12), Occupational Therapist (preK–12), Physical Therapist (preK–12), Physical Therapist Assistant (preK–12), Recreational Therapist (preK–12), Rehabilitation Counselor (preK–12), School Counselor (preK–12), School Nurse (preK–12), School Psychologist (preK–12), School Social Worker (preK–12), Secondary Vocational-Technical (7–12), Special Education (preK–12), Speech Language Pathologist (preK–12), School Business Official, Health Assistant (preK–12), School Licensed Practical Nurse (preK–12)

II. Endorsements Offered
Agriculture, Bilingual, Business Education, Family and Consumer Science, Health Education, Information Technology Coordinator, Language Arts, Library/Media, Mathematics, Modern and Classical Language, Performing Arts, Physical Education, Psychology, Reading, Science, Social Studies, Technology Education (Industrial Arts), Teaching English to Speakers of Other Languages, Visual Arts

New York

Note: As of March 2, 2010, New York is no longer printing paper certificates for time-limited certificates (Initial, Provisional, etc.). Certification status should be verified by using TEACH Online Services; see Office of Teaching Initiatives (OTI) at http://www.highered.nysed.gov/tcert

I. Stages and Titles of Teaching Certificates
    A. Initial Certificate (valid 5 years; nonrenewable; leads to Professional certificate)
        1. First-stage certificate issued in specific subject/grade titles for classroom teaching and school building leaders
        2. Requirements include completion of
            a. Baccalaureate degree;
            b. Registered program of preparation or its equivalent;
            c. Qualifying scores on applicable New York State Teacher Certification Examinations;
            d. Two clock hours of study in the identification and reporting of suspected child abuse;
            e. Two clock hours of study in school violence prevention and intervention; *and*
            f. Fingerprint clearance.
        3. Conditional Initial certificate (valid 2 years; leads to Initial certificate)
            a. First-level certificate for classroom teachers: issued to those holding comparable teaching certificate from another state party to Interstate Reciprocity Agreement, but who have not yet met New York State testing requirements.
            b. Certified teachers from other states who hold a National Board for Professional Teaching Standards (NBPTS) certificate qualify for an Initial certificate in the same or equivalent title.
    B. Professional Certificate (valid continuously with completion of 175 hours of professional development every 5 years)
        1. Second-stage certificate issued in specific subject/grade titles for classroom teaching and school building leaders
        2. Requirements for classroom teaching certificates:
            a. Satisfying the requirements for the Initial certificate (see I, A, immediately above),
            b. Completion of a master's degree or higher in the content core of the Initial certificate or in a related content area; or in any field with 12 semester hours of graduate study in the content core or related area; or completion of any graduate teacher certification program; *and*
            c. Three years of K–12 teaching experience, the first year of which must be a

mentored year if employed in a public school district (unless possessing 2 years of prior teaching experience).

    3. Certain titles, such as those in specific career and technical subjects, have slightly different requirements. See http://www.highered.nysed.gov/tcert

C. Provisional Certificate (valid 5 years; nonrenewable)

    1. The entry-level certificate for pupil personnel professionals, issued in specific subject/grade titles

    2. Requirements include completion of:

        a. Baccalaureate degree;

        b. Registered program of preparation or its equivalent;

        c. Two clock hours of study in the identification and reporting of suspected child abuse;

        d. Two clock hours of study in school violence prevention and intervention; *and*

        e. Fingerprint clearance.

    2. Some titles have additional professional license or experience requirements.

    3. Certified school counselors from other states who hold an NBPTS certificate qualify for a Provisional certificate in the same title.

D. Permanent Certificate (valid for life, unless revoked for cause by the New York State Education Department)

    1. The advanced-level certificate for pupil personnel certificates, as well as for classroom teachers and school administrators who hold a valid Provisional certificate

    2. Requirements include:

        a. Completion of a master's degree in field of certification or in a field functionally related thereto, and

        b. Two years of K–12 experience.

    3. In certain fields there are additional professional licensing or graduate study requirements.

II. Requirements for Teaching Certificates

A. Early Childhood Education (Birth–Grade 2), Childhood Education (Grades 1–6), and Middle Childhood Education Generalist (Grades 5–9). Valid for teaching in the elementary grades and middle school as indicated.

    1. Initial Certificate Requirements:

        a. Baccalaureate degree from a regionally accredited institution of higher education (IHE) or from an institution authorized by the Board of Regents to confer degrees and whose programs are registered by the State Education Department, with minimum 2.5 grade point average (GPA).

        b. Semester hour distribution includes:

            i. General Education Core .... 30 hours in the liberal arts and sciences

           ii. Content Core .... 30 hours in one or more of the liberal arts and sciences

          iii. Pedagogy Core .... 21 semester hours, 6 at the developmental level of the certificate

        c.   College-supervised student teaching experience or employment as teacher within the grades and subject area of the certificate...................40 days

        d.   Qualifying scores on the New York State Teacher Certification Examinations' Liberal Arts and Science Test (LAST), Assessment of Teaching Skills—Written (ATS—W), and Multi-Subject Content Specialty Test (CST)

  2. Professional Certificate General Requirements:

        a.   Satisfaction of requirements for the Initial certificate; see II, A, 1, directly above;

        b.   Master's degree in subject of certificate or in a related area, or in any field with 12 hours in subject of certificate or related area;
           and

        c.   Three years of K–12 teaching experience.

        d.   For a listing of specific requirements, including semester hour distribution and minimum course grade requirements, consult the certification section of the OTI, website at http://ohe32.nysed.gov/tcert

B. Middle Childhood Education Specialist (Grades 5–9) and Adolescence Education (Grades 7–12). Valid for teaching in the middle and high school as indicated.

  1. Initial Certificate Requirements

        a.   See II, A, 1, a–d, directly above, except that:

            i.   Content Core must include 30 hours in the subject of the certificate sought (English language arts; language other than English; biology; chemistry; earth science; physics; mathematics; or social studies); and

            ii.   Content Specialty Test must be in the subject of the certificate.

  2. Professional Certificate

        a.   See II, A, 2, a–d, directly above

C. Library Media Specialist (All grades)

  1. Initial Certificate requirements:

        a.   See II, A, 1, a, directly above,

        b.   Semester hour distribution includes:

            i.   General Education Core ....30 hours in the liberal arts and sciences

            ii.   Content Core ....30 hours of graduate study in library science (including instructional and assistive technology)

            iii.   Pedagogy Core ....21 semester hours,

        c.   College supervised practicum.........40 days (20 days in an elementary school and 20 days in a secondary school),

          and

        d.   See II, A, 1, d, directly above.

  2. Professional Certificate

        a.   See II, A, 2, a–d, directly above

D. Other Subject Areas

  1. See OTI website at http://www.highered.nysed.gov/tcert for details on:

        a.   Special Subjects—Agriculture, Business and Marketing, Dance, Family and Consumer Sciences, Health Education, Music, Physical Education, Technology Education, Theater, Visual Arts (all grades)

  2.   Students with Disabilities (Birth–Grade 2), (Grades 1–6), (Grades 5–9) Generalist

  3.   Students with Disabilities—Specialist Middle Level Education (Grades 5–9) and Specialist in Adolescence Education (Grades 7–12)

  4.   Literacy (Birth–Grade 6) and (Grades 5–12)

  5.   Blind and Visually Impaired (all grades)

  6.   Deaf and Hard of Hearing (all grades)

  7.   Speech and Language Disabilities (all grades)

  8.   English to Speakers of Other Languages (all grades)

  9.   Educational Technology Specialist (all grades)

  10. Specific Career and Technical Subjects (Grades 7–12)

III.   Requirements for Administrative/Supervisory Certificates

    A.   School District Leader (continuously valid with completion of 175 hours of professional development every 5 years)

        1.   Valid for central office, district-wide professional school leader

        2.   Requirements include:

            a.   Master's or higher degree;

            b.   Completion of a New York States–registered program leading to School District Leader certification, including 60 hours of graduate study, which may include graduate study completed prior to admission to the program;

            c.   Passing scores on both parts of the School District Leader assessment, with an institutional recommendation;

            d.   Three years of paid, full-time administrative/pupil personnel services/classroom teaching experience;
                and

            e.   Fingerprint clearance and citizenship.

    B.   School Building Leader (valid for building level and/or single subject area administrator and/or supervisor in elementary, middle and/or secondary schools)

        1.   Initial Certificate (valid 5 years, nonrenewable)

            a.   See III, A, directly above, except that assessment is School District Leader assessment.

            b.   For detailed requirements, consult http://www.eservices.nysed.gov/teach/certhelp/CertRequirementHelp.do

        2.   Professional Certificate (continuously valid with completion of 175 hours of professional development every 5 years). Requirements include:

        a.   Master's or higher degree;

        b.   Completion of a New York State–registered program leading to School Building Leader certification;

        c.   Passing scores on both parts of the School Building Leader assessment, with an institutional recommendation;

      d.   Three years of paid, full-time administrative/pupil personnel services/classroom teaching experience;
          and

      e.   Fingerprint clearance and citizenship

  C. School District Business Leader (valid for central office, district-wide professional school business leader)

    1. Initial certificate. Requirements include:

      a.   See III, A, 2, a and b, directly above;

      b.   Passing scores on both parts of the School District Business Leader assessment, with an institutional recommendation;

      c.   Fingerprint clearance;
          and

      d.   Citizenship.

      e.   For a more detailed description of requirements, including those for certification through reciprocity consult http://www.eservices.nysed.gov/teach/certhelp/CertRequirementHelp.do

    2. Professional certificate (continuously valid with completion of 175 hours of professional development every 5 years)

      a.   For a detailed description of requirements, including those for certification through reciprocity, go to http://www.eservices.nysed.gov/teach/certhelp/CertRequirementHelp.do

IV.   Requirements for Support Services Certificates

  A. School Counselor

    1. Provisional Certificate (valid, 5 years; nonrenewable). Requirements include:

      a.   Bachelor's degree from a higher education institution approved by the Commissioner;

      b.   30 semester hours of graduate study in the field of school counseling;
          and

      c.   College-supervised practicum in school counseling.

    2. Permanent Certificate (valid for life unless annulled for cause). Requirements include:

      a.   Satisfaction of requirements for provisional certificate (see IV, A, 1, directly above);

      b.   An additional 30 semester hours of graduate study in school counseling;

      c.   Master's degree from a higher education institution approved by the Commissioner;
          and

      d.   Two years of elementary, middle, and/or secondary school experience in pupil personnel services.

  B. School Psychologist

    1. Provisional Certificate (valid 5 years; nonrenewable). Requirements include:

      a.   Bachelor's degree from a higher education institution approved by the Commissioner;

      b.   Sixty semester hours of graduate study in the field of school psychology;

and

  c. College-supervised internship in the field of school psychology.

 2. Permanent Certificate (valid for life unless annulled for cause). Requirements include:

  a. Satisfaction of requirements for provisional certificate (see IV, B, 1, directly above);

  b. Master's degree from a higher education institution approved by the Commissioner;
   and

  c. Two years of elementary, middle, and/or secondary school experience in pupil personnel services.

C. School Social Worker

 1. Provisional Certificate (valid 5 years; nonrenewable). Requirements include:

  a. Bachelor's degree from a higher education institution approved by the Commissioner;

  b. Thirty semester hours of graduate study in social work;
   and

  c. College-supervised internship in social work.

 2. Permanent Certificate (valid for life unless annulled for cause). Requirements include:

  a. Satisfaction of requirements for provisional certificate (See IV, C, 1, directly above);

  b. Master of Social Work degree from a higher education institution approved by the Commissioner;

  c. New York State registration as a Certified Social Worker;
   and

  d. Two years of elementary, middle, and/or secondary school experience in pupil personnel services.

D. Other Support Services Certificates

 1. For information on School Attendance Teacher, School Dental Hygiene Teacher, and School Nurse-Teacher, go to http://eservices.nysed.gov/teach/certhelp/CertRequirementHelp.do

V. Maintaining Certification

A. Professional Certificate

 1. Holders employed in public school must complete 175 hours of professional development every 5 years.

  a. First professional development cycle begins on July 1 following effective date of certificate.

  b. Employing district approves all professional development activities.

 2. Holders not employed in public school must complete professional development every 5 years, but 175 hour obligation is reduced by 10 percent for every year of period during which not employed in public school.

  a. See A, 1, a, directly above.

 3. All holders must keep records of professional development activities; requirements vary according to place of employment.

4. Reporting
   a. School district reports professional development hours on behalf of public school employees
   b. Certificate holder must report professional development hours directly to Office of Teaching Initiatives annually if not employed by public school district or BOCES during any given year of professional development period.
      i. Holder reports professional development hours to the State Education Department, Office of Teaching Initiatives through the TEACH Online Services system.

VI. Testing
   A. Individuals seeking a teaching certificate must achieve qualifying scores on an appropriate set of New York State Teacher Certification Examinations (NYSTCE) assessments, depending on the certificate title, unless certified by NBPTS.
   B. For certification examination information, including online registration for tests, test study guides, test schedule and locations, test frameworks, unofficial posting of test scores, and other testing information, go to http://www.nystce.nesinc.com
   C. Tests and passing scores
      1. Liberal Arts and Sciences Test (LAST): 220 passing score
      2. Assessment of Teaching Skills—Written (ATS—W): 220 passing score
      3. Content Specialty Test (CST): 220 passing score
      4. Assessment of Teaching Skills—Performance (ATS—P): P (pass) passing score
      5. Communication and Quantitative Skills Test (CQST)
      6. Bilingual Education Assessment (BEA): (Pass)
      7. Assessment of Teaching Assistant Skills (ATAS): 220
      8. School Leadership Assessments: 220

North Carolina

License qualifications for all teachers with 0–2 years of teaching experience (currently licensed as Standard Professional 1) and for out-of-state teachers with 3 or more years of teaching experience who have net testing requirements (currently licensed as Standard Professional 2) were under review at the time of publication. For current status, consult http://www.NCPublicSchools.org/licensure

Licensure Categories

I. Standard Professional 1 (intended for teachers with less than 3 years of teaching experience; valid 3 years). Applicant must have:
   A. Completed a state-approved teacher education program from a regionally accredited college or university
      or
      Completed another state's approved alternative route to licensure,
      and
   B. Met the federal requirements to be designated as "Highly Qualified."
II. Standard Professional 2 (intended for teachers with 3 or more years of teaching experience; valid 5 years)
   A. License is issued to teachers who have 3 or more years of teaching experience in another state and who are fully licensed and "Highly Qualified" in another state,
      and
      1. Who meet North Carolina's Praxis testing requirements (consult http://www.NCPublicSchools.org/licensure)
         or
      2. Who have certification from the National Board for Professional Teaching Standards (NBPTS).
III. Lateral Entry Provisional Licenses (valid 3 years)
   A. Issued to an individual who is employed in a North Carolina public school system and who affiliates with a college or university with an approved teacher education program in the license area or with one of the Regional Alternative Licensing Centers in North Carolina.
      1. An individual plan of study is prescribed for the lateral entry teacher
   B. Applicants must hold at least a bachelor's degree from a regionally accredited institution,
      and
      1. One of the following:
         a. Bachelor's degree or higher that is relevant to the subject being taught;
            or
         b. 24 semester hours of course work in core area with the following exceptions:
            i. Elementary Education or Exceptional Children (Teacher of Record) requires prior to employment a passing score on the Praxis II subject assessment

        ii. English as a Second Language requires a degree in English, *or* 24 semester hours in English, *or* linguistics, *or* a passing score on the Praxis II subject assessment;
        or

    c. Passing score on the Praxis II subject assessment test(s) for the area of license;
    or

    d. For world languages except English, passing score on the American Council on the Teaching of Foreign Languages (ACTFL) examination;
    and

  2. One of the following:

    a. 2.5 GPA or above;
    or

    b. At least 5 years of relevant experience;
    or

    c. Passing score on the Praxis I, *or* a total SAT score of 1100, *or* a total ACT score of 24, *plus* 1 of the following:

        i. GPA of 3.0 in the major field of study,
        or

        ii. GPA of 3.0 in all courses in senior year,
        or

        iii. GPA of 3.0 on a minimum of 15 semester hours of courses completed within the last 5 years after the bachelor's degree or higher.

C. Lateral Entry License holders must complete at least 6 semester hours of course work each year and satisfy Praxis II testing requirements.

Licensure Renewal Process

I. Standard Professional 2 licenses must be renewed every 5 years.

  A. Each license holder is responsible for knowing and satisfying renewal requirements.

  B. Failure to renew the license makes a teacher ineligible for employment unless validation of the expired license is requested by an employing school system.

II. Renewal and Reinstatement Guidelines

  A. Credit required to renew license

    1. 10 semester hours or 15 units of renewal credit, with course work directly related to an individual's professional responsibilities as an educator or to area(s) of licensure

      a. One unit of renewal credit is equivalent to one-quarter hour or 1 in-service credit from a North Carolina public school system, with 1 unit generally reflecting 10 contact hours and 1 semester hour equivalent to 1.5 units of credit.

    2. All credit must be earned by the expiration date of the existing license for it to remain current.

    3. To renew an expired license, 10 semester hours or 15 units of renewal credit must be earned within the most recent 5-year period.

B. Additional requirements for those in a North Carolina public school system or a North Carolina school that has an approved license renewal plan

1. Teachers of grades K–12 must complete 3 renewal credits in their academic subject areas—including strategies to teach those subjects—during each 5-year renewal cycle.
2. Individuals teaching in grades K–8 must earn 3 units of renewal credit in reading methods during each 5-year renewal cycle.
3. Principals and assistant principals must, during each 5-year cycle, earn 5 units of renewal credit focused on the principal's role in teacher effectiveness, teacher evaluations, teacher support programs, teacher leadership, teacher empowerment, and teacher retention.

C. Activities accepted for renewal credit

1. College or university courses
   a. Transcripts are required as documentation; grade reports are not accepted.
2. Local in-service courses or workshops
   a. The administrative unit certifies credits
3. Classes and workshops approved by a Local Education Agency (LEA)
   a. Documentation of completion is provided by the agency sponsoring the activity.
4. Teaching experience
   a. One renewal credit is awarded for each year of full time teaching completed during the 5-year renewal cycle. Part-time experience can be considered for renewal credit if it amounts to the equivalent of 1 year of full time teaching.

Administrators/Special Service Personnel

I. Requirements for all areas
A. Obtain a valid Standard Professional 2 (SP2) License
B. Student services personnel who have completed an approved preparation program *and*
   1. Satisfied North Carolina's testing requirements are issued an SP 2 license
   2. Not satisfied North Carolina's testing requirements are issued an SP 1 license
      a. When North Carolina's testing requirements are satisfied, the license is converted to an SP2.
C. Student services personnel who are fully licensed in another state will be issued the SP 2 license when they:
   1. Meet North Carolina's Praxis testing requirements,
      or
      Earn National Board certifications;
      or
   2. After 1 year of satisfactory student services experience in North Carolina and with 3 or more years of student services school experience in another state, the employing LEA recommends licensure and verifies an offer of reemployment, which the individual is not required to accept.

License Areas and Requirements

I. School Administrator—Superintendent
    A. Eligibility to serve as a superintendent must be verified by the State Board of Education prior to election by a local board of education
    B. Minimum of 1 year of experience (or the equivalent) as a principal
    C. Advanced graduate level (6th-year degree) in school administration
    D. Meet the required score on the Interstate School Leaders Licensure Assessment (SLLA) test administered by Educational Testing Service (ETS),
        or
    E. At least a bachelor's degree from a regionally accredited college or university and 5 years of leadership or managerial experience considered relevant by the employing local board of education.
II. School Administrator—Principal
    A. Completion of an approved program in school administration at the master's level or above
    B. Meet the required score on the SLLA test administered by ETS
    C. No provisional principal license is issued for service as a principal
III. School Administrator—Assistant Principal
    A. Completion of an approved program in school administration at the master's level or above
    B. Meet the required score on the SLLA test administered by ETS
    C. Provisional principal license is issued for service as an assistant principal if the local board determines there is a shortage of individuals with principal licensure
    D. Affiliation with a master's school administrator program must occur before the expiration of the provisional license. Provisional principal licenses can be extended for up to 2 additional school years, during which time program requirements and SLLA test must be completed.
IV. Curriculum Instructional Specialist
    A. Completion of an approved program for a curriculum instructional specialist at the master's degree level or above
    B. Praxis Educational Leadership: Administrative and Supervision required score
V. Career-Technical Director
    A. Completion of an approved program for a career-technical education director at the master's level or above
VI. Exceptional Children Program Administrator (licensure is a supervisory classification)
    A. Master's degree in an exceptional children area or an advanced (6th-year) degree in school psychology,
        and
        Three graduate semester hours in each of the following:
        1. Administration
        2. Curriculum development
        3. Supervision,
            and
            Praxis Educational Leadership: Administrative and Supervision;

or

B. A master's degree in administration and/or curriculum instruction,
    and
    Nine semester hours of course work in exceptional children,
    and
    Praxis Educational Leadership: Administrative and Supervision.

VII.   Instructional Technology Specialist — Computers
    A. Completion of a college or university program at the master's level or above

VIII. Instructional Technology Specialist — Telecommunications
    A. Completion of a college or university program at the master's level or above

IX.   Media Supervisor
    A. Three graduate semester hours in each of the following:
        1. Administration
        2. Curriculum development
        3. Supervision

X.   Media Coordinator
    A. One of the following:
        1. Completion of an approved program for a media coordinator at the master's degree level or above
        2. Completion of an approved program after July 1, 1984, allows a provisional license upon employment with requirement to update to master's degree level
        3. A provisional media coordinator license
    B. Praxis Library Media Specialist

XI.   Counselor
    A. Completion of an approved program in school counseling at the master's level or above
    B. Praxis School Guidance and Counseling test required score

XII.   School Social Worker
    A. Completion of an approved program in school social work at the bachelor's level or above

XIII. School Psychologist
    A. Completion of an approved program in school psychology at the sixth-year level
    B. Praxis School Psychology required score

XIV. Speech-Language Pathologist
    A. One of the following:
        1. Speech-language license from the American Speech-Language Hearing Association
            or
        2. License from the North Carolina Board of Examiners for Speech and Language Pathologists and Audiologists
            or
        3. Completion of an approved program in speech pathology at the master's level or above.
    B. Praxis Speech-Language Pathology required score

XV.   Audiologist
    A.   One of the following:
        1.   Audiology license from the American Speech-Language-Hearing Association
            or
        2.   License from the North Carolina Board of Examiners for Speech and Language Pathologist and Audiologist
            or
        3.   Completion of an approved program in audiology at the master's level or above.
    B.   Praxis Audiology required score

North Dakota

Types of Licenses

I. North Dakota Century Code Authority
   A. Individual must hold valid North Dakota license issued by the North Dakota Education Standards and Practices Board (ESPS) in order to be permitted or employed to teach in any state public school.
   B. Nonpublic schools must employ licensed teachers to be approved and in compliance with compulsory attendance laws.

II. Licensure Level
   A. Level I indicates that individual still has educational or employment requirements to meet before receiving regular Level II license, or that they are not currently maintaining contracted employment.
   B. Level II indicates that individual has met all basic requirements for regular North Dakota Educators' Professional License.
   C. Level III indicates that individual has earned advanced degrees beyond bachelor's level (master's, specialist, or doctoral) or National Board for Professional Teaching Standards (NBPTS) advanced licensure.

III. Types of Educator's Licenses and Procedures
   A. 40-Day Provisional: Issued to applicants who have been offered a job and have completed entire application process with exception of background investigation. Letter from school administrator indicating desire to issue contract without background investigation being complete and letter from applicant indicating any criminal background history are needed by ESPB prior to issuing this license.
   B. Initial License (valid 2 years): Issued to first-time applicants who have met all state requirements for licensure
   C. Regular (valid 5 years): Issued to individuals who have met all requirements for a state Educator's Professional License and have successfully taught for 18 months (full-time equivalent) in state
   D. Alternate License (valid 1 year): Issued in documented shortage area. License is initiated by letter from local school administrator indicating search for qualified applicant and desire for this license to be issued. Requirements include:
      1. Initial License
      2. Bachelor's degree in appropriate content area
      3. Plan of study from college of education where applicant will complete 8 semester hours each year toward teaching degree.
   E. Out-of-State Reciprocal (valid 2 years): Issued to individuals who hold valid license from another state but have not met this state's standards and rules. Plan of study is developed for each individual indicating course work needed. Individual has 4 years to complete all requirements.

Elementary School

I. North Dakota Educator's Professional License
    A. Bachelor's degree from an accredited college approved to offer teacher education
    B. Professional requirements, credits in professional education, including student teaching, overall grade-point average 2.5, semester hours.................................. 34
    C. Valid for 2 years for teaching in the level of preparation
    D. A 5-year renewal may be issued with 2 years of successful full-time teaching experience in the state. Each renewal of the 5-year license requires 4 semester hours of work.
    E. Submission of PPST/Praxis I scores in reading, writing, and mathematics that meet or exceed North Dakota cut scores
    F. Submission of Praxis II content and pedagogy test scores that meet or exceed North Dakota cut scores
    G. Background investigation, including Bureau of Criminal Investigation and the F.B.I.

Secondary School

I. North Dakota Educator's Professional License
    A. Same as Elementary School, I, A–D
    B. Semester hours 32
    C. Submission in core academic areas only of Praxis II test scores that meet or exceed North Dakota cut scores

Superintendent

I. Provisional Credential
    A. Valid until the end of the second school year following the year in which the provisional credential is issued; not renewable
    B. Issued as the initial credential to an individual who does not meet the qualifications for a professional credential
    C. Issued to those who have a level I principal's credential but lack the course work, the experience, or both that are necessary for the professional credential
    D. Applicant must fulfill all the following standards:
        1. Hold a valid North Dakota teaching license during the life of the credential
        2. Have at least 3 years of teaching experience, verified in a letter of recommendation by a supervisor or employer who has firsthand knowledge of the individual's professional work
        3. Have at least 2 years of administrative experience comprising at least half time as an elementary or secondary principal, a central office administrator, or an administrator of an approved school with a 12-year program. This experience is to be verified by a supervisor or employer who has firsthand knowledge of the individual's professional work.

    4.   Complete the requirements for the level I elementary or secondary principal credential and 8 additional hours of designated course work specific to the superintendency; see state Department of Public Instruction (DPI), Appendix 1

II.   Professional Credential

    A.   Issued to coincide with the period for which the individual is licensed to teach by the (ESPB) and may be renewed; an individual holding a lifetime educator's professional license must renew the credential every 5 years,
and

    B.   Issued upon satisfying credential standards; see I, D, 1–4, directly above

III.   Renewal Requirements

    A.   Applicant must fulfill one of the following:

        1.   Provide a copy of official transcripts showing satisfactory completion of at least 8 semester hours of graduate work in education, of which 4 semester hours are in the area of educational administration,
or

        2.   Provide a copy of official transcripts showing satisfactory completion of at least 4 semester hours of graduate work and verification of attendance or participation in at least 6 administrative educational conferences or workshops from a state-approved list with specific verification.

Secondary Principal

I.   Provisional Credential

    A.   Issued as the initial credential to an individual who does not meet the qualifications for a level I or level II professional credential and is employed as a secondary principal; valid until the end of the second school year following the year in which the provisional credential is issued; not renewable

    B.   Issued to a person enrolled in a state-approved program in educational leadership who has completed 8 semester hours of course work in that area

    C.   Issued upon satisfying the following credentials standards with specific verification of each:

        1.   Valid North Dakota educator's professional license issued by the ESPB allowing the individual to teach at the secondary level

        2.   At least 3 years of teaching or administrative experience (as defined by DPI) or a combination thereof in secondary schools:

            a.   Equal to full-time equivalency: at least 6 hours for a 180-day school term

            b.   Positions must have been stated on a professional contract

II.   Level I Professional Credential

    A.   Issued to coincide with the period for which the individual is licensed to teach by the ESPB and may be renewed at the end of that period; an individual holding a lifetime educator's professional license must renew their credential every 5 years,
and

    B.   Issued upon satisfying the following credentials standards:

        1.   See I, C, 1 and 2, directly above

2. The level I credential requires 1 of the following:
    a. Master's degree in educational administration from a state-approved program with designated subjects,
        or
    b. Master's degree with a major certifiable by the ESPB in addition to 20 semester hours of credit that include designated courses specific to the secondary level contained within a master's degree in educational administration from a state-approved program

III. Level II Professional Credential
    A. Issued to coincide with the period for which the individual is licensed to teach by the ESPB; an individual holding a lifetime educator's professional license must renew their credential every 5 years
    B. Renewal of the level II professional credential is available only for principals serving secondary schools with 100 or fewer students,
        and
    C. Issued upon satisfying the following credentials standards:
        1. See I, C, 1 and 2, directly above
        2. The level II credential requires 20 semester hours of graduate credit taken in a master's degree program from a state-approved program with designated subjects in educational administration.

IV. Renewal Requirements
    A. To renew the level I and level II professional credentials, an individual shall submit 1 of the following:
        1. A copy of official transcripts of 8 semester hours of graduate work in education acquired after the date of the original credentialing or last renewal, of which 4 semester hours are in the area of educational administration,
            or
        2. A copy of official transcripts of 4 semester hours of graduate work in education acquired after the date of the original credentialing or last renewal and verification of attendance or participation in at least 6 educational conferences or workshops from a designated list with specific verification.

Elementary Principal

I. Provisional Credential
    A. Issued as the initial credential to an individual who does not meet the qualifications for a level I or level II professional credential and is employed as an elementary principal; valid until the end of the second school year following the year in which the provisional credential is issued; not renewable
    B. Issued upon completion of 8 semester hours of course work in educational leadership from a state-approved program in educational administration
    C. Issued upon meeting the following credential standards with specific documentation and verification of each:
        1. A valid North Dakota teaching license issued by the ESPB allowing the individual to teach at the elementary level

2.   At least 3 years of teaching or administrative experience (as defined by DPI) or a combination thereof in elementary schools:
  a.   Equal to full-time equivalency: at least 5 and one-half hours daily, for a 180-day school term
  b.   Positions must have been stated on a professional contract

II.   Level I Professional Credential
  A.   Issued to coincide with the period for which the individual is licensed to teach by the ESPB; an individual holding a lifetime educator's professional license must renew their credential every 5 years
  B.   Issued upon satisfying the following credential standards:
    1.   See I, C, 1 and 2, directly above
    2.   The level I credential requires 1 of the following:
      a.   Master's degree in educational administration that includes designated course work specific to the elementary level from a state-approved program,
      or
      b.   Master's degree with a major certifiable by the ESPB. Twenty semester hours of credit that includes designated courses specific to the elementary level contained within a master's degree in educational administration from a state-approved program are required.

III.   Level II Professional Credential
  A.   Issued to coincide with the period for which the individual is licensed to teach by the ESPB; however, an individual holding a lifetime educator's professional license must renew their credential every 5 years
  B.   Renewal of the level II professional credential is available only for principals serving elementary schools enrolling 100 or fewer students
  C.   Issued upon satisfying the following credential standards:
    1.   See I, C, 1 and 2, directly above
    2.   Level II credential requires 20 semester hours of graduate credit in a master's degree program from a state-approved program in educational administration with designated courses.

IV.   Renewal Requirements
  A.   To renew the level I and level II professional credentials, an individual must submit 1 of the following:
    1.   A copy of official transcripts of 8 semester hours of graduate work in education acquired after the date of the original credentialing or last renewal, of which 4 semester hours are in the area of educational administration,
    or
    2.   A copy of official transcripts of 4 semester hours of graduate work in education acquired after the date of the original credentialing or last renewal and verification of attendance or participation in at least 6 educational conferences or workshops from a designated list with specific verification.

School Counselor

I. School Counselor Credentials
A. Credential designations
  1. SC03 for grades K–12
  2. Counselor Designate credential CD 16 (will not be issued after June 30, 2010)
B. Credential is valid only while the individual holds a North Dakota educator's professional license or a professional school counseling restricted license.
  1. A credential must be renewed each time the individual's educator's professional license is renewed.
  2. Holders of a lifetime North Dakota educator's professional license must renew the credential every 5 years.
  3. To renew the credential, submit a copy of college transcripts documenting 4 semester hours of graduate course work in education, of which 2 semester hours must be in counseling.
    a. Two semester hours of required counseling course work may be replaced by 30 clock hours of continuing education hours in counseling with a signed verification of attendance or participation by the conference or workshop sponsor, the employer, or a school district business manager.
C. SC03 credential standards–counselor must:
  1. Hold a valid educator's professional license or a professional school counseling restricted license
    and
  2. Have a master s degree in counseling, education, or a related human service field and the following graduate core counseling course work content from a state-approved school counseling program:
    a. Elementary school counseling;
    b. Secondary school counseling;
    c. Supervised school counseling internship consisting of a minimum of 450 contact hours, of which at least 150 are at both the elementary and secondary level;
    d. Counseling program management;
    e. Counseling theories;
    f. Assessment techniques;
    g. Group counseling;
    h. Career counseling and assessment;
    i. Social and multicultural counseling;
    j. Ethics and law;
      and
    k. Counseling techniques.
D. If a school is unable to employ a credentialed counselor, the school may employ a licensed teacher to serve as the counselor on a plan of study approved by the department of public instruction (DPI) to satisfy accreditation requirements, Contact DPI for details at http://www.dpi.state.nd.us

Library Media

Contact the Department of Public Instruction (see Appendix 1) for a detailed listing of required course work, official application forms, and instructions.

I.   Librarian (LM03)
   A.   Bachelor's degree with a licenseable major or minor or an endorsement in elementary, middle-level, or secondary education
   B.   Valid North Dakota Educator's Professional License
   C.   Complete course work in library media from a state-approved program as detailed in
        Subsection 1 of Section 67-11-04-05, semester hours* 15
   D.   Validity Length
        1.   Valid only while the individual holds a valid North Dakota educator's professional license
        2.   Must be renewed each time professional license is renewed; graduate semester hours in library media and information science from a state-approved program 2
             a.   Individual holding a lifetime North Dakota educator's professional license must renew the credential every 5 years
II. Library Media Specialist (LM02)
   A.   See I, A, directly above
   B.   Valid North Dakota Educator's Professional License
   C.   Complete course work in library media from a state-approved program as detailed in
        Subsection 1 of Section 67-11-04-05, semester hours* 15
        Subsection 2 of Section 67-11-04-05, semester hours* 9
   D.   See I, D, directly above
III. Library Media Director (LM01)
   A.   Master's degree in library science, media education, education, or educational administration from a state-approved program
   B.   Valid North Dakota Educator's Professional License (based on bachelor's degree with a licenseable major or minor or an endorsement in elementary, middle-level, or secondary education)
   C.   Complete course work in library media from a state-approved program as detailed in
        Subsection 1 of Section 67-11-04-05, semester hours* 15
        Subsection 2 of Section 67-11-04-05, semester hours* 9
        Subsection 3 of Section 67-11-04-05, semester hours (graduate in school library or school administration).. 6
IV. Plan of Study Option to qualify for library media director, library media specialist, or librarian credentials
   A.   If school is unable to employ credentialed librarian, as required by enrollment of students served, may employ licensed teacher to serve as librarian if licensed teacher has completed at least 6 semester hours in library media course work and has submitted a written plan of study showing at least 6 graduate or undergraduate

semester hours in library media course work to be completed annually until credential is earned.

    B.   Once plan is approved, licensed teacher must document a minimum of 6 semester hours of library media course work each year until qualified for required credential

V.   Renewal Requirements (LM03, LM02, LM01)

All are renewed by submitting application form and documenting completion of 2 semester hours of graduate credit in library media and information science.

Speech Therapist

Contact the Education Standards and Practices Board (see Appendix 1) for detailed information.

*   graduate or undergraduate

Ohio

Ohio's standards are performance-based and lead to licensing based on assessments (administered under the authority of the state board of education) of the performance of teachers during their participation in the Ohio Resident Educator Program, beginning with the 2011–2012 school year. Applicants for any license or permit must complete both an Ohio and an FBI criminal background check, conducted by the Bureau of Criminal Identification and Investigation. For full details, consult Educator Licensure at www.ode.state.oh.us

Resident Educator

I. Resident Educator License (valid 4 years)
    A. Holds degree required by license
    B. Deemed to be of good moral character
    C. Successfully completed approved program of preparation
    D. Recommended by dean or head of teacher education at institution approved to prepare teachers
    E. Successfully completed Praxis II examination in content and professional knowledge
        1. For world languages, the American Council on the Teaching of Foreign Languages (ACTFL) oral proficiency interview and writing proficiency test is also required.
    F. Demonstrated skill in integrating educational technology in instruction of children
    G. Completed course work in teaching of reading, semester hours............................ 12
        1. For early childhood, middle childhood, and intervention specialist license, this must include at least one separate 3-semester-hour course in teaching of phonics
        2. For multiage and adolescence to young adult licenses, 3 semester hours in teaching of reading

Entry-Year Program for Teachers

I. Requirements
    A. Candidate holds 4-year resident educator license
    B. Candidate completes the 4-year Ohio Resident Educator Transition Program including:
        1. Year-long program of mentoring and support;
            and
        2. Assessment of beginning teacher's acquisition of knowledge and skills through use of formative assessments.

Professional Licenses

I. Professional Teacher License (valid 5 years)
    A. Holds provisional license
    B. Holds baccalaureate degree

   C.   See Resident Educator License, I, B, C, and E, above

   D.   Successful completion of Ohio Resident Educator Program

II. Professional Teacher License Areas

   A.   Early childhood license (PreK–3)

      1.   Minimum course work in teaching of reading, semester hours 12

   B.   Middle childhood license (4–9)

      1.   Middle childhood teacher preparation program shall include preparation in humanities (including the arts) and areas of concentration in at least 2 of the following: reading and language arts, mathematics, science, and social studies

      2.   See II, A, 1, directly above

   C.   Adolescence to young adult license (7–12)

      1.   Preparation in teaching field shall constitute at least an academic major or its equivalent with sufficient advanced course work in all areas to be taught

      2.   Licenses are issued in following teaching fields:

         a.   Earth sciences, integrated language arts, integrated mathematics, integrated science, integrated social studies, life sciences, and physical sciences (including physical sciences: chemistry; physical sciences: physics; or chemistry and physics)

   D.   Multiage license (PreK–12)

      1.   See II, C, 1, directly above

      2.   Licenses are issued in the following teaching fields:

         a.   Computer information science, dance, drama/theater, foreign language, health, library/media, music, physical education, teaching English to speakers of other languages (TESOL), and visual arts

   E.   Other professional teacher license areas include intervention specialist, early childhood intervention specialist, and a variety of career–technical areas. Please consult Educator Licensure at www.ode.state.oh.us for details.

Professional Pupil Services Licenses

  I. Professional Pupil Services License (valid 5 years)

   A.   Deemed to be of good moral character

   B.   Completed approved program of preparation

   C.   Recommended by dean or head of teacher education

   D.   Completed examination prescribed by state board of education

II. License Areas

   A.   School audiologist

      1.   Master's degree and current license to practice audiology

      2.   See I, A–D, directly above

   B.   School counselor

      1.   Master's degree and 2 years of successful teaching experience under resident educator or professional teacher license; *or* 3 years of experience as licensed school counselor in another state; *or* 1-year induction under supervision of licensed school counselor

      2.   See I, A–D, directly above

C. School psychologist
   1. Master's degree and approved program of preparation, successful completion of Praxis II examination, successful completion of 9-month, full-time internship in approved school setting
   2. See I, A–D, directly above
D. Other professional pupil personnel license areas include school social worker; school speech-language pathologist; school nurse; and orientation and mobility specialist. Please consult Educator Licensure at www.ode.state.oh.us for details.

Professional Administrator Licenses

I. Professional Administrator License
   A. Deemed to be of good moral character
   B. Holds master's degree
   C. Recommended by dean or head of teacher education at institution approved to prepare teachers
   D. Successfully completed examination prescribed by state board of education
II. License Areas
   A. Principal License
      1. Added to valid professional teaching license after successful completion of an approved program of preparation for principal licensure and the prescribed examination.
      2. Valid for working with
         a. Ages 3–12 and grades PK–6
         b. Ages 8–14 and grades 4–9
         c. Ages 10–21 and grades 5–12
   B. Administrative Specialist License
      1. Added to valid professional teacher license or professional pupil services license and valid for working in central office or supervisory capacity
      2. Prior to issuance, applicant must have completed 2 years of successful teaching experience under professional teacher's license and must have successfully completed approved program of preparation.
   C. Superintendent License
      1. Added to valid professional teacher license of individual who holds principal or administrative specialist license
      2. Prior to issuance, applicant must have completed 3 years of successful experience in position requiring principal or administrative specialist license and must have successfully completed approved preparation program for superintendents.

Oklahoma

Note: As of press time, the newly enacted Oklahoma House Bill #3029 waives requirements of educator residency for fiscal years 2011 and 2012, thus exempting school districts from participation in a residency program during that time frame. Accordingly, resident teacher programs and committees mentioned in the text below are currently on hold. Refer to the Oklahoma State Department of Education website for the most current information at http://sde.state.ok.us/Teacher/ProfStand/CertGuide

Traditional Licensure and Certification

I. Traditional Teaching License (valid 5 years)
   A. License is a credential initially issued to educators who have completed a teacher education program after February 1, 1982, and who have zero years of teaching experience in an accredited school.
   B. Requirements for licensure
      1. Holds a bachelor's degree from an accredited institution of higher education (IHE) that has approval or accreditation for teaching education,
      2. Successfully completed a higher education teacher education program approved by the Oklahoma Commission for Teacher Preparation (OCTP)—see Appendix 1 for contact information,
      3. Has met all other requirements as may be established by the Oklahoma State Board of Education (OSBE),
      4. Has made necessary application and paid competency examination fees in amount and as prescribed by OCTP,
      5. Successfully completed 3 competency examinations, including:
         a. Oklahoma General Education Test (OGET)
         b. Oklahoma Subject Area Test(s) (OSAT)
         c. Oklahoma Professional Teaching Examination (OPTE),
            and
      6. Has on file with the OSBE both a current Oklahoma and national criminal history record search from the Oklahoma State Bureau of Investigation (OSBI) and Federal Bureau of Investigation (FBI), respectively.
   C. A licensed teacher will participate in the Resident Teacher Program during the initial year of teaching in Oklahoma. See Oklahoma State Department of Education website for the most current information on resident teacher programs and committees at http://sde.state.ok.us/Teacher/ProfStand/CertGuide
      1. Employing school district shall establish a resident teacher committee consisting of a mentor teacher, an administrator, and a faculty member from an IHE to provide guidance and assistance to the beginning teacher, ultimately making a recommendation regarding certification.

II. Traditional Teaching Certificate (valid 5 years, renewable)

   A. Certificate is a credential issued to educators who have completed the Resident Teacher Program of verified teaching experience under a valid teaching credential in a state- or regionally-accredited school. See Oklahoma State Department of Education website for the most current information on resident teacher programs and committees at http://sde.state.ok.us/Teacher/ProfStand/CertGuide

   B. Requirements for certification
      1. Holds a license to teach,
      2. Has served a minimum of 1 school year as a resident teacher;
      3. Has been recommended for certification by a Resident Teacher Committee; *and*
      4. Has made the necessary application and paid the certification fee; *or*
      5. Holds an out-of-state certificate and meets standards set by the Oklahoma State Board of Education (OSBE); *or*
      6. Holds certification from the National Board for Professional Teaching Standards.
      7. For those who do not have a teacher education degree, see alternative routes to teaching below.

   C. Additional subjects may be added by to certificate by testing except for early childhood, elementary, and special education.

   D. Special Education teachers new to the profession after December 3, 2004, are required to have a Special Education certificate as well as an appropriate certificate in 1 of the following areas: early childhood, elementary education, middle or secondary education in math, science, or language arts.

   E. Credentialing for Educators with Out-of-State Licensure
      1. Applicants who hold a full teaching credential in any state are eligible for Oklahoma certification in equivalent subject areas with the possibility of having to take Oklahoma tests.
         a. Applicants who completed a teacher education program after February 1, 1982, and do not have at least 1 year of teaching experience will be required to participate in the Resident Teacher Program. See Oklahoma State Department of Education website for the most current information on resident teacher programs and committees at http://sde.state.ok.us/Teacher/ProfStand/CertGuide
         b. Applicants who completed a teacher education program prior to February 1, 1982, or completed a teacher education program after that date and have at least 1 year of teaching experience, will be issued a 5-year provisional certificate in order to complete the Oklahoma testing requirements (OGET, OSAT[s], and OPTE) and to complete 1 year of successful employment in an Oklahoma accredited school.
            i. Applicants who have passed teacher test(s) in another state may request a review of these test(s) for comparability to Oklahoma

test(s) by the OCTP to determine if any of the out-of-state tests are comparable and acceptable. Contact the OCTP (see Appendix 1) for full details.

    c. Applicants who graduated after February 1, 1982, and have zero years of teaching experience will be issued an Oklahoma license in order to complete the Resident Teacher Program required of beginning teachers. No 5-year standard license will be issued until all tests have been completed and the Resident Teacher Committee has made its recommendation for certification to the OSBE. See Oklahoma State Department of Education website for the most current information on resident teacher programs and committees at http://sde.state.ok.us/Teacher/ProfStand/CertGuide

  2. Oklahoma does have certification agreements limited to educator preparation program requirements with certain participating states/jurisdictions; see Appendix 3 for full listing.

    a. Contact individual states regarding ancillary requirements such as minimum grade-point average, standardized testing, mentoring experience, or graduation from an accredited institution.

  3. If applicants hold a full credential in any state, they are eligible for Oklahoma certification in equivalent subject areas, once Oklahoma testing requirements are met.

III. Specialist Certificate (valid 5 years, renewable)

  A. Specialist certification is awarded for library-media specialist, school counselor, school psychometrist, school psychologist, speech-language pathologist, and reading specialist.

  B. In addition to meeting initial licensure requirements (see I, A–C, directly above), specialist certification requires completion of a graduate degree program meeting the professional education association standards specific to the profession.

    1. Specialist certification may not be added through testing alone.

  C. Application for certification in the specialist areas listed above should be initiated through the director of teacher education at the recommending IHE.

IV. Administrator Certificate

  A. Principal Standard Certificate (valid 5 years, renewable)

    1. Holds a standard master's degree,

    2. Completed an Oklahoma-approved building-level leadership skills program in educational administration,

    3. Achieved a passing score on common core and principal specialty areas of the principal OSATs,
      and

    4. Completed 2 years of successful teaching experience in an OSBE-accredited Oklahoma public or private school.

  B. Superintendent Standard Certificate (valid 5 years, renewable)

    1. Holds principal certification
      or
      Completed an Oklahoma-approved building-level leadership skills program in educational administration that includes a standard master's degree,

2. Achieved a passing score on superintendent OSAT,
3. Completed an Oklahoma-approved district-level leadership skills program in educational administration,
   and
4. Completed 2 years of administrative experience in an OSBE-accredited Oklahoma public or private school.

C. For alternative administrator certification for principal or superintendent (valid 3 years, nonrenewable)
   1. Holds a standard master's degree,
   2. Completed 2 years of relevant work experience in a supervisory or administrative capacity,
   3. Achieved passing scores on the required administrator OSAT(s),
      and
   4. Has on file with the director of teacher education at an Oklahoma-accredited IHE a declaration of intent to earn standard certification through completion of an approved alternative administrative preparation program within 3 years.

Alternative Routes to Teaching

I. Alternative Placement Program
   A. Provides an opportunity for individuals with nonteaching degrees to teach in Oklahoma accredited schools.
   B. Eligibility requirements:
      1. Minimum of a baccalaureate degree from an accredited college/university,
      2. Major in a field of study corresponding to an area of Oklahoma certification for secondary, elementary/secondary, or career and technology education certificate (see OSDE, Appendix 1, for full listing),
      3. At least a 2.5 grade-point average,
         and
      4. Document 3 years of post-baccalaureate work experience if no post-baccalaureate course work.
   C. Once approved to seek an alternative license, applicant must:
      1. Complete the OGET and desired OSAT tests; contact OCTP (see Appendix 1) for details,
      2. Have on file with the OSBE a current approved OSBI/FBI criminal history fingerprint check,
         and
      3. Receive a recommendation for certification from the Oklahoma Teacher Competency Review Panel, as well as receive OSBE approval.
   D. Once the OSDE issues license, applicant must:
      1. Complete the Oklahoma Resident Teacher Program. See Oklahoma State Department of Education website for the most current information on resident teacher programs and committees at http://sde.state.ok.us/Teacher/ProfStand/CertGuide

    2.   Within 3 years, pass the OPTE and complete a professional education component as follows:

        a.   With a bachelor's degree, 18 college credit hours or 270 clock hours

        b.   With a post-baccalaureate degree, 12 college credit hours or 180 clock hours

           and

    3.   Apply for a standard certificate.

II. American Board for Certification of Teacher Excellence (ABCTE)

    A.   Funded with a U.S. Department of Education grant, ABCTE offers a flexible and cost-effective certification program designed to inspire career changers to enter teaching.

    B.   Requirements

        1.   Bachelor's degree from accredited IHE,

        2.   Accepted by the ABCTE,

        3.   Pass ABCTE desired middle-level or secondary-level subject test and professional teacher test,

           and

        4.   Have on file with the OSBE a current approved OSBI/FBI criminal history fingerprint check.

    C.   When requirements are completed, OSDE issues middle-level or secondary-level license (valid 1 year)

        1.   Licensee must participate in 1-year mentoring program and apply for a standard certificate. See Oklahoma State Department of Education website for the most current information on resident teacher programs and committees at http://sde.state.ok.us/Teacher/ProfStand/CertGuide

III. Teach for America

    A.   This is a national corps of outstanding recent college graduates and professionals of all academic major and career interests who commit 2 years to teach in urban and rural public schools and become leaders in the effort to expand educational opportunity. For full details, go to: http://www.teachforamerica/org.

    B.   Once accepted into the program, applicant could be assigned to teach in Oklahoma.

IV. Additional Alternative Certificates

Oklahoma also offers alternative certificates in the following programs; contact the OSDE (see Appendix 1) for full details.

    A.   Four-Year-Olds and Younger Certificate

    B.   Career Development Program for Paraprofessionals to be Certified Teachers

    C.   Troops to Teachers Defense Authorization Act

Oregon

Teaching Licenses

I. Initial Teaching License (valid 18 months, by which time individual must qualify for Initial I Teaching License; not renewable). Note: Initial Teaching License is usually first license issued to out-of-state applicants who need time to complete requirements for Initial I Teaching License.

   A. Initial Teaching License—Unrestricted

      1. Baccalaureate degree from regionally accredited U.S. institution or approved foreign equivalent related to teaching at 1 or more levels in 1 or more specialties

      2. Completion of approved teacher-education program in endorsement area(s) requested

      3. Furnish fingerprints and provide satisfactory responses to character question contained in licensure application

   B. Restricted Transitional Teaching License (valid 3 years; nonrenewable)

      1. Issued to applicants who have not held unrestricted license for full-time teaching in any state or have not completed approved teacher-education program but do hold baccalaureate degree in subject matter relevant to position being sought; see I, A, 1, above

      2. Restricted to district and requires coapplication with district

      3. Furnish fingerprints and provide satisfactory responses to character question contained in licensure application

II. Initial I Teaching License (valid 3 years, renewable twice under conditions described below)

   A. Baccalaureate degree from regionally accredited U.S. institution or an approved foreign equivalent of such degree

   B. Completion of approved teacher-education program in endorsement area(s) requested,

      or

      Current license issued by another state, not limited due to course work, and valid for endorsement(s) requested on Oregon license

   C. Completion of civil rights examination approved by Oregon Teacher Standards and Practices Commission (TSPC).

   D. Professional knowledge

      1. Passing score on each required test of subject mastery for license endorsement, except for tests waived due to approved special academic preparation, together with 5 years of experience teaching specialty in U.S. public or regionally accredited private school before holding any Oregon license

         a. Transcript review required for academic preparation in lieu of testing.

      2. Passing scores on Praxis I Series: PPST Mathematics (175); PPST Reading (174); and PPST Writing (171),

      or

California Basic Educational Skills Test (CBEST) (123),
or

Washington Educator Skills Test-Basic skills (WEST-B),
or

Hold regionally accredited doctoral degree.

    E.   Renewable under following conditions only:
1. First renewal (at 3 years)
   a. All candidates must show progress of at least 3 semester hours or 4.5 quarter graduate hours germane to license, which must be completed within 10 years from date Initial License was first granted.
   b. Educator must qualify for Initial II license upon expiration of 9 years following first Initial I license issue date. Candidate may apply for 1-year unconditional extension if unable to meet all requirements within 9-year period.
   c. Teacher may choose to become eligible for Continuing Teaching License in lieu of obtaining Initial II license.

    F.   Furnish fingerprints and provide statisfactory responses to character question contained in licensure application.

III.   Initial II Teaching License (valid 3 years; renewable repeatedly under requirements below)
    A.   Requirements if Initial I teaching license granted on basis of baccalaureate degree from teacher preparation program
1. Complete master's or higher degree in arts and sciences, or advanced degree in the professions, from regionally accredited U.S. institution or approved foreign equivalent of such
   or
   Complete specified graduate course work germane to license or to public school employment, including at least 10 semester hours or 15 quarter hours each of subject matter course work; of graduate educational-related course work; and of graduate electives

    B.   Requirements if Initial I teaching license granted on basis of post-baccalaureate degree from teacher-preparation program; complete one of the following:
1. Six semester hours or 9 quarter hours graduate academic credit from regionally accredited college or university. Graduate credit must be completed after Initial I teaching license is first issued and be germane to license or to public school employment; may include pedagogy, or content related to existing endorsement or authorization, or content related to new endorsement or authorization;
   or
2. Commission-approved school district program equivalent to III, B, 1, directly above;
   or
   Any commission-approved professional assessment.
3. In all cases, combination of post-baccalaureate program and additional hours required must be equivalent to master's degree, or to 45 quarter hours, or to 30 semester hours.

    C.   Renewal of Initial II teaching license requirements
1. Completion of all requirements in either III, B, 1, or III, B, 2, directly above, *and*
2. Professional development plan in accordance with current regulations.

  IV. Continuing Teaching License (CTL) (valid 5 years; option to renew)
    A.   Meet all requirements for Initial II Teaching License
    B.   Hold accredited master's degree or higher in arts and sciences, or advanced degree in the professions (all underlying degrees must also be from accredited institutions)
    C.   Have taught 5 years of at least one-half time on any non-provisional license appropriate for assignment (in any state)
    D.   Demonstrate minimum competencies, knowledge and skills by
1. Completion of TSPC-approved CTL program, or accredited doctorate degree in education
2. Certification by National Board of Professional Teaching Standards
or
Certificate of Clinical Competence awarded by Speech and Hearing Association for those holding communication discorders endorsement,
or
Completion of TSPC-approved school district program or any TSPC-approved professional assessment [not yet developed]

   V. Limited Teaching License (valid 3 years and renewable)
    A.   Valid at any level and designated for one or more highly specialized subjects of instruction for which Oregon does not issue a specific endorsement.
    B.   Valid for substitute teaching at any level but only in subjects listed on license.
    C.   Accredited associate's degree or its approved equivalent in objectively evaluated post-secondary education related to the intended subject of instruction is required.
    D.   Furnish fingerprints and provide satisfactory responses to character question contained in licensure application

  VI. Emergency Teaching License (valid for up to 1 year) when districts can demonstrate an emergency need

Teaching Authorizations

A first regular license, whether transitional or initial, is authorized for grade levels on basis of professional education, experience, previous licensure, and specialized academic course work. Oregon has following levels:

    I.   Early Childhood Authorization (grade 4 and below)
   II. Elementary Authorization (grades 3 through 8)
  III. Middle-Level Authorization (grades 5 through 9 of school designated as elementary school, middle school, or junior high school)
  IV. High School Authorization (grades 9 through 12 of school designated as high school)
    A.   This level requires qualification for at least 1 specialty endorsement appropriate to secondary schools.

Subject Matter Endorsements

I. Educator must receive currently specified passing score on each of 1 or more tests of subject mastery for license endorsement.
   A. Praxis II: subject assessments in agriculture, art, biology, general business, chemistry, chemistry/physics, educational media, family and consumer sciences, French, German, health, integrated science, language arts, marketing, basic and advanced mathematics, music, physical education, physics, reading, social studies, Spanish, speech, technology education, and ESOL
   B. Since there are no Praxis exams in drama, adapted physical education, Latin, Russian, and Japanese, transcript review is required for these endorsement areas. Contact TSPC (see Appendix 1)

Personnel Licenses

I. Transitional School Counselor License (valid 3 years; not renewable) Contact TSPC (see Appendix 1) for full details
II. Initial I School Counselor License (valid 3 years plus time to applicant's next birthday; renewable once)
   A. Valid as designated for regular counseling at specific grade levels; see TSPC (Appendix 1) for details
   B. Eligibility Requirements:
       1. Two academic years of experience as a full-time licensed teacher
           a. In a public school or regionally accredited private school in any state or other U.S. jurisdiction,
               or
           b. Completion of approved practicum at any level.
       2. Master's or higher degree in counseling, education, or related behavioral sciences from approved institution
       3. Completion of approved initial graduate program in school counseling
       4. Completion of approved practicum
       5. A passing score as currently specified on test of professional knowledge for school counselors
           or
           5 years of full-time counseling experience on a nonprovisional license valid for the assignment before holding an Oregon license
       6. A passing score as currently specified on test of basic verbal and computational skills, unless
           a. Applicant held an Oregon educator license before 1985,
               or
           b. Applicant has regionally accredited doctoral degree.
       7. Passing score on test of knowledge of U.S. and Oregon civil rights laws at conclusion of approved course or workshop
       8. Furnish fingerprints and provide satisfactory responses to the character question contained in the licensure application

C. Initial School Counselor License Renewal
1. See Teaching Licenses, II, E, above
D. Authorizations: contact TSPC (see Appendix 1) for details

III. Initial II School Counselor License (valid 3 years; renewable repeatedly under the following requirements below)
A. Valid as designated for regular counseling at specific grade levels; see TSPC (Appendix 1) for details
B. Eligibility Requirements:
1. Six semester hours or 9 quarter hours of graduate-level academic credit must be completed after the Initial I School Counselor License has first been issued and be germane to the School Counselor License or directly germane to public school employment.
C. Renewal of the Initial II School Counselor License requires a professional development plan.
D. A school counselor may choose to become eligible for the Continuing School Counselor License in lieu of obtaining the Initial II School Counselor License.
E. This rule applies to all Initial School Counselor Licenses issued after January 1999. See TSPC (Appendix 1) for certain specific time-frame requirements.

IV. Continuing School Counselor License (valid 5 years; renewable)
A. Valid for counseling at all age or grade levels and for substitute teaching at any level in any specialty
B. Eligibility Requirements
1. Completed, beyond initial graduate program in school counseling, the following:
a. Advanced program in counseling competencies consisting of at least 6 semester hours or 9 quarter hours of graduate credit or equivalent,
and
b. Practica in counseling early childhood or elementary students and middle-level or high school students
i. If institution does not award credit directly, all advanced counseling competencies must be validated through approved assessments.
ii. Such assessments may be waived when applicant holds regionally accredited doctoral degree in educational, vocational, or clinical counseling, or else in clinical or counseling psychology.
C. Continuing School Counselor License Renewal
1. Two requirements must be met during preceding 5-year period, as follows:
a. Completion of 1 academic year as full-time licensed educator, or 2 consecutive years as half-time licensed educator, or 180 days of substitution in counseling or teaching, on any appropriate license in an approved Oregon school,
and
b. Establishment, maintenance, and reporting of continuing professional development plan.

Administrative Licenses

I. Transitional Administrator (valid 3 years; ordinarily not renewable)
    A. Master's or higher degree in arts and sciences or advanced degree in the professions from regionally accredited institution or approved foreign equivalent
    B. Depending upon applicant's experience as educator, or training and/or experience as administrator, license may or may not be restricted to employing district. Contact TSPC (see Appendix 1) for additional details.
II. Transitional Superintendent License (valid 3 years; nonrenewable)
    A. Valid for superintendency when issued to person who has been a superintendent on regular assignment in any state; also valid for substitute teaching at any authorization level in any specialty
    B. Eligibility Requirements
        1. Applicant must have been employed as a superintendent for at least 5 years in any state and hold valid superintendent's license from that state
        2. Furnish fingerprints and provide satisfactory responses to character question contained in licensure application
        3. While holding license, applicants must
            a. Complete Oregon school law and finance class, *and*
            b. Complete the required civil rights exam.
    C. Qualifying for Continuing Superintendent License
        1. See II, B, 1–3, directly above
        2. Complete 3 consecutive years of successful experience as superintendent at least half time or more in state of Oregon.
III. Initial Administrative License (valid 3 years plus time to applicant's next birthday, renewable under the requirements below)
    A. Master's or higher degree in arts and sciences or advanced degree in the professions from regionally accredited U.S. institution, or approved foreign equivalent of such degree, together with equally accredited bachelor's degree
    B. Completion in Oregon or another U.S. jurisdiction, either as part of master's degree or separately, of initial graduate program in school administration at institution approved for administrator education by TSPC
    C. Completion of TSPC-approved civil rights workshop
    D. Three academic years of experience as full-time licensed educator, on any license appropriate for assignment, in public or regionally accredited private school in any state, or other U.S. jurisdiction, or in approved Oregon schools
    E. Passing score on test of knowledge of U.S. and Oregon civil rights laws at conclusion of TSPC-approved course or workshop
    F. Through required course of study, assessments, and practica, candidate for Initial Administrator License must demonstrate knowledge, skills, and competencies as specified by Oregon's TSPC.
    G. Renewal: Initial Administrator License may be renewed up to 2 times if applicant makes progress toward completion of Continuing Administrator License by completing at least 6 semester hours or 9 quarter hours of academic credit in

approved Continuing Administrator License Program upon each renewal. A transcript of completed course work is required for renewal.

IV. Continuing Administrator License (valid 5 years; renewable)

A. Completion, beyond both master's degree and the integrated or separate initial graduate program in school administration, of advanced program in administrative competencies consisting of at least 18 semester hours or 27 quarter hours of graduate credit or equivalent

B. Three years of successful experience on transitional or initial licenses administering at least half time in one or more of TSPC-approved schools in Oregon

C. Through required course of study, assessments, and administrative experience, candidate must demonstrate competencies specified by TSPC.

D. Passing score as currently specified by TSPC on test of professional knowledge for school administrators

Pennsylvania

I. Instructional (Classroom Teaching) Certificates
   A. Intern Certificate
      1. Earned baccalaureate degree (not in education)
         a. Cumulative grade-point average of 3.0
      2. Completed appropriate professional education courses in an approved Intern program
      3. Recommendation by preparing Pennsylvania institution
      4. Successful completion of the required basic skills tests, subject matter tests and, except for secondary or mid-level, fundamental subjects test
      5. Valid for no more than 3 years
      6. Applicant will be issued an Instructional I Certificate upon completion of the approved Intern program and a satisfactory evaluation on Pennsylvania Department of Education (PDE) form 430.
   B. Instructional Level I Certificate (Provisional)
      1. Completion of state-approved program of studies
      2. See I, A, 1, a, directly above
      3. Recommendation by preparing institution
      4. Valid for 6 service years in a Pennsylvania public school entity
      5. Successful completion of required tests. See VII, A, below
   C. Instructional Level II Certificate (Permanent)
      1. Completion of a PDE-approved induction program
      2. Three years of satisfactory teaching in Pennsylvania on Instructional I Certificate
      3. Completion of 24 semester hours of post-baccalaureate study, of which 6 semester hours are defined by PDE
      4. The 24 semester hours may be satisfied in whole or in part through PDE approved in-service programs.
      5. Satisfactory results on assessments
II. Educational Specialist (Nonteaching Professional) Certificates
   A. Educational Specialist I (Provisional)
      1. See I, B, 1–5, above
      2. Required Praxis tests
      3. See I, A, 1, a, above
   B. Educational Specialist II (Permanent)
      1. Three years of satisfactory service in single area of Educational Specialist I Certificate
      2. See I, C, 1, 3, 4, and 5 above
   C. Areas of authorization (all are for K–12, unless otherwise noted)
      1. Dental hygienist, elementary school counselor (K–6), home and school visitor, instructional technology specialist, school nurse, school psychologist, and secondary school counselor (7–12)

III. Supervisory Certificates

Note: Educational Leadership: Administration and Supervision test is required.

    A. Supervisory

        1. Five years of satisfactory certificated experience in area in which certification is sought

        2. Completion of approved program of graduate study preparing for supervision and direction of professional and nonprofessional employees

    B. Supervisory (for Curriculum and Instruction or Pupil Personnel Services)

        1. Five years of satisfactory certificated service in program area

            a. For Curriculum and Instruction: 5 years of instructional experience

            b. For Pupil Personnel Services: 5 years of pupil personnel experience

        2. Completion of graduate program in endorsement area

        3. Recommendation of preparing institution

IV. Administrative Certificates

Note: Educational Leadership: Administration and Supervision test is required.

    A. Administrative (Principal, K–12)

        1. Five years of certificated school experience

        2. Completion of a state-approved program and recommendation of the preparing institution

        3. Valid for 5 service years

    B. Letters of Eligibility—Superintendent

        1. See IV, A, 2, directly above,

           or

           Have been prepared through an out-of-state equivalent program

        2. Six years of certificated school service in K–12 schools, including 3 years of certificated supervisory or administrative experience

        3. Recommendation of preparing institution

    C. Letter of Eligibility—Intermediate Unit Executive Director

        1. Completion of a state-approved program and recommendation of the preparing institution

        2. Six years of professional experience, 3 of which were supervisory or administrative

V. Vocational Certificates

    A. Vocational Instructional Intern Certificate

        1. High school graduation or equivalent

        2. Pass appropriate occupational competency exam or credentials review for competency areas where occupational competency exams do not exist

        3. Acceptance for enrollment in approved vocational teacher preparation program

        4. Recommendation of preparing institution

        5. Valid for 3 *calendar* years, during which period holder must complete 18 semester hours within "vocational teacher" approved program and Praxis I tests (Reading and Writing)

    B. Vocational Instructional I (Provisional)

        1. Valid only in areas for which occupational competency credential is held

2.   Two years of wage-earning experience, in addition to earning period, required to establish competency in occupation to be taught
3.   Successful completion of Praxis I tests (Reading and Writing) and occupational competency test
4.   Completion of 18 credit hours, including at least 3 credits or 90 hours (or equivalent combination) regarding accommodations and adaptations for diverse learners in inclusive setting (applies to all certificates issued on or after January 1, 2013); remaining credit hours must be in approved program of vocational teacher education; also requires recommendation of preparing institution
5.   Valid for 6 teaching years, during which time candidate must complete requirements for Vocational Instructional II Certificate
C.   Vocational Instructional II (Permanent)
1.   Evidence of 3 years of satisfactory service on Vocational Instructional I Certificate
2.   Completion of 60 semester hours, including at least 6 credits or 180 hours (or equivalent combination) regarding accommodations and adaptations for students with disabilities in inclusive setting,
and
At least 3 credits or 90 hours (or equivalent combination) in teaching English language learners; remaining hours must be in approved program in appropriate vocational field
3.   Successful completion of Praxis I Mathematics test and PDE Form 430 Evaluation
4.   Completion of a PDE-approved induction program
5.   Satisfactory results on Level II assessment
D.   Supervisor of Comprehensive Vocational Education
Note: Educational Leadership: Administration and Supervision test is required.
1.   Have 3 years of satisfactory certificated service in a vocational field
2.   Have completed an approved preparation/certification program for supervision in the fields of vocational education, and have received recommendation of preparing institution
3.   Valid for 99 years
VI.   Certification for Graduates of Out-of-State Institutions
A.   Recommending institution has state-approved preparation/certification program in area of certification requested
B.   Competency recommendation from dean or department of education chairperson of preparing institution or possession of teaching certificate comparable to Pennsylvania Level I certificate
C.   Completed preparation program is comparable to approved programs offered by Pennsylvania institutions (certification issued for major subject areas only)
D.   Minimum 3.0 GPA
E.   Successful completion of required tests
VII.   Teacher Certification Testing Program
A.   Initial Certificate (Instructional I)
1.   Basic skills or designated basic skills tests or equivalent; consult http://www.education.state.pa.us

   2. In addition, for all instructional areas that cover K–6 or K–12:

    a. Fundamental subjects: Content Knowledge test

   3. PDE Form 430 during student teaching

   4. Designated subject assessment test

  B. Dual certification

   1. Examinations in both areas of specialization

   2. Completion of approved programs in both areas except for teachers holding valid Pennsylvania Instructional I or II Certificate who wish to add another area to that certificate (other than elementary education, early childhood education, special education, health and physical education, reading specialist, or cooperative education

   3. Appropriate subject assessment test(s)

  C. Vocational Instructional I Certificate

   1. Praxis I PPSTs in reading and writing; may also take computerized version

  D. Vocational Instructional II Certificate

   1. PDE Form 430 evaluation

   2. PPST Mathematics

VIII. Other Conditions (once a certificate is issued)

  A. Candidates for employment are required by local school entity to produce background clearance as required by Act 34 and child abuse clearance as required by Act 151; and Pennsylvania state police background check for Pennsylvania residents plus FBI background check for out-of-state applicants. Applicants may not teach without these clearances.

  B. All educators must maintain their certifications as active by

   1. Earning 6 collegiate credits,

    or

   2. 6 PDE-approved inservice credits,

    or

   3. 180 continuing education hours,

    or

   4. Any combination of the above every 5 calendar years

Rhode Island

Certification Redesign and Transition

Rhode Island is currently in the process of redesigning its educator certification system and will issue renewable 1-year transitional certificates until the redesign is complete. During this transition, educators renewing their certificates in 2011 will not be required to complete their I-Plan and will be issued a prorated 1-year professional transitional certificate, to be renewed on a yearly basis until the new renewal regulations are developed and promulgated by the Board of Regents. Consult http://www.ride.ri.gov for current status and full information on application procedures and fees.

Certification Overview

I. Certificate of Eligibility for Employment: CEE (valid 3 years; renewable)
   A. Initial certificate issued to applicants who satisfy the following requirements for certification:
      1. Hold a bachelor's degree from accredited or approved institution of higher education
      2. Demonstrate subject matter competency in core academic subject(s) by completing appropriate major or its equivalent, *or* by passing a rigorous content knowledge test
      3. Completion of a preparation program or all of the appropriate education course work
   B. Enables individuals to apply for local school district positions that match the CEE validity
   C. Renewable every 3 years by payment of appropriate certification fee
   D. Holders of previous Rhode Island certificates
      1. Holders of Provisional or Extended Provisional certificate without work experience in Rhode Island will receive a CEE upon renewal of their current certificate.
      2. Holders of a Professional certificate, in addition to a Provisional or Extended Provisional certificate, will receive Professional certificates in all certificate areas.
         a. Certificates not in use will be inactive Professional certificates.
   E. To obtain a Professional certificate, appointing authority provides CEE holder with verification of employment once a position is secured.
II. Professional Certificate (valid 5 years; renewable)
   A. Current holders of a Professional certificate who meet certification requirements for a new area will be issued a Professional certificate in that area.
      1. For current holders of a Professional certificate who are not currently employed in Rhode Island, the certificate remains inactive until employment is secured.
   B. Holders of previous Rhode Island certificates

1. Current holders of Provisional and/or Extended Provisional certificates do not need 3 years of documented service to apply for a Professional certificate, although they must provide verification of employment from appointing authority to obtain it.
2. Current holders of Life certificates are not affected by these system changes.

III. Certificate Renewal

A. For renewal of a Professional Certificate that expires in 2009, applicant must complete 6 graduate credits in any area in addition to 3 other undergraduate or graduate college credits,

or

Complete 45 hours of approved professional development.

Requirements for Certificates Issued

I. Early Childhood Certificate (Preschool–Grade 2)
A. Certificate of Eligibility for Employment (CEE). See Certification Overview, I, A–E, above. Applicants must also:
B. Graduate from approved program for preparation of early childhood teachers within previous 5 years from date of application

or

Present transcript evidence of 6 semester hours of student teaching in early childhood grades and at least 24 semester hours of course work including: child growth and development; curriculum and methods in early childhood education; reading readiness and developmental reading; health and nutrition for the young child; child, family, and community relationships; and identification of and service to special needs children
   1. Certified teachers with at least 2 years of teaching experience seeking early childhood certification may fulfill student teaching requirement by completing 1-year supervised internship at early childhood level. For full details, contact the Rhode Island Office of Educator Quality and Certification (EQAC) (see Appendix 1).
C. Applicants who have not previously been certified in Rhode Island must have a score of 171 on the Early Childhood and 169 on the Early Childhood Content Knowledge tests. Scores of 145 on the Elementary Content Knowledge Test and 148 on the Elementary Content Areas Exercises Test also meet the test requirement for this area of certification.
D. Professional Certificate. See Certification Overview, II, A–B, above

II. Elementary Certificate (Grades 1–6)
A. Certificate of Eligibility for Employment (CEE). See Certification Overview, I, A–E, above
B. See I, B, directly above, except that preparation program must be for elementary school teachers and course work must include the following areas: child growth and development; methods and materials of teaching math, science, social studies, reading, language arts in the elementary schools; the arts; identification and service to special needs children; and foundations of education

     C.   See I, C, directly above

     D.   Professional Certificate. See Certification Overview, II, A and B, above

III.   Middle School Endorsement (Grades 5–8 in middle school content areas of mathematics, English, science, social studies, or foreign languages; Grades 7–8 in junior high schools)

     A.   Valid Rhode Island elementary, secondary, special subjects, elementary/middle special educator, or middle/secondary special educator certificate

        1.   Endorsement exemptions: special subjects teachers, elementary/middle special educators, and middle/secondary special educators are permitted to teach their specific areas in a middle school without obtaining middle level endorsement.

        2.   Teachers of content areas listed in III, directly above, must obtain middle level endorsement.

           a.   Members of interdisciplinary instructional teams may lead integrated instruction provided that other members of the team are certified in each content area taught by the team.

     B.   Completion of approved college program of studies designed for preparation of middle level educators, to include collaboratively supervised field experience(s) that ensure specific competencies

     C.   A college major, minor, or 21 semester hours in 1 of the following academic areas: mathematics, English, science, or social studies

        1.   Check with EQAC (see Appendix 1) for specific course distribution requirements

     D.   Applicants who do not possess a major or its equivalent (30 semester hours) in an academic area must achieve the passing score in the following content knowledge test(s):

        1.   English—Middle School English Language Arts (#0049)—162

        2.   Mathematics—Middle School Mathematics (#0069)—158

        3.   Science—Middle School Science (#0439)—154

        4.   Social Studies—Citizenship Education: Content Knowledge (#0087)—160

     E.   For full details on competencies in III, A, directly above, as well as on implementation procedures and exemptions, contact EQAC (see Appendix 1).

IV.   Secondary Teaching Certificate (Grades 7–12, for teaching special content areas in junior/senior high school)

     A.   Certificate of Eligibility for Employment (CEE). See Certification Overview, I, A–E, above

     B.   See I, B, directly above, except that preparation program must be for secondary school teachers. Applicants who have not completed an approved program can be certified by transcript analysis by presenting evidence of 6 semester hours of student teaching in the secondary grades and no fewer than 18 semester hours of course work to include work in each of the following areas: adolescent psychology; secondary methods, measurements, and evaluation; identification of and service to special needs students; teaching of reading in the content area; and foundations of education

        1.   For full details on academic requirements, contact EQAC (see Appendix 1).

     C.   Applicants not previously certified in Rhode Island must achieve a score of at least 167 on Principles of Learning and Teaching, 7–12, test.

     D.   Professional Certificate. See Certification Overview, II, A and B, above

V.   Administrative Certification

A.   Elementary Principal's Certificate (valid for principal/assistant principal in public elementary or middle schools)

1.   Certificate of Eligibility for Employment (CEE). See Certification Overview, I, A–E, above, except that the degree from an accredited institution of higher education must be at the master's level,

and

Applicants must be eligible for a Rhode Island elementary teaching certificate and document 3 years of teaching experience in the elementary grades.

2.   See I, B, directly above, except that preparation program must be for elementary school principals and course work must include the following areas: school/community relations; elementary curriculum development; organization and administration of the elementary school; supervision of instruction; supervision and evaluation of professional staff; educational research; program evaluations; fiscal planning and management; school law (federal and state laws and regulations)

3.   Professional Certificate. See Certification Overview, II, A and B, above

B.   Secondary Principal's Certificate (valid for principal/assistant principal in public secondary or middle schools)

1.   Certificate of Eligibility for Employment (CEE). See Certification Overview, I, A–E, above, except that the degree from an accredited institution of higher education must be at the master's level,

and

Applicants must be eligible for a Rhode Island secondary teaching certificate and document 3 years of teaching experience in the secondary grades.

2.   See V, A, 2, directly above, except that preparation program must be for secondary school principals and course work must be for secondary schools

3.   Professional Certificate. See Certification Overview, II, A and B, above

C.   Superintendent of Schools Certificate (valid for superintendent/assistant superintendent in public schools)

1.   Certificate of Eligibility for Employment (CEE). See Certification Overview, I, A–E, above, except that the degree from an accredited institution of higher education must be an advanced degree, such as doctorate, certificate of advanced graduate study, or master's level,

and

Applicants must be eligible for a Rhode Island teaching certificate and document 8 years of both teaching and administrative experience.

2.   See V, A, 2, directly above, except that course work must include at least 36 semester hours of graduate-level courses, including the following areas: school/community relations; curriculum construction; organization and administration of schools; supervision of instruction; supervision and evaluation of professional staff; educational research; program evaluation; school plant planning; and school finance

3.   Professional Certificate. See Certification Overview, II, A and B, above

VI. School Counselor Certification
    A. School Counselor Certificate (Grades PK–12)
        1. Certificate of Eligibility for Employment (CEE). See Certification Overview, I, A–E, above
        2. See V, A, 2, directly above, except that preparation program must be for school counseling, and the degree from an accredited institution of higher education must be at the master's level,
            and
            Applicants must be eligible for a Rhode Island teaching certificate and document 2 years of teaching experience at the elementary or secondary level,
            and
            Course work must include the following areas: introduction to pupil personnel service; techniques of counseling; psychological and educational assessment; vocational and educational placement; and at least a 3-semester-hour internship in school counseling
        3. Professional Certificate. See Certification Overview, II, A and B, above
    B. Supervisor of School Counselors Certificate (Grades PK–12)
        1. Certificate of Eligibility for Employment (CEE). See Certification Overview, I, A–E, above
        2. See VI, A, 2, directly above, except that applicants must be eligible for a Rhode Island school counselor's certificate and document 3 years of school counselor experience,
            and
            Course work must include at least 9 semester hours of graduate-level work in educational administration in the areas of administration and organization of counseling programs; supervision of personnel; and curriculum development and evaluation
        3. Professional Certificate. See Certification Overview, II, A and B, above
VII. Special Subjects Certificate (Grades PK–12) for art, dance, health, physical education, home economics, technology education, library/media, music, and theatre
    A. Certificate of Eligibility for Employment (CEE). See Certification Overview, I, A–E, above
    B. See I, B, directly above, except that preparation program must be for special subjects teachers and 18 semester hours of course work must include the following areas: human growth and development; foundations of education; methodology (must include at least 1 course in the special subjects field); measurement and evaluation; identification of and service to special needs students; and the teaching of reading in the content area
        1. For full details on academic requirements, contact EQAC (see Appendix 1).
    C. Applicants not previously certified in Rhode Island must achieve a score of at least 167 on Principles of Learning and Teaching, K–6 or 7–12, test. Only one test is required.
    D. Professional Certificate. See Certification Overview, II, A and B, above

South Carolina

Certification Grade Spans

I. Current certication grade spans
    A. Early Childhood: (PreK–3)
    B. Elementary: (2–6)
    C. Middle Level: (5–8) in English, science, mathematics, or social science
    D. Secondary: (9–12) in specific subjects
    E. Special Education: (K–12) in mental disabilities, emotional disabilities, learning disabilities, severe disabilities, visually impaired, hearing impaired, and multicategorical
    F. Other: (K–12) in art, health, music, physical education, world languages

Types of Credential Classification

I. Initial Certificate (valid 3 years)
    A. To qualify for initial certificate, applicant must:
        1. Earn bachelor's or master's degree from an institution and programs approved by the Department of Education Division of Educator Quality & Leadership (DEQL); see Appendix 1. Professional education credit must be earned through an institution that has teacher education program approved for initial certification.
        2. Submit required teaching area examination score(s) as adopted by the DEQL for purposes of certification. The required score on examination of general professional knowledge (pedagogy), as approved by DEQL, is also required.
        3. Undergo criminal records check by South Carolina Law Enforcement Division and national criminal records check supported by fingerprinting conducted by Federal Bureau of Investigation.
    B. Beyond initial 3-year validity period, teachers who do not yet meet requirements for professional certification but who are employed by a public school district may have their certificates renewed annually by request of employing school district.
II. Professional Certificate (valid 5 years)
    A. To qualify for each successive level of professional certification (bachelor's degree, bachelor's degree plus 18 hours, master's degree, master's degree plus 30 hours, and doctorate), an applicant must:
        1. Meet all criteria for initial area of certification and have earned bachelor's degree that meets regulations for teacher certification and program approval, and successfully complete DEQL induction program, all ancillary requirements, and formal evaluation approved by DEQL,
            or

2. Successfully complete requirements for reciprocity according to Interstate Agreement on Qualifications of Educational Personnel,
   or
3. Hold valid National Board teaching certification.

III. Alternative Route Certificate (valid 1 year; renewable)
   A. Issued to individuals who qualify under the Program for Alternative Certification for Educators (PACE) guidelines as adopted by DEQL
   B. Renewable twice by successfully completing annual program requirements as approved by DEQL
   C. Eligibility for professional certificate requires successful completion of all program requirements within 3-year program period, including additional testing requirements and formal evaluation approved by DEQL.

IV. Alternative American Board for Certification of Teaching Excellence (ABCTE)
   A. Educators holding an ABCTE (American Board for Certification of Teaching Excellence) certification will receive a South Carolina statement of eligibility.
   B. Upon confirmation of an offer of employment as a teacher in a South Carolina public school, a 1-year South Carolina Alternate Route Certificate will be issued.
   C. The ABCTE certificate may be renewed annually for 2 additional years upon verification of successful teaching.
   D. Eligibility for professional certificate requires completion of 3 years of successful teaching in a South Carolina public or charter school and additional testing requirements.

Levels of Credential Classification and Renewal Credit Plan

I. Bachelor's degree
   A. Hold a bachelor's degree that meets State Board of Education regulations for teacher certification and program approval
   B. Meet all criteria for an initial area of certification

II. Bachelor's degree plus 18 hours
   A. See Certification Grade Spans, directly above
   B. Earn 18 hours of graduate credit within 7 years from the time the course work is started
      1. If not completed within 7 years, applicant must request college/university revalidation of course credits

III. Master's degree
   A. Hold a master's degree that meets State Board of Education regulations for teacher certification and program approval

IV. Master's degree plus 30 hours
   A. Earn 30 semester hours of graduate credit above the master's degree with 21 hours in 1 area of concentration, which may or may not be the initial area of certification. Course work must be completed within 7 years from the time it was started.
      1. See II, B, 1, directly above,

or

B. Earn additional master's or specialist's degree that meets State Board of Education regulations for teacher certification and program approval.

V. Renewal Credit Plan

   A. All educators' professional certificates are valid for 5 years, expiring on June 30 of expiration year.

   B. Educator must earn a minimum of 120 renewal credits during validity period

      1. Current employment status of educator will determine specific renewal steps. See DEQL (contact information in Appendix 1) for full details of renewal credit matrix.

Administration

I. Elementary School Principal and Supervisor

   A. Hold master's degree

   B. Hold valid South Carolina Educator's Professional Certificate at elementary level

   C. Meet minimum qualifying score(s) on area examinations required by State Board of Education

   D. Verify 3 years of teaching experience, including at least 1 year of teaching in grades pre-K–6

   E. Complete an advanced program approved by State Board of Education for training of elementary principals and supervisors

II. Secondary School Principal and Supervisor

   A. See I, A–C, directly above, except at secondary level

   B. Verify 3 years of teaching experience, including at least 1 year of teaching in grades 9–12

   C. Complete advanced program approved by State Board of Education for training of secondary principals and supervisors

III. District Superintendent

   A. Hold master's degree

   B. Hold valid South Carolina Professional Certificate at elementary, middle, or secondary level

   C. Meet minimum qualifying score(s) on area examination(s) required by State Board of Education

   D. Verify 3 years of experience as a pre-K–12 or postsecondary teacher and 2 years as a school or school district administrator, postsecondary administrator, or school business administrator

   E. Complete advanced program approved by State Board of Education for training of school superintendents

IV. District Superintendent (Alternative Route)

   A. Initial certificate for 1 year (renewable annually for 2 additional years at request of local school board based on verification of successful performance reviews)

B. Professional certificate issued upon completion of specified program of study, minimum qualifying scores on required certification examination(s), and recommendation by local school board after 3 years of successful service as superintendent

C. Alternative Route requirements
1. Hold master's degree
2. Verify at least 10 years of successful experience in senior position(s) of leadership such as chief executive officer in a business, corporation or agency; military officer; or other position with responsibilities similar to those of a district superintendent
3. Recommendation for certification by local school board in South Carolina public school district interested in employing individual as superintendent
4. Local school board to submit plan of study that applicant must complete within 3 years including, at a minimum, areas of curriculum and instruction, school finance, and school law. Candidate must also submit a passing score on area examination(s) required by State Board of Education for district superintendents within first year of employment as a superintendent.

South Dakota

Teacher Certification

Please note that South Dakota has aligned all teacher education programs to national standards where applicable. A complete record of standards can be obtained at http://doe.sd.gov/oatq/teacheredprograms.asp

I.   General Requirements for All Certification Levels:
   A.   Verification from accredited institution that applicant has met the standards of an approved program and can be recommended for certification
   B.   Notarized citizenship statement and verification that applicant has not been convicted of any crime involving moral turpitude, including traffic in narcotics
   C.   Completion of human relations (HR) and South Dakota Indian studies (SDIS) courses
   D.   If an applicant meets all the stated requirements for certification with the exception of SDIS and HR, a 5-year certificate can be issued with the understanding that both SDIS and HR must be completed as course work to renew the initial certificate.

II. Initial Certification Requirements (valid 5 years):
   A.   A completed online initial application form (online form is at http./doe.sd.gov/oatq/teachercert.asp)
   B.   Official transcripts from each accredited postsecondary institution attended
   C.   Official copy of all passing test scores including any subtest scores provided on the state certification exams
   D.   Teachers new to the profession or to the state are required to pass Praxis II tests specific to the content areas they will be teaching.
      1.   The department may issue a 1-year certificate allowing an applicant to complete required Praxis.
      2.   Testing information is at http://doe.sd.gov/oatq/praxis/.asp
   E.   Teachers new to the profession also must take the Principles of Learning and Teaching test that most accurately matches their level of preparation.
   F.   Teachers who have had any contracted teaching experience on a valid certificate outside of their basic teaching program requirements, including student teaching, practicum, or internship, can either show verification of teaching experience at http://doe.sd.gov/oatq/teachercert.asp or submit a copy of Praxis II PLT test scores.
   G.   Institutional statement completed and submitted by the certifying office of the college/university where preparation was made
   H.   Applicants whose programs are more than 5 years old must provide documentation of 6 semester hours in the applicant's field of study from an accredited 4-year institution in the 5 years immediately preceding the date of application.
      1.   The department may issue a 1-year certificate allowing an applicant to complete required college credits.

III. K–8 Elementary Education Program Requirements:
   A.   General and Initial Certification requirements (see I and II, directly above)

B.   Course work sufficient to constitute an elementary education major
C.   Demonstrated competencies in all of the following areas:
   1.   Knowledge of the developmental characteristics of the elementary-level learner and of the student with disabilities
   2.   Knowledge of curriculum development that uses South Dakota and other established K–12 academic standards to design a successful instructional program that facilitates student achievement
   3.   Integration of technology into teaching and learning
   4.   Verification that the applicant has completed studies and field experiences in all of the following:
     a.   Design of curriculum and instructional strategies for middle-level learners
     b.   Developmental characteristics of the middle-level learner
     c.   Concepts of middle-level education or the middle-level learner

IV.   7–12 Secondary Education Program Requirements
A.   General and Initial Certification requirements (see I and II, directly above)
B.   Course work sufficient to constitute an academic major
C.   Demonstrated competencies in all of the following areas:
   1.   Competency in the teaching of content area literacy and instructional methods in the content area specific to the discipline
   2.   Knowledge of the developmental characteristics of the secondary-level learner and of the student with disabilities
   3.   Knowledge of curriculum development that uses South Dakota and other established K–12 academic standards to design an instructional program that facilitates student achievement
   4.   Integrating technology into teaching and learning
   5.   Concepts of middle-level education or the middle-level learner
   6.   Verification that the candidate has completed studies and field experiences in the following:
     a.   Design of curriculum and instructional strategies for middle-level learners
     b.   Developmental characteristics of the middle-level learner

V.   5–8 Middle-Level Education Program Requirements
A.   General and Initial Certification requirements (see I and II, directly above)
B.   Course work sufficient to constitute a middle school education major
C.   Demonstrated competencies in all of the following areas:
   1.   Teaching middle-level reading
   2.   Integrating technology into teaching and learning
   3.   Knowledge of the developmental characteristics of the middle-level learner and of the student with disabilities
   4.   Knowledge of curriculum development that uses South Dakota and other established K–12 academic standards to design an instructional program that facilitates student achievement
   5.   Integrating technology into teaching and learning

VI.   Alternative Certification
A.   Limited to 7–12 or K–12 age/grade span authorizations issued at the approved education program level

B. To be eligible for the program, an applicant must have the following:
1. A bachelor's degree or higher, with the bachelor's degree obtained at least 2 years prior to admittance into the alternative certification program
2. An overall grade-point average of 2.5 or higher on an undergraduate transcript
3. A college major in the subject area to be taught or has 5 years experience in a related field
4. An offer of employment from a South Dakota accredited school system that operates a mentoring program approved by the department
5. A criminal background investigation done by the school district
6   Adherence to the Code of Professional Ethics, as adopted by the Professional Teachers Practices and Standards Commission
7. A screening interview with school personnel and the department's program coordinator, *and*
8. An official copy of all test scores, including any subtest scores provided by the testing company on the state certification exams for each subject or area authorization, and for the pedagogy exam for each age or grade span in which the alternative certification applicant will be certified.

Reading Specialist

I. K–12 reading specialist program shall require all of the following:
A. A master's degree with an emphasis in reading
B. Three years of teaching experience in a K–12 setting
C. The required courses and experiences of a K–12 reading specialist program shall meet the International Reading Association (IRA) standards, 2003 edition.
D. The program shall require candidates to demonstrate the content, pedagogical, and professional knowledge and skills identified in the IRA standards.

Certification Changes for Endorsement Programs

I. For the most part, South Dakota cannot award an endorsement without a valid South Dakota teaching certificate.
II. An additional authorization can be issued on a certificate, or a transcript analysis may be requested by completing the South Dakota Department of Education's Additional Authorizations application.
III. An additional authorization may be issued on a certificate with:
A. Verification of completion of an approved education program by a certifying officer or verification of completion of education endorsement program requirements by a certifying officer or by the department. Course work for education endorsement programs must be completed with a grade of "C" or higher at an accredited postsecondary institution. Course work earned at accredited community colleges and postsecondary vocational schools must be approved by the department or the certifying officer prior to enrollment in the course,
or

B. An official copy of all Praxis II test scores including any subtest scores provided by the testing company on the state certification exam for each subject or area authorization for endorsement programs for which the applicant is applying.

C. Submission of official transcript

Administration

I. Elementary and Secondary Principal Certificate Authorization
   A. Preschool through grade 12, preschool through grade 8, or grade 7 through grade 12 principal programs shall require all of the following:
      1. Master's degree in education
      2. Three years of verified experience on a valid certificate in an accredited K–12 school, 1 year of which includes classroom teaching experience or direct services to students
         a. The 3 years of verified experience may be waived if candidate receives passing score on Educational Leadership Praxis II test.
      3. Demonstrated competence related to the age/grade span for which authorization is sought
      4. Internship to include all job responsibilities at the age/grade span for which authorization is sought
         a. For a preschool through grade 12 principal program, the internship must include time spent in at least 2 of the levels of elementary school, junior high/middle school, or secondary school.
   B. The required courses and experiences of a preschool through grade 8 or 7–12 principal program shall meet the Educational Leadership Constituent Council (ELCC) standards, 2001 edition.
   C. The program shall require candidates to demonstrate the applicable content, pedagogical, and professional knowledge and skills identified in the ELCC.
   D. The principal programs may be developed with multiple options to earn eligibility for a preschool through grade 12 principal program within the same master's degree or as an additional certification-only principal program.
II. Superintendent Certificate Authorization
   A. Preschool through grade 12 career school superintendent program shall require:
      1. Completion of an education specialist or doctoral degree
      2. Three years of verified experience on a valid certificate in an accredited K–12 school
         a. One year to include classroom teaching experience or direct services to students
         b. Experience to allow for participation of the cooperating superintendent
      3. Internship in all job responsibilities
   B. Required courses and experiences of a preschool through grade 12 career school superintendent program shall meet ELCC standards, 2001.
   C. The program shall require candidates to demonstrate the applicable standards identified in the ELCC.

III. Administrative Endorsement Requirements
  A. Principal endorsement, preschool–grade 8, grade 7–grade 12, or preschool–grade 12
    1. Bachelor's degree in education
    2. Minimum of 15 graduate semester hours of course work, plus practicum or internship experiences, or a combination thereof, which address the specific competencies mandated by law
    3. Three years of verified experience in an accredited K–12 school, 1 year of which includes classroom teaching experience or direct service to students
      a. The 3 years of verified experience may be waived if candidate receives passing score on Educational Leadership Praxis II test.
    4. Valid for 5 years only, unless applicant has also completed a master's degree in education within the past 10 years
  B. School superintendent endorsement, preschool–grade 12
    1. Master's degree, plus 15 graduate semester hours which address the specific competencies mandated by law
    2. Three years of verified experience on a valid certificate in an accredited K–12 school, 1 year of which includes classroom teaching experience or direct services to students
    3. Valid for 10 years only; and within the first 5 years of validity, holder must complete 6 additional graduate semester hours addressing specific competencies mandated by law; and by end of validity, all legal requirements must be satisfied.
  C. Principal endorsement program, preschool–grade 12
    1. Master's degree with a preschool–grade 8 or 7–12 principalship
    2. Completion of course work specific to the preschool–grade 8 or 7–12 principal endorsement sought
    3. Three years of verified experience in an accredited K–12 school, 1 year of which includes classroom teaching experience or direct services to students
      a. The 3 years of verified experience may be waived if candidate receives passing score on Educational Leadership Praxis II test.

School Counselor Certificate Authorization

I. A preschool through grade 12 school counselor education program shall require a master's degree in school guidance or counseling.
  A. The required courses and experiences of a preschool through grade 12 school counselor education program shall meet the Council on Accreditation of Counseling and Related Education Programs (CACREP) standards, 2001 edition.
  B. The program shall require candidates to demonstrate the applicable content, pedagogical, and professional knowledge and skills identified in the CACREP standards.

Certificate Renewal

I. Individuals who wish to renew a current South Dakota teaching certificate or update a lapsed certificate need specific items to complete an online application; for details, contact the Department of Education (see Appendix 1)

II. Certified staff with advanced certification or degrees, including National Board certification, master's degrees, specialist degrees, and doctoral degrees, must document the following:
  A. Six semester hours or 9 quarter hours from an accredited postsecondary institution,
      or
  B. Six renewal credits,
      or
  C. Ninety hours of CEUs,
      or
  D. A combination of the above, equivalent to 6 semester hours or 9 quarter hours
III. Applicants with continuing professional development plans
  A. Must verify completion of any plan requirements in excess of 6 semester hours and update professional development plans to establish remaining requirements for subsequent renewal
      1. Renewal requirements must address legally mandated preparation standards and must be completed between issuance date of currently valid certificate and application for renewal
IV. Applicants renewing an initial 5-year certificate
  A. Must verify completion of 2 departmentally approved 3 semester-hour courses, 1 in human relations and another in South Dakota Indian studies.
V.   Applicants renewing an updated certificate must verify completion of any deficiencies in excess of 6 semester hours that were identified at the reissuance of the lapsed certificate.

Reciprocity

I.   South Dakota has reciprocity with any accredited out-of-state teacher preparation program that is also offered in South Dakota.
II. Reciprocity applicants must provide a sign-off from the university from which they obtained their degree along with supporting transcript documentation.
III. Successful applicants will be granted a 1-year certificate, during the course of which they must complete and pass both the Praxis II pedagogy and content tests for each area of certification.

Tennessee

Types of Teacher Licenses

I. Apprentice License (valid 5 years; renewable)
   A. Initial license issued to applicant who completes approved teacher preparation program or who meets reciprocal requirements with less than 1 year of teaching experience
   B. Five-year validity to allow 3 years of teaching in Tennessee public or state-accredited private school; validity expires after 3 years of teaching in approved Tennessee school

II. Out-of-State Teacher's License (valid 5 years; renewable)
   A. Initial license issued to out-of-state applicant who meets Tennessee licensure requirements; equivalent to Apprentice License
   B. Requires at least 1 year of acceptable teaching experience in another state

III. Professional License (valid 10 years; renewable)
   A. Accrue minimum of 3 years of acceptable experience in an approved school and receive positive local evaluation in Tennessee public or state-accredited private school
      1. Three years of experience may combine in-state with out-of-state experience, but last year must be in Tennessee public school to participate in local evaluation process

IV. Transitional License (1 year; renewable no more than 2 times)
   A. Applies only to candidates holding at least a bachelor's degree who may or may not have yet completed all required licensure exams.
   B. Requirements:
      1. Bachelor's degree from a regionally accredited institution of higher education and content in one of the following 3 ways:
         a. Acceptable major in the endorsement area,
            or
         b. Verification of at least 24 semester hours in the teaching content area,
            or
         c. Pass the required PRAXIS II content exam(s) for the endorsement area sought.
      2. Statement signed by a Tennessee director of schools stating intent to employ the candidate as directed by the Transitional License application
      3. Verification by the institution of higher education or approved education organization of enrollment in and/or admission to the Transitional License program

V. Apprentice Occupational Education License (valid 3 years; renewable)
   A. Issued in two areas:
      1. Health Science and Technology
      2. Trade and Industry
   B. Contact Office of Teacher Licensing (see Appendix 1) for complete list of endorsement areas and related requirements for each

VI. Professional Occupational Education License (valid 10 years; renewable)
   A. Hold Apprentice Occupational Education License
   B. Evaluation by approved university of candidate's knowledge and skills to determine specific course work required
VII. Apprentice Special Group Licenses (valid 5 years)
   A. Initial license issued for the following areas (Grades PreK–12): school counselor, school psychologist, school social worker, speech language pathologist, and school audiologist
VIII. Professional School Service Personnel License
   A. Serve in endorsement area (see VII, A, directly above) for a minimum of 3 years
      1. Last year of 3 years of service in Tennessee public or state-accredited private school with receipt of positive local evaluation

Teacher License Requirements

 I. Tennessee College/University Program Route to Licensure
   A. Hold a bachelor's and/or master's degree from a teacher preparation program at a regionally accredited college/university
      1. Program to include all required professional courses, student teaching, and/or internship
   B. Pass all appropriate portions of the Praxis Series Exam
   C. Receive recommendation from college/university to Tennessee Office of Teacher Licensing
 II. Out-of-State Route to Licensure
   A. Complete a teacher preparation program or meet reciprocity requirements
   B. Hold a bachelor's and/or master's degree from a regionally accredited college/university
   C. Pass all appropriate portions of the Praxis Series Exam, unless:
      1. Fully certified/licensed in another state before July 1, 1984,
         or
      2. Hold full, valid license in an endorsement area available in Tennessee from a state having a reciprocal agreement with Tennessee and meet all guidelines defined in reciprocal agreement; submit documentation to Office of Teaching Licensing (see Appendix 1) for determination of possible eligibility without testing.
III. Endorsements
   Administrator (Aspiring PreK–12; Beginning PreK–12; Professional PreK–12; Exemplary preK–12); Bible 7–12; Biology 7–12; Business Education 7–12; Business Technology 7–12; Early Child Care Services 9–12; Chemistry 7–12; Coop Coordinator; Dance K–12, Driver Education 7–12; Early Childhood Education PreK–3; Early Development/Learning PreK–K; Earth Science 7–12; Economics 7–12; Elementary K–6; English 7–12; English as Second Language PreK–12; Family & Consumer Sciences 5–12; Food Production & Management Services 9–12; Food Service Supervisor; Foreign Language Other (7–12; PreK–12); French (7–12; PreK–12); Geography 7–12; German (7–12; PreK–12); Gifted Education PreK–12; Government 7–12; Health & Wellness K–12; History 7–12; JROTC; Latin (7–12; PreK–12); Library Information Specialist PreK–12; Marketing 7–12;

Mathematics 7–12; Middle Grades (4–8); Music (Instrumental/General K–12; Vocal/General K–12); Physical Education K–12; Physics 7–12; Psychology 9–12; Reading Specialist PreK–12; Russian (PreK–12; 7–12); School Counselor PreK–12; School Psychologist PreK–12; School Audiologist PreK–12; Speech Language Pathologist PreK–12; School Social Worker PreK–12; Sociology 9–12; Spanish (7–12; PreK–12); Special Education (Comprehensive K–12; Early Childhood Education PreK–3; Hearing PreK–12; Modified K–12; Speech/Language Teacher PreK–12; Vision PreK–12); Speech Communications 7–12; Superintendent; Supervisor of Attendance; Supervisor of Materials; Technology/Engineering Education 5–12; Theatre K–12; Visual Arts K–12; Agriculture Education 7–12

Administrator (PreK–12)

I. Beginning Administrator License or Instructional Leadership License— Beginning (valid 5 years)
  A. Complete approved graduate program in school administration and supervision at accredited institution of higher education (IHE)
  B. Passing grades on state-required test/assessment
  C. Receive recommendation for license by an approved leadership preparation program
II. Professional Administrator License (valid 10 years; renewable)
  or
  Instructional Leadership License—Professional (valid 5 years; renewable)
  A. Hold Beginning Administrator License or Instructional Leadership License—Beginning
  B. Obtain employment as assistant principal, principal, or supervisor of instruction in Tennessee public or state-accredited private school
  C. Complete customized professional development program jointly developed by administrator, superintendent, Tennessee IHE, and mentor
  or
  Complete state beginning administrator academy program based upon Tennessee Instructional Leadership Standards (TILS)
  D. Receive successful local evaluation by superintendent or designee based upon TILS
  E. Serve successfully in administrator position at least 2 years.

Librarian

I. Licensing requirements
  A. Complete graduate-level program leading to a master's degree with major in library information; or have master's degree and complete graduate-level library licensing program
  B. Receive recommendation for licensure from college/university attended
  C. Receive passing scores on appropriate parts of Praxis series examination

Texas

For full and specific details on securing certificate copies as well as on certification testing and requirements, contact the Texas Education Agency (TEA), Educator Certification at http://www.tea.state.tx.us

Certification Overview

I. General Certification Requirements
   A. Hold bachelor's degree from institution of higher education that at the time was accredited or otherwise approved by an accrediting organization recognized by the Texas Higher Education Coordinating Board
      1. Texas institutions do not offer a degree in education, so every teacher must have an academic major as well as teacher-training courses.
         a. Only exemption is for individuals seeking Career and Technical Education certification to teach certain courses, such as welding or computer-aided drafting
   B. Complete teacher training through an approved program, offered through colleges and universities, school districts, regional service centers, community colleges, and other entities
   C. Successfully complete appropriate teacher certification tests for subject and grade level. Specific Texas Examinations of Educator Standards (TExES) and Examination for the Certification of Educators in Texas (ExCET) and other tests are required, depending on applicant's background and certification sought; contact TEA at http://www.tea.state.tx.us for list of certification tests and information on which tests are required.
II. Routes to Educator Certification
   A. University-based Programs
      1. Undergraduate certificate earned as part of baccalaureate degree program
      2. Post-baccalaureate programs designed to prepare baccalaureate degree holders seeking educator certification.
   B. Alternative Programs for Educator Preparation
      1. TEA-approved programs available at some institutions of higher education. These may involve university course work or other professional development experiences as well as intense mentoring and supervision during candidate's first year in role of educator.
      2. Some regional education service centers, large school districts, and private entities offer alternative programs of preparation.
   C. Additional Certification Based on Examination: for teachers holding a classroom teaching certificate and bachelor's degree
      l. Such teachers may add classroom certification areas by successfully completing appropriate certification examination(s) for area(s) sought.

2. Certification by examination not available for:
    a. Initial certification
    b. Career and Technical Education, except for marketing; certification based on skill and work experience
    c. Certification other than classroom teacher (e.g., counselor, principal, school librarian, educational diagnostician)
    d. Certificate for which no certification examination has been developed
D. Certification Based on Credentials from Another Jurisdiction
    1. Applicants holding an acceptable certificate or credential from another state, U.S. territory, or country may apply for a Texas certificate. Credential must be equivalent to a certificate issued by TEA and must not have been revoked, suspended, or pending such action.
    2. One-Year Certificate in one or more subject areas may be issued to applicant who holds a standard credential issued by jurisdiction outside Texas and who meets specified requirements as determined by TEA credentials review. Applicant may also request exemption from Texas test based on comparable test in another jurisdiction.
E. Temporary Teacher Certificate: Applicant holding bachelor's degree or higher from accredited institution of higher education with academic major related to at least 1 area of Texas public school curriculum and to 8–12 certificate structure that currently has TExES exam may apply for transcript review by TEA. Training may be provided by an approved school district.

Certificate Types, Classes, and Renewal

I. Types of Certificates: Designates period of validity, personnel, and requirements for each certificate (CPE stands for continuing professional education)
    A. Standard (valid 5 years, renewable with 150 CPE hours)
        1. Replaced lifetime provisional and professional certificates, and educators holding lifetime certificates have been exempted from renewal process.
            a. Note: Since educators adding certificates after September 1, 1999, will be issued a Standard Certificate that must be renewed, it is likely that many current educators will hold both lifetime and Standard Certificates.
        2. Standard teacher certificate requirements
            a. See Certification Overview, I and II, above
    B. One-year (nonrenewable)
        1. Issued for out-of-state or out-of-country candidates
    C. Probationary (valid 1 year; renewable for up to 2 more years)
        1. Issued to individual enrolled in educator preparation program and serving in supervised internship to satisfy field experience requirements of the certificate.
            a. Holder must be employed by accredited Texas public or private school in position appropriate for certificate sought.
        2. Probationary principal certificate eligibility requirements
            a. Hold at least a bachelor's degree,

b.   Meet admission requirements of educator preparation program, *and*

c.   Qualify for internship as defined by the program.

3.   Probationary superintendent eligibility requirements

a.   Hold a Texas standard principal certificate or its equivalent from another state or country, provided applicant passed TEA-approved principal certificate examination, *and*

b.   Hold at least a master's degree.

4.   Renewal contingent on enrollment of applicant in educator preparation program and employment in appropriate position, with mentoring and supervision throughout validity period.

D.   Temporary Teacher (valid for 2 years, nonrenewable)

1.   May be issued for grades 8–12 in curriculum areas that currently have TexES exam

2.   Requires passing scores on 8–12 Pedagogy and Professional Responsibilities (PPR) TExES exam and on appropriate 8–12 TExES content exam

3.   Applicant must pass national fingerprint-based criminal history background check.

4.   Successfully complete TEA transcript review

5.   Applicant must obtain a teaching position and be trained by an approved school district.

E.   Emergency Permit (valid for 1 school year, renewable for no more than 2 additional school years)

1.   Issued to degreed individual who does not have any appropriate certificate required for assignment

F.   Non-Renewable Permit (valid for 1 year, nonrenewable)

1.   Issued to degreed individual who has completed educator preparation program but has not yet passed TExES test(s)

II.   Classes of Certificates

A.   Superintendent (valid 5 years; renewable with 200 CPE hours)

B.   Principal (valid 5 years; renewable with 200 CPE hours)

C.   Classroom teacher (valid 5 years; renewable with 150 CPE hours)

D.   Instructional educator other than classroom teacher, including reading specialist (valid 5 years; renewable with 200 CPE hours)

E.   Master teacher, including master reading, math, science, and technology teacher (valid 5 years; renewable with 200 CPE hours)

F.   School librarian (valid 5 years; renewable with 200 CPE hours)

G.   School counselor (valid 5 years; renewable with 200 CPE hours)

H.   Educational diagnostician (valid 5 years; renewable with 200 CPE hours)

I.   Educational aide I, II, and III (valid 5 years; no renewal CPE requirements)

III.   Certificate Renewal

A.   Standard Requirements

1.   Hold a valid Standard Certificate that has not been, nor is in the process of being, sanctioned by TEA,

2. Successfully complete a criminal history review,
3. Not be in default on a student loan or in arrears of child support,
4. Complete the required number of clock hours of continuing professional education (CPE),
   and
5. Submit online application to TEA with appropriate renewal fee.

Administrator Certification

I. Principal Certificate (valid 5 years; renewable with 200 CPE hours)
   A. Requirements for certificate
      1. Successfully complete a TEA-approved principal preparation program and be recommended for certification by that program
      2. Successfully pass TExES Principal certification exam
      3. Hold master's degree from institution of higher education that at the time was accredited or otherwise approved by an accrediting organization recognized by the Texas Higher Education Coordinating Board
      4. Hold a valid classroom teaching certificate
      5. Have 2 years of creditable teaching experience as classroom teacher
   B. Induction for New Principals
      1. Principals or assistant principals employed for first time as campus administrators (including first time in state) shall participate in an induction period of at least 1 year.

II. Superintendent Certificate (valid 5 years; renewable with 200 CPE hours)
   A. Requirements for certificate
      1. Satisfactorily pass TExES superintendent certification exam
      2. Successfully complete a TEA-approved superintendent preparation program and be recommended for certification by that program
      3. Hold master's degree from an accredited institution of higher education that at the time was accredited or otherwise approved by an accrediting organization recognized by the Texas Higher Education Coordinating Board
      4. Hold a principal certificate or the equivalent issued under this title or by another state or country
   B. Induction for New Superintendents
      1. One-year mentorship for first-time superintendents (including those new to state)
         a. Include at least 36 clock hours of professional development directly related to identified standards
      2. Mentorship program must be completed within the first 18 months of employment as superintendent

Utah

Educator Licenses

I. Letter of Authorization (valid for up to I year; renewable annually, not to exceed 3 years)—Temporary license issued to meet special needs at the request of local school authorities

    A. Educators involved in an alternative route to licensure (ARL) hold a temporary license until they complete the first year of an approved alternative preparation program.

        1. ARL candidates who submit documentation of progress and a successful end-of-year evaluation are moved from "temporary" to "ARL" license status for years 2 and 3 of the prelicensure program.

    B. Local boards may request from the state board a letter of authorization for educators employed by the local board who have not completed requirements for areas of concentration or endorsements.

    C. An authorization is approved for 1 school year and may be renewed for a total of 3 school years.

II. Level 1 Licensure (valid for 3 years; renewal dependent on experience)

    A. Requires one of the following:

        1. Completion of an approved educator preparation program,
          or

        2. Completion of an approved alternative preparation program,
          or

        3. Eligibility under the Compact for Interstate Qualification of Educational Personnel.

            a. A Level 1 license is issued to a graduate of an educator preparation program from an accredited institution of higher education in another state who meets Utah's requirements.

            b. If the applicant has 3 or more continuous years of previous educator experience in a public or accredited private school, a Level 2 license may be issued upon the recommendation of the employing Utah Local Education Agency (LEA) after at least 1 year of teaching in Utah.

    B. All applicants for a Level 1 license or an endorsement in a No Child Left Behind (NCLB) core academic subject area must take and pass a state-approved content examination.

    C. License is valid for 3 years

        a. License holders with 3 years of teaching experience in Utah may not renew the license, but rather must meet the requirements for upgrade to a Level 2 license (See III, A, below)

      b.   A 1-year extension may be requested by the employing district/charter school if the individual has not yet met the requirements for upgrade.

    D.   Renewal for those without 3 years of teaching in Utah requires 100 Professional Development points every 3 years and a fingerprint background check within a year.

III.   Level 2 License (valid 5 years; renewable)

    A.   Prior to upgrade from Level 1 to Level 2, holders of Level 1 Utah Educator Licenses issued after June 30, 2009, must complete all requirements of the Early Years Enhancement (EYE) program, a structured support program providing novice teachers with 3 years of school, district, and state support.

        1.   All new educators are required to participate in EYE, and all requirements must be completed within the first 3 years of service in Utah.

        2.   Requirements for EYE include:

            a.   Hold a Level 1 Utah Educator License,

            b.   Complete a professional portfolio,

            c.   Receive 2 successful professional evaluations per year for 3 years in a Utah public or accredited private school,

            d.   Achieve a score of 160 or better on the Praxis II Principles of Learning and Teaching at the appropriate level of educational preparation,

            e.   Work with a trained mentor for 3 years,

            f.   Complete any additional district/school requirements,

            g.   Receive a district/school recommendation for upgrade to Level 2, *and*

            h.   Achieve NCLB Highly Qualified (HQ) status in at least one licensure area.

        3.   Because this program continues to change and develop, refer to the most recent version of its requirements at http://www.schools.utah.gov/cert

    B.   Renewal requires completion of:

        1.   200 Professional Development points every 5 years, which may include 35 points per year for 3 out of the last 5 years,

        2   Teaching experience, *and*

        3.   A fingerprint background check within a year.

IV.   Level 3 License (valid for 7 years; renewable)

    A.   Requires eligibility to hold a Level 2 License and one of the following in the educator's field of practice:

        1.   Doctoral degree, *or*

        2.   National Board for Professional Teaching Standards (NBPTS) Certificate, *or*

        3.   American Speech-Language-Hearing Association (ASHA) Certificate of Clinical Competence.

    B.   Renewal same as Level 2; see III, B, above; and in addition:

        1.   For NBPTS holders, renewal of that certificate plus 3 years of successful employment, or combination of employment and professional development, is required.

2. For speech-language pathologists, verification of continued membership in ASHA is required.

V. District/Charter School-Specific Competency-Based License (nonrenewable)

A. Only district school board chair or charter school board chair may submit application on behalf of educator, demonstrating that other licensing routes for the applicant are untenable or unreasonable.

B. Request must be made within 60 days after the date of individual's first day of employment:

C. Teachers of one or more core academic subjects shall provide specific documentation of eligibility.

1. Core academic subjects include English, reading or language arts, mathematics, science, foreign languages, civics and government, economics, arts, history, and geography.

2. Specific documentation of eligibility includes possession of a bachelor's degree and either:

a. For Grades K–6 satisfactory results of approved test including subject knowledge and teaching skills in the required core academic subjects, *or*

b. For Grades 7–12 competency in each core academic subject to be taught, as demonstrated by completion of an academic major, a graduate degree, course work equivalent to an undergraduate academic major, advanced certification or credentialing, or results/scores of a rigorous state core academic subject test in each core academic subject in which the teacher teaches.

D. Teacher of non-core subjects shall provide documentation of both:

1. A bachelor's degree, associate degree, or skill certification; and

2. Skills, talents, or abilities specific to teaching assignment.

E. The district/charter school specific competency-based license is only valid in the district/charter school requesting the license.

Concentrations and Endorsements

I. Each educator license must have at least one area of concentration from the following list:
Early childhood K–3, elementary K–6, elementary 1–8, secondary 6–12, administrative/supervisory, school counselor, school psychologist, school social worker, special education K–12, preschool special education (Birth–Age 5), communication disorders/audiology, or speech language pathology

II. Licenses may also bear appropriate endorsements relating to subject or specific assignments (e.g., biology, English as a second language, hearing or visually impaired, mild/moderate disabilities, severe disabilities, Spanish, library media, etc.)

Vermont

I. Eligibility requirements

    A. Graduation from a Vermont-approved educator preparation program with a recommendation for licensure from the institution;
       or

    B. Graduation from an approved teacher preparation program from a state with which Vermont has signed an interstate reciprocity contract. The qualifications of persons certified in a state with which Vermont does not have reciprocity, as well as all educators seeking vocational and support services licensure, will be evaluated on an individual basis;
       or

    C. An out-of-state applicant shall be issued a comparable license and endorsement(s) if he or she:

       1. Is licensed through an alternative route in a state with which Vermont has signed an interstate reciprocity contract,
          and

       2. Has provided satisfactory service under a non-conditional license as an educator in a school in an assignment covered by the endorsement sought on at least a half time basis for not fewer than 27 months during the 7 years immediately preceding the application for a Vermont license,
          and

       3. Meets the contract and ancillary requirements as defined in the contract.

    D. Alternative Routes to Licensure

       1. Peer Review process

          a. An Evaluation Panel (which shall include individuals qualified in the endorsement field sought) is established to review the applicant's qualifications. It evaluates the applicant's portfolio, interviews the applicant, then completes Peer Review evaluation indicating which competencies are met.

          b. Applicants must also achieve passing scores on required Praxis examinations; see testing requirements in II, G, 1–3, below.

       2. Other Approved Alternative Route

          a. An individual who holds at least a baccalaureate degree may be licensed by completing an alternative preparation process approved by the Vermont State Board of Education in consultation with the Vermont Standards Board for Professional Educators (VSBPE).

    E. Transcript Review. The VSBPE shall evaluate on an individual basis by transcript review any applicant for Vermont licensure who holds a valid license in a state not participating in a reciprocity contract or whose category of licensure is not covered by the reciprocity contract.

F.   An applicant for Vermont licensure who is certified by the National Board for Professional Teaching Standards (NBPTS) shall be issued a license in the applicable endorsement area.

II.   General requirements for all licensure candidates

A.   The applicant must hold a baccalaureate degree from a regionally accredited or Vermont-approved institution and must have successfully completed a major, or its equivalent, in the liberal arts and sciences or in the content area of the endorsement sought.

1.   Candidates for a career and technical education endorsement are not subject to this requirement.

2.   Candidates for a school nurse endorsement must have graduated from a nationally accredited 4-year nursing program.

a.   Candidates for an associate school nurse endorsement are not subject to the baccalaureate requirement.

B.   Demonstrated ability to communicate effectively in speaking, writing, and other forms of creative expression, and ability to apply basic mathematical skills, critical thinking skills, and creative thinking skills

C.   Documentation of the specified content knowledge, performance standards, and additional requirements, if any, for the endorsement(s) being sought

D.   Evidence of at least 12 consecutive weeks of student teaching or an equivalent learning experience as determined by VSBPE policy or by the requirements of the endorsement. For specific details on school nurse licensure, consult http://education .vermont.gov/new/html/maincert.html

E.   The educator has knowledge and skills in the content of his or her endorsement(s) at a level that enables students to meet or exceed the standards represented in both the fields of knowledge and the vital results of *Vermont's Framework of Standards and Learning Opportunities.*

F.   The educator fulfills general competencies in teaching; for details, consult http:// education.vermont.gov/new/html/maincert.html

G.   Testing requirements

1.   Praxis I Pre-Professional Skills Text (PPST) for initial licenses, including school psychologist, guidance counselor, school nurse, and all other support services personnel

a.   Meet either 3 individual Praxis I passing scores (reading—177, writing—174, and mathematics—175),

or

Composite score of 526

or

b.   Alternative test measurements. Meet total and minimum scores for either: Graduate Record Exam (GRE)—Total 1100; verbal/English 500; math/quantitative 500,

or

Scholastic Aptitude Test (SAT)—Total 1100; verbal/English 500; math/quantitative 500,

or

American College Test (ACT)—verbal/English 22; math/quantitative 22

2. Praxis II for applicants seeking initial license or additional endorsement in any of the following areas:

    a. Mathematics, social studies, English, science, elementary education, art, music, physical education, modern or classical languages, reading, ESL

    b. For middle grades: English, mathematics, science, or history/social science

3. Exemptions from Praxis testing requirements only if:

    a. Applicant qualifies for licensure under interstate reciprocity,
        and
        Has at least 3 years of employment experience under a non-conditional license within the past 7 years as licensed educator in endorsement area being sought,
        or

    b. Applicant is otherwise qualified for licensure or endorsement,
        and
        Has achieved National Board certification in the applicable endorsement area

Licensure Levels and Types with Renewal Requirements

I. Level I: Professional Educator License (valid 3 years; renewable)

   A. Issued to an applicant who has satisfactorily met all requirements for licensure

      1. See general requirements for all licensure candidates, II, A–G, above.

II. Level II: Professional Educator License (valid 7 years; renewable)

   A. Issued, upon recommendation of a local or regional standards board, to educator who has:

      1. Successfully practiced in endorsement area for 3 years under Level I license,
          and

      2. Submitted approved Individual Professional Development Plan (IPDP) developed through analysis of professional practice and student learning data that articulates the educator's professional development goals for the ensuing licensure period,
          and

      3. Provided verification from a supervising administrator that the educator has demonstrated the competencies required by the endorsement at a professional level.

   B. Applicants for licensure through interstate reciprocity may be eligible for an endorsement on a Level II license upon presentation of satisfactory evidence of 3 successful years of practice in the endorsement area under a nonconditional license.

III. Apprenticeship License. For individuals seeking Career and Technical Education Endorsements (valid 3 years). For full requirements, consult http://education.vermont.gov/new/html/maincert.html

IV. Teaching Intern License (valid 2 years)

   A. Issued with an endorsement to an individual enrolled in an alternate route to licensure program approved by the VSBPE

V. Provisional License or Endorsement (valid 2 years)
   A. A superintendent may apply to the VSBPE for a provisional license or an endorsement when the local district is unable to find an appropriately licensed and/or endorsed applicant after making all reasonable efforts to do so, or when a licensed or endorsed applicant does not possess the qualities necessary for the specific assignment.
   B. The application for a provisional license or endorsement shall include a plan for obtaining a Level I license or endorsement and an explanation of how the applicant will be mentored and supervised during the 2-year period of the provisional license.
   C. Qualifications
      1. Possess a baccalaureate degree and meet at least 1 of the following criteria:
         a. Possess any valid educator license from another state,
            or
            Possess any expired Vermont educator license or any expired license from another state, provided the license expired no longer than 10 years ago,
            or
            Have a major in the content area of the provisional endorsement sought,
            or
            Have successfully completed the licensure content assessment for the provisional endorsement sought.
   D. A provisional license or endorsement shall not be renewed for any individual unless the VSPBE, or its designee, determines that extenuating circumstances existed that prevented the individual from completing the approved plan for Level I licensure.
   E. No provisional school psychologist endorsements will be issued.
VI. Emergency Licenses and Endorsements (valid for school year issued; not renewable)
   A. See V, A, directly above, except for emergency license or endorsement.
   B. Except for applications for emergency school nurse endorsements, emergency licenses and endorsements shall be issued only to individuals who hold a baccalaureate degree or its equivalent but do not meet the qualifications for a provisional license (see V, C, directly above).
   C. The application for an emergency license shall include an explanation of how the applicant will be mentored and supervised.
   D. No emergency endorsements will be issued for school nursing, school psychologist, educational speech-language pathologist, school counseling, school social worker, junior ROTC instructor, or driver's education instructor.
VII. Renewal Requirements
   All educators shall address competency standards in their individualized professional development plans submitted for license renewal.
   A. Level I Renewal
      1. To receive a 3-year renewal, the educator shall show professional growth through completion of a minimum of 3 professional development credits in the endorsement area.

2. Level I endorsement holders who have practiced in Vermont in the endorsement area for 3 years shall seek a recommendation from their local or regional standards board for a Level II endorsement.

    a. An educator who does not receive a recommendation for a Level II endorsement upon initial application shall renew the Level I endorsement for 3 years and reapply for a Level II license prior to the expiration of the renewal.

    b. Level I endorsement of an educator who does not receive a recommendation for a Level II endorsement after the second application shall become lapsed.

    c. Level I license holders employed as educators in Vermont but who have not practiced in a particular endorsement area for 3 years shall seek a recommendation for renewal of that Level I endorsement through their local or regional standards board.

    d. Educators may renew Level 1 endorsements under which they are not currently teaching by completing 3 professional development credits for each renewal. There is no limit to the number of times these endorsements may be renewed.

B. Level II Renewal

1. Level II license holders shall seek a recommendation for renewal of their Level II license and endorsement(s) from their local or regional standards board.

2. The local or regional standards board shall recommend renewal of a Level II endorsement if the applicant presents a professional portfolio that includes:

    a. Current Individual Professional Development Plan (IPDP)

    b. Documentation of professional growth pursuant to the IPDP goals, including documentation of a minimum of 9 relicensing credits, at least 3 of which must address the specific content knowledge and performance standards of each endorsement recommended for renewal

    c. Evidence of any required additional licenses or credentials specific to a particular endorsement

    d. Approved IPDP developed through analysis of professional practice and student learning data that articulates the educator's professional development goals for the ensuing licensure period

    e. A portfolio submitted by an educator for National Board Certification shall be considered as equivalent to a relicensure portfolio for renewing the comparable endorsement.

Endorsements

I. In order to be valid, each professional educator's license shall have 1 or more endorsements.

II. Endorsements limited in time, grade level, or scope may be issued by the VSBPE based on the applicant's background and experience, permitting practice in a specialized area within a broader endorsement field, or restrict assignment to specific grade levels or to a specific period of time.

III. The holder of any license who wishes to qualify for an additional endorsement via transcript review shall present evidence of meeting the content knowledge and performance standards and additional requirements, if any, of the endorsement.

    A. A minimum of 18 credit hours in the endorsement field is required.

IV. Endorsements may be obtained in the following areas:

    A. Administrator Endorsements

        1. Assistant Director for Adult Education

        2. Career and Technical Center Director

        3. Director of Special Education

        4. Principal

        5. Superintendent

        6. Supervisor

    B. Art (Grades PreK–6, 7–12, or PreK–12); Associate School Nurse (Grades PreK–12); Business Education (Grades 5–12); Career & Technical Education School Counseling Coordinator (Grades 9–12); Computer Science (Grades 7–12); Cooperative Career and Technical Education Coordinator (Grades 9–12); Dance (Grades PreK–12); Design and Technology Education (Grades 5–12); Driver & Traffic Safety Education (Grades 9–12); Early Childhood Education (Grades Birth to Grade 3, K–3, Birth to Age 6); Educational Technology Specialist (Grades PreK–12); Elementary Education (Grades K–6); English (Grades 7–12); English as a Second Language (ESL) (Grades PreK–6, 7–12, or PreK–12); Family and Consumer Sciences (Grades 5–12); Health Education (Grades PreK–6, 7–12, or PreK–12); Junior Reserve Officer Training Corps (ROTC) Instructor (Grades 9–12); Library Media Specialist (Grades PreK–12); Mathematics (Grades 7–12); Middle Grades (with 1 or more of the required content areas of Mathematics, English/Language Arts, Science, and Social Studies) (Grades 5–9); Modern and Classical Languages (Grades PreK–6, 7–12, or PreK–12); Music (Grades PreK–6, 7–12 or PreK–12); Physical Education (Grades PreK–6, 7–12, or PreK–12); Reading/English Language Arts Coordinator (for holder of endorsement in either Early Childhood, Elementary Ed, Middle Grades, Secondary Education, or Special Education) (Grades PreK–12); Reading/English Language Arts Specialist (for holder of endorsement in either Early Childhood, Elementary Ed, Middle Grades, Secondary Education, or Special Education) (Grades PreK–12); School Counselor (Grades PreK–12); School Nurse (Grades PreK–12); School Psychologist (Grades PreK–12); School Social Worker (Grades PreK–12); Science (Grades 7–12); Social Studies (Grades 7–12); Theater Arts (Grades PreK–12); Career and Technical Special Needs Coordinator (Grade 8 to Adulthood); Consulting Teacher (Grades K–8, Grades 7–Age 21, or K through Age 21); Early Childhood Special Educator (Birth to Age 6); Intensive Special Education Teacher (Age 3 through Age 21); Special Educator (Grades K–8, Grades 7–Age 21, or K through Age 21); Educational Speech Language Pathologist (Age 3 through Age 21); Teacher of the Blind and Visually Impaired (Age 3 through Age 21); Teacher of the Deaf and Hard of Hearing (Age 3 through Age 21)

Virginia

<u>**General Requirements for Licensure**</u>

I. Applicants for licensure must:
   A. Be at least 18 years of age
   B. Pay appropriate fees and complete application process
   C. Have earned a baccalaureate degree (with the exception of the Technical Professional License) from a regionally accredited institution of higher education (IHE) and meet requirements for the license sought. Persons seeking initial licensure who graduate from Virginia IHEs shall only be licensed as instructional personnel if the Board of Education (Board) approves their IHE's endorsement areas.
   D. Possess good moral character

II. All candidates seeking an initial Virginia teaching license who hold at least a baccalaureate degree from a regionally accredited college or university must obtain passing scores on professional teacher assessments within the 3-year validity of the initial provisional license except:
   A. Candidates for the the Career Switcher Program that requires assessments as prerequisites
   B. Candidates seeking a Technical Professional License, the International License, School Manager License, or the Pupil Personnel Services License
   C. Individuals who hold valid out-of-state licenses (full credential with no deficiencies) and who have completed a minimum of 3 years of full time, successful teaching experience in a public or accredited nonpublic school (K–12) in another state

III. Those seeking an initial endorsement in early/primary education preK–3, elementary education preK–6, special education—general curriculum, special education—hearing impairments, special education—visual impairments, and individuals seeking an endorsement as a reading specialist must obtain passing scores prescribed by the Board on reading instructional assessment.

IV. For all individuals seeking an initial endorsement authorizing them to serve as principals and assistant principals in the public schools, a school leaders assessment prescribed by the Board of Education must be met:
   A. Individuals seeking an initial administration and supervision endorsement who are interested in serving as central office instructional personnel are not required to take and pass the school leaders assessment prescribed by the Board of Education.

V. Individuals seeking initial licensure must:
   A. Demonstrate proficiency in the use of educational technology for instruction
   B. Complete study in child abuse recognition and intervention in accordance with curriculum guidelines developed by the Board of Education in consultation with the Department of Social Services
   C. Receive professional development in instructional methods tailored to promote

student academic progress and effective preparation for the Standards of Learning end-of-course and end-of-grade assessments.

Types of Licenses

I. Provisional License (3-year; nonrenewable). Requirements:
   A. Undergraduate degree from a regionally accredited college or university (with the exception of those individuals seeking the Technical Professional License)
   B. Provisional License can be issued only at the request of an accredited Virginia public or private school.
II. Collegiate Professional License (5-year; renewable). Requirements:
   A. Satisfy all requirements for licensure, including an earned undergraduate degree from a regionally accredited college or university, and submit the professional teacher assessments prescribed by the Board of Education
III. Postgraduate Professional License (5-year; renewable). Requirements:
   A. Qualification for the Collegiate Professional License
   B. An appropriate earned graduate degree from a regionally accredited college or university
IV. Division Superintendent License (5-year; renewable). Requirements:
   A. Master's degree from a regionally accredited college or university
   B. Applicant's name must be listed on the Board of Education's list of eligible division superintendents.
V. Other 5-year licenses include Technical Professional License, School Manager License, Pupil Personnel Services License, International Educator License, and Local Eligibility License. For more information, contact the Virginia Board of Education (see Appendix 1).

Alternate Routes to Licensure

I. Career Switcher alternate route to licensure for career professions:
   A. Available to career switchers who seek teaching endorsements preK through grade 12 with the exception of special education.
   B. An individual seeking a Provisional License through the career switcher program must meet the following prerequisite requirements:
      1. Completed application
      2. Baccalaureate degree from a regionally accredited college or university
      3. Completion of requirements for an endorsement in a teaching area or the equivalent through verifiable experience or academic study
      4. A minimum of 5 years of full-time work experience or its equivalent
      5. Virginia qualifying scores on the professional teacher assessments as prescribed by the Board of Education
   C. The Provisional Career Switcher License is awarded at the end of Level I preparation and is valid for 1 year. The candidate must complete all components of the career switcher alternate route for career professions.
   D. Level I requirements must be completed during the course of a single year and may be offered through a variety of delivery systems, including distance learning

programs. Career Switcher programs must be certified by the Virginia Department of Education.

1. Level I preparation includes:
   a. Minimum of 180 clock hours of instruction, including field experience
2. Level II preparation during first year of employment includes:
   a. Seeking employment in Virginia with the 1-year Provisional Career Switcher License
   b. Continued Level II preparation during the first year of employment with a minimum of 5 seminars that should include a minimum of 20 cumulative instructional hours
   c. One year of successful, full-time teaching experience in a Virginia public or accredited nonpublic school under a 1-year Provisional License, under the direction of a trained mentor
   d. Upon completion of Levels I and II of the Career Switcher alternate route to licensure program and submission of a recommendation from the Virginia educational employing agency, the candidate will be eligible to apply for a 5-year renewable license.
3. Level III preparation, if required, includes:
   a. Postpreparation, if required, to be conducted by the Virginia employing educational agency to address the areas where improvement is needed as identified in the candidate's professional improvement plan
   b. Upon completion of Levels I, II, and III of the Career Switcher alternate route to licensure program and submission of a recommendation from the Virginia educational employing agency, the candidate will be eligible to receive a 5-year renewable license.
E. Verification of program completion will be documented by the certified program provider and the division superintendent or designee.

II. Other Alternate Routes to Licensure are available for individuals employed by an educational agency, at institutions of higher education or Virginia school divisions, and in the areas of special education and experiential learning. For more information, contact the Virginia Board of Education (see Appendix 1).

Endorsements for Early/Primary Education, Elementary Education, and Middle Education

Note: These endorsement requirements apply to individuals seeking licensure outside of state-approved programs and through the Alternative Route to Licensure. IHEs with approved programs in Virginia are not subject to specific semester-hour requirements since they incorporate state competencies into their programs.

I. General endorsement requirements:
   A. Completion of an approved program, including:
      1. A degree from a regionally accredited college or university in the liberal arts and sciences (or equivalent)

2. Professional teacher assessments requirement prescribed by the Board of Education
3. Specific endorsement requirements
4. Professional studies requirements,

or

B. If employed by a Virginia public or nonpublic school, completion of the Alternate Route to Licensure.

II. Professional studies requirements: 18 semester hours
A. Human growth and development (birth through adolescence): 3 semester hours
B. Curriculum and instructional procedures: 3 semester hours
    1. Early/primary education preK–3 or elementary education preK–6 curriculum and instructional procedures: 3 semester hours
    2. Middle education 6–8 curriculum instructional procedures: 3 semester hours
    3. Secondary education curriculum instructional procedures: 3 semester hours
C. Classroom and behavior management: 3 semester hours
D. Foundations of education: 3 semester hours
E. Reading:
    1. Early/primary preK–3 and elementary education preK–6 language acquisition and reading: 6 semester hours
    2. Middle education—language acquisition and reading in the content areas: 6 semester hours
    3. Special education—language acquisition and reading: 6 semester hours
    4. Secondary education—reading in the content area: 3 semester hours
F. Supervised classroom experience:
    1. Full-time classroom experience for a minimum of 300 clock hours (including pre- and postclinical experiences) with at least 150 clock hours spent supervised in direct teaching activities
    2. One year of successful full-time teaching experience in the endorsement area in a public or accredited nonpublic school may be accepted in lieu of the supervised teaching experience.

III. Early/primary education preK–3 endorsement requirements:
A. Graduation from an approved teacher preparation program in early/primary education preK–3,

or

B. A degree from a regionally accredited college or university in the liberal arts and sciences (or equivalent) and completed course work that covers the early/primary education preK–3 competencies and fulfills the following 48 semester-hour requirements: English (12 semester hours), mathematics (9 semester hours), science (9 semester hours in at least 2 science disciplines), history (6 semester hours), social science (6 semester hours), arts and humanities (6 semester hours).

IV. Elementary education preK–6 endorsement requirements:
A. Graduation from an approved teacher preparation program in elementary education preK–6,

or

B. The candidate for the elementary education preK–6 endorsement must have a bachelor's degree or higher from a regionally accredited college or university majoring in the liberal arts and sciences (or equivalent) and fulfill the following 57 semester-hour requirements: English (12 semester hours), mathematics (12 semester hours), science (12 semester hours in at least 2 science disciplines), history (9 semester hours), social science (6 semester hours), arts and humanities (6 semester hours).

V. Middle education 6–8 endorsement requirements:

A. Graduation from an approved teacher preparation discipline-specific program in middle education 6–8 with at least 1 area of academic preparation from the areas of English, mathematics, science, and history and social sciences,
or

B. A degree from a regionally accredited college or university in the liberal arts and sciences (or equivalent); and completed a minimum of 21 semester hours in at least 1 area of academic preparation (concentration) that will be listed on the license; and completed minimum requirements for those areas in which the individual is not seeking an area of academic preparation. Areas: English (21 semester hours), mathematics (21 semester hours), science (21 semester hours), history and social sciences (21 semester hours).

Endorsements for PreK–12 and Secondary Grades 6–12, Special Education, and Adult Education

Note: These endorsement requirements apply to individuals seeking licensure outside of state-approved programs and through the Alternative Route to Licensure. IHEs with approved programs in Virginia are not subject to specific semester-hour requirements since they incorporate state competencies into their programs.

I. Individuals seeking licensure with preK–12 endorsements, special education, secondary grades 6–12 endorsements, and adult education may meet requirements through the completion of an approved program or, if employed by a Virginia public or nonpublic school, through the Alternative Route to Licensure. Components of the licensure program include a degree in the liberal arts and sciences (or equivalent), professional teacher assessment requirements prescribed by the Board of Education, specific endorsement requirements, and professional studies requirements. For further details on course distributions in each subject field, as well as for additional teaching endorsement areas, contact the Virginia Department of Education (see Appendix 1).

A. Art, semester hours 36
B. Biology, semester hours 32
C. Chemistry, semester hours 32
D. Earth science, semester hours 32
E. English, semester hours 36
F. English as a second language, semester hours 24
G. Foreign language (6–12), semester hours 30
H. Health and physical education (PreK–12), semester hours 45

I.   History and social science, semester hours 51
J.   Library media (preK–12), semester hours 24
K.   Mathematics, semester hours 36
L.   Music (choral/instrumental), semester hours 42
M.   Physics, semester hours 32

II.   Professional studies requirements: 15 semester hours
    A.   See Endorsements for Early/Primary Education, II, A–F, above, with an emphasis on preK–12, Secondary Grades 6–12, Special Education, and Adult Education

Support Personnel Licensure Requirements

I.   Administration and Supervision, preK–12
    A.   Level I endorsement
        1.   Master's degree from a regionally accredited college or university
        2.   Three years of successful, full-time experience in a public school or accredited nonpublic school in an instructional personnel position that requires licensure in Virginia
        3.   Completed an approved program in administration and supervision from a regionally accredited college or university
        4.   Completed a minimum of 320 clock hours of a supervised internship that provided exposure to multiple sites (elementary, middle, high, central office, agency) with diverse student populations
        5.   Satisfied the requirements for the school leaders licensure assessment prescribed by the Board of Education
        6.   Recommendation from a Virginia school division superintendent
    B.   Out-of-state administration and supervision endorsement
        1.   Master's degree from a regionally accredited college or university
        2.   Current, valid out-of-state license (full credential) with an endorsement in administration and supervision
    C.   Level II endorsement
        1.   Successful service as a building-level administrator for at least 5 years in a public school or accredited nonpublic school
        2.   Successful completion of a formal induction program as a principal or assistant principal
        3.   Recommendation from a Virginia school division superintendent
        4.   Two or more of the following Board of Education criteria: improved student achievement; effective instructional leadership; positive effect on school climate or culture; earned doctorate in educational leadership or evidence of formal professional development in the areas of school law, school finance, supervision, human resource management, and instructional leadership; completion of a high-quality professional development project designed by the division superintendent

II.   Division Superintendent
    A.   Option 1
        1.   An earned doctorate degree in educational administration or educational leadership from a regionally accredited college or university

      2.   Five years of educational experience in a public or accredited nonpublic school, of which 2 must be teaching experience at the preK–12 level and 2 must be in administration/supervision at the preK–12 level,
or

  B. Option 2
      1.   An earned master's degree from a regionally accredited college or university plus 30 completed hours beyond the master's degree
      2.   Completed requirements for administration and supervision preK–12 endorsement that includes demonstration of competency. For more information, contact the Virginia Board of Education (see Appendix 1),
or

  C. Option 3
      1.   An earned master's degree from a regionally accredited college or university
      2.   A current, valid out-of-state license with an endorsement as a division/district superintendent
      3.   Five years of educational experience in a public or accredited nonpublic school, of which 2 must be teaching experience at the preK–12 level and 2 must be in administration/supervision,
or

  D. Option 4
      1.   Master's degree, or its equivalent, from a regionally accredited college or university
      2.   Have held a senior leadership position such as chief executive officer or senior military officer
      3.   Be recommended by a school board interested in employing the individual as superintendent.

III. School Counselor PreK–12. Endorsement requirements:
  A. An earned master's degree from an approved counselor education program, with at least 100 clock hours of clinical experiences in the preK–6 setting and 100 clock hours of clinical experiences in the grades 7–12 setting,
and
Two years of successful full-time teaching experience or 2 years of successful experience in guidance and counseling in a public or accredited nonpublic school. Two years of successful full-time experience in guidance and counseling under a Provisional License may be accepted to meet this requirement.

IV. Additional Support Personnel. Each of the licenses listed below has specific requirements. For details, contact the Virginia Department of Education (see Appendix 1)
  A. Mathematics Specialist for Elementary and Middle Education
  B. Reading Specialist
  C. School Manager
  D. School Psychologist
  E. School Social Worker
  F. Special Education—Speech-Language Pathologist, PreK–12
  G. Vocational Evaluator

Washington

General Certificate Information

I. The teacher certificate authorizes service in the primary role of teacher.

II. The administrator certificate authorizes service in the primary role of building-level administration (principal), program administration (program administrator), and district-wide general administration (superintendent).

III. The educational staff associate (ESA) certificate authorizes service as school psychologist, counselor, social worker, school nurse, physical therapist, occupational therapist, or speech-language pathologist or audiologist.

IV. Levels of Certificates available to first-time applicants:
   A. Teaching Certificates
      1. Residency Teaching Certificate
      2. Professional Teaching Certificate
   B. Administrator Certificates
      1. Residency Administrator Certificate—Principal and Program Administrator
      2. Professional Administrator Certificate—Principal and Program Administrator
      3. Initial Administrator Certificate—Superintendent Only
      4. Continuing Administrator Certificate—Superintendent Only
   C. Educational Staff Associate Certificates
      1. Residency ESA Certificate—School Counselor, Psychologist, Social Worker
      2. Professional ESA Certificate—School Counselor, Psychologist, Social Worker
      3. Initial ESA Certificate—School Nurse, Occupational Therapy, Physical Therapy, School Speech Language Pathologist/Audiologist
      4. Continuing ESA Certificate—School Nurse, Occupational Therapy, Physical Therapy, School Speech Language Pathologist/Audiologist

V. Candidates for all certificates must complete course work in issues of abuse, which must include information related to:
   A. Identification of physical, emotional, sexual, and substance abuse;
   B. The impact on learning and behavior;
   C. The responsibilities of a teacher, administrator, or ESA to report abuse or to provide assistance to victimized children;
      and
   D. Methods of teaching about abuse and its prevention.

Teaching Certificates

I. Residency Teaching Certificate (valid minimum of 7 years). Subject to change September 1, 2011; consult Washington's Professional Certification Office at http://www.k12.wa.us/certification for current status and details.

A. Baccalaureate degree from regionally accredited institution and completion of state-approved teacher education program

B. Completion of 1 endorsement

C. Passed a WEST-B (Washington Educator Skills Test-Basic skills reading, writing, and math) and a WEST-E (Washington Educator Skills Test-Endorsements) content test in each endorsement area

D. Until September, 2011, valid until completion of 2 consecutive years of successful service in the role with the same Washington public or approved-private school and 3-year contract signed. The certificate may then be reissued for the next 5 years. Within this 5-year period, teachers are expected to earn the Washington state–approved second-level teaching certificate, the Professional Teaching Certificate (see II, A–C, directly below).

E. Certificate Endorsements

   1. Endorsements indicate the content area(s) and/or specializations for which the teacher is prepared.
   2. Teachers may obtain endorsements on their Washington certificate in several ways:
      a. Program. By completing a college/university program approved to offer the endorsement. This can be in-state or out-of-state.
      b. National Board for Professional Teaching Standards. By earning National Board certification in a Washington endorsement area
      c. Testing. Through WEST-E testing in an area compatible with an endorsement for which they already qualify and are experienced

II. Professional Teacher Certificate (valid for 5 years; renewed upon completion of 150 clock hours every 5 years)

A. Specific Washington state–approved second-level professional certificate program that all teachers are expected to earn within the 5-year reissuing of the Residency Teaching Certificate (see I, D, directly above),

B. As of September 1, 2011, to earn a professional certificate, you must:

   1. Have 2 years of teaching experience,
      and
   2. Pass the new professional certificate assessment (portfolio of evidence). Teachers can register to take the assessment any time prior to the expiration of their residency certificate, but typically do so during their third or fourth year of teaching in Washington schools.
      a. Registration for the assessment will be available by January 2010. For full details about the new portfolio of evidence requirements, go to www.pesb.wa.gov

C. Existing professional certificates will remain valid until the expiration date stated on the certificate.

   1. Renewal requires 150 clock hours every 5 years.

Administrator Certificates

I. Residency Administrator Certificate—Principal and Program Administrator (valid until completion of 2 consecutive years of successful service in the role in Washington)

   A. Master's degree from regionally accredited institution
   B. Completion of an administrator preparation program in the administrative role, or, if no state-approved program, completion of 3 years of successful experience in another state in the administrative role while holding a regular certificate issued by another state
   C. For Principal: Hold or have held a regular teaching certificate or ESA certificate
   D. For Principal: Verification of successful school-based instructional experience in an educational setting
 II. Professional Administrator Certificate—Principal and Program Administrator
   A. Completion of a ProCert. Program for administration through a Washington college or university
III. Initial Administrator Certificate—Superintendent Only (valid 7 years)
   A. Master's degree from regionally accredited institution
   B. Completion of an administrator preparation program for superintendent or, if no state-approved college/university program, 3 years of successful experience as a superintendent, deputy superintendent, or assistant superintendent while holding a regular certificate issued by another state
   C. Must hold a valid regular teaching certificate, ESA, principal, or program administrator certificate
IV. Continuing Administrator Certificate—Superintendent Only (valid for 5-year periods; renewed upon completion of 150 clock hours professional development)
   A. Completed all requirements for the Initial Superintendent's Certificate
   B. Master's degree, plus 60 quarter hours (40 semester hours) of graduate-level course work in education completed after the baccalaureate degree, or a doctorate in education
   C. Completed 180 days of service as a superintendent, deputy superintendent, or assistant superintendent, 30 days of which must have been in the same school district

Educational Staff Associate Certification

  I. Residency Educational Staff Associate (ESA) Certificate for school counselor, school psychologist, and school social worker (valid minimum of 7 years)
   A. Completion of master's degree with major in the appropriate specialization
   B. Completion of state-approved program for certification in the appropriate ESA role, *or*
      If no program, must have completed 3 years of experience under that certificate, *or*
      For school psychologist only: must hold NCSP Certificate issued after December 31, 1991, by the National School Psychology Certification Board; if the other state didn't require a certificate, must have 3 years of experience in that role.
   C. Completion of a comprehensive written examination required in the master's degree program. If a candidate has been awarded a master's degree without a comprehensive written examination, the candidate, as a condition for certification, must arrange to take such an examination with any accredited college or university and provide the superintendent of public instruction with an affidavit from the chair of the department of the academic field that he or she has successfully completed this comprehensive examination.

1. School Counselor
    a. Successful completion of a proctored, written comprehensive examination of the knowledge included in the course work for the required master's degree, given by a regionally accredited institution of higher education, *or*
    b. The candidate may meet this requirement by receiving a passing score on the Praxis II guidance and counseling examination administered by Educational Testing Service (ETS).
2. School Psychologist
    a. Successful completion of a proctored, written comprehensive examination of the knowledge included in the course work for the required master's degree, given by a regionally accredited institution of higher education, *or*
    b. The candidate may meet this requirement by receiving a passing score on the Praxis II school psychology examination administered by ETS.
3. School Social Worker
    a. Successful completion of a proctored, written comprehensive examination of the knowledge included in the course work for the required master's degree, given by a regionally accredited institution of higher education, *or*
    b. The candidate may meet this requirement by receiving a passing score on the Praxis II school social work examination administered by ETS.

II. Professional ESA Certificate for school counselor, school psychologist, and school social worker (valid minimum of 5 years). Requirements:
  A. Hold a certificate from the National Board for Professional Teaching Standards (NBPTS) if a school counselor;
      or
      Successfully complete an approved professional ESA certificate program, including course on the issue of abuse; see III, A, 5, immediately below for full description of required course content.
  B. Professional ESA school counselor certificate issued on the basis of holding a valid NBPTS school counselor certificate will have a validity of 5 years or the validity of the NBPTS certificate, whichever is greater.

III. Continuing Educational Staff Associate (ESA)
  A. For school counselor, school psychologist, and school social worker (candidates must hold a valid initial certificate at time of application). Requirements:
    1. Candidate must have completed 180 days of experience in the role (or the equivalent of 180 days of full-time service), of which 30 days must be in the same district.
    2. Candidate must have completed role-specific academic requirements. (It is not, however, necessary for a candidate holding a master's degree or doctorate in another field to obtain the specified master's degree if he or she has completed all course work requirements relevant to the required master's degree.)
      a. School counselor: hold a master's degree with a major in counseling

        b.   School psychologist: Hold a master's degree with a major or specialization in school psychology

        c.   School social worker: hold a master's degree in social work.

    3.   Candidate must have completed a college-level course that includes peer review at a college/university in Washington while employed in the role.

    4.   Candidate must have completed a written comprehensive exam relevant to the field of specialization.

    5.   Candidate must have taken course work in issues of abuse, which must include information related to identification of physical, emotional, sexual, and substance abuse; the impact on learning and behavior; the responsibilities of an ESA to report abuse or to provide assistance to victimized children; and methods of teaching about abuse and its prevention.

  B.   For school nurse, school occupational therapist, school physical therapist, and school speech language pathologist or audiologist

    1.   Continuing ESA is the advanced level regular certificate available for these positions. For full details, go to www.k12.wa.us/certification/ESA

IV.   Initial Educational Staff Associate (ESA) for school counselor, school psychologist, school social worker, school nurse, school occupational therapist, school physical therapist, and school speech language pathologist or audiologist

  A.   Initial ESA is the first-level regular certificate for these positions. For full details, go to www.k12.wa.us/certification/ESA

West Virginia

General Information and Requirements

I. West Virginia licenses include:
   A. Professional Certificate
   B. Alternative Teaching Certificate
   C. Temporary Certificate
   D. Career/Technical Education Certificate
   E. Temporary Career/Technical Education Certificate
   F. Permit
   G. Adult License
   H. Authorization
   I. Paraprofessional Certificate (granted to service personnel)
II. Valid grade levels
   A. Preschool Education (Birth–PreK)
   B. Early Education (PreK–K)
   C. Early Childhood (K–4)
   D. Middle Childhood (5–9)
   E. Adolescent (9–12)
   F. Adult

Licenses for Professional Educators

I. General requirements for all applicants for certificates detailed in this section:
   A. Applicant must be a U.S. citizen, unless otherwise noted; of good moral character; physically, mentally, and emotionally qualified to perform the duties of a teacher; and 18 years old.
   B. FBI background check for initial certificates
   C. State background check for initial certificates
II. Temporary Teaching Certificate (valid 1 year) requirements:
   A. Bachelor's degree or master's degree from an accredited institution of higher education (IHE) or an equivalent degree from an IHE in a foreign country
   B. Out-of-State applicants must submit proof of:
      1. Successful completion of an out-of-state approved teacher education program from an accredited IHE.
      or
   B. Foreign academic credentials,
      or
   C. Valid Out-of-State Certificate.
III. Initial Professional Certificate (valid 3 years) requirements:
   A. Minimum proficiency levels in state board–approved tests

1. Basic skills: Praxis I—Pre-Professional Skills in Reading, Writing, and Mathematics
2. Content specialization(s): appropriate Praxis II test(s)
3. Professional knowledge: Praxis II that includes at least a portion of the grade levels indicated on license sought

   and either

B. Successful completion of a regionally accredited IHE's state-approved program and the recommendation of the designated official at the college or university through which the program was completed,

   or

C. A valid out-of-state professional certificate

   or

D. Successful completion of a state-approved alternative delivery program that incorporates the preprofessional skills, content, and professional education standards approved by the state board.

E. Requirements for renewal of any Professional Teaching Certificate issued prior to January 1, 2008:
   1. Six semester hours of appropriate college/university course work, with a minimum 3.0 GPA, related to the public school program,
      a. Three of the 6 semester hours must meet 1 of the following criteria:
         i. Courses relevant to a master's degree in a curriculum related to the public school program,

            or
         ii. Courses related to improvement of instruction and the applicant's current endorsement area,

            or
         iii. Courses needed to qualify for an additional endorsement,

            or
         iv. Credit prescribed by the county as a result of an applicant's evaluation,

            or

            Master's degree plus 30 Salary Classification,

            or

            Has reached 60 years of age and presents a photocopy of the birth certificate
   2. Recommendation of the employing county's superintendent.

F. Requirements for renewal of any Professional Teaching Certificate issued after January 1, 2008:
   1. Recommendation of the employing county's superintendent

      and
   2. See requirements listed in III, E, 1 and 2, directly above
   3. In addition, 3 of the 6 semester hours must be a course related to the improvement of instruction through the use of instructional technologies

IV. Professional Five-Year Teaching Certificate (valid 5 years; nonrenewable) requirements:

A. Successful completion of the Beginning Educator Internship for classroom, unless the applicant holds a valid out-of-state certificate and has 5 years of teaching experience in another state

B.   Six semester hours of appropriate college/university course work reflecting a 3.0 GPA and related to the public school program, unless the applicant holds a minimum of a master's degree plus 30 Salary Classification based on the awarding of a master's degree

C.   Two years of experience, 1 of which must be completed in West Virginia, within 1 endorsement or a combination of the endorsements, on the Initial Professional Teaching Certificate

D.   Recommendation of superintendent in the county in which the educator teaches or last taught

V.   Permanent Professional Teaching Certificate (valid unless surrendered, suspended or revoked) requirements:

A.   Hold or be eligible for the Professional Teaching Certificate (valid 5 years);
and

Master's degree related to the public school;
and

Five years of educational experience, including 2 within the specialization(s) for which the permanent certificate is requested.
or

B.   Hold a valid Professional Five-Year Teaching Certificate,
and

Two Renewals of the Professional Five-Year Teaching Certificate based on:

1.   Six semester hours of appropriate renewal credit reflecting a 3.0 GPA,

2.   Minimum of a master's degree plus 30 Salary Classification based on the awarding of a master's degree,
or

3.   Age 60,
or

Hold certification through the National Board for Professional Teaching Standards (NBPTS),
or

Valid out-of-state certificate,
and

C.   Recommendation of superintendent in the county in which the educator teaches or last taught.

VI. Individuals who hold a valid out-of-state teaching certificate, have completed a state-approved educator preparation program, and hold a bachelor's degree from a regionally accredited IHE should visit http://wvde.state.wv.us/certification for specific information.

Specializations

I.   Recognized Programmatic Level

A.   Preschool Education (Birth–PreK), Early Education (PreK–K), Early Childhood (K–4), Middle Childhood (5–9), Adolescent (9–12), Adult (Adult)

II. Grade-Level Options for General Education Specializations Current Programs:

A.   Agriculture (5–Adult); American Sign Language (PreK–Adult), any Modern Foreign Language (PreK–Adult, 5–Adult); Art (PreK–Adult, 5–Adult, 5–9); Biology (9–Adult); Business Education (5–Adult, 9–Adult); Chemistry (9–Adult); Chemistry/Physics (9–Adult); Chinese (PreK–Adult, 9–Adult); Computer Science Education (PreK–Adult); Dance (PreK–Adult, 5–Adult); Driver Education (9–Adult); Early Childhood Education (K–4); Early Education (PreK–K); Elementary Education (K–6); English (5–Adult, 5–9); English as a Second Language (PreK–Adult); Family & Consumer Science (5–Adult); French (PreK–Adult, 5–Adult); General Math through Algebra I (5–Adult, 5–9); General Science (5–Adult, 5–9); German (PreK–Adult, 5–Adult); Health (PreK–Adult, 5–Adult); Instructional Technology (PreK–Adult); Japanese (PreK–Adult, 5–Adult); Journalism (5–Adult, 9–Adult); Latin (PreK–Adult, 5–Adult); Marketing (9–Adult); Mathematics (5–Adult, 5–9); Middle Childhood Education (MCE) (5–9); Music (PreK–Adult); Oral Communications (5–Adult, 9–Adult); Physical Education (PreK–Adult, 5–Adult, 5–9); Physics (9–Adult); Preschool Education (Birth–PreK); Reading (PreK–Adult); Reading Specialist* (PreK–Adult); Russian (PreK–Adult, 5–Adult); School Library/Media (PreK–Adult); Social Studies (5–Adult, 5–9); Spanish (PreK–Adult, 5–Adult); Technology Education (5–Adult); Theater (PreK–Adult); Wellness (Health–Physical Education) (PreK–Adult)

III.   Grade-Level Options for Special Education Specializations:
Autism (K–6, 5–Adult); Emotional/Behavior Disorders (K–6, 5–Adult); Gifted (1—12); Deaf and Hard of Hearing (PreK–Adult); Mentally Impaired Mild/Moderate (K–6, 5–Adult); Multi–Categorical (E/BD, MI, SLD) (K–6, 5–Adult); Preschool Special Needs (PreK–K); Severe Disabilities (PreK–Adult); Specific Learning Disabilities (K–6, 5–Adult); Visually Impaired (PreK–Adult)

IV.   Grade-Level Options for Student Support Specializations (all are PreK–Adult):
Athletic Trainer, Counselor,* School Nurse, School Psychologist,* Social Services and Attendance, Speech Language Pathologist,* Speech Assistant

V.   Grade-Level Options for Administrative Specializations (all are PreK–Adult):
General Supervisor,* Principal,* Superintendent*

*   Master's degree required

Administrative Certificates

I.   Initial Professional Administrative Certificate (valid for 5 years)

A.   The Initial Professional Administrative Certificate shall be endorsed for Superintendent, Principal, and/or Supervisor of Instruction and shall indicate the specialization(s) and grade levels in which the holder can be legally assigned within the public schools.

B.   General Requirements:

1.   Successful completion of an IHE's state approved program and the recommendation of the designated official at the college or university through which the program was completed,
or

2.   Applicants holding a valid out-of-state Administrative Certificate need only present the official transcripts evidencing graduation from a state-approved

teacher education program at a regionally accredited college or university and a copy of his/her valid out-of-state Administrative Certificate.

    C. See Licenses for Professional Educators, III, E, 1 and 2, above

    D. See Licenses for Professional Educators, III, F, 1–3, above

II. Permanent Professional Administrative Certificate (remains valid unless surrendered, suspended or revoked for just cause)

    A. Requirements for converting the Initial Professional Administrative Certificate to the Permanent Professional Administrative Certificate:

        1. Six semester hours of appropriate renewal credit related to the public school program,

or

Master's degree plus 30 Salary Classification,

and

        2. Five years of educational experience,

and

        3. Recommendation of the employing county's superintendent.

III. Temporary Administrative Certificate

    A. Endorsed for Superintendent, Principal, and/or Supervisor of Instruction and shall indicate the specialization(s) and grade levels in which the holder may be assigned within the public schools

    B. Issued to administrators who graduate from an out-of-state IHE or who are transferring credential from another state or country to complete the requirements for testing, if applicable, and to complete the Evaluation Leadership Institute.

Student Support Certificates

  I. School Counselor

    A. Temporary Professional Student Support Certificate

        1. Issued to applicant who meets requirements for a Temporary Teaching Certificate

    B. Initial Professional Student Support Certificate (valid 3 years)

        1. Issued to applicant who meets the following criteria:

            a. Master's degree in Counseling from an accredited IHE

            b. Successful completion of an accredited School Counseling Program

    C. Professional Student Support Certificate (valid 5 years).

        1. Issued to applicant who meets the requirements for a Professional Five-Year Teaching Certificate

    D. Permanent Professional Student Support Certificate

        1. Issued to an applicant who meets the requirements for a Permanent Professional Teaching Certificate

  II. School Psychologist

    A. Temporary Professional Student Support Certificate

        1. Issued to applicant who meets requirements for a Temporary Teaching Certificate

    B.   Initial Professional Student Support Certificate
       1.   Issued to applicant who completes master's degree in a field related to education from an accredited institution of higher education
    C.   See I, C and D, directly above
III.   Speech-Language Pathologist
    A.   Temporary Student Support Certificate
       1.   Issued to applicant who meets requirements for a Temporary Teaching Certificate
    B.   Initial Professional Student Support Certificate
       1.   Issued to applicant who earns a master's degree in an approved program in Speech-Language Pathology from an accredited institution of higher learning
    C.   See I, C and D, directly above
IV.   Renewal of the Professional Student Support Certificate
    A.   Application for renewal of the Professional Student Support Certificate for School Counselor, School Psychologist, and Speech-Language Pathologist must be submitted after January 1 of the year in which the license expires.
    B.   The applicant for licensure must submit evidence of satisfying the following:
       1.   Completed 6 semester hours of appropriate college/university course work related to the public school program with a minimum 3.0 GPA
       2.   See Licenses For Professional Educators, V, B and C, above, except that requirements must be met in the 5-year period immediately preceding the date of application
  V.   Professional Five-Year Student Support Certificate
    A.   Six semester hours of appropriate college/university course work reflecting a 3.0 GPA and related to the public school program,
       or
       Minimum of a master's plus 30 Salary Classification,
       and
    B.   Two years of experience within 1 endorsement or a combination of endorsements, on the Initial Professional Student Support Certificate,
       and
    C.   Recommendation of superintendent.
VI.   Permanent Professional Student Support Certificate
    A.   Professional Five-Year Student Support Certificate,
       and
    B.   Master's degree related to the public school program,
       and
    C.   Five years of educational experience,
       or
       Professional Five-Year Student Support Certificate,
       and
    D.   Six semester hours of appropriate renewal credit reflecting a 3.0 GPA,
       or
       Minimum of a master's degree plus 30 Salary Classification,
       or

Has reached 60 years of age,
or

E.   NBPTS certification,
and

F.   Recommendation of superintendent.

Wisconsin

Educator Standards

I. Teacher Standards: To receive a license to teach in Wisconsin, an applicant shall complete an approved program and demonstrate proficient performance in the knowledge, skills, and dispositions under all of the following standards:

   A. The teacher understands the central concepts, tools of inquiry, and structures of the disciplines he or she teaches and can create learning experiences that make these aspects of subject matter meaningful for pupils.

   B. The teacher understands how children with broad ranges of ability learn and provides instruction that supports their intellectual, social, and personal development.

   C. The teacher understands how pupils differ in their approaches to learning and the barriers that impede learning and can adapt instruction to meet the diverse needs of pupils, including those with disabilities and exceptionalities.

   D. The teacher understands and uses a variety of instructional strategies, including the use of technology, to encourage children's development of critical thinking, problem solving, and performance skills.

   E. The teacher uses an understanding of individual and group motivation and behavior to create a learning environment that encourages positive social interaction, active engagement in learning, and self-motivation.

   F. The teacher uses effective verbal and nonverbal communication techniques as well as instructional media and technology to foster active inquiry, collaboration, and supportive interaction in the classroom.

   G. The teacher organizes and plans systematic instruction based upon knowledge of subject matter, pupils, the community, and curriculum goals.

   H. The teacher understands and uses formal and informal assessment strategies to evaluate and ensure the continuous intellectual, social, and physical development of the pupil.

   I. The teacher is a reflective practitioner who continually evaluates the effect of his or her choices and actions on pupils, parents, professionals in the learning community, and others, and who actively seeks out opportunities to grow professionally.

   J. The teacher fosters relationships with school colleagues, parents, and agencies in the larger community to support pupil learning and well-being and acts with integrity, fairness, and in an ethical manner.

II. Administrator standards: To receive a license in a school administrator category, an applicant shall complete an approved program in school administration and demonstrate proficient performance in the knowledge, skills, and dispositions under all of the following standards:

   A. The administrator has an understanding of and demonstrates competence in the teacher standards.

   B. The administrator leads by facilitating the development, articulation, implementation, and stewardship of a vision of learning that is shared by the school community.

C. The administrator manages by advocating, nurturing, and sustaining a school culture and instructional program conducive to pupil learning and staff professional growth.

D. The administrator ensures management of the organization, operations, finances, and resources for a safe, efficient, and effective learning environment.

E. The administrator models collaborating with families and community members, responding to diverse community interests and needs, and mobilizing community resources.

F. The administrator acts with integrity, fairness, and in an ethical manner.

G. The administrator understands, responds to, and interacts with the larger political, social, economic, legal, and cultural context that affects schooling.

III. Pupil Services Standards: To receive a license in a pupil services category (school counselors, school social workers, school psychologists, and school nurses), an applicant shall complete an approved program and demonstrate proficient performance in the knowledge, skills, and dispositions under all of the following standards:

A. The pupil services professional understands the 10 Teacher Standards (see I, directly above).

B. The pupil services professional understands the complexities of learning and has knowledge of comprehensive, coordinated practice strategies that support pupil learning, health, safety, and development.

C. The pupil services professional has the ability to use research, research methods, and knowledge about issues and trends to improve practice in schools and classrooms.

D. The pupil services professional understands and represents professional ethics and social behaviors appropriate for school and community.

E. The pupil services professional understands the organization, development, management, and content of collaborative and mutually supportive pupil services programs within educational settings.

F. The pupil services professional is able to address comprehensively the wide range of social, emotional, behavioral, and physical issues and circumstances which may limit pupils' abilities to achieve positive learning outcomes through development, implementation, and evaluation of system-wide interventions and strategies.

G. The pupil services professional interacts successfully with pupils, parents, professional educators, employers, and community support systems such as juvenile justice, public health, human services, and adult education.

License Stages

I. Initial Educator License (valid 5 years; nonrenewable)
   A. Prerequisites
      1. Bachelor's degree and completion of state-approved educator preparation program at a regionally accredited institution
         a. Officer of the institution's state-approved educator preparation program must certify applicant
         b. Additional requirements/experience may be required for specific license areas.

2. Graduates of professional educator programs in a state or U.S. territory other than Wisconsin who have never held a Wisconsin educator license must submit an "out-of-state" application even if they currently reside in Wisconsin.

3. See "Testing Requirements," below, for full details

B. Professional Development Plan (PDP) addressing 2 or more standards required for advancement

    1. Pre-service portfolio may be used to inform Initial Educator PDP development

    2. PDP goal is approved by a majority of 3-member Initial Educator PDP team, including an administrator, an institution of higher education (IHE) representative, and a peer (not a mentor). The PDP team also verifies completion of the PDP.

    3. Support to educator is provided by mentor, and feedback is provided from initial educator team.

    4. School district must provide:

        a. Collaboratively developed ongoing orientation to Initial Educator

        b. Support seminars reflecting the standards and district goals

        c. A trained mentor holding an appropriate license. The mentor is an educator and colleague trained to provide support, assistance, and feedback to initial educators and is not part of the formal employment evaluation process.

II. Professional Educator License (valid 5 years; renewable)

A. Educators licensed before June 2004 have been grandparented as Professional Educators

    1. Grandparenting choice for license renewal: 6 credits or PDP

B. Professional Development Plan shows proficiency in Wisconsin standards; used for license renewal by post-8/31/04 program completers.

    1. Professional Development Team verifies PDP completion to the Wisconsin Department of Public Instruction (DPI).

        a. PDP Review Team is composed of at least 3 licensed teachers, pupil service professionals, and/or administrators selected by their peers.

        b. Convened at the discretion of the educator

    2. Required components of PDP

        a. Reflection

        b. Describe school and assignment

        c. Rationale for and goals addressing standards

        d. Plan to assess achievement of goals

        e. Plan to meet the goals, including objectives, activities, timelines, and collaboration

    3. Required evidence of successful completion of PDP

        a. Annual review of PDP by educator

        b. Summary and reflection statement

        c. Demonstrated increase in proficiency in standards

        d. Growth indicators

        e. How professional knowledge was improved by meeting goals

        f. How student learning was improved by meeting goals

III. Master Educator License Optional (valid 10 years; renewable): Optional
   A. Mastery of Wisconsin standards in high-stakes portfolio assessment through the Wisconsin Master Educator Assessment Process (WMEAP) requiring:
      1. Related master's degree
      2. Demonstrated improvement in pupil learning
      3. Assessment by DPI-trained WMEAP Team
      4. Professional contributions
      or
   B. National Board of Professional Teaching Standards Certification
IV. Administrative License (valid 5 years)
   A. Required of superintendents, directors of instruction, principals, directors of special education and pupil services, instructional library media supervisors, local vocational education coordinators, school business managers, and instructional technology coordinators.
   B. Prerequisites
      1. Completion of approved graduate education program leading to licensure in specific administrative category
      2. Except for school business manager license, all applicants must hold, or be eligible to hold, a Wisconsin:
         a. Professional educator teaching license and have 3 years of successful teaching experience,
            or
         b. Professional educator license in a pupil services category (school counselor, psychologist, or social worker), have 3 years successful experience in that category, and 540 hours of classroom instruction experience.
      3. Satisfactory background check is required of all applicants.

Testing Requirements

I. Praxis I: Pre-Professional Skills Tests (PPST)
   A. Required for admission to all professional education programs and usually taken during first or second year of undergraduate work
   B. Teachers applying for licenses in Wisconsin who complete professional education programs after August 31, 1992, at colleges and universities located in other states must submit passing scores on this or equivalent basic skills tests.
   C. Qualifying scores for PPST or Computerized PPST tests are: reading—175; writing—174; and mathematics—173.
II. Praxis II: Subject Assessments
   A. All students who complete professional education programs after August 31, 2004, must take the Praxis II subject assessment specified for their license area(s).
      1. All state-approved professional education programs in Wisconsin require student assessments of content knowledge that are determined by passing scores on the Praxis II.

2. This requirement may not be waived for any reason, including but not limited to these:

    a. Educators licensed prior to September 2004 returning to complete a license program in a new subject,

    b. Educators licensed prior to September 2004 returning to complete programs to add on age levels that were not covered by their previous licenses,

    c. All educators who complete initial licensing programs after August 31, 2004, and all subsequent programs (requiring a Praxis II test) that they complete,

    and

    d. Students completing licensing programs at the undergraduate and graduate levels.

3. Educators who complete state-approved professional education programs after August 31, 2004, in other states must document passing grades on the specific Praxis II test(s) required to obtain an Initial or Professional Educator License in their area.

    a. A 1-year, nonrenewable license may be issued to out-of-state applicants who need to take and pass the appropriate Praxis II test(s).

B. Contact the team at the Wisconsin Department of Public Instruction (see Appendix 1) or http://dpi.wi.gov/tepdl/testing.html for qualifying scores for specific licenses.

Wyoming

General Licensure Information

I. All teachers and administrators employed in a Wyoming school district must be licensed in accordance with state law. The Wyoming Professional Teaching Standards Board (PTSB) requires all Wyoming educators to have completed an approved teacher preparation program from an accredited institution of higher education (IHE) in order to become licensed to teach in a Wyoming school district.

II. There are 2 routes to teacher licensure in Wyoming.

    A. Traditional Route to Teacher Licensure requires the completion of a teacher preparation program from a regionally or nationally accredited IHE.

    B. Alternative Route to Teacher Licensure offers an alternative program for secondary licensure through the Northern Plains Transition to Teaching (NPTT) program located at Montana State University-Bozeman. The NPTT allows applicants to obtain work in a Wyoming school district while completing the teacher preparation course work necessary to become fully licensed.

Requirements for Initial Licensure

I. To obtain initial, first-time licensure, applicants must meet all the following requirements:

    A. Complete an approved teacher preparation program at a regionally or nationally accredited college or university. The program must:

        1. Include student teaching

        2. Lead to an institutional recommendation for licensure

    B. Submit an institutional recommendation for licensure, signed by an authorized official, recommending the applicant for licensure in the applicable endorsement area(s)

    C. Submit official college transcripts documenting completion of teacher preparation program

    D. Undergo fingerprinting and complete a background check

    E. Demonstrate knowledge of the U.S. and Wyoming constitutions either through course work or by successfully passing an exam

    F. Pass approved Praxis II exams in 2 teaching areas:

        1. Elementary Education—A passing score of 160 or better on Praxis II exam 0011 "Elementary Education: Curriculum, Instruction, and Assessment"

        2. Social Studies Composite—A passing score of 158 or better on Praxis II exam 0081 "Social Studies: Content Knowledge"

    G. Submit a complete application packet and pay appropriate fees

II. To obtain licensure through the NPTT program:

A. Applicant must currently hold a bachelor's degree in a secondary teaching area, *and*

Be employed by a Wyoming school district.

B. If the district is unable to find a fully licensed and qualified teacher, it has the option of offering the position to someone who has a bachelor's degree in that teaching area—on the condition that the applicant enrolls in the NPTT program.

III. Troops to Teachers

A. Wyoming also participates in the Troops-to-Teachers (TTT) program through the regional office located in Montana. Visit the TTT site (http://www.montana.edu/ttt) for more information.

IV. Out-of-State Applicants

A. All out-of-state applicants are required to submit the documentation listed below in addition to their complete application packet, fingerprint cards, institutional recommendation (if applicable), and U.S. and Wyoming constitution requirements.

1. Verification of work history for the past 6 years, signed by the applicant's present or most recent school administrator or board chair

2. Copy of the applicant's current, valid teaching certificate or license from the state in which he or she taught

3. Copy of the applicant's test scores from Praxis II exam(s) or an equivalent exam from his or her state

4. In accordance with the NASDTEC Interstate Agreement, PTSB may require an out-of-state applicant to complete additional requirements to obtain a Wyoming teaching license.

Endorsements by Grade/Age Level

Endorsement(s) for which an applicant qualifies will appear on the Initial License. As determined by program approval standards, the endorsement(s) will allow teachers to provide instruction in the classroom or the school personnel to provide services in the areas identified on the certificate. Teaching endorsements are valid at the level for which they are issued.

I. Birth to 5: Early Childhood/Special Education

II. Birth to Age 8 (or Grade 3): Early Childhood

III. Age 3–5: Preschool Early Childhood (excluding Kindergarten)

IV. Elementary Level K–6: art; elementary teacher; English as a second language; music; music instrumental; music vocal; reading; physical education; adaptive physical education; principal; director; school counselor; institutional teacher, world languages

V. Middle Level 5–8: art; English as a second language; health; language arts; mathematics; music; music instrumental; music vocal; reading; physical education; adaptive physical education; science; social studies; Spanish; principal; director; school counselor

VI. Secondary level 6–12: agriculture; anthropology; art; biology; business; chemistry; computer science; drama; driver's education; earth science; economics; English; English as a second language; family consumer science; geography; health; history; journalism;

mathematics; music; music instrumental; music vocal; physical education; adaptive physical education; physical science; physics; political science; psychology; reading; social studies comprehensive; sociology; speech; trade and technical; principal; director; school counselor; at-risk/alternative teacher; institutional teacher; world language (Chinese, Japanese, French, Latin, German, Russian, Italian, Spanish)

VII. K–12: art; audiology; educational diagnostician; English as a second language; health; gifted and talented; library media; music; music instrumental; music vocal; physical education; adaptive physical education; reading; superintendent; principal; director; institutional administrator; institutional teacher; school nurse; school counselor; school psychologist; school social worker; educational sign language interpreter; speech language therapist; world languages

VIII. Special Education K–6/ 5–8/ 6–12/ K–12: exceptional specialist—generalist; exceptional specialist—behavioral & emotional disabilities; exceptional specialist—cognitive disability; exceptional specialist—deaf and hard of hearing; exceptional specialist—learning disability; exceptional specialist—physical and health disability; exceptional specialist—visual disability

Additional School Personnel

I. School Administrator (valid 5 years)
  A. An individual who holds a standard Wyoming educator license may apply to add a school administrator endorsement to his or her license.
  B. This endorsement allows individuals to serve as an administrator or superintendent in any Wyoming school in accordance with his or her level of preparation.
  C. The following school administrator endorsements are offered by PTSB:
    1. District superintendent
    2. School principal
    3. Program director
  D. Requirements:
    1. Hold Wyoming licensure in a teaching field
    2. Have completed an educational leadership program, from a nationally or regionally accredited college/university, that leads to an institutional recommendation in educational leadership, school principal, educational administrator, or other equivalent endorsement areas
  E. Educators who are applying concurrently for initial licensure and a school administrator endorsement must submit a complete application for Initial, First-Time Licensure.

II. School Librarian (valid 5 years)
  A. An individual with this endorsement is eligible to serve as a school librarian in a Wyoming K–12 classroom.
  B. Endorsement requires completion of a bachelor's degree in school library science, K–12.

III. School Counselor (valid 5 years)
  A. Endorsement requires an institutional recommendation indicating completion of a master's degree in school counseling

IV. School Psychologist (valid 5 years)
    A. Endorsement requires an institutional recommendation indicating completion of a master's degree in school psychology
 V. School Social Worker (valid 5 years)
    A. Endorsement requires an institutional recommendation indicating completion of a master's degree in school social work
VI. Speech Pathologist (valid 5 years)
    A. Endorsement requires an institutional recommendation indicating completion of a master's degree in speech pathology

Appendix 1

How to Contact State Offices of Certification

Alabama
Teacher Education and Certification
   Office
State Department of Education
5201 Gordon Persons Building
P.O. Box 302101
Montgomery, AL 36130-2101
334-242-9977
334-353-8567
334-242-0498 (fax)
http://www.alsde.edu/Portal/Public/
   Pages/News/aspx
tcert@alsde.edu

Alaska
Alaska Dept. of Education & Early
   Development
Attn: Teacher Certification
801 West 10th Street, Suite 200,
   P.O. Box 110500
Juneau, AK 99811-0500
907-465-2831
907-465-2800 (TTY/TTD)
907-465-2441 (fax)
http://www.eed.state.ak.us/teacher
   certification
tcwebmail@alaska.gov

Arizona
Arizona Dept. of Education
Certification Unit
P.O. Box 6490
Phoenix, AZ 85005-6490
602-542-4367 (8:30 – 4:30)
http://www.azed.gov/certification
Certification@AZED.gov

Arkansas
Office of Professional Licensure
State Dept. of Education
Four Capitol Mall, Room 107B
Little Rock, AR 72201-1071
501-682-4342 (8 – 4:30)
501-682-4898 (fax)
http://Arkansased.org
ron.tolson@arkansas.gov

California
Commission on Teacher
   Credentialing
1900 Capitol Avenue
Sacramento, CA 95811-4213
916-445-7254 (12 – 4:45 pm, pst)
916-327-3166 (fax)
www.ctc.ca.govcredentials
   @ctc.ca.gov

Colorado
Educator Licensing
Department of Education
201 East Colfax Avenue, Room 106
Denver, CO 80203-1799
303-866-6628
303-866-6722 (altern tchr fax)
303-866-6866 (fax)
http://www.cde.state.co.us/index_
   license.htm
educator.licensing@cde.state.co.us

Connecticut
Bureau of Educator Standards &
   Certification
Department of Education
P.O. Box 150471, Room 243
Hartford, CT 06115-0471
860-713-6969 (12 – 4, M, T, Th, F)
860-713-7017 (fax)
www.sde.ct.gov/sde
teacher.cert@ct.gov

Delaware
Educator Licensure and
   Certification
Department of Education
401 Federal Street, Suite 2
Dover, DE 19901
302-735-4120
888-759-9133 (toll free)
http://www.doe.k12.de.us
Submit on website

District of Columbia
Office of Educator Licensure and
   Accreditation
OSSE - Division of Elementary and
   Secondary Education
810 First St., NE, 5th Floor
Washington, DC 20002
202-741-5881
www.osse.dc.gov
educator.licensurehelp@dc.gov

Florida
Bureau of Educator
   Certification
Department of Education
325 W. Gaines
Turlington Bldg., Suite 201
Tallahassee, FL 32399-0400
800-445-6739 (in U.S.)
850-245-5049 (outside U.S.)
http://www.fldoe.org/edcert

Georgia
Professional Standards
   Commission
Certification Section
Two Peachtree St., Ste. 6000
Atlanta, GA 30303
404-232-2500
800-869-7775 (beyond Atlanta)
404-232-2560 (fax)
http://www.gapsc.com

Hawaii
Hawaii Teacher Standards Board
650 Iwilei Road, Suite 201
Honolulu, HI 96817
808-586-2603 (7:45–4:30)
808-586-2606 (fax)
http://www.htsb.org
licensingsection@htsb.org

Idaho
Certification/Professional Standards
  Commission
State Department of Education
650 W. State St., P.O. Box 83720
Boise, ID 83720-0027
208-332-6881
800-432-4601 (toll-free)
208-334-2228 (fax)
http://www.sde.idaho.gov/site/
  teacher_certification
jbjensen@sde.idaho.gov

Illinois
Illinois State Board of Education
Certification Division
100 N. First Street
Springfield, IL 62777-0001
217-557-6763
http://www.isbe.net/certification/
  default.htm
Submit on website

Indiana
Educator Licensing and
  Development
Indiana Department of Education
151 W. Ohio Street
Indianapolis, IN 46204
317-232-9010
866-542-3672
317-232-9023 (fax)
http://www.doe.in.gov/
  educatorlicensing
licensinghelp@doe.in.gov

Iowa
Board of Educational Examiners
Grimes State Office Building
400 East 14th Street
Des Moines, IA 50319-0147
515-281-3245
515-281-7669 (fax)
http://www.boee.iowa.gov

Kansas
Teacher Education and Licensure
Kansas State Department of
  Education
120 SE 10th Avenue
Topeka, KS 66612-1182
785-291-3678
785-296-2288 (automated syst)
785-296-4318 (fax)
http://www.ksde.org

Kentucky
Education Professional Standards
  Board
Division of Certification
100 Airport Road, 3rd Floor
Frankfort, KY 40601
502-564-4606
888-598-7667
502-564-7080 (fax)
http://www.epsb.ky.gov
dcert@ky.gov

Louisiana
Louisiana Department of Education
Certification, Preparation &
  Recruitment
P.O. Box 94064
Baton Rouge, LA 70804-9064
877-453-2721 (toll-free)
225-342-3499 (fax)
http://www.doe.state.la.us/divisions/
  cert/certification.html

Maine
Certification Office
Department of Education
23 State House Station
Augusta, ME 04333-0023
207-624-6603
207-624-6604 (fax)
www.maine.gov/education
cert.doe@maine.gov

Maryland
Certification Branch
Maryland State Department of
  Education
200 West Baltimore Street
Baltimore, MD 21201-2595
410-767-0412
866-772-8922 (toll-free)
410-333-6442 (TTY-TDD)
http://www.mdcert.org

Massachusetts
Department of Elementary and
  Secondary Education (ESE)
Office of Educator Licensure
75 Pleasant Street
Malden, MA 02148
781-338-6600
781-338-3000 (24/7 automated)
781-338-3391 (fax)
http://www.doe.mass.edu/educators

Michigan
Office of Professional Preparation
  Services
Michigan Department of Education
608 West Allegan
P.O. Box 30008
Lansing, MI 48909
517-373-3310
517-373-4410
http://www.michigan.gov/mde

Minnesota
Educator Licensing
State Department of Education
1500 Highway 36 West
Roseville, MN 55113-4266
651-582-8691
651-582-8201 (TTY)
651-582-8809 (fax)
http://education.state.mn.us/mde/
  Teacher_Support/Educator_
  Licensing/index.html
mde.educator-licensing@state.mn.us

Mississippi
Office of Educator Licensure
Mississippi Department of
  Education
359 North West Street, P.O. Box 771
Jackson, MS 39205-0771
601-359-3483
601-359-2778 (fax)
http://www.mde.k12.ms.us/
  ed_licensure/index.html
teachersupport@mde.k12.ms.us

Missouri
Educator Certification
Dept. of Elementary & Secondary
    Education
P.O. Box 480
Jefferson City, MO 65102-0480
573-751-0051/3847
573-522-8314 (fax)
http://www.dese.mo.gov/
    divteachqual/teachcert/
    index.html
webreplyteachcert@dese.mo.gov

Montana
Educator Licensure
Office of Public Instruction
P.O. Box 202501
Helena, MT 59620-2501
406-444-3150
http://www.opi.mt.gov/cert
cert@mt.gov

Nebraska
Teacher Certification
Nebraska Department of Education
301 Centennial Mall South
P.O. Box 94987
Lincoln, NE 68509-4987
402-471-0739
402-471-2496 (elec voice mail)
402-471-9735 (fax)
http://www.education.ne.gov/tcert
nde.tcertweb@nebraska.gov

Nevada
Teacher Licensure, Southern Nevada
Nevada Department of Education
9890 South Maryland Parkway,
    Suite 221
Las Vegas, NV 89183
702-486-6458 (8 am–5 pm)
702-486-6450 (fax)
http://nvteachers.doe.nv.gov
license@doe.nv.gov

Nevada Department of Education-
    Carson City
Teacher Licensure, Northern Nevada
700 East Fifth Street
Carson City, NV 89701
775-687-9115
775-687-9101 (fax)

New Hampshire
Bureau of Credentialing
State Department of Education
Division of Program Support
101 Pleasant Street
Concord, NH 03301-3860
603-271-2408
603-271-4134 (fax)
http://www.ed.state.nh.us
lmiller@ed.state.nh.us

New Jersey
New Jersey Department of
    Education
Office of Licensure and Credentials
P.O. Box 500
Trenton, NJ 08625-0500
609-292-2070 (2–5 pm M–F)
609-292-3768 (fax)
http://www.state.nj.us/education/
    educators/license

New Mexico
Professional Licensure Bureau
New Mexico Public Education
    Department
300 Don Gaspar
Santa Fe, NM 87501-2786
505-827-6587 (for app status)
505-827-5821 (help desk)
505-827-4148 (fax)
http://www.ped.state.nm.us/licensure
LicensureUnit@state.nm.us

New York
Office of Teaching Initiatives
New York State Education
    Department
89 Washington Avenue, 5N EB
Albany, NY 12234
518-474-3901 (9 – 4:30 M–F)
800-855-2880 (TTY)
518-474-6950 (fax)
http://www.highered.nysed.gov/tcert

North Carolina
Department of Public Instruction
Licensure Section
6365 Mail Service Center
Raleigh, NC 27699-6365
919-807-3310 (out of state)
800-577-7994 (in-state only)
http://www.NCPublicSchools.org/
    licensure/

North Dakota
Education Standards & Practices
    Board
Teacher Licensure
2718 Gateway Ave., Suite 303
Bismarck, ND 58503-0585
701-328-9641
701-328-9647 (fax)
http://www.state.nd.us/espb
espbinfo@nd.gov

North Dakota Dept. of Public
    Instruction
School Approval & Accreditation
Teacher Credentials
600 E. Boulevard Ave., Dept. 201
Bismarck, ND 58505-0440
701-328-1718
701-328-0201 (fax)
http://www.dpi.state.nd.us

Ohio
Office of Educator Licensure
Ohio Department of Education
25 South Front St., Mail Stop 105
Columbus, OH 43215-4183
614-466-3593
877-644-6338 (toll-free)
www.ode.state.oh.us
Educator.Licensure@ode.state.oh.us

Oklahoma
Professional Standards and
    Certification
State Department of Education
2500 N. Lincoln Blvd., Rm. 212
Oklahoma City, OK 73105-4599
405-521-3337
405-522-1520 (fax)
http://www.sde.state.ok.us
karen_nickell@sde.state.ok.us

Oregon
Teacher Standards and Practices
    Commission
465 Commercial St. NE
Salem, OR 97301
503-378-3586
503-378-6961 (TDD)
503-378-4448 (fax)
http://www.tspc.state.or.us
contact.tspc@state.or.us

Pennsylvania
Bureau of School Leadership and
    Teacher Quality
Department of Education
333 Market Street
Harrisburg, PA 17126-0333
717-787-3356 (8:00 – 4:30)
717-772-2864 (TDD)
717-783-6736 (fax)
http://www.education.state.pa.us
ra-teachercert@state.pa.us

Rhode Island
Office of Educator Quality and
    Certification
State Department of Education
255 Westminster St.
Providence, RI 02903-3400
401-222-4600
http://www.ride.ri.gov
eqac@ride.ri.gov

South Carolina
Division of Educator Quality &
    Leadership
Department of Education
Landmark II Office Building
3700 Forest Drive, Suite 500
Columbia, SC 29204
803-734-8466 (hotline, 1 – 4:30pm)
877-885-5280 (toll-free)
http://www.scteachers.org
certification@scteachers.org

South Dakota
Department of Education
Office of Accreditation & Teacher
    Quality
800 Governors Drive
Pierre, SD 57501-2291
605-773-3134
605-773-6139 (fax)
http://doe.sd.gov/oatq/teachercert
    .asp
certification@state.sd.us

Tennessee
Tennessee Department of Education
Office of Teacher Licensing
4th Floor, Andrew Johnson Tower
710 James Robertson Parkway
Nashville, TN 37243-0377
615-532-4885
615-532-1448 (fax)
http://www.tennessee.gov/
    education / lic
education.licensing@tn.us

Texas
Texas Education Agency
Educator Certification and Standards
1701 N. Congress Ave., WBT 5-100
Austin, TX 78701-1494
512-936-8400
888-863-5880 (toll-free)
512-936-8277 (fax)
http://www.tea.state.tx.us

Utah
Teaching and Learning Licensing
State Office of Education
250 East 500 South
P.O. Box 144200
Salt Lake City, UT 84114-4200
801-538-7740
801-538-7973 (fax)
http://www.schools.utah.gov/cert

Vermont
Educator Licensing Office
Educator Quality
Department of Education
120 State Street
Montpelier, VT 05620-2501
802-828-2445 (8 am – 4:30 pm)
802-828-5107 (fax)
http://education.vermont.gov/new/
    html /maincert.html
DOE-LicensingInfo@state.vt.us

Virginia
Division of Teacher Education
    Licensure
Department of Education
P.O. Box 2120
Richmond, VA 23218-2120
804-225-2022
804-530-4510 (fax)
www.doe.virginia.gov/teaching/
    licensure/index.shtml
licensure@doe.virginia.gov

Washington
Professional Office Certification
Old Capitol Building
600 Washington Street, S.E.
P.O. Box 47200
Olympia, WA 98504-7200
360-725-6400
360-664-3631 (TTY)
360-586-0145 (fax)
http://www.k12.wa.us/certification
cert@k12.wa.us

West Virginia
Office of Professional Preparation
Building 6, Room 252
1900 Kanawha Blvd., East
Charleston, WV 25305-0330
304-558-7010
800-982-2378 (10 – 12; 1 – 4)
304-558-7843 (fax)
http://wvde.state.wv.us /certification
mfmiller@access.k12.wv.us

Wisconsin
Teacher Education, Professional
    Development & Licensing
Department of Public Instruction
125 S. Webster St., P.O. Box 7841
Madison, WI 53707-7841
608-266-1027
800-266-1027
608-264-9558 (fax)
http://dpi.wi.gov/tepdl /
licensing@dpi.wi.gov

Wyoming
Professional Teaching Standards
    Board
State of Wyoming
1920 Thomes Avenue, Suite 400
Cheyenne, WY 82002
307-777-7291 (in state)
800-675-6893 (toll-free)
307-777-8718 (fax)
http://ptsb.state.wy.us
ptsbtemp@state.wy.us.

Appendix 2

Addresses for Certification Information for U.S. Possessions and Territories

American Samoa
Ms. Esther Ili
Teacher Quality Assistant Director
American Samoa Government
Department of Education
Teacher Quality Office
Pago Pago, AS 96799
Phone: (684) 699-6557
Fax: (684) 699-6446
E-mail: kaleolanikamanakaili@
   yahoo.com

Federated States of Micronesia
Ms. Emma Nelson
Title II Coordinator
FSM National Department of
   Education
P.O. Box PS 87
Palikir, Pohnpei, FM 96941
Phone: (691) 320-2091
Fax: (691) 320-5359
E-mail: nelemma43@yahoo.com

Guam
Mr. John Anderson
Education Certification Officer
Guam Commission for Educator
   Certification
UOG Station-SOE
Mangilao, GU 96923
Phone: (671) 735-2554
Fax: (671) 735-2569
E-mail: john.anderson@gcec.guam
   .gov

Marshall Islands
Mr. Aliksa Andrike
RMI Ministry of Education
P.O. Box #3
Majuro, MH 96960
Phone: (692) 625-2251
Fax: (692) 625-3861
E-mail: a_andrike@yahoo.com

Northern Marianas
Coreen Palacios
Personnel Specialist
CNMI Public School System
Phone: (670) 237-3059
Fax: (670) 664-3707
E-mail: coreen.palacios@
   cnmipss.org

Palau
Mr. Emery Wenty
Director of Education
Ministry of Education
P.O. Box 189
Koror, PW 96940
Phone: (680) 488-2952
Fax: (680) 488-8465
E-mail: ewenty@palaumoe.net

Puerto Rico
Mr. Miguel Gaud
Puerto Rico Department of
   Education
P.O. Box 190759
San Juan, PR 00919-0759
Phone: (787) 773-2077
Fax: (787) 250-0275
E-mail: gaud_m@de.gobierno.pr

Virgin Islands
Ms. Alscess Lewis-Brown
Director, Human Resources
USVI Department of Education
1842 Kongens Gade
St. Thomas, USVI 00802
Phone: (340) 773-5844
Fax: (340) 776-5687
E-mail: teachusvi@doe.vi

**United States Department of
   Defense Education Activity**
Human Resources Regional Service
   Center
Recruitment & Staffing Unit
703-588-3983 (phone)
703-588-5383 (fax)
http://www.dodea.edu/offices/hr/
   employees/licensure/default.htm
Personnel.Helpline@hq.
   dodea.edu

Appendix 3

Parties to the Interstate Agreement

Many of the states (as well as U.S. possessions, territories, and the Department of Defense) are parties to the National Association of State Directors of Teacher Education and Certification Interstate Contract. This agreement allows educators who hold certificates or licenses in one of the participating states to obtain analogous certification or licensure in any of the other participating states. Applicants should note that individual states may have special conditions upon granting certification, for example, demonstrated knowledge of state history. Such conditions, and even whether there is reciprocity for all classes of educational personnel, vary from state to state. Many of these conditions are noted in the individual state requirements found in this volume, but not all.

The listing below shows which states are parties to the agreement, current as of press time, according to type of certification: teachers, administrators, support personnel, and vocational personnel. Applicants seeking reciprocal certification in another state should contact the certification office (see Appendix 1) there for full information.

Alabama

Teacher — AK, AS, AZ, AR, CA, CO, CT, DE, DODEA, DC, FL, GA, GU, HI, ID, IL, IN, IA, KS, KY, LA, ME, MD, MA, MI, MN, MS, MO, MT, NE, NV, NH, NJ, NM, NY, NC, ND, NMI, OH, OK, OR, PA, PR, RI, SC, SD, TN, TX, UT, VT, VA, WA, WV, WI, WY

Administrator — AK, AS, AZ, AR, CA, CO, CT, DE, DODEA, DC, FL, GA, GU, HI, ID, IL, IN, IA, KS, KY, LA, ME, MD, MA, MI, MN, MS, MO, MT, NE, NV, NH, NJ, NM, NY, NC, ND, NMI, OH, OK, OR, PA, PR, RI, SC, SD, TN, TX, UT, VT, VA, WA, WV, WI, WY

Support — AK, AS, AZ, AR, CA, CO, CT, DE, DODEA, DC, FL, GA, GU, HI, ID, IL, IN, IA, KS, KY, LA, ME, MD, MA, MI, MN, MS, MO, MT, NE, NV, NH, NJ, NM, NY, NC, ND, NMI, OH, OK, OR, PA, PR, RI, SC, SD, TN, TX, UT, VT, VA, WA, WV, WI, WY

Vocational — None

Alaska

Teacher — None

Administrator — None

Support — None

Vocational — None

Arizona

Teacher — AL, AK, AR, CA, CO, CT, DE, DODEA, DC, FL, GA, HI, ID, IL, IN, IA, KS, KY, LA, ME, MD, MA, MI, MN, MS, MO, MT, NE, NV, NH, NJ, NM, NY, NC, ND, OH, OK, OR, PA, RI, SC, SD, TN, TX, UT, VT, VA, WA, WV, WI, WY

Administrator — None

Support — None

Vocational — None

Arkansas

Teacher — AL, AK, AZ, CO, CT, DE, DODEA, DC, FL, GA, GU, HI, ID, IL, IN, IA, KS, KY, LA, ME, MD, MA, MI, MN, MS, MO, MT, NE, NH, NJ,

NM, NY, NC, ND, OH, OK, OR, PA, RI, SC, SD, TN, TX, UT, VT, VA, WA, WV, WI, WY

Administrator   AL, AK, AZ, CO, CT, DE, DODEA, DC, FL, GA, GU, HI, ID, IL, IN, IA, KS, KY, LA, ME, MD, MA, MI, MN, MS, MO, MT, NE, NH, NJ, NM, NY, NC, ND, OH, OK, OR, PA, RI, SC, SD, TN, TX, UT, VT, VA, WA, WV, WI, WY

Support   None

Vocational   None

California
Teacher   AL, AK, AS, AZ, AR, CO, CT, DE, DC, FL, GA, GU, HI, ID, IL, IN, IA, KS, KY, LA, ME, MD, MA, MI, MN, MS, MO, MT, NE, NV, NH, NJ, NM, NY, NC, ND, OH, OK, OR, PA, PR, RI, SC, SD, TN, TX, UT, VT, VA, WA, WV, WI, WY

Administrator   AL, AK, AS, AZ, AR, CO, CT, DE, DC, FL, GA, GU, HI, ID, IL, IN, IA, KS, KY, LA, ME, MD, MA, MI, MN, MS, MO, MT, NE, NV, NH, NJ, NM, NY, NC, ND, OH, OK, OR, PA, PR, RI, SC, SD, TN, TX, UT, VT, VA, WA, WV, WI, WY

Support   None

Vocational   None

Colorado
Teacher   AL, AK, AS, AZ, AR, CA, CT, DE, DODEA, DC, FL, GA, GU, HI, ID, IL, IN, IA, KS, KY, LA, ME, MD, MA, MI, MN, MS, MO, MT, NE, NV, NH, NJ, NM, NY, NC, ND, OH, OK, OR, PA, PR, RI, SC, SD, TN, TX, UT, VT, VA, WA, WV, WI, WY

Administrator   AL, AK, AS, AZ, AR, CA, CT, DE, DODEA, DC, FL, GA, GU, HI, ID, IL, IN, IA, KS, KY, LA, ME, MD, MA, MI, MN, MS, MO, MT, NE, NV, NH, NJ, NM; NY, NC, ND, OH, OK, OR, PA, PR, RI, SC, SD, TN, TX, UT, VT, VA, WA, WV, WI, WY

Support   AL, AK, AS, AZ, AR, CA, CT, DE, DODEA, DC, FL, GA, GU, HI, ID, IL, IN, IA, KS, KY, LA, ME, MD, MA, MI, MN, MS, MO, MT, NE, NV, NH, NJ, NM, NY, NC, ND, OH, OK, OR, PA, PR, RI, SC, SD, TN, TX, UT, VT, VA, WA, WV, WI, WY

Vocational   AL, AK, AS, AZ, AR, CA, CT, DE, DODEA, DC, FL,. GA, GU, HI, ID, IL, IN, IA, KS, KY, LA, ME, MD, MA, MI, MN, MS, MO, MT, NE, NV, NH, NJ, NM, NY, NC, ND, OH, OK, OR, PA, PR, RI, SC, SD, TN, TX, UT, VT, VA

Connecticut
Teacher   AL, AR, CA, CO, DE, DC, FL, GA, HI, ID, IL, IN, KY, ME, MD, MA, MI, MS, MT, NV, NH, NJ, NM, NY, NC, OH, OK, OR, PA, RI, SC, TN, TX, UT, VT, VA, WA, WV

Administrator   None

Support   AL, MD, MA, NH, NC, RI, SC, UT, WA, WV

Vocational   NH, NY, NC, RI, SC, UT, WV

Delaware
Teacher   AL, AK, AS, AZ, AR, CA, CO, CT, DODEA, DC, FL, GA, GU, HI, ID, IL, IN, IA, KS, KY, LA, ME, MD, MA, MI, MN, MS, MO, MT, NE, NV, NH, NJ, NM, NY, NC, ND, NMI, OH, OK, OR, PA, PR, RI, SC, SD, TN, TX, UT, VT, VA, WA, WV, WI, WY

Administrator   AL, AK, AS, AZ, AR, CA, CO, CT, DODEA, DC, FL, GA, GU, HI, ID, IL, IN, IA, KS, KY, LA, ME, MD, MA, MI, MN, MS, MO, MT, NE, NV, NH, NJ, NM, NY, NC, ND, NMI, OH, OK, OR, PA, PR, RI, SC, SD, TN, TX, UT, VT, VA, WA, WV, WI, WY

Support   DODEA, DC, FL, GA, GU, HI, ID, IL, IN, IA, KS, KY, LA, ME, MD, MA, MI, MN, MS, MO, MT, NE, NV, NH, NJ, NM, NY, NC, ND,

NMI, OH, OK, OR, PA, PR, RI, SC,
SD, TN, TX, UT, VT, VA, WA, WV,
WI, WY

Vocational   None

Department of Defense Education Activity (DODEA)

Teacher   AL, AK, AZ, AR, CA, CO, CT, DE,
DC, FL, GA, GU, HI, ID, IL, IN, IA,
KS, KY, LA, ME, MD, MA, MI,
MN, MS, MO, MT, NE, NV, NH,
NJ, NM, NY, NC, ND, OH, OK, OR,
PA, PR, RI, SC, SD, TN, TX, UT,
VT, VA, WA, WV, WI, WY

Administrator   AL, AK, AZ, AR, CA, CO, CT, DE,
DC, FL, GA, GU, HI, ID, IL, IN, IA,
KS, KY, LA, ME, MD, MA, MI,
MN, MS, MO, MT, NE, NV, NH,
NJ, NM, NY, NC, ND, OH, OK, OR,
PA, PR, RI, SC, SD, TN, TX, UT,
VT, VA, WA, WV, WI, WY

Support   None

Vocational   AL, AK, AZ, AR, CA, CO, CT, DE,
DC, FL, GA, GU, HI, ID, IL, IN, IA,
KS, KY, LA, ME, MD, MA, MI,
MN, MS, MO, MT, NE, NV, NH,
NJ, NM, NY, NC, ND, OH, OK, OR,
PA, PR, RI, SC, SD, TN, TX, UT,
VT, VA, WA, WV, WI, WY

District of Columbia

Teacher   None

Administrator   None

Support   None

Vocational   None

Florida

Teacher   AL, AK, AS, AZ, AR, CA, CO, CT,
DE, DODEA, DC, GA, GU, HI, ID,
IL, IN, IA, KS, KY, LA, ME, MD,
MA, MI, MN, MS, MO, MT, NE,
NV, NH, NJ, NM, NY, NC, ND,
NMI, OH, OK, OR, PA, PR, RI, SC,
SD, TN, TX, UT, VT, VA, WA, WV,
WI, WY

Administrator   AL, AK, AS, AZ, AR, CA, CO, CT,
DE, DODEA, DC, GA, GU, HI, ID,
IL, IN, IA, KS, KY, LA, ME, MD,
MA, MI, MN, MS, MO, MT, NE,
NV, NH, NJ, NM, NY, NC, ND,
NMI, OH, OK, OR, PA, PR, RI, SC,
SD, TN, TX, UT, VT, VA, WA, WV,
WI, WY

Support   AL, AK, AS, AZ, AR, CA, CO, CT,
DE, DODEA, DC, GA, GU, HI, ID,
IL, IN, IA, KS, KY, LA, ME, MD,
MA, MI, MN, MS, MO, MT, NE,
NV, NH, NJ, NM, NY, NC, ND,
NMI, OH, OK, OR, PA, PR, RI, SC,
SD, TN, TX, UT, VT, VA, WA, WV,
WI, WY

Vocational   None

Georgia

Teacher   AL, AK, AZ, AR, CA, CO, CT, DE,
DODEA, DC, FL, HI, ID, IL, IN,
IA, KS, KY, LA, ME, MD, MA, MI,
MN, MS, MO, MT, NE, NV, NH,
NJ, NM, NY, NC, ND, OH, OK, OR,
PA, RI, SC, SD, TN, TX, UT, VT,
VA, WA, WV, WI, WY

Administrator   AL, AK, AZ, AR, CA, CO, CT, DE,
DODEA, DC, FL, HI, ID, IL, IN, IA,
KS, KY, LA, ME, MD, MA, MI,
MN, MS, MO, MT, NE, NV, NH,
NJ, NM, NY, NC, ND, OH, OK, OR,
PA, RI, SC, SD, TN, TX, UT, VT,
VA, WA, WV, WI, WY

Support   AL, AK, AZ, AR, CA, CO, CT, DE,
DODEA, DC, FL, HI, ID, IL, IN, IA,
KS, KY, LA, ME, MD, MA, MI,
MN, MS, MO, MT, NE, NV, NH,
NJ, NM, NY, NC, ND, OH, OK, OR,
PA, RI, SC, SD, TN, TX, UT, VT,
VA, WA, WV, WI, WY

Vocational   AL, AK, AZ, AR, CA, CO, CT, DE,
DODEA, DC, FL, HI, ID, IL, IN, IA,
KS, KY, LA, ME, MD, MA, MI,
MN, MS, MO, MT, NE, NV, NH,
NJ, NM, NY, NC, ND, OH, OK, OR,
PA, RI, SC, SD, TN, TX, UT, VT,
VA, WA, WV, WI, WY

Guam

Teacher   AL, AK, AZ, AR, CA, CO, CT, DE, DODEA, DC, FL, GA, HI, ID, IL, IN, IA, KS, KY, LA, ME, MD, MA, MI, MN, MS, MO, MT, NE, NV, NH, NJ, NM, NY, NC, ND, NMI, OH, OK, OR, PA, RI, SC, SD, TN, TX, UT, VT, VA, WA, WV, WI, WY

Administrator   AL, AK, AZ, AR, CA, CO, CT, DE, DODEA, DC, FL, GA, HI, ID, IL, IN, IA, KS, KY, LA, ME, MD, MA, MI, MN, MS, MO, MT, NE, NV, NH, NJ, NM, NY, NC, ND, NMI, OH, OK, OR, PA, RI, SC, SD, TN, TX, UT, VT, VA, WA, WV, WI, WY

Support   AL, AK, AZ, AR, CA, CO, CT, DE, DODEA, DC, FL, GA, HI, ID, IL, IN, IA, KS, KY, LA, ME, MD, MA, MI, MN, MS, MO, MT, NE, NV, NH, NJ, NM, NY, NC, ND, NMI, OH, OK, OR, PA, RI, SC, SD, TN, TX, UT, VT, VA, WA, WV, WI, WY

Vocational   AL, AK, AZ, AR, CA, CO, CT, DE, DODEA, DC, FL, GA, HI, ID, IL, IN, IA, KS, KY, LA, ME, MD, MA, MI, MN, MS, MO, MT, NE, NV, NH, NJ, NM, NY, NC, ND, NMI, OH, OK, OR, PA, RI, SC, SD, TN, TX, UT, VT, VA, WA, WV, WI, WY

Hawaii

Teacher   AL, AK, AS, AZ, AR, CA, CO, CT, DE, DODEA, DC, FL, GA, GU, HI, ID, IL, IN, IA, KS, KY, LA, ME, MD, MA, MI, MN, MS, MO, MT, NE, NV, NH, NJ, NM, NY, NC, ND, NMI, OH, OK, OR, PA, PR, RI, SC, SD, TN, TX, UT, VT, VA, WA, WV, WI, WY

Administrator   None

Support   None

Vocational   None

Idaho

Teacher   AL, AK, AZ, AR, CA, CO, CT, DE, DODEA, DC, FL, GA, GU, HI, ID, IL, IN, IA, KS, KY, LA, ME, MD, MA, MI, MN, MS, MO, MT, NE, NV, NH, NJ, NM, NY, NC, ND, OH, OK, OR, PA, RI, SC, SD, TN, TX, UT, VT, VA, WA, WV, WI, WY

Administrator   None

Support   None

Vocational   None

Illinois

Teacher   AL, AK, AZ, AR, CA, CO, CT, DE, DC, FL, GA, GU, HI, ID, IN, IA, KS, KY, LA, ME, MD, MA, MI, MN, MS, MO, MT, NE, NV, NH, NJ, NM, NY, NC, ND, OH, OK, OR, PA, RI, SC, SD, TN, TX, UT, VT, VA, WA, WV, WI, WY

Administrator   AL, AK, AZ, CA, CO, CT, DE, DC, FL, GA, GU, HI, ID, IN, IA, KS, KY, LA, ME, MD, MA, MN, MS, MO, MT, NE, NV, NH, NJ, NM, NY, NC, OK, OR, PA, RI, SC, SD, TN, TX, VT, VA, WA, WV, WI, WY

Support   AL, AK, CA, CO, CT, DE, DC, FL, GA, GU, HI, ID, IN, IA, KS, KY, LA, ME, MD, MA, MI, MN, MS, MO, MT, NE, NV, NH, NJ, NM, NY, NC, OK, OR, PA, RI, SC, SD, TN, TX, VT, VA, WA, WV, WI

Vocational   None

Indiana

Teacher   AL, AK, AZ, AR, CA, CO, CT, DE, DC, FL, GA, HI, ID, IL, KY, ME, MD, MA, MI, MS, MT, NE, NV, NH, NJ, NM, NY, NC, ND, OH, OK, OR, RI, SC, TN, TX, UT, VT, VA, WA, WV, WY

Administrator   AL, AK, AZ, CO, DE, GA, MD, MA, MS, NM, NY, OK, RI, SC, TN, TX, VA, WA, WV, WY

Support	AL, AK, AZ, DC, FL, GA, MD, MA, NE, NH, NY, OK, RI, SC, TN, VA, WA, WV, WY
Vocational	None

Iowa

Teacher	None
Administrator	None
Support	None
Vocational	None

Kansas

Teacher	AL, AK, AZ, AR, CA, CO, CT, DE, DC, FL, GA, HI, ID, IL, IN, IA, KY, LA, ME, MD, MA, MI, MN, MS, MO, MT, NE, NV, NH, NJ, NM, NY, NC, ND, OH, OK, OR, PA, RI, SC, SD, TN, TX, UT, VT, VA, WA, WV, WI, WY
Administrator	AL, AK, AZ, AR, CA, CO, CT, DE, DC, FL, GA, HI, ID, IL, IN, IA, KY, LA, ME, MD, MA, MI, MN, MS, MO, MT, NE, NV, NH, NJ, NM, NY, NC, ND, OH, OK, OR, PA, RI, SC, SD, TN, TX, UT, VT, VA, WA, WV, WI, WY
Support	AL, AK, AZ, AR, CA, CO, CT, DE, DC, FL, GA, HI, ID, IL, IN, IA, KY, LA, ME, MD, MA, MI, MN, MS, MO, MT, NE, NV, NH, NJ, NM, NY, NC, ND, OH, OK, OR, PA, RI, SC, SD, TN, TX, UT, VT, VA, WA, WV, WI, WY
Vocational	None

Kentucky

Teacher	AL, AR, CA, CT, DE, DC, GA, HI, ID, IL, IN, ME, MD, MA, MI, MT, NV, NH, NJ, NY, OH, OK, PA, RI, SC, TN, TX, UT, VT, VA, WA, WV, WY
Administrator	None
Support	None
Vocational	None

Louisiana

Teacher	AL, AK, AZ, AR, CA, CO, CT, DE, DC, FL, GA, GU, HI, ID, IL, IN, IA, KS, KY, LA, ME, MD, MA, MI, MN, MS, MO, MT, NE, NV, NH, NJ, NM, NY, NC, ND, OH, OK, OR, PA, PR, RI, SC, SD, TN, TX, UT, VT, VA, WA, WV, WI, WY
Administrator	AL, AK, AZ, AR, CA, CO, CT, DE, DC, FL, GA, GU, HI, ID, IL, IN, IA, KS, KY, LA, ME, MD, MA, MI, MN, MS, MO, MT, NE, NV, NH, NJ, NM, NY, NC, ND, OH, OK, OR, PA, PR, RI, SC, SD, TN, TX, UT, VT, VA, WA, WV, WI, WY
Support	None
Vocational	AL, AK, AZ, AR, CA, CO, CT, DE, DC, FL, GA, GU, HI, ID, IL, IN, IA, KS, KY, LA, ME, MD, MA, MI, MN, MS, MO, MT, NE, NV, NH, NJ, NM, NY, NC, ND, OH, OK, OR, PA, PR, RI, SC, SD, TN, TX, UT, VT, VA, WA, WV, WI, WY

Maine

Teacher	AL, AK, AZ, AR, CA, CO, CT, DE, DC, FL, GA, HI, ID, IL, IN, IA, KS, KY, LA, MD, MA, MI, MN, MS, MO, MT, NE, NV, NH, NJ, NM, NY, NC, ND, OH, OK, OR, PA, RI, SC, SD, TN, TX, UT, VT, VA, WA, WV, WI, WY
Administrator	None
Support	AL, AK, AZ, AR, CA, CO, CT, DE, DC, FL, GA, HI, ID, IL, IN, IA, KS, KY, LA, MD, MA, MI, MN, MS, MO, MT, NE, NV, NH, NJ, NM, NY, NC, ND, OH, OK, OR, PA, RI, SC, SD, TN, TX, UT, VT, VA, WA, WV, WI, WY
Vocational	AL, AK, AZ, AR, CA, CO, CT, DE, DC, FL, GA, HI, ID, IL, IN, IA, KS, KY, LA, MD, MA, MI, MN, MS, MO, MT, NE, NV, NH, NJ, NM, NY, NC, ND, OH, OK, OR, PA, RI, SC, SD, TN, TX, UT, VT, VA, WA, WV, WI, WY

Maryland

Teacher
AL, AK, AS, AZ, AR, CA, CO, CT, DE, DODEA, DC, FL, GA, GU, HI, ID, IL, IN, IA, KS, KY, LA, ME, MA, MI, MN, MS, MO, MT, NE, NV, NH, NJ, NM, NY, NC, ND, NMI, OH, OK, OR, PA, PR, RI, SC, SD, TN, TX, UT, VT, VA, WA, WV, WI, WY

Administrator
AL, AK, AS, AZ, AR, CA, CO, CT, DE, DODEA, DC, FL, GA, GU, HI, ID, IL, IN, IA, KS, KY, LA, ME, MA, MI, MN, MS, MO, MT, NE, NV, NH, NJ, NM, NY, NC, ND, NMI, OH, OK, OR, PA, PR, RI, SC, SD, TN, TX, UT, VT, VA, WA, WV, WI, WY

Support
AL, AK, AS, AZ, AR, CA, CO, CT, DE, DODEA, DC, FL, GA, GU, HI, ID, IL, IN, IA, KS, KY, LA, ME, MA, MI, MN, MS, MO, MT, NE, NV, NH, NJ, NM, NY, NC, ND, NMI, OH, OK, OR, PA, PR, RI, SC, SD, TN, TX, UT, VT, VA, WA, WV, WI, WY

Vocational
AL, AK, AS, AZ, AR, CA, CO, CT, DE, DODEA, DC, FL, GA, GU, HI, ID, IL, IN, IA, KS, KY, LA, ME, MA, MI, MN, MS, MO, MT, NE, NV, NH, NJ, NM, NY, NC, ND, NMI, OH, OK, OR, PA, PR, RI, SC, SD, TN, TX, UT, VT, VA, WA, WV, WI, WY

Massachusetts

Teacher
AL, AK, AZ, AR, CA, CO, CT, DE, DC, FL, GA, GU, HI, ID, IL, IN, KS, KY, LA, ME, MD, MI, MS, MT, NE, NV, NH, NJ, NM, NY, NC, ND, OH, OK, OR, PA, RI, SC, TN, TX UT, VT, VA, WA, WV, WY

Administrator
AL, AK, AZ, CO, DE, DC, GA, ID, IN, MD, MS, NE, NV, NM, NY, NC, OK, OR, RI, SC, TN, TX, UT, VT, VA, WA, WV, WY

Support
AL, AK, AZ, CT, DC, FL, GA, IN, ME, MD, MS, NH, NY, NC, OK, OR, RI, SC, TN, UT, VA, WA, WV, WY

Vocational
None

Michigan

Teacher
AL, AK, AS, AZ, AR, CA, CO, CT, DE, DODEA, DC, FL, GA, GU, HI, ID, IL, IN, IA, KS, KY, LA, ME, MA, MI, MD, MN, MS, MO, MT, NE, NV, NH, NJ, NM, NY, NC, ND, NMI, OH, OK, OR, PA, PR, RI, SC, SD, TN, TX, UT, VT, VA, WA, WV, WI, WY

Administrator
None

Support
AL, AK, AS, AZ, AR, CA, CO, CT, DE, DODEA, DC, FL, GA, GU, HI, ID, IL, IN, IA, KS, KY, LA, ME, MD, MA, MI, MN, MS, MO, MT, NE, NV, NH, NJ, NM, NY, NC, ND, NMI, OH, OK, OR, PA, PR, RI, SC, SD, TN TX, UT, VT, VA, WA, WV, WI, WY

Vocational
None

Minnesota

Teacher
None

Administrator
None

Support
None

Vocational
None

Mississippi

Teacher
AL, AK, AZ, AR, CA, CO, CT, DE, DC, FL, GA, GU, HI, ID, IN, KS, LA, ME, MD, MA, MI, MT, NE, NV, NH, NJ, NM, NY, NC, ND, OH, OK, OR, PA, RI, SC, TN, TX, UT, VT, VA, WA, WV

Administrator
AL, AK, AZ, CO, DC, GA, ID, IN, MD, MA, NE, NV, NM, NY, NC, OK, OR, RI, SC, TN, TX, UT, VA, WA, WV

Support
AL, AK, AZ, DC, FL, GA, GU, ME, MD, MA, NH, NY, NC, OK, OR, RI, SC, TN, UT, VA, WA, WV

Vocational
AZ, DC, GA, ME, MD, NY, NC, OK, RI, SC, TX, UT, VA, WV

Missouri
Teacher   AL, AK, AS, AZ, AR, CA, CO, CT, DE, DODEA, DC, FL, GA, GU, HI, ID, IL, IN, IA, KS, KY, LA, ME, MD, MA, MI, MN, MS, MO, MT, NE, NV, NH, NJ, NM, NY, NC, ND, NMI, OH, OK, OR, PA, PR, RI, SC, SD, TN, TX, UT, VT, VA, WA, WV, WI, WY

Administrator   None

Support   None

Vocational   None

Montana
Teacher   AL, AK, AZ, AR, CA, CO, CT, DE, DC, FL, GA, HI, ID, IL, IN, IA, KS, KY, LA, ME, MD, MA, MI, MN, MS, MO, NE, NV, NH, NJ, NM, NY, NC, ND, OH, OK, OR, PA, RI, SC, SD, TN, TX, UT, VT, VA, WA, WV, WI, WY

Administrator   AL, AK, AZ, AR, CA, CO, CT, DE, DC, FL, GA, HI, ID, IL, IN, IA, KS, KY, LA, ME, MD, MA, MI, MN, MS, MO, NE, NV, NH, NJ, NM, NY, NC, ND, OH, OK, OR, PA, PR, RI, SC, SD, TN, TX, UT, VT, VA, WA, WV, WI, WY

Support   None

Vocational   AL, AK, AZ, AR, CA, CO, CT, DE, DC, FL, GA, HI, ID, IL, IN, IA, KS, KY, LA, ME, MD, MA, MI, MN, MS, MO, NE, NV, NH, NJ, NM, NY, NC, ND, OH, OK, OR, PA, PR, RI, SC, SD, TN, TX, UT, VT, VA, WA, WV, WI, WY

Nebraska
Teacher   AL, AK, AS, AZ, AR, CA, CO, CT, DE, DODEA, DC, FL, GA, GU, HI, ID, IL, IN, IA, KS, KY, LA, ME, MD, MA, MI, MN, MS, MO, MT, NE, NV, NH, NJ, NM, NY, NC, ND, NMI, OH, OK, OR, PA, PR, RI, SC, SD, TN, TX, UT, VT, VA, WA, WV, WI, WY

Administrator   None

Support   None

Vocational   None

Nevada
Teacher   AL, AK, AS, AZ, AR, CA, CO, CT, DE, DODEA, DC, FL, GA, GU, HI, ID, IL, IN, IA, KS, KY, LA, ME, MD, MA, MI, MN, MS, MO, MT, NE, NV, NH, NJ, NM, NY, NC, ND, OH, OK, OR, PA, PR, RI, SC, SD, TN, TX, UT, VT, VA, WA, WV, WI, WY

Administrator   AL, AK, AZ, GA, ID, MD, MA, MS, NE, NM, OK, OR, TN, TX, UT, VA, WA, WV, WY

Support   None

Vocational   None

New Hampshire
Teacher   AL, AK, AS, AZ, AR, CA, CO, CT, DE, DODEA, DC, FL, GA, GU, HI, ID, IL, IN, IA, KS, KY, LA, ME, MD, MA, MI, MN, MS, MO, MT, NE, NV, NH, NJ, NM, NY, NC, ND, OH, OK, OR, PA, PR, RI, SC, SD, TN, TX, UT, VT, VA, WA, WV, WI, WY

Administrators   None

Support   None

Vocational   None

New Jersey
Teacher   AL, AK, AZ, AR, CA, CO, CT, DE, DC, FL, GA, HI, ID, IL, IN, IA, KS, KY, LA, ME, MD, MA, MI, MS, MT, NV, NH, NM, NY, NC, ND, OH, OK, OR, PA, RI, SC, TN, TX, UT, VT, VA, WA, WV, WY

Administrator   None

Support   None

Vocational   None

New Mexico

Teacher   AL, AK, AS, AZ, AR, CA, CO, CT, DE, DODEA, DC, FL, GA, GU, HI, ID, IL, IN, IA, KS, KY, LA, ME, MD, MA, MI, MN, MS, MO, MT, NE, NV, NH, NJ, NY, NC, ND, NMI, OH, OK, OR, PA, PR, RI, SC, SD, TN, TX, UT, VT, VA, WA, WV, WI, WY

Administrator   AL, AK, AS, AZ, AR, CA, CO, CT, DE, DODEA, DC, FL, GA, GU, HI, ID, IL, IN, IA, KS, KY, LA, ME, MD, MA, MI, MN, MS, MO, MT, NE, NV, NH, NJ, NM, NY, NC, ND, NMI, OH, OK, OR, PA, PR, RI, SC, SD, TN, TX, UT, VT, VA, WA, WV, WI, WY

Support   None

Vocational   None

New York

Teacher   AL, AK, AS, AZ, AR, CA, CO, CT, DE, DODEA, DC, FL, GA, GU, HI, ID, IL, IN, IA, KS, KY, LA, ME, MD, MA, MI, MN, MS, MO, MT, NE, NV, NH, NJ, NM, NC, ND, NMI, OH, OK, OR, PA, PR, RI, SC, SD, TN, TX, UT, VT, VA, WA, WV, WI, WY

Administrator   None

Support   Support AL, AK, AS, AZ, AR, CA, CO, CT, DE, DODEA, DC, FL, GA, GU, HI, ID, IL, IN, IA, KS, KY, LA, ME, MD, MA, MI, MN, MS, MO, MT. NE, NV, NH, NJ, NM, NC, ND, NMI, OH, OK, OR, PA, PR, RI, SC, SD, TN, TX, UT, VT, VA, WA, WV, WI, WY

Vocational   AL, AK, AS, AZ, AR, CA, CO, CT, DE, DODEA, DC, FL, GA, GU, HI, ID, IL, IN, IA, KS, KY, LA, ME, MD, MA, MI, MN, MS, MO, MT. NE, NV, NH, NJ, NM, NC, ND, NMI, OH, OK, OR, PA, PR, RI, SC, SD, TN, TX, UT, VT, VA, WA, WV, WI, WY

North Carolina

Teacher   AL, AK, AS, AZ, AR, CA, CO, CT, DE, DODEA, DC, FL, GA, GU, HI, ID, IL, IN, IA, KS, KY, LA, ME, MD, MA, MI, MN, MS, MO, MT, NE, NV, NH, NJ, NM, NY, ND, NMI, OH, OK, OR, PA, PR, RI, SC, SD, TN, TX, UT, VT, VA, WA, WV, WI, WY

Administrator   AL, AK, AS, AZ, AR, CA, CO, CT, DE, DODEA, DC, FL, GA, GU, HI, ID, IL, IN, IA, KS, KY, LA, ME, MD, MA, MI, MN, MS, MO, MT, NE, NV, NH, NJ, NM, NY, ND, NMI, OH, OK, OR, PA, PR, RI, SC, SD, TN, TX, UT, VT, VA, WA, WV, WI, WY

Support   AL, AK, AS, AZ, AR, CA, CO, CT, DE, DODEA, DC, FL, GA, GU, HI, ID, IL, IN, IA, KS, KY, LA, ME, MD, MA, MI, MN, MS, MO, MT, NE, NV, NH, NJ, NM, NY, ND, NMI, OH, OK, OR, PA, PR, RI, SC, SD, TN, TX, UT, VT, VA, WA, WV, WI, WY

Vocational   AL, AK, AS, AZ, AR, CA, CO, CT, DE, DODEA, DC, FL, GA, GU, HI, ID, IL, IN, IA, KS, KY, LA, ME, MD, MA, MI, MN, MS, MO, MT, NE, NV, NH, NJ, NM, NY, ND, NMI, OH, OK, OR, PA, PR, RI, SC, SD, TN, TX, UT, VT, VA, WA, WV, WI, WY

North Dakota

Teacher   AL, AK, AS, AZ, AR, CA, CO, CT, DE, DODEA, DC, FL, GA, GU, HI, ID, IL, IN, IA, KS, KY, LA, ME, MD, MA, MI, MN, MS, MO, MT, NE, NV, NH, NJ, NM, NY, NC, NMI, OH, OK, OR, PA, PR, RI, SC, SD, TN, TX, UT, VT, VA, WA, WV, WI, WY

Administrator   None

Support   None

Vocational   None

Northern Mariana Islands

Teacher   None

Administrator None

Support   None

Vocational   None

Ohio

Teacher   AL, AK, AZ, AR, CA, CO, CT, DE,
               DC, FL, GA, HI, ID, IL, IN, IA, KS,
               KY, ME, MD, MA, MI, MS, MT,
               NE, NH, NJ, NY, NC, OK, OR, PA,
               RI, SC, SD, TN, UT, VT, VA, WA,
               WV, WI

Administrator None

Support   None

Vocational   None

Oklahoma

Teacher   AL, AK, AS, AZ, AR, CA, CO, CT,
               DE, DODEA, DC, FL, GA, GU, HI,
               ID, IL, IN, IA, KS, KY, LA, ME, MD,
               MA, MI, MN, MS, MO, MT, NE,
               NV, NH, NJ, NM, NY, NC, ND, NMI,
               OH, OR, PA, PR, RI, SC, SD, TN,
               TX, UT, VT, VA, WA, WV, WI, WY

Administrator AL, AK, AS, AZ, AR, CA, CO, CT,
               DE, DODEA, DC, FL, GA, GU, HI,
               ID, IL, IN, IA, KS, KY, LA, ME, MD,
               MA, MI, MN, MS, MO, MT, NE, NV,
               NH, NJ, NM, NY, NC, ND, NMI,
               OH, OR, PA, PR, RI, SC, SD, TN,
               TX, UT, VT, VA, WA, WV, WI, WY

Support   AL, AK, AS, AZ, AR, CA, CO, CT,
               DE, DODEA, DC, FL, GA, GU, HI,
               ID, IL, IN, IA, KS, KY, LA, ME, MD,
               MA, MI, MN, MS, MO, MT, NE, NV,
               NH, NJ, NM, NY, NC, ND, NM,
               OH, OR, PA, PR, RI, SC, SD, TN,
               TX, UT, VT, VA, WA, WV, WI, WY

Vocational   AL, AK, AS, AZ, AR, CA, CO, CT,
               DE, DODEA, DC, FL, GA, GU, HI,
               ID, IL, IN, IA, KS, KY, LA, ME, MD,
               MA, MI, MN, MS, MO, MT, NE, NV,

NH, NJ, NM, NY, NC, ND, NMI,
OH, OR, PA, PR, RI, SC, SD, TN,
TX, UT, VT, VA, WA, WV, WI, WY

Oregon

Teacher   AL, AK, AS, AZ, AR, CA, CO,
               CT, DE, DODEA, DC, FL, GA,
               GU, HI, ID, IL, IN, IA, KS, KY, LA,
               ME, MD, MA, MI, MN, MS, MO,
               MT, NE, NV, NH, NJ, NM, NY, NC,
               ND, NMI, OH, OK, PA, PR, RI, SC,
               SD, TN, TX, UT, VT, VA, WA, WV,
               WI, WY

Administrator AL, AK, AS, AZ, AR, CA, CO,
               CT, DE, DODEA, DC, FL, GA,
               GU, HI, ID, IL, IN, IA, KS, KY, LA,
               ME, MD, MA, MI, MN, MS, MO,
               MT, NE, NV, NH, NJ, NM, NY, NC,
               ND, NMI, OH, OK, PA, PR, RI, SC,
               SD, TN, TX, UT, VT, VA, WA, WV,
               WI, WY

Support   AL, AK, AS, AZ, AR, CA, CO, CT,
               DE, DODEA, DC, FL, GA, GU, HI,
               ID, IL, IN, IA, KS, KY, LA, ME, MD,
               MA, MI, MN, MS, MO, MT, NE,
               NV, NH, NJ, NM, NY, NC, ND, NMI,
               OH, OK, PA, PR, RI, SC, SD, TN,
               TX, UT, VT, VA, WA, WV, WT, WY

Vocational   AL, AK, AS, AZ, AR, CA, CO, CT,
               DE, DODEA, DC, FL, GA, GU, HI,
               ID, IL, IN, IA, KS, KY, LA, ME, MD,
               MA, MI, MN, MS, MO, MT, NE,
               NV, NH, NJ, NM, NY, NC, ND, NMI,
               OH, OK, PA, PR, RI, SC, SD, TN,
               TX, UT, VT, VA, WA, WV, WI, WY

Pennsylvania

Teacher   AL, AK, AZ, AR, CA, CO, CT, DE,
               DODEA, DC, FL, GA, HI, ID, IL,
               IN, IA, KS, KY, LA, ME, MD, MA,
               MI, MN, MS, MO, MT, NE, NV,
               NH, NJ, NM, NY, NC, ND, OH,
               OK, OR, PR,. RI, SC, SD, TN, TX,
               UT, VT, VA, WA, WV, WI, WY

Administrator None

Support   None

Vocational   None

Puerto Rico

Teacher	None
Administrator	None
Support	None
Vocational	None

Rhode Island

Teacher	AL, AK, AZ, AR, CA, CO, CT, DE, DC, FL, GA, GU, HI, ID, IL, IN, KY, LA, ME, MD, MA, MI, MS, MT, NE, NV, NH, NJ, NM, NY, NC, ND, OH, OK, OR, PA, SC, TN, TX, UT, VT, VA, WA, WV, WY
Administrator	AL, AK, AZ, DE, GA, GU, IN, LA, MD, MA, MS, NE, NH, NM, NY, OK, OR, SC, TN, TX, UT, VT, VA, WA, WV, WY
Support	AL, AK, AZ, CO, CT, DC, FL, GA, GU, IN, LA, ME, MD, MA, MI, MS, NH, NY, NC, OK, OR, SC, TN, TX, UT, VA, WA, WV, WY
Vocational	AZ, CT, DC, GA, MD, MS, NH, NY, OK, SC, TN, TX, UT, VA, WV, WY

South Carolina

Teacher	AL, AK, AS, AZ, AR, CA, CO, CT, DE, DODEA, DC, FL, GA, GU, HI, ID, IL, IN, IA, KS, KY, LA, ME, MD, MA, MI, MN, MS, MO, MT, NE, NV, NH, NJ, NM, NY, NC, ND, NMI, OH, OK, OR, PA, PR, RI, SD, TN, TX, UT, VT, VA, WA, WV, WI, WY
Administrator	AL, AK, AS, AZ, AR, CA, CO, CT, DE, DODEA, DC, FL, GA, GU, HI, ID, IL, IN, IA, KS, KY, LA, ME, MD, MA, MI, MN, MS, MO, MT, NE, NV, NH, NJ, NM, NY, NC, ND, NMI, OH, OK, OR, PA, PR, RI, SD, TN, TX, UT, VT, VA, WA, WV, WI, WY
Support	AL, AK, AS, AZ, AR, CA, CO, CT, DE, DODEA, DC, FL, GA, GU, HI, ID, IL, IN, IA, KS, KY, LA, ME, MD,

	MA, MI, MN, MS, MO, MT, NE, NV, NH, NJ, NM, NY, NC, ND, NMI, OH, OK, OR, PA, PR, RI, SC, SD, TN, TX, UT, VT, VA, WA, WV, WI, WY
Vocational	None

South Dakota

Teacher	AL, AK, AZ, AR, CA, CO, CT, DE, DC, FL, GA, HI, ID, IL, IN, IA, KS, KY, LA, ME, MD, MA, MI, MN, MS, MO, MT, NE, NV, NH, NJ, NM, NY, NC, ND, OH, OK, OR, PA, RI, SC, TN, TX, UT, VT, VA, WA, WV, WI, WY
Administrator	AL, AK, AZ, AR, CA, CO, CT, DE, DC, FL, GA, HI, ID, IL, IN, IA, KS, KY, LA, ME, MD, MA, MI, MN, MS, MO, MT, NE, NV, NH, NJ, NM, NY, NC, ND, OH, OK, OR, PA, RI, SC, TN, TX, UT, VT, VA, WA, WV, WI, WY
Support	AL, AK, AZ, AR, CA, CO, CT, DE, DC, FL, GA, HI, ID, IL, IN, IA, KS, KY, LA, ME, MD, MA, MI, MN, MS, MO, MT, NE, NV, NH, NJ, NM, NY, NC, ND, OH, OK, OR, PA, RI, SC, TN, TX, UT, VT, VA, WA, WV, WI, WY
Vocational	AL, AK, AZ, AR, CA, CO, CT, DE, DC, FL, GA, HI, ID, IL, IN, IA, KS, KY, LA, ME, MD, MA, MI, MN, MS, MO, MT, NE, NV, NH, NJ, NM, NY, NC, ND, OH, OK, OR, PA, RI, SC, TN, TX, UT, VT, VA, WA, WV, WI, WY

Tennessee

Teacher	AL, AK, AZ, AR, CA, CO, CT, DE, DC, FL, GA, GU, HI, ID, IL, IN, IA, KS, KY, LA, ME, MD, MA, MI, MN, MS, MO, MT, NE, NV, NH, NJ, NM, NY, NC, ND, OH, OK, OR, PA, PR, RI, SC, SD, TX, UT, VT, VA, WA, WV, WI, WY
Administrator	AL, AK, AZ, AR, CA, CO, CT, DE, DC, FL, GA, GU, HI, ID, IL, IN, IA,

KS, KY, LA, ME, MD, MA, MI,
MN, MS, MO, MT, NE, NV, NH,
NJ, NM, NY, NC, ND, OH, OK, OR,
PA, PR, RI, SC, SD, TX, UT, VT,
VA, WA, WV, WI, WY

Support   AL, AK, AZ, AR, CA, CO, CT, DE,
DC, FL, GA, GU, HI, ID, IL, IN, IA,
KS, KY, LA, ME, MD, MA, MI,
MN, MS, MO, MT, NE, NV, NH,
NJ, NM, NY, NC, ND, OH, OK, OR,
PA, PR, RI, SC, SD, TX, UT, VT,
VA, WA, WV, WI, WY

Vocational AL, AK, AZ, AR, CA, CO, CT, DE,
DC, FL, GA, GU, HI, ID, IL, IN, IA,
KS, KY, LA, ME, MD, MA, MI,
MN, MS, MO, MT, NE, NV, NH,
NJ, NM, NY, NC, ND, OH, OK, OR,
PA, PR, RI, SC, SD, TX, UT, VT,
VA, WA, WV, WI, WY

Texas

Teacher   AL, AK, AS, AZ, AR, CA, CO, CT,
DE, DC, FL, GA, GU, HI, ID, IL,
IN, IA, KS, KY, LA, ME, MD, MA,
MI, MN, MS, MO, MT, NE, NV,
NH, NJ, NM, NY, NC, ND, NMI,
OH, OK, OR, PA, PR, RI, SC, SD,
TN, UT, VT, VA, WA, WV, WI, WY

Administrator AL, AK, AS, AZ, AR, CA, CO, CT,
DE, DC, FL, GA, GU, HI, ID, IL,
IN, IA, KS, KY, LA, ME, MD, MA,
MI, MN, MS, MO, MT, NE, NV,
NH, NJ, NM, NY, NC, ND, NMI,
OH, OK, OR, PA, PR, RI, SC, SD,
TN, UT, VT, VA, WA, WV, WI, WY

Support   AL, AK, AS, AZ, AR, CA, CO, CT,
DE, DC, FL, GA, GU, HI, ID, IL,
IN, IA, KS, KY, LA, ME, MD, MA,
MI, MN, MS, MO, MT, NE, NV,
NH, NJ, NM, NY, NC, ND, NMI,
OH, OK, OR, PA, PR, RI, SC, SD,
TN, UT, VT, VA, WA, WV, WI, WY

Vocational AL, AK, AS, AZ, AR, CA, CO, CT,
DE, DC, FL, GA, GU, HI, ID, IL,
IN, IA, KS, KY, LA, ME, MD, MA,
MI, MN, MS, MO, MT, NE, NV,

NH, NJ, NM, NY, NC, ND, NMI,
OH, OK, OR, PA, PR, RI, SC, SD,
TN, UT, VT, VA, WA, WV, WI, WY

Utah

Teacher   AL, AK, AZ, AR, CA, CO, CT, DE,
DC, FL, GA, GU, HI, ID, IL, IN, IA,
KS, KY, LA, ME, MD, MA, MI,
MN, MS, MO, MT, NE, NV, NH,
NJ, NM, NY, NC, ND, OH, OK, OR,
PA, RI, SC, SD, TN, TX, VT, VA,
WA, WV, WI, WY

Administrator AL, AK, AZ, AR, CA, CO, CT, DE,
DC, FL, GA, GU, HI, ID, IL, IN, IA,
KS, KY, LA, ME, MD, MA, MI,
MN, MS, MO, MT, NE, NV, NH,
NJ, NM, NY, NC, ND, OH, OK, OR,
PA, RI, SC, SD, TN, TX, VT, VA,
WA, WV, WI, WY

Support   AL, AK, AZ, AR, CA, CO, CT, DE,
DC, FL, GA, GU, HI, ID, IL, IN, IA,
KS, KY, LA, ME, MD, MA, MI,
MN, MS, MO, MT, NE, NV, NH,
NJ, NM, NY, NC, ND, OH, OK, OR,
PA, RI, SC, SD, TN, TX, VT, VA,
WA, WV, WI, WY

Vocational AL, AK, AZ, AR, CA, CO, CT, DE,
DC, FL, GA, GU, HI, ID, IL, IN, IA,
KS, KY, LA, ME, MD, MA, MI,
MN, MS, MO, MT, NE, NV, NH,
NJ, NM, NY, NC, ND, OH, OK, OR,
PA, RI, SC, SD, TN, TX, VT, VA,
WA, WV, WI, WY

Vermont

Teacher   AL, AK, AZ, AR, CA, CO, CT, DE,
DC, FL, GA, GU, HI, ID, IL, IN,
KS, KY, LA, ME, MD, MA, MI,
MS, MT, NE, NV, NH, NJ, NM,
NY, NC, ND, OH, OK, OR, PA,
RI, SD, TN, TX, VA, WA, WV, WI,
WY

Administrator AL, AK, AZ, CO, DE, DC, FL, GA,
IL, IN, KS, LA, ME, MD, NJ, NM,
NY, NC, OH, OK, OR, PA, RI, SD,
TN, TX, UT, VA, WA, WY

Support	None	Support	AL, AK, AZ, CT, DC, FL, GA, GU, IN, ME, MD, MA, MS, NH, NY, NC, OK, OR, RI, SD, TN, UT, VA, WV
Vocational	None		
Virginia		Vocational	None
Teacher	AL, AK, AS, AZ, AR, CA, CO, CT, DE, DC, FL, GA, GU, HI, ID, IL, IN, IA, KS, KY, LA, ME, MD, MA, MI, MN, MS, MO, MT, NE, NV, NH, NJ, NM, NY, NC, ND, NMI, OH, OK, OR, PA, PR, RI, SC, SD, TN, TX, VT, WA, WV, WI, WY	**West Virginia**	
		Teacher	AL, AK, AZ, AR, CA, CO, CT, DE, DODEA, DC, FL, GA, HI, ID, IL, IN, IA, KS, KY, LA, ME, MD, MA, MI, MN, MS, MO, MT, NE, NV, NH, NJ, NM, NY, NC, ND, OH, OK, OR, PA, RI, SC, SD, TN, TX, UT, VT, VA, WA, WI, WY
Administrator	AL, AK, AS, AZ, AR, CA, CO, CT, DE, DC, FL, GA, GU, HI, ID, IL, IN, IA, KS, KY, LA, ME, MD, MA, MI, MN, MS, MO, MT, NE, NV, NH, NJ, NM, NY, NC, ND, NMI, OH, OK, OR, PA, PR, RI, SC, SD, TN, TX, UT, VT, WA, WV, WI, WY	Administrator	AL, AK, AZ, AR, CA, CO, CT, DE, DODEA, DC, FL, GA, HI, ID, IL, IN, IA, KS, KY, LA, ME, MD, MA, MI, MN, MS, MO, MT, NE, NV, NH, NJ, NM, NY, NC, ND, OH, OK, OR, PA, RI, SC, SD, TN, TX, UT, VT, VA, WA, WI, WY
Support	AL, AK, AS, AZ, AR, CA, CO, CT, DE, DC, FL, GA, GU, HI, ID, IL, IN, IA, KS, KY, LA, ME, MD, MA, MI, MN, MS, MO, MT, NE, NV, NH, NJ, NM, NY, NC, ND, NMI, OH, OK, OR, PA, PR, RI, SC, SD, TN, TX, UT, VT, WA, WV, WI, WY	Support	AL, AK, AZ, AR, CA, CO, CT, DE, DODEA, DC, FL, GA, HI, ID, IL, IN, IA, KS, KY, LA, ME, MD, MA, MI, MN, MS, MO, MT, NE, NV, NH, NJ, NM, NY, NC, ND, OH, OK, OR, PA, RI, SC, SD, TN, TX, UT, VT, VA, WA, WI, WY
Vocational	AL, AK, AS, AZ, AR, CA, CO, CT, DE, DC, FL, GA, GU, HI, ID, IL, IN, IA, KS, KY, LA, ME, MD, MA, MI, MN, MS, MO, MT, NE, NV, NH, NJ, NM, NY, NC, ND, NMI, OH, OK, OR, PA, PR, RI, SC, SD, TN, TX, UT, VT, WA, WV, WI, WY	Vocational	AL, AK, AZ, AR, CA, CO, CT, DE, DODEA, DC, FL, GA, HI, ID, IL, IN, IA, KS, KY, LA, ME, MD, MA, MI, MN, MS, MO, MT, NE, NV, NH, NJ, NM, NY, NC, ND, OH, OK, OR, PA, RI, SC, SD, TN, TX, UT, VT, VA, WA, WI, WY
Washington			
Teacher	AL, AK, AZ, AR, CA, CO, CT, DE, DC, FL, GA, GU, HI, ID, IL, IN, IA, KS, KY, LA, ME, MD, MA, MI, MN, MS, MO, MT, NE, NV, NH, NJ, NM, NY, NC, ND, OH, OK, OR, PA, RI, SC, SD, TN, TX, UT, VT, VA, WV, WI, WY	**Wisconsin**	
		Teacher	AL, AK, AZ, AS, AR, CA, CO, CT, DE, DC, FL, GA, HI, ID, IL, IN, IA, KS, KY, LA, ME, MD, MA, MI, MN, MS, MO, MT, NE, NV, NH, NJ, NM, NY, NC, ND, NMI, OH, OK, OR, PA, PR, RI, SC, SD, TN, TX, UT, VT, VA, WA, WY
Administrator	AL, AK, AZ, CO, DC, GA, ID, IN, MD, MA, MS, NE, NV, NC, NM, OK, OR, RI, SD, TN, TX, UT, VT, VA, WV		
		Administrator	None
		Support	None
		Vocational	None

<u>Wyoming</u>

Teacher	AL, AK, AS, AZ, AR, CA, CO, CT, DE, DODEA, DC, FL, GA, GU, HI, ID, IL, IN, IA, KS, KY, LA, ME, MD, MA, MI, MN, MS, MO, MT, NE, NV, NH, NJ, NM, NY, NC, ND, NMI, OH, OK, OR, PA, PR, RI, SC, SD, TN, TX, UT, VT, VA, WA, WV, WI	Support	AL, AK, AS, AZ, AR, CA, CO, CT, DE, DODEA, DC, FL, GA, GU, HI, ID, IL, IN, IA, KS, KY, LA, ME, MD, MA, MI, MN, MS, MO, MT, NE, NV, NH, NJ, NM, NY, NC, ND, NMI, OH, OK, OR, PA, PR, RI, SC, SD, TN, TX, UT, VT, VA, WA, WV, WI
Administrator	AL, AK, AS, AZ, AR, CA, CO, CT, DE, DODEA, DC, FL, GA, GU, HI, ID, IL, IN, IA, KS, KY, LA, ME, MD, MA, MI, MN, MS, MO, MT, NE, NV, NH, NJ, NM, NY, NC, ND, NMI, OH, OK, OR, PA, PR, RI, SC, SD, TN, TX, UT, VT, VA, WA, WV, WI	Vocational	AL, AK, AS, AZ, AR, CA, CO, CT, DE, DODEA, DC, FL, GA, GU, HI, ID, IL, IN, IA, KS, KY, LA, ME, MD, MA, MI, MN, MS, MO, MT, NE, NV, NH, NJ, NM, NY, NC, ND, NMI, OH, OK, OR, PA, PR, RI, SC, SD, TN, TX, UT, VT, VA, WA, WV, WI